SCHAUM'S OUTLINE OF

THEORY AND PROBLEMS

OF

PROGRAMMING

WITH

VISUAL BASIC

BYRON S. GOTTFRIED, Ph.D.

Professor Emeritus
University of Pittsburgh

SCHAUM'S OUTLINE SERIES
McGRAW-HILL, INC.

New York Chicago San Francisco Lisbon London
Madrid Mexico City Milan New Delhi San Juan
Seoul Singapore Sydney Toronto

To Marcia, Sharon, Gail, Susan and Aaron

BYRON S. GOTTFRIED is a Professor Emeritus of Industrial Engineering at the University of Pittsburgh. He attended Purdue University (B.S.), the University of Michigan (M.S.), and Case-Western Reserve University (Ph.D.). His primary interests are in the modeling and simulation of industrial processes. Dr. Gottfried also has active interests in computer graphics, programming languages, and innovative educational paradigms. He is the author of several college textbooks, including *Programming with Basic, Programming with Structured Basic, Programming with C* and *Programming with Pascal* in the Schaum's Outline Series, and *Spreadsheet Tools for Engineers* in McGraw-Hill's BEST Series.

Microsoft, Visual Basic and Windows are registered trademarks of Microsoft Corporation.

Schaum's Outline of Theory and Problems of
PROGRAMMING WITH VISUAL BASIC

1 2 3 4 5 6 7 8 9 10 11 12 13 14 15 16 17 18 19 20 SHP SHP 0 9 8 7 6 5 4 3 2 1

ISBN 0-07-135671-1

Sponsoring Editor: Barbara Gilson
Production Supervisor: Tina Cameron
Editing Supervisor: Maureen B. Walker

Library of Congress Cataloging-in-Publication Data applied for.

McGraw-Hill

A Division of The McGraw·Hill Companies

Preface

Visual Basic is an event-driven programming language for creating applications that run under Microsoft's *Windows* operating systems. The language appeals to two distinctly different groups: beginning programming students, who love the immediate visual gratification of creating simple, professional-looking programs that include graphics, dialog boxes and drop-down menus; and experienced programmers, who are able to create complex Windows-based applications with a minimum amount of effort. Most Visual Basic textbooks typically focus on one or the other of these two groups.

This book is intended for beginners. The book follows the style of other programming texts in the Schaum's Outline Series (the first of which, published in 1975, was my own *Programming with Basic*). As such, it is written in a manner that can easily be understood by advanced secondary or beginning college-level students. Hence, it can be used as a textbook for an introductory programming course, as a supplementary text in a programming course or as an effective self-study guide. For the most part, the required mathematical level does not go beyond high school algebra.

The material is organized in such a manner that the reader can write complete, though elementary, Visual Basic programs as soon as possible. It is very important that the reader write such programs and execute them on a computer concurrently with reading the text. This greatly enhances the beginning programmer's self-confidence and stimulates his or her interest in the subject. (Learning to program a computer is like learning to play the piano; it cannot be learned simply by studying a textbook!)

The text contains many examples. These include both simple illustrations that focus on specific programming constructs and comprehensive programming problems. In addition, sets of review questions, drill problems and programming problems are included at the end of each chapter. The review questions enable readers to test their recall of the material presented within the chapter. They also provide an effective chapter summary.

Most of the drill problems and programming problems require no special mathematical or technological background. The student should solve as many of these problems as possible. (Answers to the drill problems are provided at the end of the text.) When using this book as a text in a programming course, the instructor may wish to supplement the programming problems with additional assignments that reflect particular disciplinary interests.

Visual Basic has been modified several times since it was first introduced. This book is based upon Visual Basic Version 6 and is largely compatible with recent earlier versions of the language. However, Microsoft's preliminary description of the next version of Visual Basic, to be named *Visual Basic.NET*, indicates a number of incompatibilities with previous versions. An overview of the more significant incompatibilities, based upon Microsoft's preliminary description, is included as an appendix to this book. (Readers may expect a new edition of this book, focusing on Visual Basic.NET, in the near future.)

Last but not least, readers who complete this book will have learned a great deal about event-driven programming concepts in general as well as the specific rules of Visual Basic. Hopefully, most will be convinced that programming with Visual Basic is not only *easy*, but also *fun*.

BYRON S. GOTTFRIED

Contents

Complete Programming Examples

The projects are listed in the order in which they first appear within the text. The examples vary from simple to moderately complex.

1. Example 1.1 – *Area of a Circle*
2. Example 4.3 – *Current Data and Time*
3. Example 4.4 – *Entering and Displaying Text*
4. Example 4.5 – *Entering and Displaying Numerical and Graphical Data (A Piggy Bank)*
5. Example 4.6 – *Selecting Multiple Features (Multilingual Hello)*
6. Example 4.7 – *Selecting Exclusive Alternatives (Temperature Conversion)*
7. Example 4.8 – *Selecting Multiple Alternatives (Temperature Conversion Revisited)*
8. Example 4.9 – *Selecting from a List (Multilingual Hello Revisited)*
9. Example 4.10 – *Assigning Properties Using With Blocks*
10. Example 4.11 – *Calculating Factorials*
11. Example 4.12 – *Timed Events (A Metronome)*
12. Example 4.13 – *Using Scroll Bars (The Metronome Revisited)*
13. Example 5.2 – *Using Drop-Down Menus (Geography)*
14. Example 5.3 – *Using Menu Enhancements (Geography Revisited)*
15. Example 5.4 – *More Menu Enhancements (Geography Revisited)*
16. Example 5.5 – *Using Submenus (Geography Revisited)*
17. Example 5.6 – *Using a Pop-Up Menu*
18. Example 5.7 – *Using Dialog Boxes (Multilingual Hello Revisited)*
19. Example 5.9 – *Using Input Boxes*
20. Example 6.2 – *Stepping through a Program*
21. Example 6.3 – *An Error Handler*
22. Example 6.4 – *Generating a Stand-Alone Executable Program*
23. Example 7.2 – *Accessing a Sub Procedure (Smallest of Two Numbers)*
24. Example 7.3 – *Smallest of Three Numbers*
25. Example 7.6 – *Accessing a Function Procedure*
26. Example 7.7 – *Calculating the Sine of an Angle*
27. Example 7.10 – *Shooting Craps*
28. Example 8.6 – *Multilingual Hello Using an Array*
29. Example 8.9 – *Smallest of Two Numbers*
30. Example 8.10 – *Sorting a List of Numbers*
31. Example 8.11 – *Deviations about an Average*
32. Example 8.14 – *Deviations about an Average Using Dynamic Arrays*
33. Example 8.18 – *Selecting Multiple Features Using Control Arrays*
34. Example 8.19 – *Adding and Deleting Control Array Elements at Run Time*
35. Example 9.2 – *Text File Fundamentals*
36. Example 9.4 – *Creating a Sequential Data File: Daily High Temperatures*

Chapter 1

Introducing Visual Basic

1.1 WHAT IS VISUAL BASIC?

Visual Basic is an *object-oriented* programming development system for creating applications that run under any of the Microsoft Windows environments. It has the following two major components:

1. An extensive collection of prewritten tools, called *controls*. These controls are accessible as icons within a graphical programming environment for creating customized windows components (e.g., menus, dialog boxes, text boxes, slide bars, etc.).

2. A complete set of program commands, derived from Microsoft's implementation of the classical Basic programming language. The command set includes features that embrace contemporary programming practices.

The overall approach to Visual Basic programming is twofold:

1. Create a user interface that is appropriate to the particular application at hand.

2. Add a group of Basic instructions to carry out the actions associated with each of the controls.

1.2 EVENTS AND EVENT PROCEDURES

In traditional computer programs, the actions are carried out in a prescribed order. This order may be sequential, corresponding to the order in which the instructions are written, or it may depend on the outcome of one or more logical tests. In either case, the order of execution is determined internally within the program.

Visual Basic, on the other hand, is based upon an *event-driven* paradigm, in which each feature included within the program is activated only when the user responds to a corresponding object (i.e., an icon, a check box, an option button, a menu selection, etc.) within the user interface. The program's response to an action taken by the user is referred to as an *event*. Note that the user initiates the event, but it is the program's response that actually defines the event. The group of Basic commands that brings about this response is called an *event procedure*.

1.3 OBJECT-RELATED CONCEPTS

In addition to events and event procedures, you must understand the meaning of each of the following terms:

Forms: In Visual Basic, a window is called a *form*. Each form includes a *title bar* at the top. A form may also include a *menu bar*, a *status bar*, one or more *toolbars*, *slide bars*, etc. A *user area* (called a *client area*) occupies the remaining space within the form. Some applications are based upon a single form, while others require two or more forms. Fig. 1.1 shows a simple form containing two *command button controls* and a *text box control* (see below).

Controls: The icons with which the user interacts are called *controls*. Commonly used controls include *command buttons*, *option buttons*, *check boxes*, *labels*, *text boxes*, *picture boxes* and *menus*. The user will typically activate a control (e.g., click on a command button) to produce an event.

1

Objects: Forms and controls are referred to collectively as *objects*. Most objects are associated with events; hence, objects may include their own unique event procedures. Objects are also associated with their own *properties* and *methods* (see below).

Properties: Objects include *properties* that generally define their appearance or behavior. The choice of properties depends on the type of object. For example, the name, caption, height, width, background color, location and font are some of the more common properties associated with a command button.

Methods: Some objects also include special program statements called *methods*. A method brings about some predefined action affecting the associated object. For example, *show* is a method that can be used with a hidden form to make it visible.

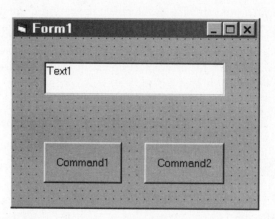

Fig. 1.1 A form containing three controls

1.4 THE VISUAL BASIC PROGRAM DEVELOPMENT PROCESS

In general terms, the process of writing a Visual Basic program consists of several steps. They are:

1. Decide what the program is supposed to do. Be as specific as possible. (Remember, however, that you may change your mind, perhaps several times, before you are finished.)

2. Create a user interface, using Visual Basic's program development tools. This generally involves two related activities:

    (*a*) Draw the controls within their respective forms.

    (*b*) Define the properties of each control.

3. Write the Visual Basic instructions to carry out the actions resulting from the various program events. This generally involves writing a group of commands, called an *event procedure*, for each control (though certain controls, such as labels, do not have event procedures associated with them).

4. Run the program to verify that it executes correctly.

5. Repeat one or more steps if the results are incorrect, or if the program does not respond as you had intended.

Be prepared to carry out several cycles before you're satisfied with the final result. Remember that computer programming is a detailed, creative process that requires patience, skill and ingenuity. At times the program development process can become frustrating (as, for example, when your program does not execute correctly, or it does not execute at all because of hidden, hard-to-find programming errors). At such times it is often best to take a break, set your work aside for a while, and come back to it later.

1.5 REQUIRED COMPUTER SKILLS

In order to use Visual Basic and derive some benefit from this book, you should have some proficiency in all of the following:

1. Familiarity with one of the Microsoft Windows operating systems (e.g., Windows 2000/98/95/NT, etc.). In particular:

    (*a*) Entering windows.

    (*b*) Using a mouse.

    (*c*) Accessing an application (specifically, Visual Basic).

    (*d*) Leaving windows.

    (*e*) Getting on-line help.

2. Managing files within Windows (locating files, opening files, editing files, saving files, copying files, moving files, deleting files, etc.).

3. Installing new applications (in case Visual Basic has not already been installed, or needs to be reinstalled).

We will not discuss these issues further – it is assumed that you already have the requisite skills. We will, however, discuss file management within Visual Basic later in this book, as the need arises.

1.6 LOGICAL PROGRAM ORGANIZATION

Virtually all nontrivial computer programs involve three major tasks. They are:

1. Entering input data (supplying information to be processed).

2. Computing the desired results (processing the input data).

3. Displaying the results (displaying the results of the computation.

Each step may be complex; its implementation may therefore require considerable time and effort.

In Visual Basic, the first and last steps (data input and data output) are accomplished through the user interface. Thus, it is important to design a user interface that will accept input data and display output in a manner that is logical and straightforward for the particular application at hand. In many applications, the design of the user interface is the most complicated part of the entire program development process, though the controls built into Visual Basic simplify this process considerably.

The second step (computation) is usually carried out by a series of Visual Basic instructions, embedded in one or more independent event procedures. The selection and order of these Visual Basic instructions are determined by an appropriate *algorithm*, i.e., a logical and orderly computational strategy for transforming the given input data into the desired output data. In many realistic applications, this step (i.e., the implementation of the algorithm) can be very complicated, challenging the abilities of very skilled programmers.

1.7 VISUAL BASIC PROGRAM COMPONENTS

In Visual Basic, a program is referred to as a *project*. Every Visual Basic project consists of at least two separate files – a *project file* (whose extension is *.vbp*), and a *form file* (with extension *.frm*). Some projects include multiple form files and other types of files, such as *class module* (*.cls*) files, *standard module* (*bas*) files, *resource* (*.res*) files, and *ActiveX control* (*.ocx*) files. Thus, the development of a Visual Basic project involves keeping track of several different files, and accessing these files individually within the Visual Basic environment, as needed.

1.8 THE VISUAL BASIC ENVIRONMENT

To enter the Visual Basic environment, click the mouse on the Visual Basic icon which appears on your Windows Desktop. This will result in the opening group of windows shown in Fig. 1.2. You may then enter the workspace for a new project by selecting New/Standard.EXE, or by selecting New Project from the File menu (see below). Or, you may open an existing project by selecting either the Existing tab or the Recent tab, and then selecting the particular project that is of interest. Still another way to open an existing project is to select Open Project from the File menu, and then select the particular project of interest.

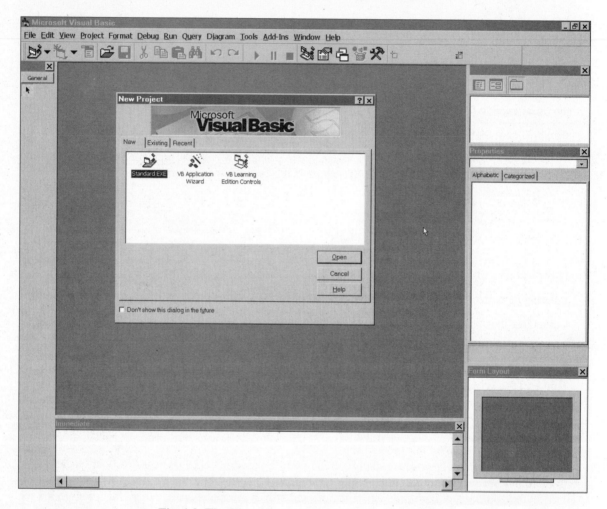

Fig. 1.2 The Visual Basic opening group of windows

If you choose to create a new project, you will see a group of windows similar to that shown in Fig. 1.3. The principal items are described below:

TITLE BAR

The top line is called the *Title Bar*. It includes the project name, an icon that closes Visual Basic at the left, and icons that minimize the group of windows, change the size of the group, or close Visual Basic on the right. We will discuss these icons later, as the need arises. For now, however, note that you can exit from Visual Basic by clicking on the left icon and then selecting Close from the resulting drop-down menu, or by clicking on the rightmost icon (×).

MENU BAR

The second line is called the *Menu Bar*. Selecting one of the choices (File, Edit, View, Project, Format, . . . Help) causes one of Visual Basic's *drop-down menus* to appear. These menus present logical groupings of Visual Basic's individual features. For example, the File menu includes selections for opening new or existing VB projects, saving the project, saving the currently active window, printing the currently active project, running (executing) a Visual Basic project, opening recently accessed projects, and so on.

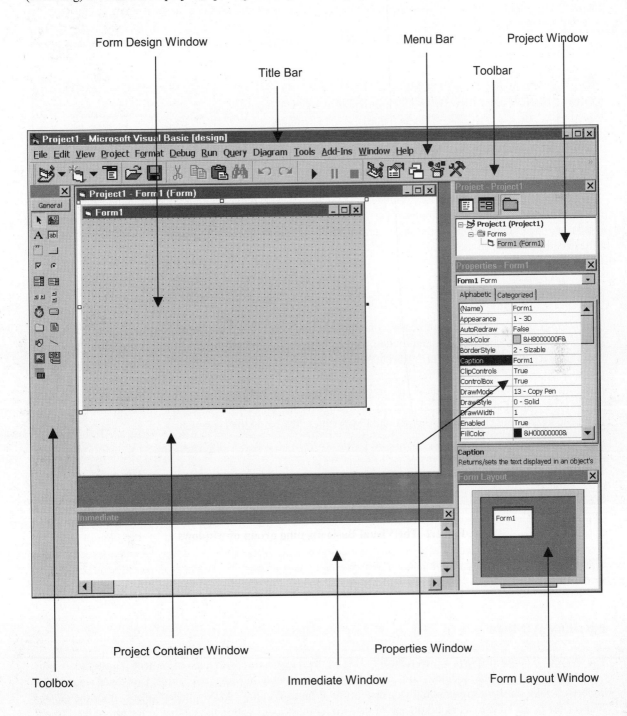

Fig. 1.3 The Visual Basic new project environment

TOOLBAR

The third line is called the *Standard Toolbar*. The icons on this line duplicate several of the more commonly used menu selections that are available via the drop-down menus accessed from the Menu Bar. For example, the Standard Toolbar contains icons that will open an existing project; save the current project; cut, copy and delete; undo the most recent changes; start, pause and end program execution; and add/delete windows from the current overall environment. All of these features can be accessed via drop-down menus. Hence, the toolbar icons do not offer any new or unique features, but their use is convenient, since the icon-based features can be selected with a single mouseclick.

Other toolbars (*Debug*, *Edit* and *Form Editor*) can be accessed by selecting Toolbars from the View menu. The Standard Toolbar can also be removed in this manner.

FORM DESIGN AND PROJECT CONTAINER WINDOWS

The *Form Design Window* is where the user interface is actually designed. This is accomplished by selecting the desired *Control Icons* from the *Toolbox* (see below) and placing them in the Form Design Window. Each control can then be moved (place the mouse over the icon and drag) or resized (activate the icon and drag one of the small surrounding squares), and its *properties* can be reassigned as required (see below).

The entire form (i.e., the entire Form Design Window) can be moved within the surrounding *Project Container Window* (by placing the mouse over the form and dragging), or it can be resized (by activating the mouse and then dragging one of the small surrounding squares). Both windows can also be closed, minimized, or resized by clicking on the appropriate icons in their respective Title Bars.

TOOLBOX

The *Toolbox* contains icons that represent commonly used controls, such as a label, text box, command button, picture box, frame, check box, option button, file list box, and so on. You can select a control from the Toolbox and place it in the current Form Design Window by double-clicking on the control icon (thus placing the control in the center of the window), or by clicking once on the control icon, then clicking on the desired location within the Form Design Window and dragging the mouse so that the control has the desired size.

Once a control has been placed in the Form Design Window, the associated *code* (i.e., the associated Visual Basic instructions) can be viewed or edited by double-clicking on the control.

PROPERTIES WINDOW

We have already learned that every object has *properties* associated with it. Each object has its own unique list of properties. The *Properties Window* allows you to assign or change the properties associated with a particular object (i.e., a particular form or control). To do so, active the object by clicking on it; then choose from the corresponding list of properties shown in the left column of the Properties Window. Once you select a property, the adjoining box in the right column may change its appearance, showing a drop-down menu so you can choose from a list of permissible values.

PROJECT WINDOW

The *Project Window* displays a hierarchical list of the files associated with a given project. These files represent individual forms and modules. You can display a form or module within the Project Container Window by double-clicking on the corresponding icon within the Project Window. Also, you can select either the *Object View* or the *Code View* by clicking on one of the two leftmost icons within the toolbar at the top of the Project Window.

CODE EDITOR WINDOW

If you select Code View within the Project Window, or if you double-click on a control icon within the Form Design Window, the *Code Editor Window* will open, displaying the Visual Basic code associated with the currently active form. Fig. 1.4 shows the Code Editor Window containing two different *event procedures* (i.e., the Visual Basic code associated with two different command buttons). Ignore the individual Visual Basic instructions for now. Notice, however, the two list boxes at the top of the window. The leftmost list box (showing Command2 in Fig. 1.4) is the *Object Listbox*; it allows you to select the event procedures associated with a particular *object* (e.g., a particular command button, form, label, text box, etc.). The rightmost list box (showing Click in Fig. 1.4) is called the *Procedure Listbox*; for the current object, it allows you to select the event procedure associated with a particular type of *event* (e.g., Click, DragDrop, KeyDown, MouseDown, etc.).

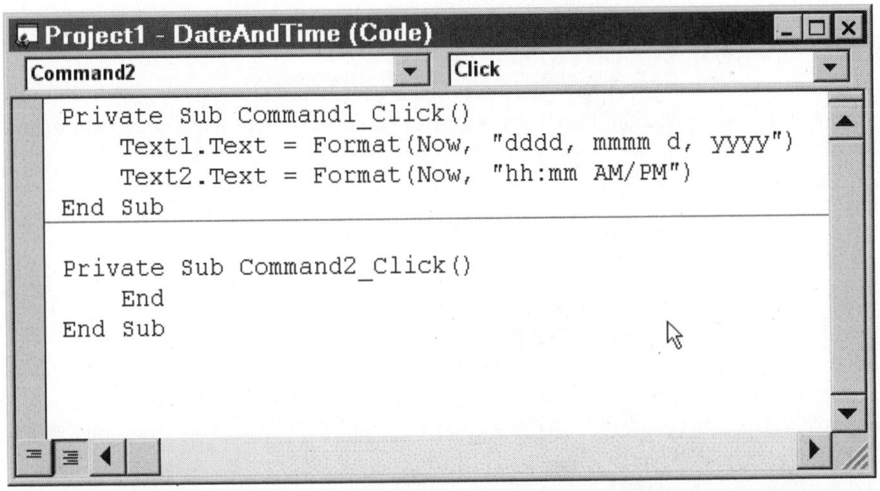

```
Project1 - DateAndTime (Code)
Command2                        Click

    Private Sub Command1_Click()
        Text1.Text = Format(Now, "dddd, mmmm d, yyyy")
        Text2.Text = Format(Now, "hh:mm AM/PM")
    End Sub

    Private Sub Command2_Click()
        End
    End Sub
```

Fig. 1.4 The Code Editor Window containing two event procedures

FORM LAYOUT WINDOW

The *Form Layout Window* allows you to specify the screen location of the forms within a project. To change the form location, simply drag the form icon to the desired position.

IMMEDIATE WINDOW

The *Immediate Window* is very useful when debugging a project. Whenever you enter a variable or expression within this window, the corresponding value will be shown immediately.

REPOSITIONING, RESIZING, DELETING, ADDING, AND DOCKING WINDOWS

Any of the individual windows can be repositioned (by activating the window and then dragging it to the desired location), resized (by activating and then dragging an edge or corner), and deleted (by clicking on the ✕ in the upper right corner). A window can be added by selecting the window name from the View menu.

The interface may become messy if several windows have been moved and/or resized. When this happens, Visual Basic allows the windows to be returned to their orderly, preassigned position. This is called *docking*. Docked windows are always aligned alongside their neighbors, and they are always visible.

To dock a window that has been moved from its preassigned position, simply double-click on the window's title bar. For any window, docking can be overridden by selecting Options/Docking from the Tools menu, and then selecting or deselecting the appropriate check boxes.

1.9 OPENING AN EXISTING VISUAL BASIC PROJECT

We have already seen that an existing project can be accessed by locating the project name listed under the Existing or the Recent tab within the New Project window (see Fig. 1.2), or by locating the project via File/Open Project. Once the project is opened, however, the Form Design Window may not be visible within the Project Container Window. To access the Form Design Window, you may have to expand the Forms icon within the Project Window as shown in Fig. 1.5, and then select the desired form. Double-click on the form icon to show the Form Design Window.

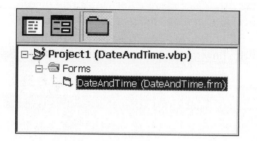

Fig. 1.5 Activating a form within the Project Container Window

1.10 SAVING A VISUAL BASIC PROJECT

Saving a project can be tricky in Visual Basic because it involves saving multiple files.

To save a new Visual Basic project for the first time, choose Save Project As from the File menu. You will be prompted separately for a form name (i.e., the name of the *.frm* file) and a project name (the *.vbp* file). Usually, the same name is given to both files.

To save an updated version of a previously saved project, click on the Save Project button in the Toolbar (see Fig. 1.6), or select Save Project from the File menu. This will cause the current version of the project files to be saved under their existing names.

Fig. 1.6 The Standard Toolbar

To save a previously saved project under a different name (this is the tricky part), you must *save each file separately under its new name*. Thus, you should first save each form file under the new name, and then save the project file under the new name. If you simply save the project file under a different name, the form files will retain their old names; this may cause problems when switching between the old version and the new version of the project.

1.11 RUNNING A VISUAL BASIC PROJECT

To execute a Visual Basic project, simply click on the Start button in the Toolbar (see Fig. 1.6), or select Start from the Run menu. The execution can be temporarily suspended by clicking on the Break button, or by selecting Break from the Run menu. The execution of a paused project can then be resumed by clicking on the Run button, or by selecting Continue from the Run menu. To end the execution, simply click on the End button, or select End from the Run menu.

1.12 GETTING HELP

Visual Basic includes many intricate concepts, predefined identifiers, detailed syntactic requirements, etc. – more than you can remember at any one time. Fortunately, Visual Basic also includes an excellent on-line help facility, which will answer most questions and provide detailed information, with examples, of various Visual Basic features.

To access the help feature, press function key F1 or select Contents, Index or Search from the Help menu. Fig. 1.7 shows the help window that is obtained by pressing F1, or by selecting Help/Index. Notice the tabs at the left side of the window, which allow you to select the Contents, Index, Search or Favorites window for viewing.

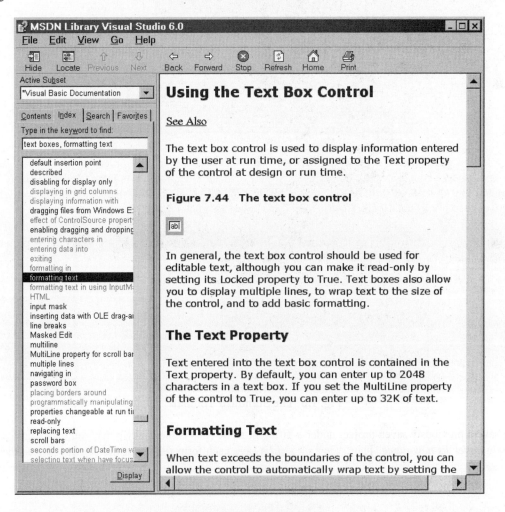

Fig. 1.7 The Help window

1.13 A SAMPLE VISUAL BASIC PROJECT

The following example shows the overall process used to create a Visual Basic project. Our primary emphasis is on the use of controls to create a user interface. When reading through this example, try to focus on the "big picture" and ignore the details, which are discussed in later chapters.

EXAMPLE 1.1 AREA OF A CIRCLE

In this example, we create a project that calculates the area of a circle. The user enters a value for the radius, and then clicks on the Go button. The corresponding area will then be displayed, as illustrated in Fig. 1.8.

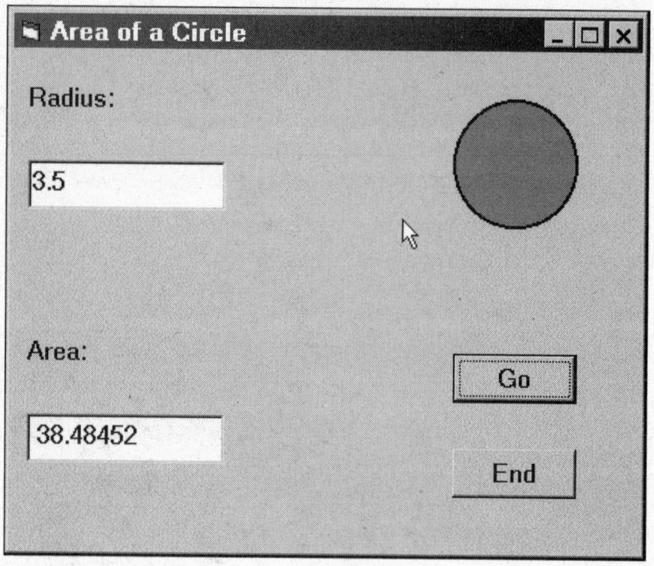

Fig. 1.8

We begin by opening Visual Basic and selecting Standard EXE from the New tab in the New Project menu (see Fig. 1.2). This causes a blank Form Design Window to be displayed, as shown in Fig. 1.9 (see also Fig. 1.3).

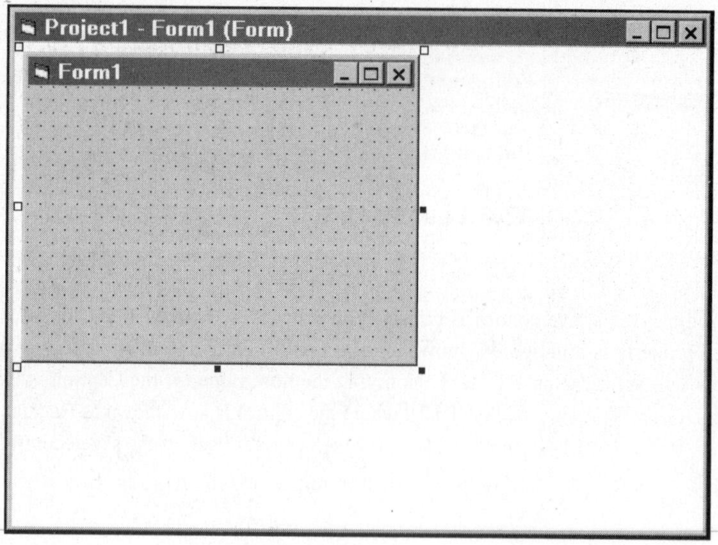

Fig. 1.9

We then place the necessary controls in the Form Design Window. In particular, we place two labels, two text boxes, two command buttons, and a geometric shape on the form, as shown in Fig. 1.10. Each control is selected from the Toolbox, which is positioned to the left of the Form Design Window (see Fig. 1.3). Note that the controls are automatically called Label1, Label2, Text1, Text2, Command1, and Command2, and the Form Design Window is called Form1. The geometric shape has no default name.

Each control can be selected two different ways. You can click on the desired control icon within the Toolbox, then click on the control's location within the Form Design Window, and then drag the mouse until the control has the desired size and shape. Or, you can double-click on the desired control icon within the Toolbox, placing the control at the center of the Form Design Window. You can then drag the control to its desired location and resize the control by dragging one of its edges or corners. (In Fig. 1.10, the controls have been placed in their approximate desired locations but they have not been resized.) If you change your mind, you can delete a control by highlighting the control (clicking on it) and then pressing the Delete key.

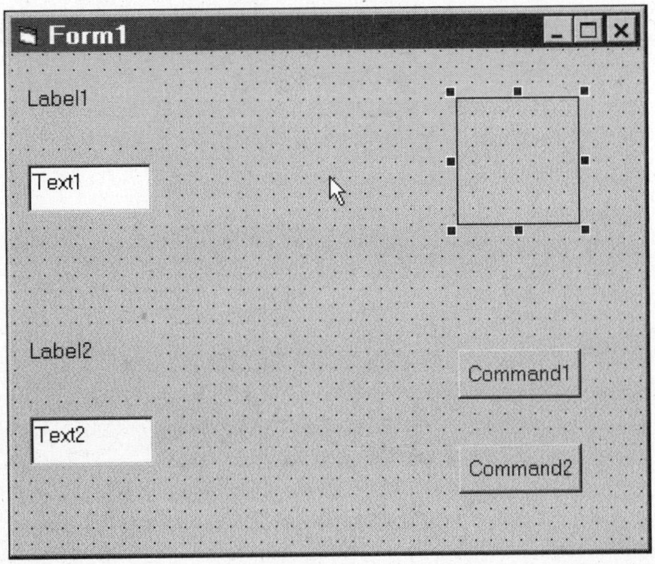

Fig. 1.10

Defining the Interface Control Properties

The next step is to define an appropriate set of properties for each control. Since the controls already have default properties associated with them, the actual process generally involves changing only a few of the defaults.

The properties associated with each control are displayed in the Properties Window (see Fig. 1.11 below). To view the properties, simply activate the control by clicking on it. You may then choose a property from the list shown in the left column of the Properties Window. The current value of that property is shown in the adjoining location within the right column.To change the value of the property, either type in a new value, or select from the list of values shown in the drop-down menu.

In Fig. 1.11, for example, the active control is Label1. The Properties Window shows the properties associated with this control. The Caption property is highlighted, showing Label1 as the current (default) value. If we change this value to Radius:, then the window will appear as in Fig. 1.11. Note that the new value for the Caption is Radius:. This new value also appears in the Form Design Window (see Fig. 1.12), where the control is now shown as Radius:.

The (nondefault) property values for each object (i.e., for the form and each of the seven controls) are summarized below.

Object	Property	Value
Form1	Name	"Circle"
	Caption	"Area of a Circle"
Label1	Caption	"Radius:"
	Font	MS Sans Serif, 10-point
Label2	Caption	"Area:"
	Font	MS Sans Serif, 10-point

Object	Property	Value
Text1	Font	MS Sans Serif, 10-point
Text2	Font	MS Sans Serif, 10-point
Command1	Caption	"Go"
	Font	MS Sans Serif, 10-point
Command2	Caption	"End"
	Font	MS Sans Serif, 10-point
Shape	Shape	3 – Circle
	BorderWidth	2
	FillStyle	0 – Solid
	FillColor	Medium Blue

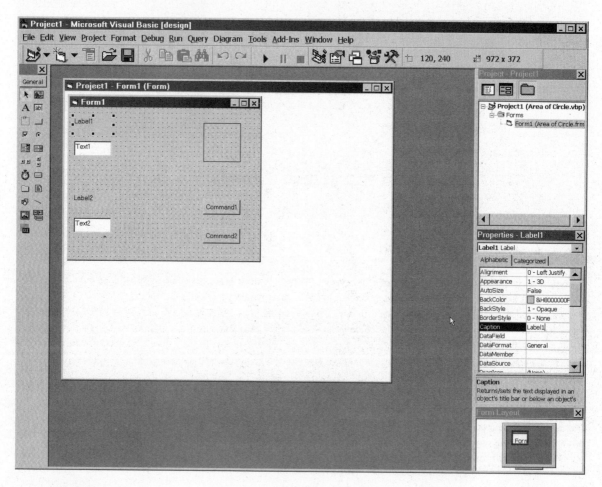

Fig. 1.11

Defining the Event Procedures

The last step is to write the Visual Basic commands that comprise the event procedures. In this example, only the command buttons, labeled Go and End in Fig. 1.13 (originally labeled Command1 and Command2, as shown in Fig. 1.12), have event procedures associated with them. Hence, we must define an event procedure for each of these command buttons.

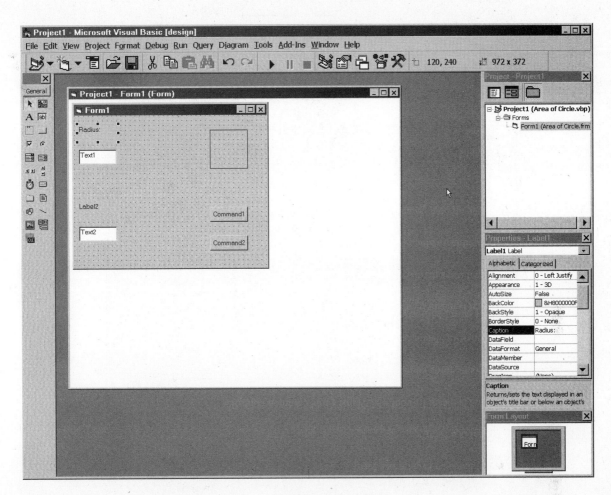

Fig. 1.12

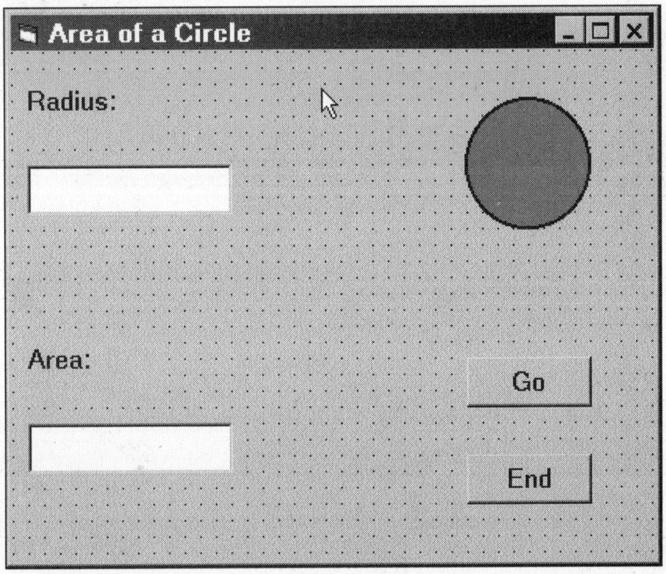

Fig. 1.13

To define the event procedure associated with the Go button, double-click on the button. This will cause the Code Editor Window to be displayed, as shown in Fig. 1.14. Within this window, the first and last line of each event procedure (e.g., Private Sub Command1_Click() and End Sub) are provided automatically, separated by a blank line. The actual Visual Basic commands must be inserted between these two lines.

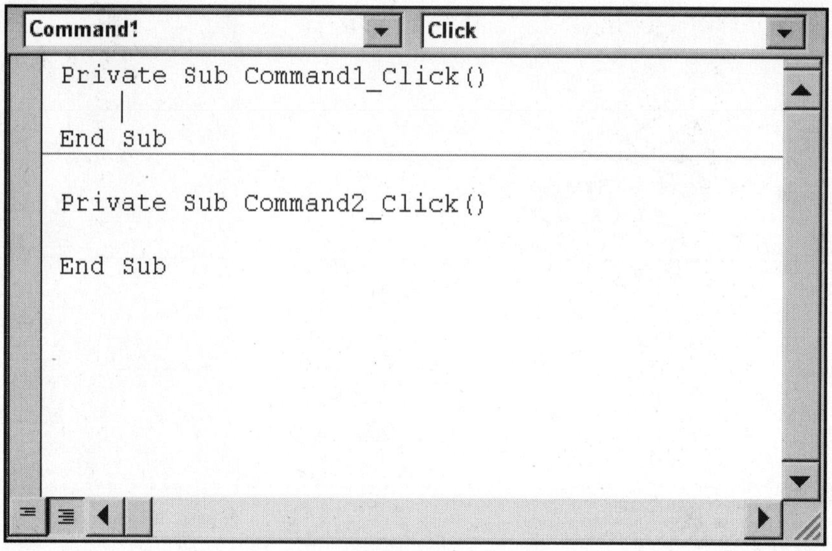

```
Command1                        ▼    Click                              ▼

   Private Sub Command1_Click()                                    ▲
     |
   End Sub

   Private Sub Command2_Click()

   End Sub

                                                                   ▼
```

Fig. 1.14

In the current example, we add the following commands to the first event procedure:

```
Dim R As Single, A As Single

R = Val(Text1.Text)
A = 3.141593 * R ^ 2
Text2.Text = Str(A)
```

The first line is a variable declaration, stating that R and A are single-precision, real variables. The remaining three lines are *assignment statements*; that is, the information represented by the item on the right-hand side of the equal sign is assigned to the item on the left-hand side. Thus, the first assignment statement assigns the current value of the radius, entered from text box Text1, to the variable R. The second assignment statement computes the area and assigns this value to the variable A. The third assignment statement converts the value of the area to a string and then assigns this string to the Text property of Text2.

Similarly, we add the command

```
End
```

to the second event procedure. This command simply terminates the computation.

Here is a more detailed explanation of the first event procedure (skip this if you wish – it will all be discussed later in this book): Text1 is the name of an object (in this case, a text box) and Text is the name of the object's associated property. Thus, Text1.Text refers to the text associated with text box Text1. Similarly, Text2.Text refers to the text associated with text box Text2. Val and Str are *library functions*. Val returns a numerical value from a string *argument*. Str does just the opposite – it returns a string from a numeric argument.

When the program is executed, the user must enter a value for the radius in text box Text1 and click on the Go button. The radius (Text1.Text) is then converted to a numerical value, represented by the variable R. The area (represented by the variable A) is then calculated, converted to a string, and assigned to Text2.Text. This string is then displayed in text box Text2.

Fig. 1.15 shows the completed event procedures for this project. Note that the added commands are indented, relative to the first and last lines of each event procedure. This is not essential, but it is considered good programming practice. The indentation allows each event procedure to be quickly identified and easily read.

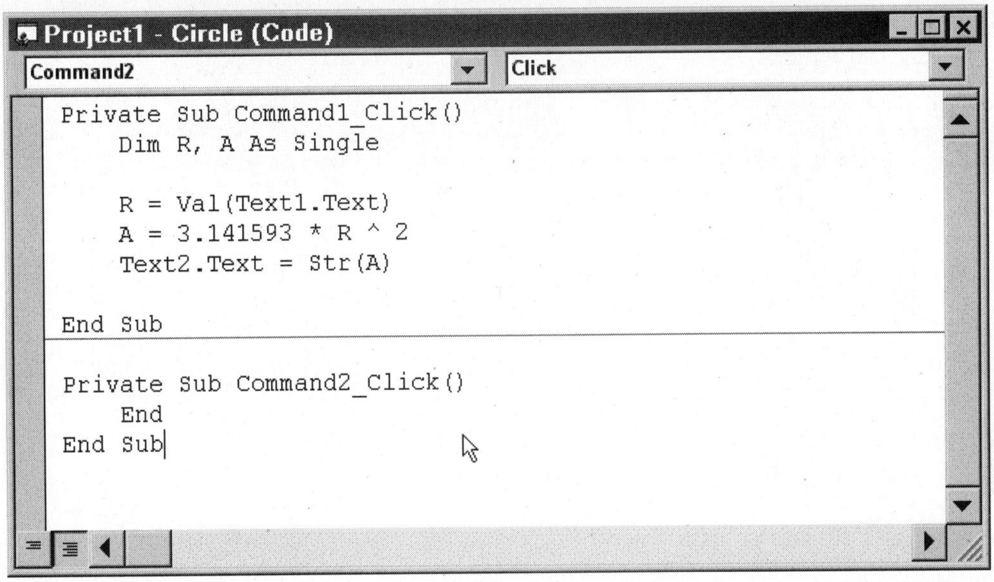

```
Project1 - Circle (Code)
Command2                          Click

Private Sub Command1_Click()
    Dim R, A As Single

    R = Val(Text1.Text)
    A = 3.141593 * R ^ 2
    Text2.Text = Str(A)

End Sub

Private Sub Command2_Click()
    End
End Sub
```

Fig. 1.15

Project Execution

When the project is executed (by clicking on the Start button in the menu bar), the window shown in Fig. 1.16 appears. Entering a value for the radius and clicking on the Go button results in a display of the corresponding area, as shown in Fig. 1.17.

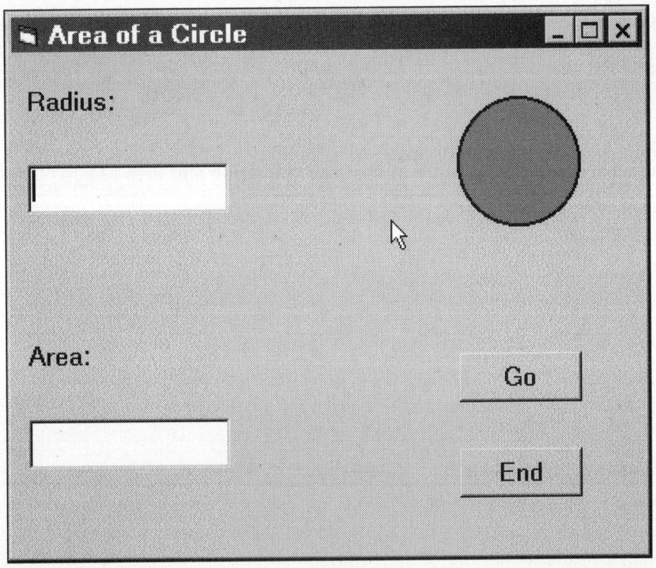

Area of a Circle

Radius:

Area:

Go

End

Fig. 1.16

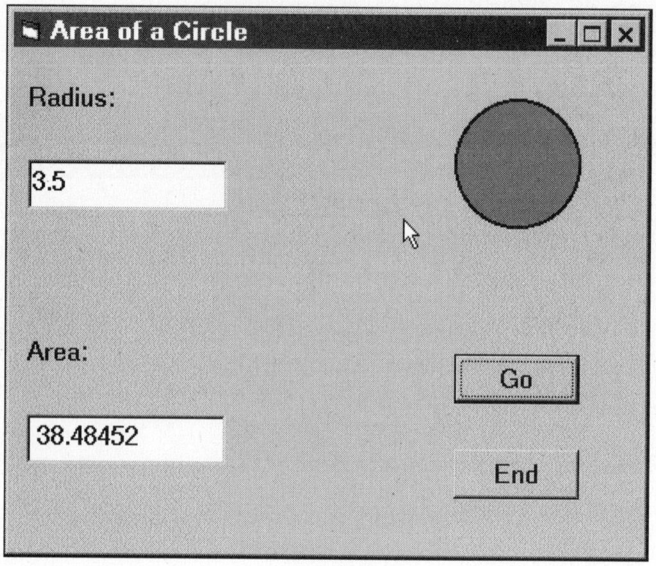

Fig. 1.17

The computation is ended by clicking on the End button. The Form Design Window shown in Fig. 1.13 then reappears.

Review Questions

1.1   What are the two major components within the Visual Basic programming development system?

1.2   What two primary activities are required when creating a Visual Basic program?

1.3   What is an event? What is an event procedure?

1.4   In Visual Basic, what is a form?

1.5   In Visual Basic, what is meant by controls? Name some common controls.

1.6   What are objects? Name some common Visual Basic objects.

1.7   What are object properties? Name some common properties of Visual Basic objects.

1.8   In Visual Basic, what is meant by a method?

1.9   Describe the principal steps involved in the Visual Basic project development process.

1.10 Most computer programs involve what three major tasks?

1.11 Open up Visual Basic on your computer. Then identify each of the following:
  (*a*) Title Bar
  (*b*) Menu Bar
  (*c*) Drop-down menus
  (*d*) Standard Toolbar

    (*e*) Form Design Window

    (*f*) Project Container Window

    (*g*) Toolbox

    (*h*) Properties Window

    (*i*) Project Window

    (*j*) Code Editor Window

    (*k*) Form Layout Window

    (*l*) Immediate Window

1.12 Summarize how each of the following operations is carried out:

    (*a*) Repositioning (relocating) a window

    (*b*) Resizing a window

    (*c*) Deleting (closing) a window

    (*d*) Adding a new window

1.13 What is meant by "docking" a window? How is window docking is carried out?

1.14 How is an existing Visual Basic project opened?

1.15 How is a Visual Basic project saved?

1.16 How is a Visual Basic project executed? How is the project paused during execution? How is it resumed? How is the execution ended?

1.17 How is the on-line help feature accessed?

Programming Problems

1.18 Re-create the project given in Example 1.1 using your own version of Visual Basic. Verify that the project executes correctly. Then change the project in the following ways:

    (*a*) Change the label captions to Enter the radius below: and The area is:.

    (*b*) Change the background colors of the form and the text boxes. (Choose your own colors.)

    (*c*) Change the command button captions to Execute and Quit.

    (*d*) Raise the lower label and the lower text box so that they are closer to the upper label and text box.

    (*e*) Move the command buttons to the bottom of the form and align them horizontally.

    (*f*) Resize the form and rearrange the controls relative to one another so that the form has an overall pleasing appearance.

    (*g*) Access the on-line help for the Val function (select Index/Val function from the Help menu). Then do the same with the Str function.

1.19 Modify the project given in Example 1.1 so that it calculates both the area and the circumference of a circle from the given value of the radius. Display each calculated value in a separate text box. Experiment with the project so that it runs correctly and has a pleasing appearance. Access the on-line help feature to obtain assistance with programming details.

Chapter 2

Visual Basic Fundamentals

In this chapter we will consider several fundamental features of Visual Basic, such as numbers, strings, data types and variables. We will then consider some fundamental Visual Basic features that will allow us to form numerical expressions, manipulate strings, assign data to variables and add remarks to a program. We will also discuss the use of *library functions*, which simplify various numerical and string manipulation operations.

After completing this chapter, you will be able to write a variety of Visual Basic commands (also referred to as *statements*) for simple problem situations.

2.1 NUMERIC CONSTANTS

Numbers are referred to as *numeric constants* in Visual Basic. Most numeric constants are expressed as *integers* (whole numbers that do not contain a decimal point or an exponent), *long integers* (similar to integers with an extended range), *single-precision real quantities* (numbers that include a decimal point, an exponent, or both), or *double-precision real quantities* (similar to single-precision real quantities with an extended range and greater precision). The following rules apply to numeric constants:

1. Commas cannot appear anywhere in a numeric constant.

2. A numeric constant may be preceded by a + or a − sign. The constant is understood to be positive if a sign does not appear.

3. An integer constant occupies two bytes. It must fall within the range −32,768 to 32,767. It cannot contain either a decimal point or an exponent.

4. A long integer constant occupies four bytes. It must fall within the range −2,147,483,648 to 2,147,483,647. It cannot contain either a decimal point or an exponent.

5. A single-precision real constant occupies four bytes. It can include a decimal point and as many as seven significant figures. However, its magnitude cannot exceed approximately 3.4×10^{38}.

   A single-precision real constant can include an exponent if desired. Exponential notation is similar to scientific notation, except that the base 10 is replaced by the letter E. Thus, the quantity 1.2×10^{-3} could be written as `1.2E-3`. The exponent itself can be either positive or negative, but it must be a whole number; i.e., it cannot contain a decimal point.

6. A double-precision real constant occupies eight bytes. It can include a decimal point and as many as fifteen significant figures. However, its magnitude cannot exceed approximately 1.8×10^{308}.

   A double-precision real constant can include an exponent if desired. Double-precision exponential notation is similar to scientific notation, except that the base 10 is replaced by the letter D. Thus, the quantity 1.6667×10^{-3} could be written as `1.6667D-3`. The exponent itself can be either positive or negative, but it must be a whole number; i.e., it cannot contain a decimal point.

All of the numeric constants discussed above are based upon the decimal (base 10) numbering system. Visual Basic also supports octal (base 8) and hexadecimal (base 16) numeric constants, though octal and hexadecimal constants are rarely used by beginning programmers. Hence, we will not work with octal or hexadecimal constants in this book.

EXAMPLE 2.1

Several Visual Basic numeric constants are shown below. Note that each quantity (each row) can be written in several different ways.

0	+0	−0	
1	+1	0.1E+1	10E−1
−5280	−5.28E+3	−.528E4	−52.8E2
1492	0.1492D+4	1.492D+3	+14.92D2
−.0000613	−6.13E−5	−613E−7	−0.613E−4
3000000	3D6	3D+6	0.3D7

2.2 STRING CONSTANTS

A *string constant* is a sequence of characters (i.e., letters, numbers and certain special characters, such as +, −, /, *, =, $, ., etc.), enclosed in quotation marks. Blank spaces can be included within a string. A quotation mark can also be placed within a string, but it must be written as *two adjacent* quotation marks (see the last line in the example below).

String constants are used to represent nonnumeric information, such as names, addresses, etc. There is no practical restriction on the maximum number of characters that can be included within a string constant. Thus, the maximum length of a string constant can be considered infinite.

EXAMPLE 2.2

Several string constants are shown below.

```
"SANTA CLAUS"                    "Please type a value for C:"

"$19.95"                         "Welcome to the 21st Century"

"X1 = "                         "3730425"

"The answer is "                "Do you wish to try again?"

"The professor said, ""Please don't snore in class"" "
```

2.3 VARIABLES

A *variable* is a name that represents a numerical quantity, a string, or some other basic data item (e.g., a date, true/false condition, etc.). The following rules apply to the naming of variables:

1. A variable name must begin with a letter. Additional characters may be letters or digits. Certain other characters may also be included, though the period and special *data-typing characters* (e.g., %, &, !, #, and $) are *not* permitted. In general, it is good programming practice to avoid the use of characters other than letters and digits.

2. A variable name cannot exceed 255 characters. As a practical matter, however, variable names rarely approach this size.

3. Visual Basic does not distinguish between uppercase and lowercase letters. Many programmers use uppercase letters as word separators within a single variable name (e.g., FreezingPoint, TaxRate, etc.)

4. Visual Basic includes a number of *reserved words* (e.g., Dim, If, Else, Select, Case, Do, etc.). These reserved words represent commands, function names, etc. They *cannot* be used as variable names.

EXAMPLE 2.3

Several variable names are shown below.

Area	Radius	X	xmax	C3
Counter	CustomerName		Account_Number	UnpaidBalance

2.4 DATA TYPES AND DATA DECLARATIONS

Visual Basic supports all common data types, including *Integer*, *Long* (i.e., long integer), *Single*, *Double* and *String*. The language also supports other data types, such as *Boolean*, *Byte*, *Currency* and *Date* data, as well as *Variant*-type data (see below) and user-defined data types.

The Dim statement is used to associate variables with specific data types. This process, which is common to all modern programming languages, is known as *data declaration*, or simply *declaration*. In general terms, the Dim statement is written as

Dim *variable name 1* As *data type 1*, *variable name 2* As *data type 2*, etc.

EXAMPLE 2.4

Several variable declarations are shown below.

```
Dim Counter As Integer

Dim Area As Single

Dim StudentName As String

Dim StudentName As String * 30

Dim TaxRate As Single, Income As Double, Taxes As Double, Dependents As Integer
```

The first line declares Counter to be an integer-type variable, and the second line declares that Area is a single-precision real variable. The third line declares StudentName to be a string variable of unspecified length; in the fourth line, however, StudentName is declared to be a string variable of fixed length, not exceeding 30 characters. Finally, the last line declares TaxRate to be a single-precision real variable, Income and Taxes as double-precision real variables, and Dependents as an integer variable.

Variants

Visual Basic allows variables to be undeclared if the programmer so chooses. In such cases, the data type of the variable is determined implicitly by the value that is assigned to the variable. Such variables are referred to as *Variant-type* variables, or simply as *variants*.

On the surface, the use of variants appears to simplify the program development process. This is a false perception, however, as the use of variants is computationally inefficient, and it compromises the clarity of a program. *Good programming practice suggests that the use of variants be avoided.* Use explicitly declared variables instead.

Named Constants

It is also possible to define named constants in Visual Basic. Named constants are similar to variables. However, variables can be reassigned different values within a program, whereas named constants remain unchanged throughout a program.

The Const statement is used to declare a named constant. This statement has the general form

> Const *constant name* As *data type* = *value*

EXAMPLE 2.5

Here are some typical named constant declarations:

```
Const TaxRate As Single = 0.28

Const Avogadro As Double = 6.0225D+23

Const MaxCount As Integer = 100
```

The first line declares TaxRate to be a single-precision real constant whose value is 0.28. The second line defines *Avogadro's number* as a double-precision real constant whose value is 6.0225×10^{23}. The last line declares MaxCount as an integer constant whose value is 100.

Note that the values assigned to TaxRate, Avogadro and MaxCount will remain unchanged throughout the program.

Suffixes

Rather than declaring a data type explicitly (using a Dim or Const statement), a variable or named constant can be associated with a data type by adding a single-character *suffix* to the end of the variable/constant name. Several of the more commonly used suffixes are listed below.

Suffix	Data Type
%	integer
&	long integer
!	single
#	double
$	string

EXAMPLE 2.6

Shown below are several variables whose data types are defined by suffixes.

Variable	Data Type
Index%	integer
Counter&	long integer
TaxRate!	single
Ratio#	double
CustomerName$	string

The use of suffixes is derived from earlier versions of the Basic language, and is included in Visual Basic largely for purposes of consistency and backward compatibility. Modern programming practice encourages the use of explicit data type declarations rather than suffixes. Hence, we will not make use of suffixes elsewhere in this book.

User-Defined Data Types

It is sometimes convenient to define a multicomponent data type whose individual components are standard data items (i.e., integers, single-precision reals, strings, etc.). Visual Basic allows such data types to be defined, and it permits variables to be associated with these data types. Moreover, the components (called *members*) within such variables can easily be accessed individually.

In general terms, the data type definition is written as

```
Type data type name
     member name 1 As data type 1
     member name 2 As data type 2
     . . . . .
End Type
```

To associate a variable with a user-defined data type, we simply write

```
Dim variable name As user-defined data type
```

The components (members) of a user-defined variable can be accessed individually as

```
variable name . member name
```

These components can be used in the same manner as ordinary variables. Thus, they can appear within expressions, and they can be assigned values (see Secs. 2.5 and 2.10).

EXAMPLE 2.7

Here is a typical user-defined data type. This data type might be useful in a customer billing application.

```
Type Customer
     CustomerName As String
     AcctNo As Integer
     Balance As Single
End Type
```

Once the data type has been defined, we can declare one or more variables of this data type, as follows.

```
Dim OldCustomer As Customer, NewCustomer As Customer
```

We can then refer to the individual variable members as

```
OldCustomer.CustomerName            NewCustomer.CustomerName

OldCustomer.AcctNo                  NewCustomer.AcctNo

OldCustomer.Balance                 NewCustomer.Balance
```

and so on.

2.5 OPERATORS AND EXPRESSIONS

Special symbols, called *arithmetic operators*, are used to indicate arithmetic operations such as addition, subtraction, division and exponentiation. These operators are used to connect numeric constants and numeric variables, thus forming *arithmetic expressions*.

The standard arithmetic operators are

Addition:	+	(plus sign)
Subtraction:	−	(minus sign)
Multiplication:	*	(asterisk)
Division:	/	(slash)
Exponentiation:	^	(caret, or upward-pointing arrow)

When arithmetic operators appear within an arithmetic expression, the indicated operations are carried out on the individual terms within the expression, resulting in a single numerical value. Thus, *an arithmetic expression represents a specific numerical quantity*.

EXAMPLE 2.8

Several arithmetic expressions are presented below.

```
2 * j + k - 1                          2 * (j + k - 1)

first + second - third                 (a ^ 2 + b ^ 2) ^ 0.5

4 * Pi * Radius ^ 3 / 3                 (5 / 9) * (F - 32)

b ^ 2 - (4 * a * c)                    (2 * x - 3 * y) / (u + v)
```

Each expression represents a numerical quantity. Thus, if the variables a, b and c represent the quantities 2, 5 and 3, respectively, the expression a + b - c will represent the quantity 4.

Visual Basic also includes two additional arithmetic operators:

Integer division	\	(backward slash)
Integer remainder	Mod	

In integer division, each of the two given numbers is first *rounded* to an integer; the division is then carried out on the rounded values and the resulting quotient is truncated to an integer. The integer remainder operation (Mod) provides the remainder resulting from an integer division.

EXAMPLE 2.9

The results of several ordinary division, integer division and integer remainder operations are shown below.

13 / 5 = 2.6	13 \ 5 = 2	13 Mod 5 = 3
8.6 / 2.7 = 3.185185	8.6 \ 2.7 = 3	8.6 Mod 2.7 = 0
8.3 / 2.7 = 3.074074	8.3 \ 2.7 = 2	8.3 Mod 2.7 = 2
8.3 / 2.2 = 3.772727	8.3 \ 2.2 = 4	8.3 Mod 2.2 = 0

An arithmetic expression can be composed of a single numerical constant or a single numerical variable as well as some combination of constants, variables and operators. In any event, *every numerical variable that appears in an arithmetic expression must be assigned a specific value before it can appear in the expression*. Otherwise, the expression could not be evaluated to yield a specific numerical result.

2.6 HIERARCHY OF OPERATIONS

Questions in meaning may arise when several operators appear in an expression. For example, does the expression 2 * x – 3 * y correspond to the algebraic term $(2x) - (3y)$ or to $2(x - 3y)$? Similarly, does the expression a / b * c correspond to $a/(bc)$ or to $(a/b)c$? These questions are answered by the *hierarchy of operations* and the *order of execution within each hierarchical group*.

The hierarchy of operations is

1. *Exponentiation.* All exponentiation operations are performed first.

2. *Multiplication and division.* These operations are carried out after all exponentiation operations have been performed. Multiplication does not necessarily precede division.

3. *Integer division.* Integer division operations are carried out after all multiplication and (ordinary) division operations.

4. *Integer remainder.* Integer remainder operations are carried out after all integer divisions operations.

5. *Addition and subtraction.* These operations are the last to be carried out. Addition does not necessarily precede subtraction.

Within a given hierarchical group, the operations are carried out from left to right.

EXAMPLE 2.10

The arithmetic expression

        a / b * c

is equivalent to the mathematical expression $(a/b)\,c$, since the operations are carried out from left to right.

Similarly, the arithmetic expression

        b ^ 2 – 4 * a * c

is equivalent to the mathematical expression $b^2 - (4ac)$. In this case, the quantity b ^ 2 is formed initially, followed by the product 4 * a * c [first 4 * a, then (4 * a) * c]. The subtraction is performed last, resulting in the final numerical quantity (b ^ 2) – (4 * a * c).

A more extensive listing of the Visual Basic operators and their respective hierarchical ordering is given in Chapter 3.

2.7 INSERTING PARENTHESES

We may wish to alter the normal hierarchy of operations in a numeric expression. This is easily accomplished by inserting pairs of parentheses at the proper places within the expression. Then the operations within the innermost pair of parentheses will be performed first, followed by the operations within the second innermost pair, and so on. Within a given pair of parentheses, the natural hierarchy of operations will apply unless specifically altered by other pairs of parentheses embedded inside the given pair.

Remember to use *pairs* of parentheses. A careless imbalance of right and left parentheses is a common error among beginning programmers.

EXAMPLE 2.11

Suppose we want to evaluate the algebraic term

$$[\,2(a+b)^2 + (3c)^2\,]^{\,m\,/\,(n+1)}$$

A Visual Basic expression corresponding to this algebraic term is

```
(2 * (a + b) ^ 2 + (3 * c) ^ 2) ^ (m / (n + 1))
```

If there is some uncertainty in the order in which the operations are carried out, we can introduce additional pairs of parentheses, giving

```
((2 * ((a + b) ^ 2)) + ((3 * c) ^ 2)) ^ (m / (n + 1))
```

Both expressions are correct. The first expression is preferable, however, since it is less cluttered with parentheses and therefore easier to read.

2.8 SPECIAL RULES CONCERNING ARITHMETIC EXPRESSIONS

Special problems can arise if an arithmetic expression is not correctly written. Such problems can be avoided by remembering the following rules.

1. *Preceding a variable by a minus sign is equivalent to multiplication by −1.*

EXAMPLE 2.12

The arithmetic expression

```
-x ^ n
```

is equivalent to −(x ^ n) or −1 * (x ^ n), since exponentiation has precedence over multiplication. Hence, if x and n are assigned values of 3 and 2, respectively, then −x ^ n will yield a value of −9.

2. Except for the condition just described, *operations cannot be implied.*

EXAMPLE 2.13

The algebraic expression $2\,(x_1 + 3x_2)$ must be written in Visual Basic as

```
2 * (x1 + 3 * x2)
```

Note that the multiplication operators must be shown explicitly. Thus, the arithmetic expressions 2 (x1 + 3 * x2) and 2 * (x1 + 3 x2) are incorrect.

3. In an expression involving exponentiation, *a negative quantity can be raised to a power only if the exponent is an integer. (Do not confuse the exponent in an arithmetic expression with the exponent that is a part of a single- or double-precision real constant.)* To understand this restriction, we must see how exponentiation is carried out. If the exponent is an *integer* quantity, the quantity to be exponentiated is multiplied by itself an appropriate number of times. But if the exponent is *not* an integer quantity, Visual Basic computes the *logarithm* of the quantity being exponentiated, multiplies this logarithm by the exponent, and then computes the antilog. Since the logarithm of a negative number is not defined, we see that the operation is invalid if the quantity being exponentiated is negative.

EXAMPLE 2.14

Consider the arithmetic expression

        (c1 + c2) ^ 3

The quantity represented by (c1 + c2) is multiplied by itself twice, thus forming the cubic expression. It does not matter whether the quantity (c1 + c2) is positive or negative.

On the other hand, the arithmetic expression

        (b ^ 2 – 4 * a * c) ^ .5

will be valid only if (b ^ 2 – 4 * a * c) represents a positive quantity.

Finally, consider what happens in the arithmetic expression a ^ n when either a or n is zero. If n has a value of zero, then a ^ n will be assigned a value of 1, regardless of the value of a. If a has a value of zero and n is nonzero, however, then a ^ n will be evaluated as zero.

2.9 STRING EXPRESSIONS

Numerical operations cannot be performed on string constants or string variables. However, strings and string variables can be *concatenated* (i.e., combined, one behind the other). In Visual Basic we use either the ampersand (&) or the plus sign (+) as a string concatenation operator (the ampersand is favored).

EXAMPLE 2.15

Suppose the string variables str1 and str2 have been assigned the following values:

        Str1 = "TEN"

        Str2 = "THOUSAND"

Then the string expression

        Str1 & " " & str2 & " DOLLARS"

will cause the three individual strings to be concatenated, resulting in the single string

        TEN THOUSAND DOLLARS

Note that we could also have written the string expression as

        Str1 + " " + str2 + " DOLLARS"

2.10 ASSIGNING VALUES TO VARIABLES

The equal sign (=) is used to assign a numeric or string value to a variable. The general form is

        Variable = Expression

where the value of the expression on the right is assigned to the variable on the left. Note that the expression can consist of a constant, a single variable, or a more complex expression.

EXAMPLE 2.16

Shown below are several unrelated assignment statements.

```
X = 12.5

Cmax = X

Area = 3.141593 * Radius ^ 2

Label = "Name: "

Str = FirstStr + LastStr
```

In each statement, the value of the expression on the right of the equal sign is assigned to the variable on the left.

If the variable on the left of the equal sign and the expression on the right differ in their respective data types, Visual Basic will attempt to convert from the data type of the expression to the data type of the variable. Note that this may result in a data loss in some situations. For example, if the expression on the right is a real quantity and the variable on the left is an integer, the fractional part of the expression will be dropped when it is assigned to the integer variable. Moreover, some types of mixed-data-type assignments are incompatible and therefore not allowed. For example, a string expression cannot be assigned to a numeric variable.

EXAMPLE 2.17

Consider the Visual Basic statements shown below.

```
Dim Radius As Single, Area As Single, Counter As Integer, CircleID as String
Radius = 3
CircleID = "Red"

Area = 3.141593 * Radius ^ 2
Counter = Area
Area = CircleID
```

The first assignment statement (Area = 3.141593 * Radius ^ 2) does not present any problems, since we are assigning a single-precision real quantity to a single-precision real variable. However, the second assignment statement results in a data loss, because the single-precision value of Area (in this case, 28.27434) is assigned to the integer variable Counter. The decimal portion of Area is dropped, and Counter takes on the integer value 28.

The last assignment statement attempts to assign a string to a numeric variable. This operation is not permitted. Hence, the last assignment statement will result in a runtime error.

It is important to understand the difference between an assignment statement and an algebraic equation. Many assignment statements look like algebraic equations. On the other hand, there are certain kinds of assignments that would make no sense if viewed as algebraic equations.

EXAMPLE 2.18

Consider the following assignment statement.

```
J = J + 1
```

The assignment term J = J + 1 obviously does not correspond to an algebraic equation, since the equation $j = j + 1$ makes no sense. What we are doing here is to increase the value of the numeric variable J by one unit. Thus, the assignment term is entirely logical if we interpret it as follows: add 1 to the value originally represented by the variable J, and assign this new value to J. Thus, the new value of J will replace the old value. This operation is known as *incrementing*.

2.11 DISPLAYING OUTPUT – THE Print STATEMENT

The Print statement is used to display information within the currently active form, beginning in the upper left corner. This statement is not used often in Visual Basic projects. However, it is very convenient for displaying the results of very simple programs, and it provides a way to view the results of small program segments during the development of a large project.

The Print statement consists of the keyword Print, followed by a list of output items. The output items can be numeric constants, string constants, or expressions. Successive items must be separated either by commas or semicolons. Commas result in wide separation between data items; semicolons result in less separation. Each new Print statement will begin a new line of output. An empty Print statement will result in a blank line.

EXAMPLE 2.19

A Visual Basic program contains the following statements.

```
Dim Student As String, X As Integer, C1 As Single, C2 As Single
. . . . .
Student = "Aaron"
X = 39
C1 = 7
C2 = 11
. . . . .
Print "Name:", Student, X, (C1 + C2) / 2
```

The Print statement will generate the following line of output:

```
Name:           Aaron           39              9
```

If the Print statement had been written with semicolons separating the data items, e.g.,

```
Print "Name:"; Student; X; (C1 + C2) / 2
```

then the output data would be spaced more closely together, as shown below.

```
Name: Aaron  39  9
```

Now suppose the original Print statement had been replaced by the following three successive Print statements:

```
Print "Name:"; Student
Print
Print X,, (C1 + C2) / 2
```

Notice the repeated comma in the last Print statement.

The output would appear as

```
Name: Aaron

39                         9
```

The empty Print statement would produce the blank line separating the first and second lines of output. Also, the repeated comma in the last Print statement would increase the separation between the two data items.

2.12 LIBRARY FUNCTIONS

Visual Basic contains numerous *library functions* that provide a quick and easy way to carry out many mathematical operations, manipulate strings, and perform various logical operations. These library functions are prewritten routines that are included as an integral part of the language. They may be used in place of variables within an expression or a statement. Table 2.1 presents several commonly used library functions.

A library function is accessed simply by stating its name, followed by whatever information must be supplied to the function, enclosed in parentheses. A numeric quantity or string that is passed to a function in this manner is called an *argument*. Once the library function has been accessed, the desired operation will be carried out automatically. The function will then return the desired value.

Table 2.1   Commonly Used Library Functions

Function	Application	Description
Abs	y = Abs(x)	Return the absolute value of x; $y = |x|$.
CDbl, CInt, CSng, CStr, CVar, etc.	y = CInt(x)	Convert x to the appropriate data type (CDbl converts to double, CInt to integer, CSng to single, etc.).
Chr	y = Chr(x)	Return the character whose numerically encoded value is x. For example, in the ASCII character set, Chr(65) = "A".
Cos	y = Cos(x)	Return the cosine of x (x must be in radians).
Date	y = Date	Return the current system date.
Exp	y = Exp(x)	Return the value of e to the x power; $y = e^x$.
Format	y = Format(x, "*frmt str*")	Return the value of x in a format designated by "*frmt str*" (format string). Note that the format string may take on several different forms.
Int	y = Int(x)	Return the largest integer that algebraically does not exceed x. For example, Int(-1.9) = -2.
Lcase	y = Lcase(x)	Return the lowercase equivalent of x.
Left	y = Left(x, n)	Return the leftmost n characters of the string x.
Len	y = Len(x)	Return the length (number of characters) of x.
Log	y = Log(x)	Return the natural logarithm of x; $y = \log_e(x)$, $x > 0$.
Mid	y = Mid(x, n1, n2)	Return the middle $n2$ characters of the string x, beginning with character number $n1$.
Right	y = Right(x, n)	Return the rightmost n characters of the string x.
Rnd	y = Rnd	Return a random number, uniformly distributed within the interval $0 \leq y < 1$.
Sgn	y = Sgn(x)	Determine the sign of x; ($y = +1$ if x is positive, $y = 0$ if $x = 0$, and $y = -1$ if x is negative).
Sin	y = Sin(x)	Return the sine of x (x must be in radians).
Sqr	y = Sqr(x)	Return the square root of x; $y = \sqrt{x}$, $x > 0$.
Str	y = Str(x)	Return a string whose characters comprise the value of x. For example, Str(-2.50) = "-2.50".
Tan	y = Tan(x)	Return the tangent of x (x must be in radians).
Time	y = Time	Return the current system time.
Ucase	y = Ucase(x)	Return the uppercase equivalent of x.
Val	y = Val(x)	Return a numeric value corresponding to the string x, providing x has the appearance of a number. For example, Val("-2.50") = -2.5.

Note: The symbol e represents the base of the natural (Naperian) system of logarithms. It is an irrational number whose approximate value is 2.718282.

EXAMPLE 2.20

Suppose we wanted to calculate the square root of the value represented by the expression Area / 3.141593, using the library function Sqr. To do so, we could write

```
Radius = Sqr(Area / 3.141593)
```

Notice that the argument of Sqr is the numeric expression (Area / 3.141593).
    Of course, we could also have written

```
Radius = (Area / 3.141593) ^ 0.5
```

The library function is not required in this situation – it is merely used for convenience. In many situations, however (such as calculating the log of a number, or calculating the length of a string), the use of library functions may be the only straightforward way to carry out the calculation.

    Most of the functions listed in Table 2.1 have a straightforward interpretation. A few, however, require some additional explanation. The next several examples should clarify any confusion.

EXAMPLE 2.21

The Int function can be confusing, particularly with negative arguments. The values resulting from several typical function calls are shown below.

```
Int(2.3) = 2                        Int(-2.3) = -3

Int(2.7) = 2                        Int(-2.7) = -3
```

    Remember that Int produces a value whose magnitude is equal to or *smaller* than its argument if the argument is *positive*, and equal to or *larger* (in magnitude) than its argument if the argument is *negative*.

    Some functions, such as Log and Sqr, require positive arguments. If a negative argument is supplied, an error message will be generated when an attempt is made to evaluate the function.

EXAMPLE 2.22

A Visual Basic program contains the statements

```
x = -2.7
. . . . . .
y = Sqr(x)        (Notice the negative value assigned to x.)
```

When the program is executed, the following error message will be displayed:

```
Run-time error '5':
Invalid procedure call or argument
```

The execution will then cease.
    Similarly, the statement

```
y Log(x)
```

will produce the same error message when the program is executed.

EXAMPLE 2.23

The Format function allows a data item to be displayed in many different forms. Several possibilities are shown below. Many other variations are possible.

Expression	Result	
Print Format(17.66698, "##.##")	17.67	
Print Format(7.66698, "##.##")	7.67	(note the leading blank space)
Print Format(0.66667, "##.###")	.667	(note the leading blank spaces)
Print Format(0.66667, "#0.###")	0.667	(note the leading blank space)
Print Format(12345, "##,###")	12,345	
Print Format(12345, "##,###.00")	12,345.00	
Print Format("Basic", "&&&&&&&&")	Basic	
Print Format("Basic", "@@@@@@@@")	Basic	(note the leading blank spaces)
Print Format(Now, "mm-dd-yyyy")	1-20-2001	
Print Format(Now, "mm/dd/yy")	1/20/01	
Print Format(Now, "hh:mm:ss am/pm")	04:47:51 pm	

Note that Now is a predefined Visual Basic variable that represents the current date and time, as determined by the computer's real-time clock.

The use of library functions is not confined to assignment statements – a library function may appear anywhere in an expression in place of a constant or a variable. Moreover, the arguments need not be constants or simple variables – expressions (which may include references to other functions) can be used as valid function arguments, provided they are of the proper data type.

We will encounter additional library functions elsewhere in this book, in conjunction with features to be discussed in later chapters.

2.13 PROGRAM COMMENTS

Comments provide a convenient means to *document* a program (i.e., to provide a program heading, to identify important variables, to distinguish between major logical segments of a program, to explain complicated logic, etc.). A comment consists of a single apostrophe ('), followed by a textual message. Comments can be inserted anywhere in a Visual Basic program. They have no effect on the program execution.

EXAMPLE 2.24

A Visual Basic program includes the following statements:

```
'Program to Calculate the Roots of a Quadratic Equation
. . . . . .
X1 = (-b + root) / (2 * a)      'calculate the first root
X2 = (-b - root) / (2 * a)      'calculate the second root
Print X1, X2
```

The entire first line is a comment, which serves as a program heading. On the other hand, the last two lines each have a comment attached at the end of an executable statement. Note that each comment begins with a single apostrophe.

Review Questions

2.1   How do integer and long-integer constants differ from one another?

2.2   How do integer and single-precision real constants differ from one another?

2.3   How do single-precision and double-precision real constants differ from one another?

2.4   Summarize the rules that apply to numeric constants.

2.5   Present a detailed comparison between a number written in scientific notation and a number written in Visual Basic as a floating-point constant.

2.6   What is a string constant? How are string constants written?

2.7   What is the maximum permissible length of a string constant?

2.8   Summarize the rules for naming numeric and string variables.

2.9   What is the maximum permissible length of a variable name?

2.10   What are reserved words? Can a reserved word be used as a variable name?

2.11   Is Visual Basic case-sensitive (i.e., does it distinguish between uppercase and lowercase letters)?

2.12   What common data types are supported by Visual Basic?

2.13   What is the purpose of the Dim statement? How is a Dim statement written?

2.14   What is a variant? What are the advantages and disadvantages associated with the use of variants?

2.15   What is the purpose of the Const statement? How does it differ from a Dim statement? How is a Const statement written?

2.16   In Visual Basic, how does a named constant differ from a variable?

2.17   What are the commonly used variable-name suffixes in Visual Basic? What does each suffix represent?

2.18   Summarize the syntax for defining a multicomponent user-defined data type. How are variables of this data type declared?

2.19   Within a multicomponent user-defined data type, what is a member?

2.20   What arithmetic operators are available in Visual Basic? What is their natural hierarchy? In what order are operations carried out within a hierarchical group?

2.21   What is a numeric expression? What does a numeric expression represent?

2.22   How can the natural hierarchy of operations be altered within a numeric expression?

2.23   Describe a particular problem that can arise in exponentiation operations. Give a reason for the problem and describe how the problem can be avoided.

2.24   What is a string expression? How do string expressions differ from numeric expressions?

2.25 What operations can be carried out on strings?

2.26 How is a numerical or string value assigned to a variable?

2.27 Summarize the rules for writing an assignment statement.

2.28 What happens if the variable on the left-hand side of an assignment statement and the expression on the right-hand side differ in their respective data types? Describe all possible situations.

2.29 Discuss the similarities and differences between an assignment statement and an algebraic equation.

2.30 Describe the customary use of the `Print` statement in Visual Basic.

2.31 What is the purpose of an empty `Print` statement?

2.32 Suppose a `Print` statement includes five output items, separated by commas. How can the statement be rewritten so that the output items appear on the same line, with minimum spacing between them?

2.33 Suppose a `Print` statement includes five output items. How can the statement be rewritten so that the first three data items appear on one line and the remaining two data items appear on a second line?

2.34 What are library functions? What useful purpose do they serve?

2.35 Name several of the more common library functions. State the purpose of each.

2.36 What is an argument? Must an argument have the same data type as the quantity returned by the function?

2.37 What is the purpose of the `Int` function? What does the `Int` function return if it receives a negative argument?

2.38 What happens if a negative value is supplied to a library function that requires a positive argument?

2.39 What is the purpose of the `Format` function? What type of arguments does this function require?

2.40 Can a library function accept an expression as an argument? Can it accept a reference to another library function as an argument?

2.41 What is the purpose of a comment within a Visual Basic program? How are comments written?

2.42 Can a comment be included on a line containing a program statement?

Problems

2.43 Express each of the following quantities as a numeric constant.

    (a) 7,350

    (b) −12

    (c) 10^6

    (d) $-2{,}053.18 \times 10^3$

    (e) 0.00008291

    (f) 9.563×10^{12}

    (g) 1/6

2.44 Each of the following numeric constants is written incorrectly. Identify the errors.

    (a) `7,104`

    (b) `-+4920`

    (c) `2.665E+42`

    (d) `0.333333333333`

    (e) `4.63D-0.8`

2.45 Each of the following items represents a string constant. Identify which, if any, are written incorrectly.

(*a*) `"July 4, 1776"`

(*b*) `"2 + 5 = 7"`

(*c*) `Another game?`

(*d*) `"75.50"`

(*e*) `"Divide "X" by 100"`

(*f*) `"One hundred twenty-nine and 73/100 dollars"`

(*g*) `"Programming with Visual Basic is lots of fun`

2.46 Identify which of the following variable names are written incorrectly.

(*a*) `xmax`

(*b*) `Qbar$`

(*c*) `Big C`

(*d*) `Big_C`

(*e*) `#space`

(*f*) `x.3`

(*g*) `Answer?`

(*h*) `root1`

(*i*) `Str1`

(*j*) `input3`

2.47 Write a single (one-line) declaration for each of the following situations:

(*a*) Declare `x1` and `x2` as single-precision real variables.

(*b*) Declare `CustomerName` and `Address` as string variables.

(*c*) Declare `Counter` as an integer variable, and `Sum` and `Variance` as double-precision real variables.

(*d*) Declare `Factor` as a named single-precision constant whose value is 0.80.

(*e*) Declare `City` as a named string constant whose value is "`New York`".

2.48 Repeat Prob. 2.47 using variable-name suffixes rather than explicit declarations.

2.49 Define a multicomponent data type called `MachinePart` having the following components:

`Color`	(string)
`PartNo`	(long integer)
`Length`	(single-precision real)
`Cost`	(single-precision real)

Then declare a variable called `EnginePart` of this data type. Assign the following values to the components of `EnginePart`: color: black; part number: 64,389; length: 88.042; cost: 22,515.87.

2.50 Write an arithmetic expression that corresponds to each of the following algebraic formulas.

(*a*) $3x + 5$

(*b*) $i + j - 2$

(*c*) $x^2 + y^2$

(*d*) $(x + y)^2$

(*e*) $(u + v)^{k-1}$

(*f*) $(4\,t)^{1/6}$

(*g*) $t^{(n+1)}$

(*h*) $(x + 3)^{1/k}$

2.51 Determine the value of each of the following expressions.

(*a*) 17 / 3

(*b*) 17 \ 3

(*c*) 17 Mod 3

(*d*) 7.8 / 1.8

(*e*) 7.8 \ 1.8

(*f*) 7.8 Mod 1.8

(*g*) 7.1 / 1.3

(*h*) 7.1 \ 1.3

(*i*) 7.1 Mod 1.3

(*j*) 7.1 / 1.8

(*k*) 7.1 \ 1.8

(*l*) 7.1 Mod 1.8

2.52 Write a string concatenation expression to join each of the following groups of string variables and constants.

(*a*) StrA, StrB and StrC

(*b*) Client, Street and City, with a blank space between each string

(*c*) "Hello, " and StudentName

2.53 Write an assignment statement for each of the following situations.

(*a*) Assign a value of 2.54 to the variable C.

(*b*) Assign a value of 12 to the variable xmin.

(*c*) Assign the value represented by the variable N to the variable Nstar.

(*d*) Assign the string "January 31" to the variable Date.

(*e*) Assign the string represented by the variable Str1 to the variable Tag.

(*f*) Assign the value represented by the expression (A ^ 2 + B ^ 2 + C ^ 2) to the variable squares.

(*g*) Increase the value assigned to the variable count by 0.01.

(*h*) Assign the value represented by the expression (I + J) to the variable I.

(*i*) Assign the string "PITTSBURGH, PA." to the variable City.

(*j*) Assign the value of the expression X / (A + B − C) to the variable Ratio.

(*k*) Decrease the value assigned to the variable K by 2.

(*l*) Double the value assigned to the variable Prize.

2.54 Write an assignment statement that corresponds to each of the following algebraic equations.

(*a*) $z = (x / y) + 3$

(*b*) $z = x / (y + 3)$

(*c*) $w = (u + v) / (s + t)$

(*d*) $f = [2ab / (c + 1) - t / (3(p + q))]^{1/3}$

(*e*) $y = (a_1 - a_2 x + a_3 x^2 - a_4 x^3 + a_5 x^4) / (c_1 - c_2 x + c_3 x^2 - c_4 x^3)$

(*f*) $P = Ai (1 + i)^n / [(1 + i)^n - 1]$

2.55 What particular difficulty might be experienced in executing the statement

    x = (y − z) ^ 0.25

2.56 Consider the statement

    P = −Q ^ 4

If Q = 2, what value will be assigned to P?

2.57 Consider the statement

    P = Q ^ 4

If Q = −2, what value will be assigned to P? (Compare with the answer to the previous problem.)

2.58 Write an appropriate statement, or group of statements, for each situation described below.

(*a*) Display the values of `C1`, `C2`, `C3`, `C4` and `C5` all on one line.

(*b*) Display the values of `A`, `B` and `C` on one line and the values of `X`, `Y` and `Z` on another line, with a blank line separating them.

(*c*) Display the values of `A`, `B`, `C`, `X`, `Y` and `Z` all on one line, spaced as closely as possible.

(*d*) Display the values of `X`, `Y` and `Z` on one line. Precede each numeric value with an appropriate label.

(*e*) Display the values of `N$` and `N` next to one another, followed by the value of the following expression: `A ^ 2 + B ^ 2`.

2.59 Show how the output will appear in each of the following situations.

(*a*) `Print "Name: ", employee, pay, tax, net`

    where `employee = George Smith`   `pay = 7000`   `tax = 1500`   `net = 5500`

(*b*) `Print "Name: "; employee; pay; tax; net`

    where the variables have the same values as in part (*a*).

(*c*) `Print A1, B1, C1, D1`
     `Print A2, B2, C2, D2`

    where   `A1 = 3`   `A2 = 5`
          `B1 = 6`   `B2 = 10`
          `C1 = 9`   `C2 = 15`
          `D1 = 12`   `D2 = 20`

(*d*) `Print A1; B1; C1; D1;`
     `Print A2; B2; C2; D2`

    where the variables have the same values as in part (*c*).

(*e*) `Print A1 + B1; D2 / C2; (A1 * B2) / (B2 * C2)`

    where the variables have the same values as in part (*c*).

2.60 Using appropriate library functions, write assignment statements that correspond to each of the following algebraic equations.

(*a*) $w = \log_e (v)$

(*b*) $p = qe^{-qt}$

(*c*) $w = ||u - v| - |u + v||$

(*d*) $r = (p + q)^{1/2}$

(*e*) $y = ae^{bx} \sin cx$

(*f*) $y = (|\sin x - \cos x|)^{1/2}$

2.61 Using appropriate library functions, write a Visual Basic statement for each of the following situations.

(*a*) Determine the sign of the quantity $(ab - cd) / (f + g)$.

(*b*) Determine if the value of the integer variable `N` is even or odd, assuming that `N` has a positive value. (*Hint:* Compare the value of `N / 2` with the truncated value of `N / 2`.)

(*c*) In problem (*b*) above, what will happen if `N` has a negative value?

(*d*) Determine the largest integer that algebraically does not exceed z, where $z = x^2 - y^2$. Assign this value to the integer variable `IZ`.

(*e*) In problem (*d*) above, if $x = 2.5$ and $y = 6.3$, what value will be assigned to `IZ`?

2.62 Determine the result of each of the following expressions. Assume that the variable `Address` has been assigned the string `"1600 Pennsylvania Avenue"`.

(a) `Len(Address)`
(d) `Mid(Address, 5, 8)`

(b) `UCase(Address)`
(e) `Str(1/5)`

(c) `Right(Address, 5)`
(f) `Val("1.25")`

2.63 In each of the following cases, show how the comment (or remark) can be placed in a Visual Basic program.

(a) Add the program heading `Area and Circumference of a Circle`

(b) Add the program heading `Averaging of Air Pollution Data`

(c) Add the comments `Area` and `Circumference` to the statements

```
Area = Pi * Radius ^ 2
Circumference = 2 * Pi * Radius
```

(d) Insert the full-line comment `Loop to Calculate Cumulative Sum`

(e) Add the comment `Calculate an Average Value` to the statement

```
Avg = Sum / n
```

Chapter 3

Branching and Looping

Visual Basic includes a number of features that allow us to select among alternative pathways, or to repeat the execution of a particular block of statements. For example, we can choose to execute one of several different blocks of statements, depending on the value of an expression. This process is known as *selection*. Or, we can choose one of two different paths, depending on the outcome of a logical test (i.e., depending whether a *logical expression* is *true* or *false*). This process is known as *branching*.

Many programs require that a group of instructions be executed repeatedly, until some particular condition has been satisfied. This process is known as *looping*. Sometimes the number of passes through the loop will be known in advance (*unconditional* looping). In other situations the looping action will continue indefinitely, until some logical condition has been satisfied (*conditional* looping).

In this chapter we will see how Visual Basic allows us to carry out selection, branching and looping operations.

3.1 RELATIONAL OPERATORS AND LOGICAL EXPRESSIONS

In order to carry out branching operations in Visual Basic, we must be able to express conditions of equality and inequality. To do so, we make use of the following *relational operators* (also called *comparison operators*):

Equal:	=
Not equal:	<>
Less than:	<
Less than or equal to:	<=
Greater than:	>
Greater than or equal to:	>=

These operators are used to compare numeric quantities (i.e., constants, numeric variables or numeric expressions) or strings, thus forming *logical expressions* that are either *true* or *false*. The *operands* within a logical expression must be of the same type; i.e., both must be numeric or both must be strings.

EXAMPLE 3.1

Several logical expressions involving numeric quantities are shown below. Each logical expression will be either true or false, depending on the value assigned to the numeric variables.

```
X = 27

Error <= Abs(x1 - x2)

C < Sqr(A + B)

Profit > (Gross - Taxes)

FLAG <> CUTOFF
```

The first expression will be true if X has been assigned a value of 27; otherwise, the expression will be false. Similarly, the second expression will be true if the value assigned to error does not exceed the absolute value of the numeric expression x1 - x2, and so on. Notice that the second and third expressions involve the use of library functions.

Strings can be tested for equality or inequality, in much the same manner as numeric quantities. However, string expressions involving operators <, <=, > and >= refer to alphabetical ordering; that is, these operators are interpreted as "comes before" or "comes after" rather than "less than" or "greater than." The actual alphabetic ordering is determined by the system used to encode the characters (as, for example, the ASCII character set).

String comparisons are carried out on a character-by-character basis, from left to right. Uppercase characters precede lowercase characters, and blank spaces precede nonblank characters. If one string is shorter than the other and all of its characters are the same as the corresponding characters in the longer string, the shorter string is considered to precede the longer string. Thus, car precedes far, Dog precedes dog, cat precedes cats, and so on.

EXAMPLE 3.2

Several logical expressions involving strings are presented below. All variables represent strings. Each logical expression will be either true or false, depending on the particular strings that are assigned to the string variables.

```
Student = "Smith"

char <> "w"

Target < City
```

The first expression will be true if the string assigned to Student is "Smith"; otherwise, the expression will be false. Similarly, the second expression will be true if the string assigned to char is not "w", and the last expression will be true if the string assigned to Target comes earlier in the alphabet than the string assigned to City. Thus, if Target represents "Philadelphia" and City represents "Pittsburgh", the expression will be true.

3.2 LOGICAL OPERATORS

In addition to the relational operators, Visual Basic contains several *logical operators*. They are And, Or, Xor (exclusive Or), Not, Eqv (equivalent) and Imp (implies). The first three operators (And, Or and Xor) are used to combine logical expressions, thus forming more complex logical expressions. And will result in a condition that is true if *both* expressions are true. Or will result in a condition that is true if *either* expression is true, or if they are both true; Xor, however, will result in a condition that is true *only* if one of the expressions is true and the other is false. Not is used to reverse (*negate*) the value of a logical expression (e.g., from true to false, or false to true). Eqv will result in a condition that is true if both expressions have the *same* logical value (either both true or both false); and Imp will always result in a true condition unless the first expression is true and the second is false.

EXAMPLE 3.3

Shown below are several logical expressions that make use of logical operators.

```
X = 27 And Student = "Smith"

X > 0 And Student <= "Smith"

C < Sqr(A + B) Or FLAG <> CUTOFF

C < Sqr(A + B) Xor FLAG <> CUTOFF
```

```
Not(Student = "Smith") And (Account = "CURRENT")

(Student = "Smith") Eqv (Account = "CURRENT")

(Student = "Smith") Imp (Account = "CURRENT")
```

The first two logical expressions will be true only if *both* logical operands are true. Thus, the first logical expression will be true if the numeric value assigned to X is 27 and the string assigned to Student is "Smith". (Note that the first logical operand involves numeric quantities whereas the second involves strings.) Similarly, the second logical expression will be true if the numeric value assigned to X exceeds zero and the string assigned to Student is "Smith", or it precedes "Smith".

The third logical expression will be true if *either* logical operand is true; i.e., if the numeric value assigned to C is less than the square root of (A + B), or the value assigned to FLAG differs from the value assigned to CUTOFF. The expression will also be true if *both* logical operands are true. However, the fourth logical expression will be true *only* if *one* of the logical operands is true and the other is false.

The fifth logical expression involves both Not and And. In this case, the logical expression will be true only if the string assigned to Student is *not* "Smith", and the string assigned to Account *is* "CURRENT". Notice that the Not operator has reversed (negated) the condition for which the first operand will be true.

The second-last logical expression will be true if both logical operands are true ("Smith" has been assigned to Student and "CURRENT" has been assigned to Account), or if both logical operands are false. And finally, the last logical expression will be true *unless* the first logical operand is true ("Smith" has been assigned to Student) and the second is false ("CURRENT" has *not* been assigned to Account).

The complete hierarchy of arithmetic, relational and logical operators is as follows:

	Operation	*Operator*
1.	Exponentiation	^
2.	Negation (i.e., preceding a numeric quantity with a minus sign)	–
3.	Multiplication and division	* /
4.	Integer division	\
5.	Integer remainder	Mod
6.	Addition and subtraction	+ –
7.	Relationals	= <> < <= > >=
8.	Logical Not	Not
9.	Logical And	And
10.	Logical Or	Or
11.	Logical Xor	Xor
12.	Logical Eqv	Eqv
13.	Logical Imp	Imp

Within a given hierarchical group, the operations are carried out from left to right. The natural hierarchy can be altered, however, by using parentheses, as described in Sec. 2.6. In particular, note that parentheses can be used with logical expressions, just as they are used with arithmetic expressions.

EXAMPLE 3.4

Consider the logical expression

```
Balance > 0 Or Flag = 1 And Account = "Regular"
```

This expression is equivalent to

```
Balance > 0 Or (Flag = 1 And Account = "Regular")
```

Thus, the expression will be true if either `Balance` has been assigned a value greater than 0, or `Flag` has been assigned a value of 1 and `Account` has been assigned the string `"Regular"`.

On the other hand, the logical expression

```
(Balance > 0 OR Flag = 1) And Account = "Regular"
```

has a different interpretation. Now the expression will be true only if either `Balance` has been assigned a value greater than 0 and/or `Flag` has been assigned a value of 1, and in addition, `Account` has been assigned the string `"Regular"`.

Note that the first logical expression can be satisfied simply if `Balance > 0` is true. However, the second logical expression requires that *two* conditions be true; `Account = "Regular"` must be true, and one or both of the remaining conditions must also be true (either `Balance > 0` or `Flag = 1`).

3.3 BRANCHING WITH THE `If-Then` BLOCK

An `If-Then` block is used to execute a single statement or a block of statements on a conditional basis. There are two different forms. The simplest is the single-line, single-statement `If-Then`, which is written as

> `If` *logical expression* `Then` *executable statement*

The *executable statement* will be executed only if the *logical expression* is true. Otherwise, the statement following `If-Then` will be executed next. Note that the executable statement must appear on the same line as the logical expression; otherwise, an `End If` statement will be required (see below).

EXAMPLE 3.5

A typical situation utilizing an `If-Then` statement is shown below.

```
If x < 0 Then x = 0
Sum = Sum + x
```

This example causes negative values of x to be set to zero before adding the current value of x to Sum. Note that the adjustment is executed only if the logical expression `x < 0` is true. However, the second assignment statement (`Sum = Sum + x`) is always executed, regardless of the outcome of the logical test.

Here is a more general form of an `If-Then` block:

> `If` *logical expression* `Then`
>
> . . . .
> *executable statements*
> . . . .
>
> `End If`

The block of statements included between `If-Then` and `End If` will be executed if the logical expression is true. Otherwise, this block of statements will be bypassed, and the statement following `End If` will be executed next.

EXAMPLE 3.6

The following If-Then block permits a single group of statements to be executed conditionally.

```
IF income <= 14000 THEN
    tax = 0.2 * pay
    net = pay - tax
END IF
```

The assignment statements will be executed only if the logical expression income <= 14000 is true.

3.4 BRANCHING WITH If-Then-Else BLOCKS

An If-Then-Else block permits one of two different groups of executable statements to be executed, depending on the outcome of a logical test. Thus, it permits a broader form of branching than is available with a single If-Then block.

In general terms, an If-Then-Else block is written as

```
If logical expression Then
    . . . . . . . .
    executable statements
    . . . . . . . .
Else
    . . . . . . . .
    executable statements
    . . . . . . . .
End If
```

If the *logical expression* is true, the *first* group of executable statements will be executed. Otherwise, the *second* group of executable statements will be executed. Thus, one group of executable statements will always be executed. Note that If-Then, Else and End If are separate statements that are used together to create a complete If-Then-Else block.

The executable statements are usually indented with respect to the If-Then, Else and End If statements so that the structure of the block is readily identifiable. This is not a rigid syntactical requirement, but it is considered to be good programming practice and is strongly encouraged.

EXAMPLE 3.7

A typical If-Then-Else sequence is shown below. This sequence allows us to calculate either the area and circumference of a circle or the area and circumference of a rectangle, depending on the string that is assigned to the variable form.

```
pi = 3.141593
If (form = "circle") THEN            'circle
    area = pi * radius ^ 2
    circumference = 2 * pi * r
Else                                 'rectangle
    area = length * width
    circumference = 2 * (length + width)
End If
```

If the logical expression `form = "circle"` is true, then the *first* group of executable statements (the first two indented lines) will be executed. If the logical expression is false, however, the *second* group of executable statements (the indented lines that follow `Else`) will be executed.

Note that the indentation of the executable statements causes the entire If-Then-Else structure to be readily discernable. Thus, it is easy to identify which group of statements corresponds to If-Then and which corresponds to Else.

Though If-Then-Else blocks often include several executable statements after the If-Then and the Else statements, the appearance of a single executable statement is also common. The following example illustrates a typical application.

EXAMPLE 3.8

Consider the following If-Then-Else block.

```
IF (status = "single") THEN
    tax = 0.2 * pay
Else
    tax = 0.14 * pay
END IF
```

If the logical expression `status = "single"` is true, then the *first* assignment statement will be executed. If the logical expression is false, however, the *second* assignment statement will be executed.

A more general form of the If-Then-Else block can be written as

If *logical expression 1* Then
    . . . .
        executable statements
    . . . .

ElseIf *logical expression 2* Then
    . . . .
        executable statements
    . . . .

repeated ElseIf *clauses*
    . . . .

Else
    . . . .
        executable statements
    . . . .

End If

In this form, If-Then clauses are embedded within prior Else clauses. Hence, we can construct conditional execution blocks that involve complex logical conditions.

EXAMPLE 3.9 ROOTS OF A QUADRATIC EQUATION

The roots of the quadratic equation $ax^2 + bx + c = 0$ can be determined using the well-known formulas

$$x_1 = \frac{-b + \sqrt{b^2 - 4ac}}{2a}$$

$$x_2 = \frac{-b - \sqrt{b^2 - 4ac}}{2a}$$

provided the quantity $b^2 - 4ac$ is positive.

If $b^2 - 4ac$ is zero, we have a single (repeated) real root, determined as

$$x = -b\,/\,2a$$

If $b^2 - 4ac$ is negative, we have two complex roots. In this case,

$$x_1 = \frac{-b + \sqrt{4ac - b^2}\ i}{2a}$$

$$x_2 = \frac{-b - \sqrt{4ac - b^2}\ i}{2a}$$

where i represents the *imaginary number* $\sqrt{-1}$

In Visual Basic, we can accommodate these three situations with a group of `If-Then-ElseIf-Else` blocks, as shown below.

```
'Roots of a Quadratic Equation

Dim a, b, c, d, x, x1, x2, real, imag          'variant data types

d = (b ^ 2 - 4 * a * c)

If d > 0 Then                                  'real roots
    x1 = (-b + Sqr(d)) / (2 * a)
    x2 = (-b - Sqr(d)) / (2 * a)

ElseIf d = 0 Then                              'repeated root
    x = -b / (2 * a)

Else                                           'complex roots
    real = -b / (2 * a)
    imag = Sqr(-d) / (2 * a)

End If
```

We will see additional applications of `If-Then` and `If-Then-Else` blocks, in conjunction with other Visual Basic control structures, in the remaining sections of this chapter.

3.5 SELECTION: Select Case

One way to select a block of statements from several competing blocks is to use a series of `If-Then-Else` or `If-Then-ElseIf-Else` blocks. This can be tedious, however, if the number of competing blocks is moderately large. The `Select Case` structure frequently offers a simpler approach to this type of situation.

The most common form of the `Select Case` structure is written in general terms as

```
Select Case expression

Case value1
     executable statements

Case value2
     executable statements


     . . . . . . . .


Case Else
     executable statements

End Select
```

The Case Else group is optional; it may omitted if one or more Case *value* groups are present. Similarly, the Case *value* groups may be omitted if the Case Else group is present. In practice, however, a Case Else group rarely appears alone, without any preceding Case *value* groups.

When the Select Case structure is executed, the value of the *expression* is compared successively with *value1*, *value2*, etc., until a match is found. The group of *executable statements* following the matching Case statement is then executed, and control is passed to the first statement following End Select. If a match cannot be found among the available values (i.e., *value1*, *value2*, etc.), then the *executable statements* following Case Else are executed.

The Select Case structure is particularly convenient when used in conjunction with a menu entry. In such situations the selection is based upon the menu item that is chosen.

EXAMPLE 3.10

Here is a Visual Basic program segment that makes use of a Select Case structure.

```
'Raise x to a Selected Power

Dim x, z, n As Integer

Select Case n                    'select a group of statements

Case 1                           'x ^ 1
   z = x

Case 2                           'x ^ 2
   z = x ^ 2

Case 3                           'x ^ 3
   z = x ^ 3

Case Else                        'error
   MsgBox("ERROR - Please try again")

End Select
```

This program segment assumes that integer values have been assigned for x and n. The value of x, x^2 or x^3 is then assigned to z, depending on the value assigned to n. An error message will be displayed if n is assigned a value other than 1, 2 or 3. (See Sec. 4.13 for a discussion of the MsgBox function.)

The *expression* in the Select Case statement can be a string rather than a numeric expression. In this case, the *values* in the subsequent Case statements must also be strings. The original string expression will then be compared with the string values in the subsequent Case statements until a match is found. As before, Case Else provides a default in the event that a match cannot be found.

EXAMPLE 3.11

The following program segment is similar to that shown in Example 3.10, except that the selection is based upon a string rather than the value of a numeric expression. The program segment assumes that a string has been assigned to Status. If the string is Single, Married or Retired (in either uppercase or lowercase), an appropriate value will be assigned to TaxRate. If any other string is entered, an error message will be displayed.

```
'Tax rate based upon marital status
Dim Status As String, TaxRate as Single
Status = UCase(Status)
Select Case Status
Case "SINGLE"
   TaxRate = 0.20
Case "MARRIED"
   TaxRate = 0.14
Case "RETIRED"
   TaxRate = 0.12
Case Else
   MsgBox("ERROR - Please try again")
End Select
```

Some additional options are available when writing Select Case statements. For example, if the value of the *expression* in the Select Case statement is numeric, then a numeric expression may appear in a succeeding Case statement. A logical expression may also appear, provided the expression is preceded by the keyword Is. Moreover, multiple values, separated by commas, may appear in a single Case statement. Also, a *range* of values, connected by the keyword To, may appear in a single Case statement. All of these options are illustrated in the following example.

EXAMPLE 3.12

The following program segment shows a selection based upon the value of a numeric constant.

```
Dim Flag As Integer, Label As String
Select Case Flag
Case 1, 3, 5
   Label = "Odd digit between 1 and 5"
Case 2, 4, 6
   Label = "Even digit between 2 and 6"
Case 7 To 9
   Label = "Any digit between 7 and 9"
Case Is >= 10
   Label = "Too big"
Case Else
   Label = "Nonpositive number"
End Select
```

The first two `Case` statements each contain multiple values separated by commas. The third `Case` statement contains a range of values connected by the keyword `To` (i.e., `Case 7 To 9`). And finally, the fourth `Case` statement contains a logical expression preceded by the keyword `Is` (i.e., `Case Is >= 10`).

Similar options are also available if the *expression* in the `Select Case` statement is a string. A succeeding `Case` statement may contain a logical expression, preceded by the keyword `Is`. A `Case` statement may also contain multiple strings, separated by commas. Or, a `Case` statement may contain a *range* of strings, connected by the keyword `To`. The following example illustrates these options.

EXAMPLE 3.13

The following program segment presents a selection based upon a single-character string.

```
Dim Char As String, Label As String

Select Case Char

Case "A" To "Z", "a" To "z"
   Label = "Character is a LETTER"

Case "0" To "9"
   Label = "Character is a DIGIT"

Case Is < " ", Is > "~"
   Label = "Character is NONPRINTING"

Case Else
   Label = "Character is NOT ALPHANUMERIC"

End Select
```

The first `Case` statement contains two string ranges. Each range includes the keyword `To`. The individual ranges are separated by a comma.

The second `Case` statement includes a single range of strings. (Note that the digits 0 and 9 are written as strings, not numerical values.) Again, note the use of the keyword `To`.

Finally, the third `Case` statement includes two logical expressions. Each logical expression is preceded by the keyword `Is`. The individual expressions are separated by a comma.

3.6 LOOPING WITH `For-Next`

The `For-Next` structure is a block of statements that is used to carry out a looping operation; that is, to execute a sequence of statements some predetermined number of times. The structure begins with a `For-To` statement and ends with a `Next` statement. In between are the statements to be executed.

In its simplest form, a `For-Next` structure is written as

```
For index = value1 To value2
       . . . . . . . .
       executable statements
       . . . . . . . .
Next index
```

The `For-To` statement specifies the number of passes through the loop. Within this statement, *index* is a variable whose value begins with *value1*, increases by 1 each time the loop is executed, until it reaches *value2*. Note that the value of *index* will be *value2* during the last pass through the loop.

The Next statement identifies the end of the loop. It consists simply of the keyword Next, followed by the *index*. The *index* appearing in the For-To and the Next statements must be the same. (Visual Basic allows the *index* to be omitted from the Next statement in single For-Next loops, though this is considered poor programming practice.)

The *executable statements* refer to one or more consecutive statements that are executed during each pass through the loop. These statements are usually indented, so that the structure can easily be identified. The indentation is not required, though it is considered good programming practice.

EXAMPLE 3.14

A typical For-To loop structure is shown below.

```
sum = 0
For i = 1 To 10
    sum = sum + i
Next i
```

This structure will result in 10 passes through the loop. During the first pass, i will be assigned a value of 1; i will then increase by 1 during each successive pass through the loop, until it has reached its final value of 10 in the last pass. Within each pass, the current value of i is added to sum. Hence, the net effect of this program segment is to determine the sum of the first 10 integers (i.e., $1 + 2 + \ldots + 10$).

Note the indentation of the assignment statement within the loop structure.

A more general form of the For-Next structure can be written as

```
For index = value1 To value2 Step value3
    . . . . . . . .
    executable statements
    . . . . . . . .
Next index
```

Within the For-To statement, *value3* determines the amount by which *value1* changes from one pass to the next. This quantity need not be restricted to an integer, and it can be either positive or negative. If *value3* is negative, then *value1* must be greater than *value2* (because the value assigned to *index* will *decrease* during each successive pass through the loop). Note that *value3* is understood to equal 1 if it is not shown explicitly (i.e., if the Step clause is omitted).

EXAMPLE 3.15

The loop structure

```
sum = 0
For count = 2.5 To -1 STEP -0.5
    sum = sum + count
Next count
```

will cause count to take on the values 2.5, 2.0, 1.5, . . ., 0.0, -0.5, -1.0. Hence, the final value of sum will be 6.0 (because $2.5 + 2.0 + 1.5 + 1.0 + 0.5 + 0.0 - 0.5 - 1.0 = 6.0$). Note that this structure will generate a total of eight passes through the loop.

The For-Next structure is one of the most widely used features in Visual Basic. It is most often used when the number of passes through the loop is known in advance.

The following rules apply to For-Next loops.

1. The index variable can appear within a statement inside the loop, but its value cannot be altered.

2. If *value1* and *value2* are equal and *value3* is nonzero, the loop will be executed once.

3. The loop will not be executed at all under any of the following conditions:

   (a) *value1* and *value2* are equal, and *value3* is zero.

   (b) *value1* is greater than *value2*, and *value3* is positive.

   (c) *value1* is less than *value2*, and *value3* is negative.

4. Control can be transferred *out* of a loop, but *not in* (see below).

Visual Basic includes an Exit For statement. This statement permits a transfer out of a For-Next loop if some particular condition is satisfied. For example, we may wish to jump out of a loop if an error or a stopping condition is detected during the execution of the loop.

The Exit For statement is generally embedded in an If-Then structure that is included within the loop. When the Exit For statement is encountered during program execution, control is immediately transferred out of the For-Next loop, to the first executable statement following Next.

EXAMPLE 3.16

Here is a variation of Example 3.14, illustrating the use of a typical Exit For statement.

```
sum = 0
For i = 1 To 10
    sum = sum + i
    If sum >= 10 Then
        Exit For
Next i
```

This loop is set up to execute 10 times, but the execution will be terminated if the current value of sum equals or exceeds 10. In this particular case, the execution will terminate within the fourth pass (because $1 + 2 + 3 + 4 = 10$).

3.7 LOOPING WITH Do-Loop

In addition to For-Next structures, Visual Basic also includes Do-Loop structures, which are convenient when the number of passes through a loop is not known in advance (as, for example, when a loop is required to continue until some logical condition has been satisfied).

A Do-Loop structure always begins with a Do statement and ends with a Loop statement. However, there are four different ways to write a Do-Loop structure. Two of the forms require that a logical expression appear in the Do statement (i.e., at the beginning of the block); the other two forms require that the logical expression appear in the Loop statement (at the end of the block).

The general forms of the Do-Loop structure are shown below.

First form:

```
Do While logical expression
    . . . . . . . .
    executable statements
    . . . . . . . .
Loop
```

Second form:

```
Do Until logical expression
    . . . . . . . .
    executable statements
    . . . . . . . .
Loop
```

Third form: *Fourth form:*

```
Do                                                                    Do
    . . . . . . . . .                                                     . . . . . . . . .
    executable statements                                                executable statements
    . . . . . . . .                                                      . . . . . . . .
Loop While logical expression                                         Loop Until logical expression
```

The first form continues to loop as long as the *logical expression* is true, whereas the second form continues to loop as long as the *logical expression* is *not* true (until the *logical expression* becomes true). Similarly, the third form continues to loop as long as the *logical expression* is true, whereas the fourth form continues to loop as long as the *logical expression* is *not* true.

Note that there is a fundamental difference between the first two forms and the last two forms of the Do-Loop block. In the first two forms, the logical test is made at the *beginning* of each pass through the loop; hence, it is possible that there will not be *any* passes made through the loop, if the indicated logical condition is not satisfied. In the last two forms, however, the logical test is not made until the *end* of each pass; therefore, at least one pass through the loop will always be carried out.

EXAMPLE 3.17

Consider the following two Do-Loop structures.

```
flag = "False"                                  flag = "False"
    . . . . . . . .                                 . . . . . . . .
Do While flag = "True"                          Do
    . . . . . . . .                                 . . . . . . . .
Loop                                            Loop While flag = "True"
```

The left loop will not execute at all, because the logical test at the beginning of the loop structure is false. The right loop will execute once, however, because the logical test is not carried out until the end of the first pass through the loop. Moreover, if the string "True" is assigned to flag during this first pass through the right loop, then the execution will continue indefinitely, until flag is reassigned.

Note that a Do-Loop structure does not involve a formal index. Thus, the programmer must provide the logic for altering the value of the *logical expression* within the loop. Typically, an initial assignment is made before entering the loop structure. The logical expression is then altered at some point within the loop.

EXAMPLE 3.18

Here is a Do-While loop that is comparable to the For-Next loop in Example 3.14.

```
sum = 0
count = 1
Do While count <= 10
    sum = sum + count
    count = count + 1
Loop
```

This structure will result in 10 passes through the loop. Note that count is assigned a value of 1 before entering the loop. The value of count is then incremented by 1 during each pass through the loop. Once the value of count exceeds 10, the execution will cease.

Here is another way to accomplish the same thing.

```
sum = 0
count = 1
Do
    sum = sum + count
    count = count + 1
Loop While count <= 10
```

If we choose to use an `Until` clause rather than a `While` clause, we can write the control structure in either of the following ways.

```
sum = 0                              sum = 0
count = 1                            count = 1
Do Until count > 10                  Do
    sum = sum + count                    sum = sum + count
    count = count + 1                    count = count + 1
Loop                                 Loop Until count > 10
```

Note that the logical expression in these two structures (`count > 10`) is the opposite of the logical expression in the first two structures (`count <= 10`).

Control can be transferred out of a `Do-Loop` block using the `Exit Do` statement. This statement is analogous to `Exit For`, which is used with `For-Next` blocks. Thus, when an `Exit Do` statement is encountered during program execution, control is transferred out of the `Do-Loop` block to the first executable statement following `Loop`.

EXAMPLE 3.19

Here is a variation of Example 3.16, illustrating the use of a typical `Exit Do` statement.

```
sum = 0
count = 1
Do While count <= 10
    sum = sum + count
    If sum >= 10 Then
        Exit Do
    count = count + 1
Loop
```

3.8 LOOPING WITH `While-Wend`

Visual Basic supports `While-Wend` structures in addition to `Do-Loop` structures. This structure also permits conditional looping. The structure begins with the `While` statement (analogous to `Do While`), and ends with the `Wend` statement (analogous to `Loop`).

The general form of a `While-Wend` structure is

```
While logical expression
    . . . . . . . . .
    executable statements
    . . . . . . . .
Wend
```

The loop created by the While-Wend structure continues to execute as long as the *logical expression* is true. Thus, While-Wend is analogous to a Do While-Loop structure. Note that the logical expression is tested at the *beginning* of each pass through the loop.

The While-Wend structure, like the Do-While structure, does not involve a formal index. Therefore, you must assign an initial value to the *logical expression* before entering the loop. This value will then be altered within the loop, in accordance with the program logic.

EXAMPLE 3.20

Here is a While-Wend loop that is comparable to the Do-While loop in Example 3.18.

```
sum = 0
count = 1
While count <= 10
    sum = sum + count
    count = count + 1
Wend
```

3.9 THE Stop STATEMENT

The Stop statement is used to terminate the execution at any point in the program. The statement consists simply of the keyword Stop. This statement may appear anywhere in a Visual Basic program except at the very end. Multiple Stop statements may appear in the same program, as dictated by the program logic. However, modern programming practice tends to avoid the use of the Stop statement.

Review Questions

3.1   What is meant by selection?

3.2   What is branching? How does branching differ from selection?

3.3   What is looping? What is the difference between unconditional looping and conditional looping?

3.4   Name the six relational operators used in Visual Basic. What is the purpose of each?

3.5   What is a logical expression? What values can a logical expression take on?

3.6   What are operands within a logical expression?

3.7   What is the interpretation of the relational operators <, <=, > and >= when applied to string operands?

3.8   Name the three commonly used logical operators in Visual Basic. What is the purpose of each? What other logical operators are available in Visual Basic?

3.9   What is the purpose of the If-Then statement?

3.10   What is the purpose of an If-Then-Else block? Compare with the If-Then statement.

3.11   How is an If-Then-Else block ended?

3.12   Describe how one `If-Then-Else` block can be embedded within another.

3.13   What is the purpose of the `Select Case` structure?

3.14   Summarize the principal components of the `Select Case` structure. Which are required and which are optional?

3.15   For what type of application is the `Select Case` structure well-suited?

3.16   Can the expression in a `Select Case` structure be based upon a string rather than a numeric value?

3.17   How are multiple data items handled in a single `Case` statement?

3.18   How is a range of data items handled in a `Case` statement?

3.19   How is a logical expression handled in a `Case` statement?

3.20   What is the purpose of the `For-Next` structure? What is the purpose of the `Step` clause within this structure?

3.21   How is a `For-Next` structure ended?

3.22   What is the index in a `For-Next` structure? In what way must the index appearing in the `For-To` statement be related to the index appearing in the `Next` statement?

3.23   Can the index in a `For-Next` structure take on fractional values? Can it decrease in value from one pass to another?

3.24   Summarize the rules that apply to `For-Next` structures.

3.25   What is the purpose of the `Exit For` statement? How is `Exit For` used within a `For-Next` structure?

3.26   Describe the four variations of a `Do-Loop` structure. What is the purpose of each?

3.27   What is the principal difference between `Do While` and `Do Until` (or `Loop While` and `Loop Until`)?

3.28   What is the principal difference between `Do While-Loop` and `Do-Loop While` (or `Do Until-Loop` and `Do-Loop Until`)?

3.29   How can a `Do-Loop` structure be written so that at least one pass through the loop will always be executed?

3.30   Write a skeletal outline of a `Do-Loop` structure, illustrating the manner in which the logical expression is assigned its initial value and its subsequent values within the loop. Compare with a `For-Next` structure.

3.31   What is the purpose of the `Exit Do` statement? How is `Exit Do` used within a `Do-Loop` structure? Compare with a `For-Next` structure.

3.32   What is the purpose of the `While-Wend` structure? Compare with the `Do-Loop` structure.

Problems

3.33   Write an appropriate `If-Then` statement or an `If-Then-Else` block for each of the following situations.

(a)   Test the value of the variable sum. If sum exceeds 100, then adjust its value so that it equals 100.

(b)   Test the value of the variable sum. If sum exceeds 100, then display its value, adjust its value so that it equals 100 and assign the string "Maximum Amount Exceeded" to the string variable Flag.

(c)   Test the value of the variable sum. If sum is less than or equal to 100, add the value of the variable v to sum. If sum exceeds 100, however, adjust its value so that it equals 100 and assign a value of 0 to v.

3.34   Write an appropriate If-Then statement or an If-Then-Else block for each of the following situations.

(a)   Suppose the variable pay has been assigned a value of 6.00. Test the value of the variable hours. If hours exceeds 40, assign the value of 9.50 to pay.

(b)   Test the value of the variable hours. If hours is less than or equal to 40, assign 6.00 to pay and assign "Regular" to the string variable Status. If pay exceeds 40, assign 9.50 to pay and assign "Overtime" to Status.

3.35   Write an appropriate If-Then-Else block for the following situation:

Test the string variable Flag. If Flag = "True", set count equal to 0 and assign the message "Resetting the Counter" to the string variable Msg1. Then test the value of the single-precision real variable Z.

   If Z exceeds Zmax, assign the message "Maximum Value Exceeded" to the string variable Msg2, and assign the value of Zmin to Z.

   Otherwise, add the value of W to Z.

If Flag = "False", increase the value of count by 1, then test the string variable Type.

   If Type equals "A", add the value of U to Z.

   If Type equals "B", add the value of V to Z.

   Otherwise, add the value of W to Z.

   Finally, reset the value of Flag to "True".

3.36   Write a Select Case structure that will examine the value of a numeric variable called Flag and assign one of the following messages to the string variable Message, depending on the value assigned to Flag.

(a)   "Hot", if Flag has a value of 1

(b)   "Luke Warm", if Flag has a value of 2

(c)   "Cold", if Flag has a value of 3

(d)   "Out of Range", if Flag has any other value

3.37   Write a Select Case structure that will examine the value of a string variable called Color and assign one of the following messages to the string variable Message, depending on the value assigned to Color.

(a)   "Red", if either r or R is assigned to Color

(b)   "Green", if either g or G is assigned to Color

(c)   "Blue", if either b or B is assigned to Color

(d)   "Black", if Color is assigned any other string

3.38 Write an appropriate block of statements that will examine the value of a single-precision variable called `Temperature` and display one of the following messages, depending on the value assigned to `Temperature`.

(a) `"Ice"`, if the value of `Temperature` is less than 0

(b) `"Water"`, if the value of `Temperature` lies between 0 and 100

(c) `"Steam"`, if the value of `Temperature` exceeds 100

Can a `Select Case` structure be used in this instance?

3.39 Write a loop that will calculate the sum of every third integer, beginning with $i = 2$ (i.e., calculate the sum $2 + 5 + 8 + 11 + \ldots$) for all values of i that are less than 100. Write the loop in each of the following ways:

(a) Using a `For-Next` structure

(b) Using a `Do While-Loop` structure

(c) Using a `Do Until-Loop` structure

(d) Using a `Do-Loop While` structure

(e) Using a `Do-Loop Until` structure

3.40 Repeat Problem 3.39, calculating the sum of every n^{th} integer, beginning with `nstart` (i.e., `nstart`, `nstart+n`, `nstart+(2*n)`, `nstart+(3*n)`, etc.). Continue the looping process for all values of i that do not exceed `nstop`.

3.41 Modify Problem 3.40 by transferring out of the loop if `sum` exceeds some specified value represented by `maxsum`.

3.42 Generalize Problem 3.39 by generating a *series* of loops, each loop generating the sum of every j^{th} integer, where j ranges from 2 to 13. Begin each loop with a value of $i = 2$ and increase i by j, until i takes on the largest possible value that is less than 100. (In other words, the first loop will calculate the sum $2 + 4 + 6 + \ldots + 98$; the second loop will calculate the sum $2 + 5 + 8 + \ldots + 98$; the third loop will calculate the sum $2 + 6 + 10 + \ldots + 98$; and so on. The last loop will calculate the sum $2 + 15 + 28 + \ldots + 93$.

Use a nested loop structure to solve this problem, with one loop embedded within another. Calculate each sum with the inner loop, and let the outer loop control the value of j.

3.43 Write a loop that will generate every third integer, beginning with $i = 2$ and continuing for all integers that are less than 100. Calculate the sum of those integers that are evenly divisible by 5.

3.44 Repeat Problem 3.43, calculating the sum of every n^{th} integer, beginning with `nstart` (i.e., `nstart`, `nstart+n`, `nstart+(2*n)`, `nstart+(3*n)`, etc.). Continue the looping process for all values of i that do not exceed `nstop`. Calculate the sum of those integers that are evenly divisible by k, where k represents some positive integer.

3.45 Write a loop that will examine each character in a string called `Text` and determine how many of the characters are letters, how many are digits, how many are blank spaces, and how many are other kinds of characters (e.g., punctuation characters). *Hint*: Use the `Len` library function to determine the length of the string; then use the `Mid` library function within a loop to extract the individual characters, one at a time.

3.46 Write a loop that will examine each character in a string called Text and determine how many of the characters are vowels and how many are consonants. *Hint*: First determine whether or not a character is a letter; if so, determine the type of letter. Also, see the suggestion given at the end of Problem 3.45.

3.47 Write a loop that will display the characters in a string in reverse order (so that the string will appear backwards). *Hint*: See the suggestion at the end of Problem 3.45.

3.48 Describe the final value of x that is generated by each of the following Visual Basic program segments.

(*a*)
```
i = 0
x = 0
Do While (i < 20)
    If (i Mod 5 = 0) Then x = x + i
    i = i + 1
Loop
```

(*b*)
```
i = 0
x = 0
Do
    If (i Mod 5 = 0) Then x = x + 1
    i = i + 1
Loop While (i < 20)
```

(*c*)
```
x = 0
For i = 1 To 10 Step 2
    x = x + 1
Next i
```

(*d*)
```
x = 0
For i = 1 To 10 Step 2
    x = x + i
Next i
```

(*e*)
```
x = 0
For i = 1 To 10
    IF (i Mod 2 = 1) Then
        x = x + i
    Else
        x = x - 1
    End If
Next i
```

(*f*)
```
x = 0
For i = 1 To 10
    If (i Mod 2 = 1) Then
        x = x + i
    Else
        x = x - 1
    End If
    Exit For
Next i
```

(*g*) ```
x = 0
For i = 0 To 4
  For j = 0 To i - 1
      x = x + (i + j - 1)
  Next j
Next i
```

(*h*)  ```
x = 0
For i = 0 To 4
  For j = 0 To i - 1
      x = x + (i + j - 1)
      Exit For
  Next j
Next i
```

(*i*) ```
x = 0
For i = 0 To 4
  For j = 0 To i
      x = x + j
  Next j
  Exit For
Next i
```

(*j*)  ```
x = 0
For i = 0 To 4
  For j = 0 To i - 1
      k = (i + j - 1)
      If (k Mod 2 = 0) Then
          x = x + k
      ElseIF (k Mod 3 = 0) Then
          x = x + k - 2
      End If
  Next j
Next i
```

(*k*) ```
x = 0
For i = 0 To 4
  For j = 0 To i - 1
      Select Case (i + j - 1)
      Case -1, 0
          x = x + 1
      Case 1, 2, 3
          x = x + 2
      Case Else
          x = x + 3
      End Select
  Next j
Next i
```
```

Chapter 4

Visual Basic Control Fundamentals

4.1 VISUAL BASIC CONTROL TOOLS

In Chapter 1 we saw that the *Visual Basic Toolbox* (shown below in Fig. 4.1) contains a collection of control tools, such as labels, text boxes and command buttons. These controls, together with customized menus, allow us to build a broad variety of graphical user interfaces. In this chapter we will focus on several of the more commonly used *Toolbox* control tools. These tools, together with the material covered in the previous two chapters, will allow us to write complete Visual Basic programs.

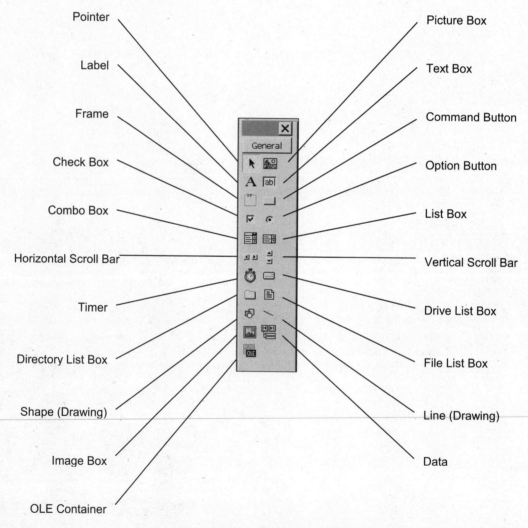

Fig. 4.1 The Visual Basic toolbox

Here, in alphabetical order, is a brief description of each control tool:

Check Box

Provides a means of specifying a Yes/No response. Within a group of check boxes, any number of boxes can be checked, including none. (See also the Option Box description.)

Combo Box

Combines the capabilities of a text box and a list box. Thus, it provides a collection of text items, one of which may be selected from the list at any time during program execution. Text items can be assigned initially, or they can be assigned during program execution. In addition, the user can enter a text item at any time during program execution.

Command Button

Provides a means of initiating an event action by the user clicking on the button.

Data

Provides a means of displaying information from an existing database.

Directory List Box

Provides a means of selecting paths and directories (folders) within the current drive.

Drive List Box

Provides a means of selecting among existing drives.

File List Box

Provides a means of selecting files within the current directory.

Frame

Provides a container for other controls. It is usually used to contain a group of option buttons, check boxes or graphical shapes.

Horizontal Scroll Bar

Allows a horizontal scroll bar to be added to a control (if a horizontal scroll bar is not included automatically).

Image Box

Used to display graphical objects, and to initiate event actions. (Note that an Image Box is similar to a Picture Box. It redraws faster and can be stretched, though it has fewer properties than a Picture Box.)

Label

Used to display text on a form. The text cannot be reassigned during program execution, though it can be hidden from view and its appearance can be altered. (See also the Text Box description.)

Line

Used to draw straight-line segments within forms. (See also the Shape tool description.)

List Box

Provides a collection of text items. One text item may be selected from the list at any time during program execution. Text items can be assigned initially, or they can be assigned during program execution. However, in contrast to a text box, the user cannot enter text items to a list box during program execution. (Note that a combo box combines the features of a list box and a text box).

OLE Container

Allows a data object to be transferred from another Windows application and embedded within the Visual Basic application.

Option Button

Provides a means of selecting one of several different options. Within a group of option buttons, one and only one can be selected. (See also the Check Box description.)

Picture Box

Used to display graphical objects or text, and to initiate event actions. (Note that a Picture Box is similar to an Image Box. It has more properties than an Image Box, though it redraws slower and cannot be stretched.)

Pointer

The pointer is not really a control tool, in the true sense of the word. When the pointer is active, the mouse can be used to position and resize other controls on the design form, and to double-click on the controls, resulting in a display of the associated Visual Basic code.

Shape

Used to draw circles, ellipses, squares and rectangles within forms, frames or picture boxes. (See also the Line tool description.)

Text Box

Provides a means of entering and displaying text. The text can be assigned initially, it can be reassigned during program execution, or it can be entered by the user during program execution. (See also the Label Box and the Combo Box descriptions.)

Timer

Allows events to occur repeatedly at specified time intervals.

Vertical Scroll Bar

Allows a vertical scroll bar to be added to a control (if a vertical scroll bar is not included automatically).

4.2 CONTROL TOOL CATEGORIES

The control tools can be grouped into the following overall categories: (Keep in mind that some control tools have multiple uses and are not restricted to the categories listed below.)

Entering Text

Text Box

Combo Box

Displaying Text

Label

Text Box

List Box

Combo Box

Displaying Graphics

Image Box

Picture Box

Frame

Managing Files

File List Box

Drive List Box

Directory List Box

Initiating Events

Command Button

Executing Timed Events

Timer

Drawing

Line Button

Shape Button

Selecting Among Alternatives

Check Box

Option Button

Frame

List Box

Viewing Windows

Frame

Horizontal Scroll Bar

Vertical Scroll Bar

Accessing Existing Data

Data

Linking with Other Objects

OLE

4.3 WORKING WITH CONTROLS

A control can be *added* to the Form Design Window two different ways:

1. By clicking on the desired control tool within the Toolbox, then clicking on the control's location within the Form Design Window.

2. By double-clicking on the desired control tool within the Toolbox, automatically placing the control at the center of the Form Design Window.

A control can be *relocated* within the Form Design Window by dragging the control to its desired location (hold down the left mouse button and drag).

A control can be *resized* within the Form Design Window by dragging one of its edges or corners.

A control can be *removed* from the Form Design Window by highlighting the control (i.e., by clicking on it) and then pressing the Delete key.

4.4 NAMING FORMS AND CONTROLS

When an object (i.e., a form or control) is added to the Form Design Window, a generic default name (e.g., Form1, List1, List2, Text1, etc.) is automatically assigned to that object. Each name includes a generic identifier

(Form, List, Text, etc.) that identifies the type of object, followed by a number that identifies the order in which that particular object type has been added to the Form Design Window. Thus, List1 is the name of the first list box added to the Form Design Window, List2 is the name of the second list box, and so on.

The default names work well for simple applications. For more complicated applications, however, it may be preferable to assign different names that suggest the purpose of each object. Thus, Students and Addresses may be preferable to List1 and List2.

Microsoft suggests that such programmer-assigned names include a three-letter prefix suggesting the type of object. Hence, we might use lstStudents and lstAddresses rather than Students and Addresses, if each object is a list box. (The use of prefixes is unnecessary when the default names are used, since the names themselves indicate the object type.)

Microsoft recommends the following prefixes for programmer-defined object names:

Object	Prefix	Object	Prefix
Combo Box	cbo	Label	lbl
Check Box	chk	Line	lin
Command Button	cmd	List Box	lst
Data	dat	Menu	mnu
Directory List Box	dir	OLE	ole
Drive List Box	drv	Option Button	opt
File List Box	fil	Picture Box	pic
Frame	fra	Shape	shp
Form	frm	Text Box	txt
Horizontal Scroll Bar	hsb	Timer	tmr
Image Box	img	Vertical Scroll Bar	vsb

4.5 ASSIGNING PROPERTY VALUES TO FORMS AND CONTROLS

The properties associated with each object type are unique, though some, such as Name, BackColor (i.e., background color), Height and Width, are common to many different object types. The meaning of most properties is readily apparent. Some, however, require further explanation, particularly certain unique properties that are required for an object's special behavior. For information about such properties, you should consult the on-line help (press F1 or click on the Help menu), related example projects, or printed reference material.

Moreover, each object will have a unique set of values assigned to its properties. These values may be assigned at *design time* (i.e., when the object is first defined, before the application is executed), or at *run time* (i.e., while the application is executing).

Design-time assignments are made by selecting a property from the list of properties shown in the Properties Window (see Fig. 1.3), and then either choosing an appropriate value from the adjoining list of values or entering a value from the keyboard. These property values will apply when the application first begins to run.

Run-time assignments are carried out using Visual Basic assignment commands, as described in Chap. 2. In general terms, a property assignment is written as

   object_name.property = value

where *object_name* refers to the name of the form or control, *property* refers to the associated property name, and *value* refers to an assignable item, such as a number or a string. The net effect is to assign the value on the right-hand side of the equal sign to the property on the left. Such assignments can provide initial values to properties that were formerly undefined, or they may replace previous assignments.

EXAMPLE 4.1 ASSIGNING VALUES TO PROPERTIES

Each of the following commands assigns a run-time value to a text box property.

```
Text1.Text = "Welcome to Visual Basic"

txtMessage.Text = "Welcome to Visual Basic"

txtMessage.Height = 300
```

The first line assigns the string "Welcome to Visual Basic" to the Text property associated with text box Text1 (default name). The second line assigns this same string to the Text property associated with text box txtMessage (programmer-assigned name). The last line assigns a numerical value to the Height property associated with txtMessage.

Each of these commands either assigns a new value during program execution, or replaces a previously assigned initial value (i.e., a value assigned during design time).

4.6 EXECUTING COMMANDS (EVENT PROCEDURES AND COMMAND BUTTONS)

An *event procedure* is an independent group of commands that is executed whenever an "event" occurs during program execution. Typically, an event occurs when the user takes some action, such as clicking on a control icon, or dragging an icon to another location. Many (though not all) Visual Basic controls have event procedures associated with them.

Each event procedure begins with a Sub statement, such as `Private Sub Command1_Click()`, and ends with an End Sub statement. Between the Sub and End Sub statements is a group of instructions, such as those discussed in the last two chapters, that are executed when the user initiates the corresponding event. The parentheses in the Sub statement may contain *arguments* – special variables that are used to transfer information between the event procedure and the "calling" routine (see Chap. 7 for more information on this topic).

Command buttons are often used to execute Visual Basic event procedures. Thus, when the user clicks on a command button during program execution, the statements within the corresponding event procedure are carried out. The statements within the event procedure may involve the properties of controls other than the command button. For example, a command-button event procedure may result in new values being assigned to the properties of a label or a text box.

EXAMPLE 4.2 A SAMPLE EVENT PROCEDURE

A typical event procedure is shown below:

```
Private Sub Command1_Click()
    Label1.Caption = "Hello, " & Text1.Text & "!  Welcome to Visual Basic."
    Label1.BorderStyle = 1
    Label1.Visible = True
End Sub
```

From the first line (i.e., the Sub statement), we see that this event procedure is associated with command button Command1, and it is a response to a click-type event. The three assignment statements within the event procedure will be executed whenever the user clicks the mouse on command button Command1 during program execution.

To enter an event procedure, double-click on the appropriate command button within the Form Design Window (see Fig. 1.3), or click once on the command button (to activate it), and then select the Code Editor by clicking on the leftmost button within the Project Window toolbar (see Fig. 4.2). You may then enter the required Visual Basic commands within the corresponding event procedure (see Fig. 1.4 or Fig. 4.6).

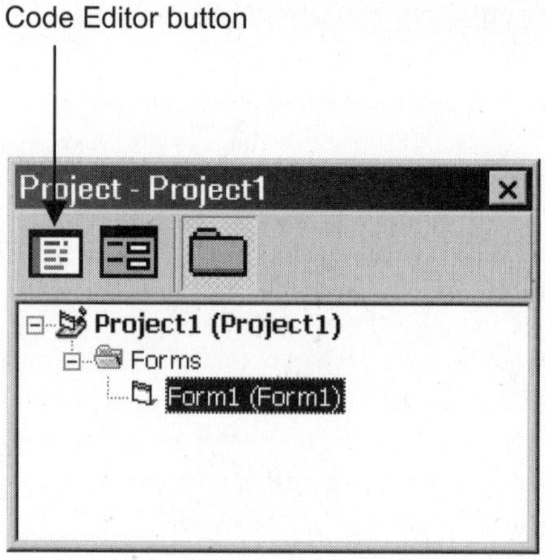

Code Editor button

Fig. 4.2 The Visual Basic Project Window

In the next section we will see how the Code Editor is used to enter an event procedure and associate that event procedure with a command button.

4.7 DISPLAYING OUTPUT DATA (LABELS AND TEXT BOXES)

The most straightforward way to display output data is with a label or a text box. A label can only display output data, though a text box can accept input data as well as display output data. For now, however, we will work only with output data.

Both of these controls process information in the form of a string. This is not a serious limitation, however, because numeric values can easily be converted to strings via the Str function (see Sec. 2.12).

To display output using a label, the basic idea is to assign a string containing the desired output information to the label's Caption property. Similarly, when displaying output using a text box, a string containing the desired output information is assigned to the text box's Text property. The following example illustrates the technique.

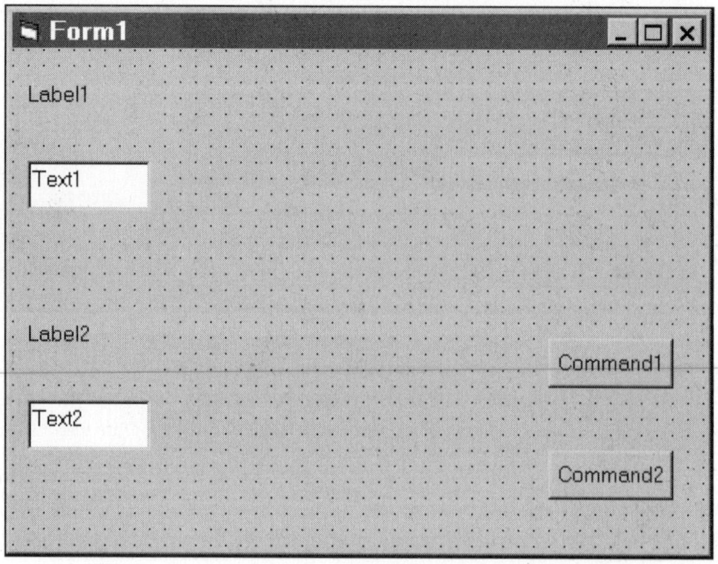

Fig. 4.3

EXAMPLE 4.3 CURRENT DATE AND TIME

In this example, we create a project that displays the current date and time. To do so, we will make use of the special Visual Basic variable Now, and the Format library function. We will use two label controls to represent permanent headings, and two text box controls to represent the date and time, respectively. In addition, we will utilize two command buttons, one to initiate and/or repeat the computation, and the other to end the computation. Fig. 4.3 shows the preliminary control layout.

The next step is to define an appropriate set of properties for the form and each control. Since the controls already have default properties associated with them, we must change only a few of the defaults. The (nondefault) property values for each object are summarized below.

Object	Property	Value
Form1	Name	"DateAndTime"
	Caption	"Date and Time"
Label1	Caption	"Today is . . ."
	Font	MS Sans Serif, 10-point
Label2	Caption	"The Current Time is . . ."
	Font	MS Sans Serif, 10-point
Text1	BackColor	Light Gray
	Font	MS Sans Serif, 12-point
Text2	Alignment	2 – Center
	BackColor	Light Gray
	Font	MS Sans Serif, 12-point
Command1	Caption	"Go"
	Font	MS Sans Serif, 10-point
Command2	Caption	"End"
	Font	MS Sans Serif, 10-point

Fig. 4.4 shows the appeareance of the form after defining the new properties and resizing the controls.

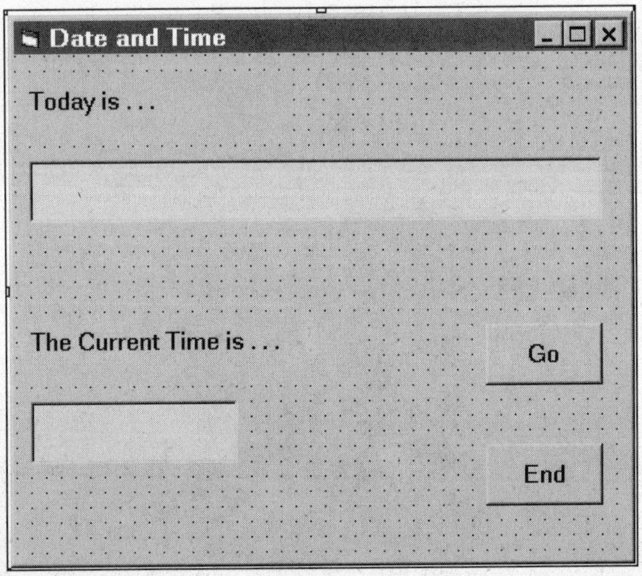

Fig. 4.4

We now define the event procedure associated with the Go button. To do so, double-click on the button, causing the Code Editor Window to be displayed, as shown in Fig. 4.5.

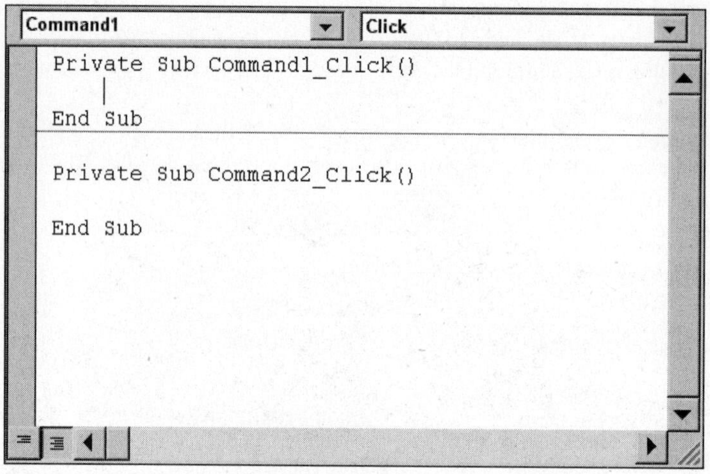

```
Command1                    ▼   Click                        ▼
    Private Sub Command1_Click()
         |
    End Sub

    Private Sub Command2_Click()

    End Sub
```

Fig. 4.5

We now add the following two assignment statements to the first event procedure:

```
Text1.Text = Format(Now, "dddd, mmmm d, yyyy")
Text2.Text = Format(Now, "hh:mm AM/PM")
```

In both of these assignment statements, the predefined variable Now represents the current date and time. The term "dddd, mmmm d, yyyy" is a *format string*, which indicates how the information represented by Now will appear (in this case, as the day of the week, followed by the month, day and year). Hence, the first command formats the value of Now so that it represents the current day and date; it then assigns this formatted information to the text property associated with the object named Text1. Similarly, the second command formats the value of Now so that it represents the current time, represented as hours and minutes, followed by AM or PM; it then assigns the time to the text property associated with the object named Text2. When the program is executed and the Go button is selected, the two text boxes will therefore display the current day and date and the current time, respectively.

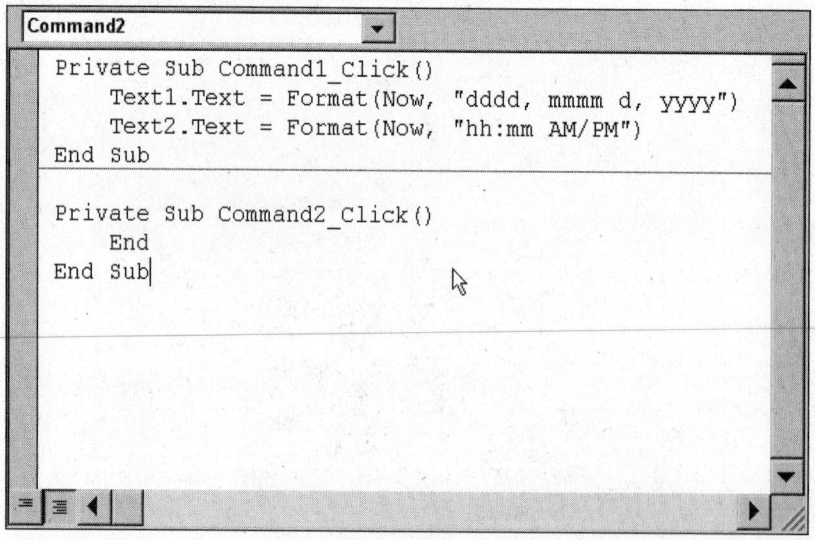

```
Command2                    ▼
    Private Sub Command1_Click()
         Text1.Text = Format(Now, "dddd, mmmm d, yyyy")
         Text2.Text = Format(Now, "hh:mm AM/PM")
    End Sub

    Private Sub Command2_Click()
         End
    End Sub
```

Fig. 4.6

Similarly, we add the command

    End

to the second event procedure. This command simply terminates the computation.

Fig. 4.6 shows the completed event procedures for this project. Note the indentation, relative to the first and last lines, of each event procedure.

When the project is executed, the window shown in Fig.4.7 appears. Clicking on the Go button results in a display of the current day and date and the current time, as shown in Fig. 4.8.

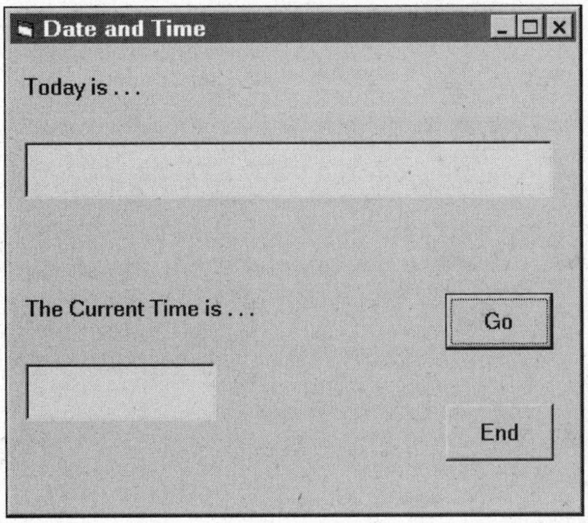

Fig. 4.7

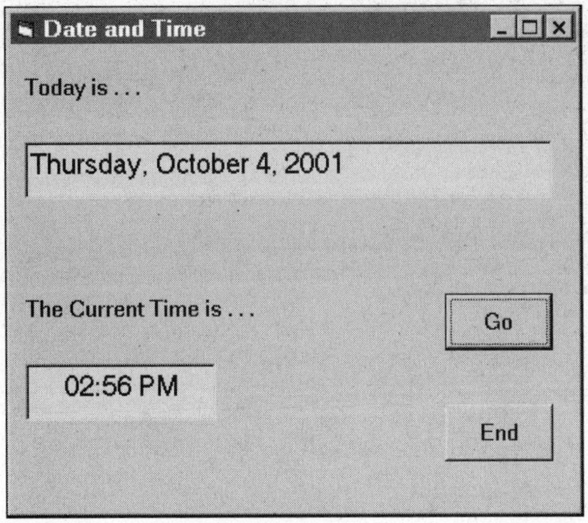

Fig. 4.8

The computation is ended by clicking on the End button. The Form Design Window shown in Fig. 4.4 then reappears.

A text box can be restricted to a single-line or it can contain multiple lines, depending on the value assigned to the MultiLine property. Multiline text boxes can be aligned in various ways (left-justified, right-justified or centered), as determined by the Alignment property; and they can include scroll bars, as determined by the ScrollBars property.

4.8 ENTERING INPUT DATA (TEXT BOXES)

Input data is generally entered through a text box. Typically, the user enters a string from the keyboard when the program is executed. This string is automatically assigned to the text box's text property. If the string represents a number, it can be converted to an actual numerical value by means of the Val function.

EXAMPLE 4.4 ENTERING AND DISPLAYING TEXT

In this example we prompt the user to enter his or her name, and then display the name as a part of a message. We will make use of a text box to enter the data, and a command button to accept the input data and to create the final display. We will also utilize two labels; one for the input prompt, and the other for the final message.

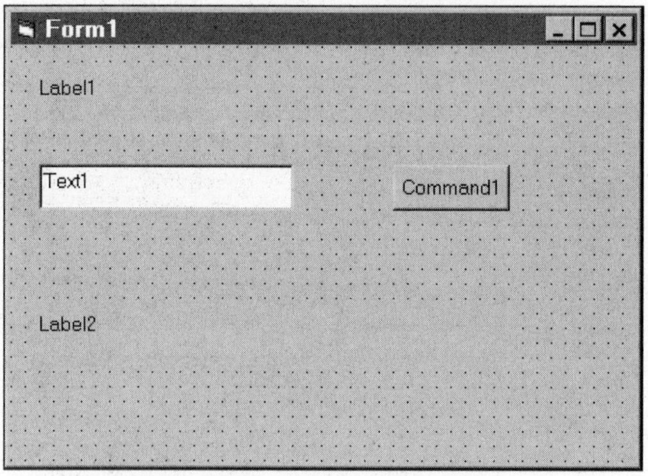

Fig. 4.9

Fig. 4.9 shows the preliminary control layout in the Form Design Window, using standard default names for the form and the controls. In this figure the controls have been stretched to their approximate final sizes, but control properties have not yet been assigned.

We now assign the following property values for each object:

Object	Property	Value
Form1	Caption	"Welcome to Visual Basic"
Label1	Caption	"Please enter your first name below:"
	Font	MS Sans Serif, 10-point
Label2	Caption	(none)
	BackColor	White
	Font	MS Sans Serif, 10-point
	Visible	False
Text1	Caption	(none)
	Font	MS Sans Serif, 10-point
Command1	Caption	"Enter"
	Font	MS Sans Serif, 10-point

After assigning the property values, the form and the controls were resized and rearranged, as shown in Fig. 4.10.

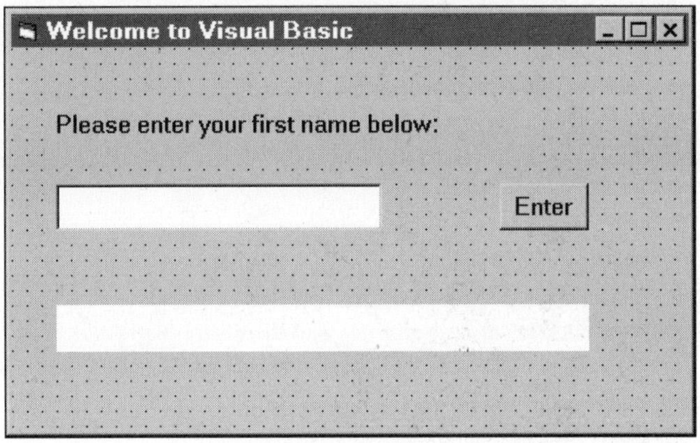

Fig. 4.10

We now add the following commands to the Click event procedure associated with the Enter button (double-click on the command button to display the event procedure in the Code Editor Window):

```
Label2.Caption = "Hello, " + Text1.Text + "!  Welcome to Visual Basic."

Label2.BorderStyle = 1

Label2.Visible = True
```

These commands reassign the property values associated with Label2. The first command combines the word Hello with the user's name and the succeeding text to form the message

Hello, < user's name>! Welcome to Visual Basic.

The second command changes the border of Label2 so that the label will appear indented, in the same manner as a text box. The third command causes Label2 to become visible to the user (it is invisible initially, because the Visible property is initially set to False).

The entire event procedure appears as shown below:

```
Private Sub Command1_Click()
    Label2.Caption = "Hello, " + Text1.Text + "!  Welcome to Visual Basic."
    Label2.BorderStyle = 1
    Label2.Visible = True
End Sub
```

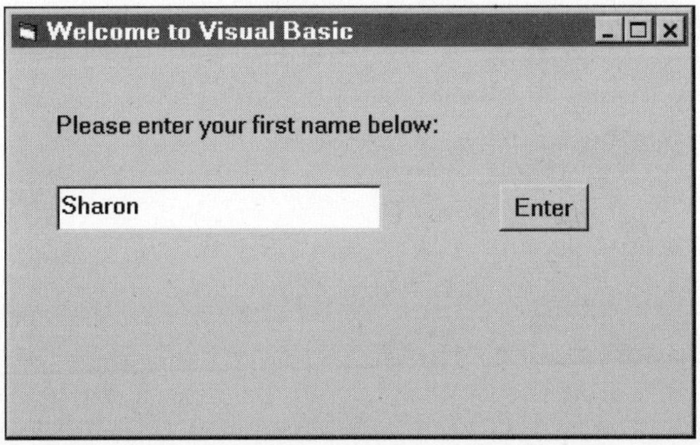

Fig. 4.11

Fig. 4.11 shows a name being entered in the text box during program execution (before clicking on the Enter button). The final screen (after clicking on the Enter button) is shown in Fig. 4.12.

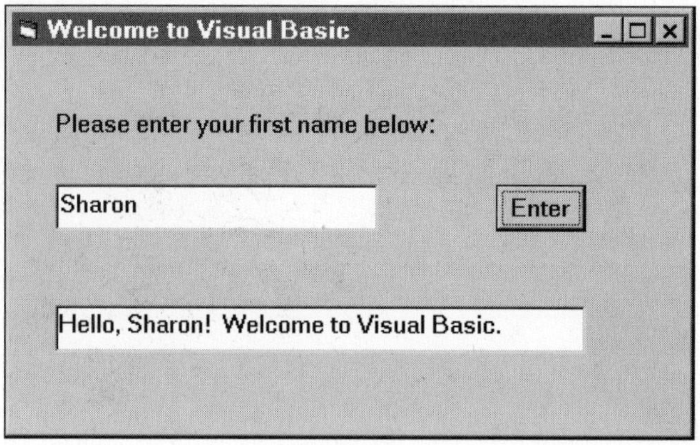

Fig. 4.12

Keep in mind that this example illustrates a technique for entering text by means of a text box, processing the text (combining it with other text), and then displaying the processed text as a second label. We could have displayed the final text within a second text box rather than the label if we had wished. We could also have used the *library functions* Input-Box and MsgBox to enter and display text, respectively. (See Sec. 5.8 for information about the InputBox function, and Secs. 4.13 and 5.7 for information regarding the MsgBox function.)

EXAMPLE 4.5 ENTERING AND DISPLAYING NUMERICAL AND GRAPHICAL DATA (A PIGGY BANK)

This example presents a program that will determine how much money is contained within a piggy bank. The user will enter the number of pennies, number of nickels, number of dimes, number of quarters, and number of half-dollars; the program will then display the total amount of money, in dollars and cents. A graphic will also be displayed, to add interest.

Our strategy will be to enter each number as text (through a text box), and then convert each text item to a numerical value using the Val function. A text box and an accompanying label will be used for each type of coin, and for the total amount of money. Note that text boxes are being used both to enter input (the number of pennies, nickels, dimes, quarters and half-dollars), and to display output (the total amount of money).

The total amount of money will be determined using the formula

$$T = 0.01P + 0.05N + 0.10D + 0.25Q + 0.50H$$

where T = the total amount of money, in dollars and cents

P = the number of pennies

N = the number of nickels

D = the number of dimes

Q = the number of quarters

H = the number of half-dollars

Fig. 4.13 shows the preliminary control layout, using standard default names for the form and the controls. The square in the upper right portion of the form represents an image box.

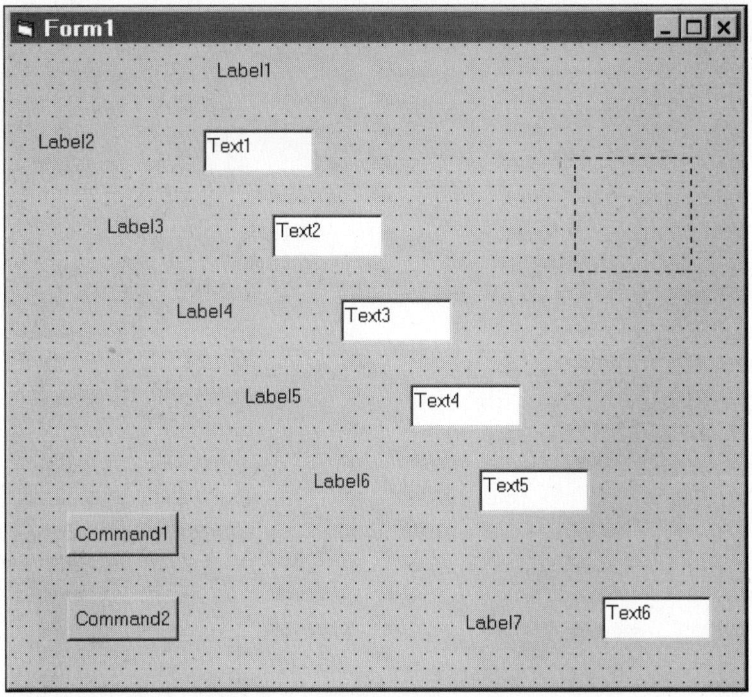

Fig. 4.13

We now assign the following property values for each object:

Object	Property	Value
Form1	Caption	"Piggy Bank"
Label1	Caption	"My Piggy Bank"
	Font	MS Sans Serif, 12-point bold
	Alignment	2 – Center
Label2	Caption	"Pennies:"
	Font	MS Sans Serif, 10-point
Label3	Caption	"Nickels:"
	Font	MS Sans Serif, 10-point
Label4	Caption	"Dimes:"
	Font	MS Sans Serif, 10-point
Label5	Caption	"Quarters:"
	Font	MS Sans Serif, 10-point
Label6	Caption	"Half-Dollars:"
	Font	MS Sans Serif, 10-point
Label7	Caption	"Total:"
	Font	MS Sans Serif, 10-point
Text1	Caption	(none)
	Font	MS Sans Serif, 10-point

(Continues on next page)

Object	Property	Value
Text2	Caption	(none)
	Font	MS Sans Serif, 10-point
Text3	Caption	(none)
	Font	MS Sans Serif, 10-point
Text4	Caption	(none)
	Font	MS Sans Serif, 10-point
Text5	Caption	(none)
	Font	MS Sans Serif, 10-point
Text6	Caption	(none)
	Font	MS Sans Serif, 10-point
Command1	Caption	"Go"
	Font	MS Sans Serif, 10-point
Command2	Caption	"Quit"
	Font	MS Sans Serif, 10-point
Image1	Picture	*<picture file* path and file name >

Note that the picture selected for the image box (Image1) can be any picture file – typically a graphics file having any of the following extensions: .bmp, .dib, .wmf, .emf, .ico, or .cur. The particular path and file name shown in this example (e.g., c:\Clipart\Moneybag.wmf) will vary from one computer to another.

Fig. 4.14 shows the Form Design Window after assigning these property values.

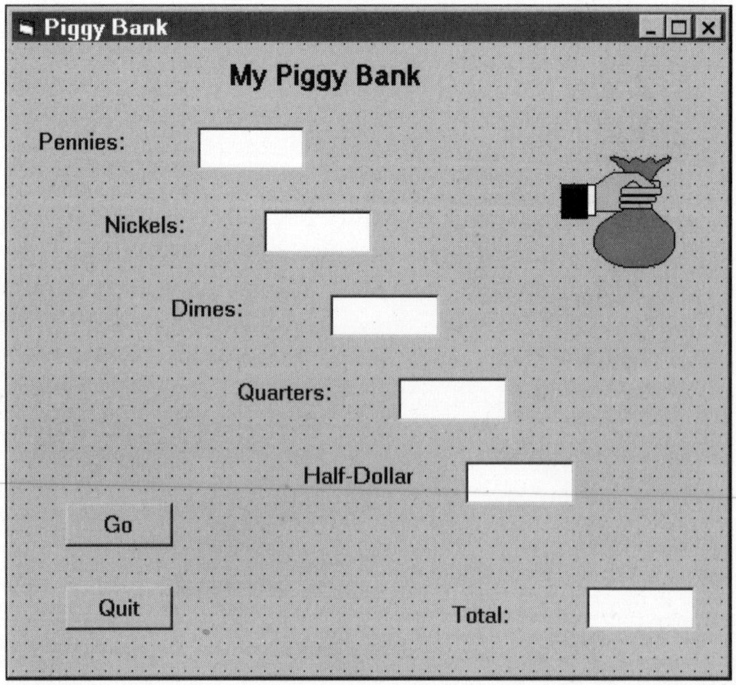

Fig. 4.14

We now add the following assignment statement to the Click event associated with the Go button (double-click on the Go button to access the event procedures):

```
Text6.Text = 0.01 * Val(Text1.Text) + 0.05 * Val(Text2.Text) + 0.1 * Val(Text3.Text) +
             0.25 * Val(Text4.Text) + 0.5 * Val(Text5.Text)
```

In addition, we add the End statement to the Click event associated with the Quit button.

The complete event procedures associated with the command buttons will appear as follows:

```
Private Sub Command1_Click()
   Text6.Text = 0.01 * Val(Text1.Text) + 0.05 * Val(Text2.Text) + 0.1 * Val(Text3.Text) +
                0.25 * Val(Text4.Text) + 0.5 * Val(Text5.Text)
End Sub

Private Sub Command2_Click()
   End
End Sub
```

Fig. 4.15 shows the appearance of the form when the program is executed using the following data:

Pennies:	12
Nickels:	8
Dimes:	7
Quarters:	5
Half-Dollars:	3

Pressing the Go button shows that the piggy bank contains $3.97.

While the program is executing, you may change any of the input values at any time. The new total value will be displayed whenever you press the Go button.

Don't forget to save your program files before exiting.

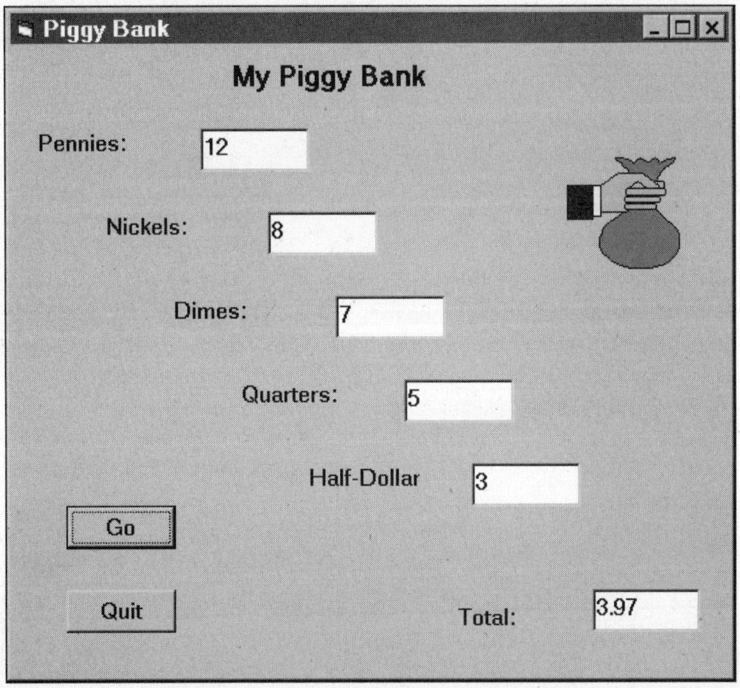

Fig. 4.15

4.9 SELECTING MULTIPLE FEATURES (CHECK BOXES)

Many programs allow the user to select among many different options. That is, the user may select one option, several different options, or no options at all. Check boxes are used for this purpose. Each option has its own check box. A check box is "checked" (i.e., selected) by clicking on it, or assigning its Value property a value of 1. Hence, for each check box, an If-Then-Else block can be written that tests the value of the check box's Value property, and an appropriate action taken if the value equals 1. The Value property can also be assigned 0 to "uncheck" the check box, or 3 to "gray-out" (i.e., deactivate) the check box. The following example illustrates the procedure.

EXAMPLE 4.6 SELECTING MULTIPLE FEATURES (MULTILINGUAL HELLO)

In this example we will display the word "Hello" in one or more foreign languages. The choices are French, German, Hawaiian, Hebrew, Italian, Japanese and Spanish. We will use check boxes to select the particular foreign languages from among the available choices. Each check box will have a corresponding label, which will display the actual greeting.

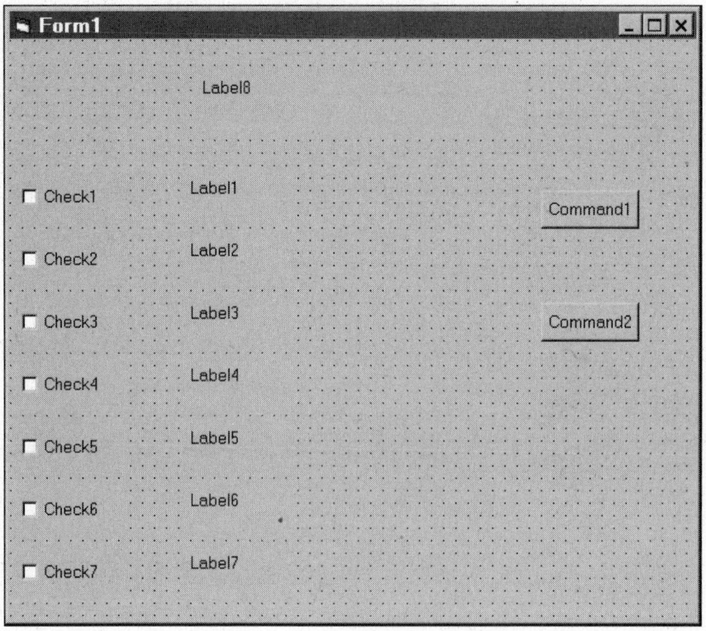

Fig. 4.16

Fig. 4.16 shows the preliminary control layout. Note that the Form Design Window includes seven check boxes (one for each language), and eight labels (a main title, and a label for each language). In addition, there are two command buttons, one of which initiates or refreshes the display and the other terminates the computation.

We now assign the following initial property values:

Object	Property	Value
Form1	Caption	"Multilingual Hello"
Check1	Caption	"French"
	Font	MS Sans Serif, 10-point
Check2	Caption	"German"
	Font	MS Sans Serif, 10-point

(*Continues on next page*)

Object	Property	Value
Check3	Caption	"Hawaiian"
	Font	MS Sans Serif, 10-point
Check4	Caption	"Hebrew"
	Font	MS Sans Serif, 10-point
Check5	Caption	"Italian"
	Font	MS Sans Serif, 10-point
Check6	Caption	"Japanese"
	Font	MS Sans Serif, 10-point
Check7	Caption	"Spanish"
	Font	MS Sans Serif, 10-point
Label1	Caption	"Bonjour"
	Font	MS Sans Serif, 14-point bold
	Visible	False
Label2	Caption	"Guten Tag"
	Font	MS Sans Serif, 14-point bold
	Visible	False
Label3	Caption	"Aloha"
	Font	MS Sans Serif, 14-point bold
	Visible	False
Label4	Caption	"Shalom"
	Font	MS Sans Serif, 14-point bold
	Visible	False
Label5	Caption	"Buon Giorno"
	Font	MS Sans Serif, 14-point bold
	Visible	False
Label6	Caption	"Konichihua"
	Font	MS Sans Serif, 14-point bold
	Visible	False
Label7	Caption	"Buenos Dias"
	Font	MS Sans Serif, 14-point bold
	Visible	False
Label8	Caption	"Say Hello, in . . ."
	Font	MS Sans Serif, 14-point bold
	Alignment	2 – Center
Command1	Caption	"Go"
	Font	MS Sans Serif, 10-point
Command2	Caption	"Quit"
	Font	MS Sans Serif, 10-point

Fig. 4.17 shows the Form Design Window, after assigning these property values, rearranging and resizing the controls.

Fig. 4.17

Finally, we add the following instructions to the event procedures associated with the Go and Quit command buttons:

```
Private Sub Command1_Click()
    If (Check1.Value = 1) Then
        Label1.Visible = True
    Else
        Label1.Visible = False
    End If

    If (Check2.Value = 1) Then
        Label2.Visible = True
    Else
        Label2.Visible = False
    End If

    If (Check3.Value = 1) Then
        Label3.Visible = True
    Else
        Label3.Visible = False
    End If

    If (Check4.Value = 1) Then
        Label4.Visible = True
    Else
        Label4.Visible = False
    End If

    If (Check5.Value = 1) Then
        Label5.Visible = True
    Else
        Label5.Visible = False
    End If
```

```
        If (Check6.Value = 1) Then
            Label6.Visible = True
        Else
            Label6.Visible = False
        End If

        If (Check7.Value = 1) Then
            Label7.Visible = True
        Else
            Label7.Visible = False
        End If
    End Sub


    Private Sub Command2_Click()
        End
    End Sub
```

The first event procedure (Command1_Click) is associated with the Go button. It includes seven independent If-Then-Else statements. Each of these statements determines whether or not a check box has been checked. If so, the corresponding label (which represents the "Hello" expression) is made visible (i.e., Label1.Visible = True, etc); otherwise, the corresponding label is made invisible (Label1.Visible = False, etc.).

In order to run this program, the user must select one or more of the check boxes and then click on the Go button. The results of a typical execution are shown in Fig. 4.18. The user may continue this process by selecting different boxes and clicking on Go after each selection. The entire process ends when the user clicks on the Quit button.

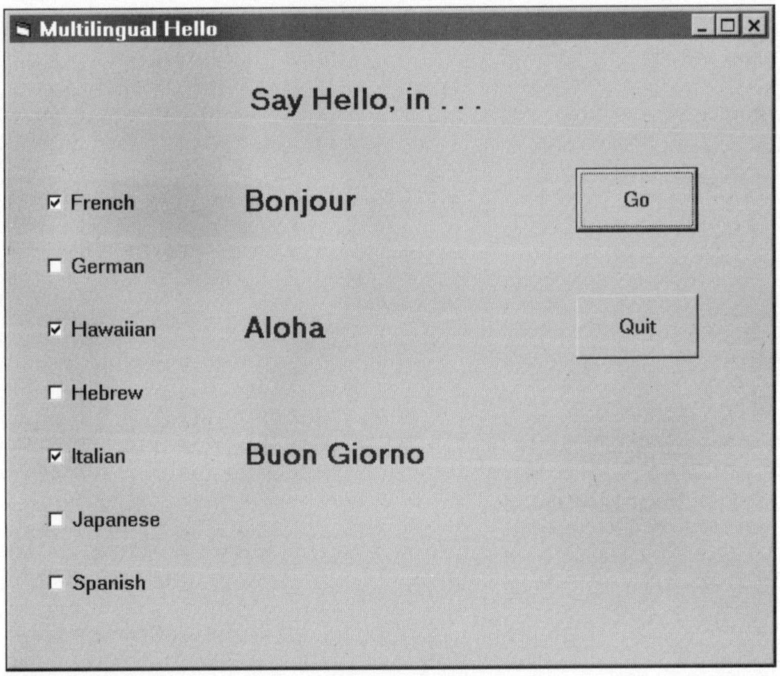

Fig. 4.18

4.10 SELECTING EXCLUSIVE ALTERNATIVES (OPTION BUTTONS AND FRAMES)

Option buttons, like check boxes, allow the user to select among several different alternatives. However, check boxes allow the selection of any number of alternatives (including none), whereas option buttons allow the selection of one and only one alternative within an option-button group. Normally, all of the option buttons within a form comprise a single option-button group. (More about this later.)

In order to select an option button, the user must click on the button, causing a small dot to appear within the outer circle. The value of the option button's Value property will then be set to True. The dot will simultaneously disappear from any previously selected button (since only one option button can be selected at any time), and its Value property will be assigned the value False. An event procedure containing an If-Then-Else block can then determine which button has been selected, and the appropriate action taken. The procedure is illustrated in the following example.

EXAMPLE 4.7 SELECTING EXCLUSIVE ALTERNATIVES (TEMPERATURE CONVERSION)

This example presents a program to convert temperatures from degrees Fahrenheit to degrees Celsius or from degrees Celsius to degrees Fahrenheit, based upon the well-known formulas

$$°C = (5/9) (°F - 32) \qquad \text{and} \qquad °F = 1.8 \, °C + 32$$

where $°C$ represents the temperature in degrees Celsius and $°F$ represents the temperature in degrees Fahrenheit.

Two option buttons will be used to select the particular conversion. In addition, we will use three labels, two text boxes (for the given temperature and the equivalent temperature, respectively), and two command buttons (to initiate or repeat the computation, and to terminate). Fig. 4.19 shows the preliminary control layout.

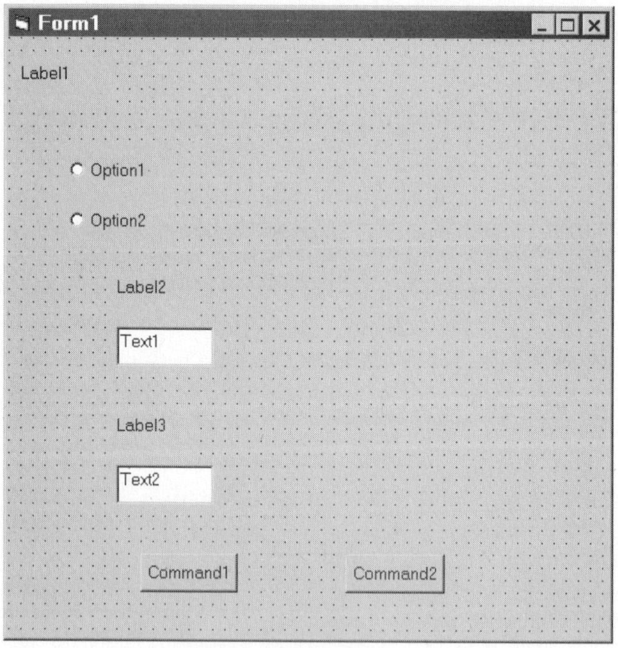

Fig. 4.19

Let us now assign the following initial values to the control properties listed below:

Object	Property	Value
Form1	Caption	"Temperature Conversion"
Label1	Caption	"Temperature Conversion"
	Font	MS Sans Serif, 12-point
Label2	Caption	"Enter original temperature in degrees Fahrenheit"

Object	Property	Value
Label3	Caption	"Equivalent temperature in degrees Celsius"
Option1	Caption	"Fahrenheit to Celsius"
	Value	True
Option2	Caption	"Celsius to Fahrenheit"
Text1	Text	(blank)
Text2	Text	(blank)
Command1	Caption	"Go"
Command2	Caption	"End"

After assigning these values to their respective control properties and resizing the controls, the Form Design Window appears as shown in Fig. 4.20.

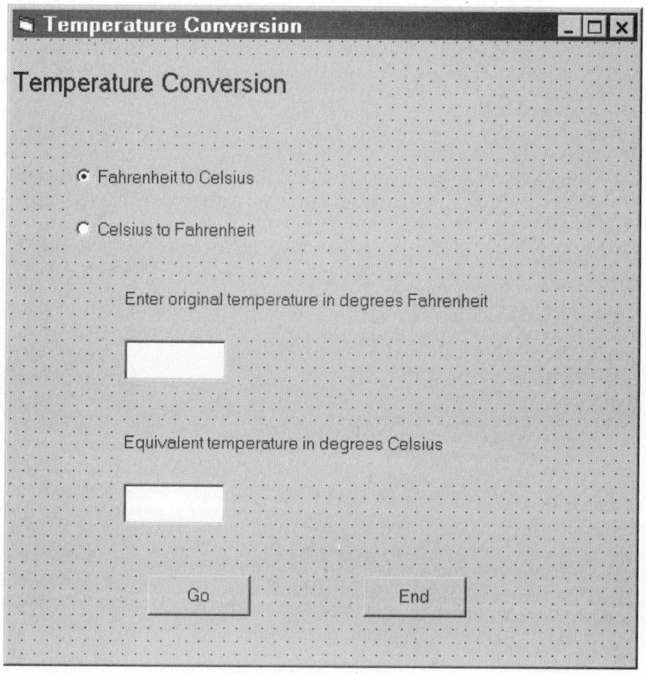

Fig. 4.20

Next, we must add the required instructions. In this example we will provide an event procedure for each option button (to provide the proper prompts), and an event procedure for each command button (to carry out the proper conversion). The event procedures are listed below.

```
Private Sub Option1_Click()
    If (Option1.Value = True) Then
        Label2.Caption = "Enter original temperature in degrees Fahrenheit"
        Text1.Text = ""

        Label3.Caption = "Equivalent temperature in degrees Celsius"
        Text2.Text = ""
    End If
End Sub
```

```
Private Sub Option2_Click()
    If (Option2.Value = True) Then
        Label2.Caption = "Enter original temperature in degrees Celsius"
        Text1.Text = ""

        Label3.Caption = "Equivalent temperature in degrees Fahrenheit"
        Text2.Text = ""
    End If
End Sub

Private Sub Command1_Click()
    Dim TempIn As Double, TempOut As Double

    TempIn = Val(Text1.Text)
    If (Option1 = True) Then
        TempOut = (5 / 9) * (TempIn - 32)
    Else
        TempOut = 1.8 * TempIn + 32
    End If
    Text2.Text = Str(TempOut)
End Sub

Private Sub Command2_Click()
    End
End Sub
```

Fig. 4.21 shows the appearance of the form when the program is first executed, before the first actual calculation. In this figure the user has entered a given value of 68 degrees Fahrenheit, but has not yet clicked on the Go button.

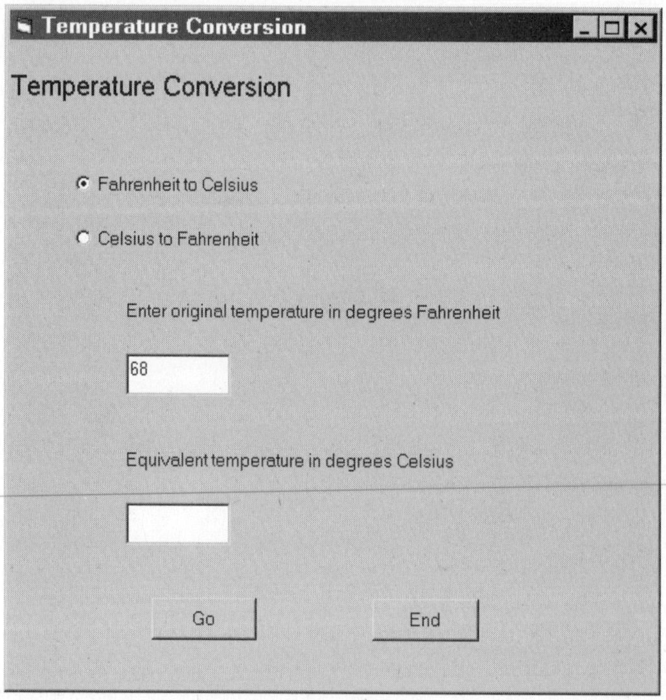

Fig. 4.21

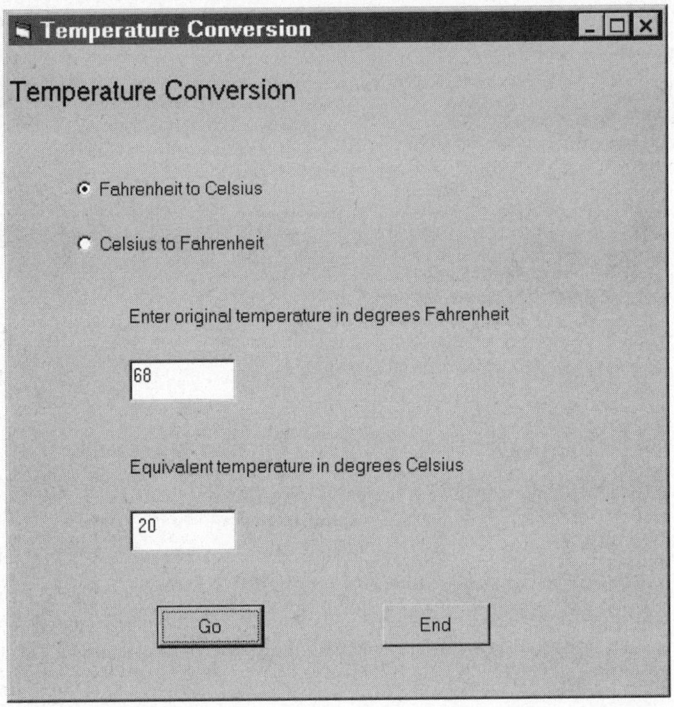

Fig. 4.22

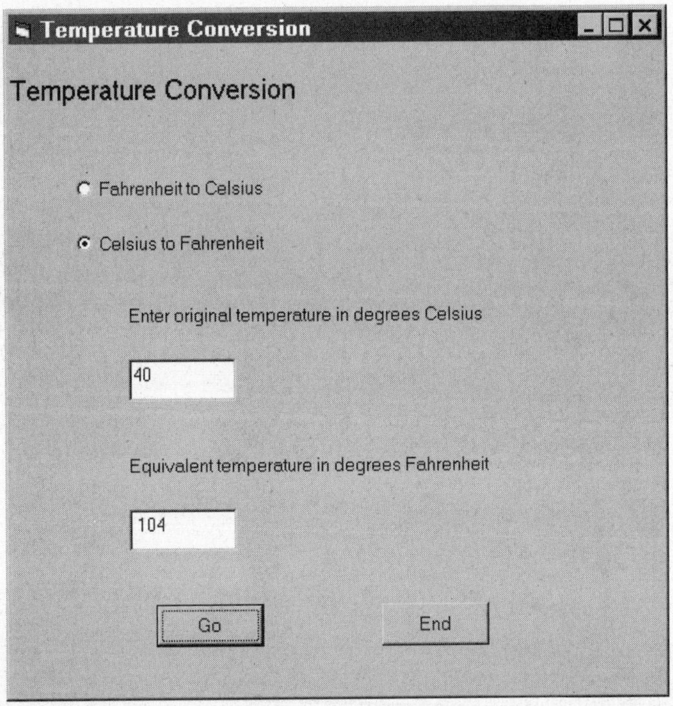

Fig. 4.23

In Fig. 4.22 we see the resulting output, after clicking on the Go button. Thus, a temperature of 68 degrees Fahrenheit is equivalent to 20 degrees Celsius. Fig. 4.23 shows the result of an opposite calculation, in which a temperature of 40 degrees Celsius is determined to be equivalent to 104 degrees Fahrenheit.

Many applications require several different groups of option buttons, where the selection of an option button within each group is independent of the selections made in other groups. This can be accomplished by placing each option-button group within a separate *frame*. (Existing option buttons can be moved into a frame using cut-and-paste techniques.)

The use of option-button groups within frames is illustrated in the next example.

EXAMPLE 4.8 SELECTING MULTIPLE ALTERNATIVES (TEMP. CONVERSION REVISITED)

Let us now extend the temperature conversion program presented in Example 4.7 to include the following additional features:

1. Display the equivalent temperature in either full precision (maximum number of decimal places) or rounded to the nearest integer.

2. Display the equivalent temperature in either a large (12-point) font or a small (8-point) font.

3. Display the absolute temperature, in addition to the converted temperature (i.e., display the temperature in degrees Kelvin in addition to degrees Celsius, or in degrees Rankin in addition to degrees Fahrenheit). Note that $°K = °C + 273.15$, and $°R = °F + 459.67$.

To implement these features, we will place the original two option buttons (indicating the type of conversion) within a frame. We will also place two more option buttons (to select the precision) within a second frame, and an additional two option buttons (to select the font size) within a third frame. In addition, we will use a check box to display the absolute temperature as an option. We will also add a new label and a new text box, to label and display the absolute temperature. Fig. 4.24 shows the preliminary Form Design Window layout.

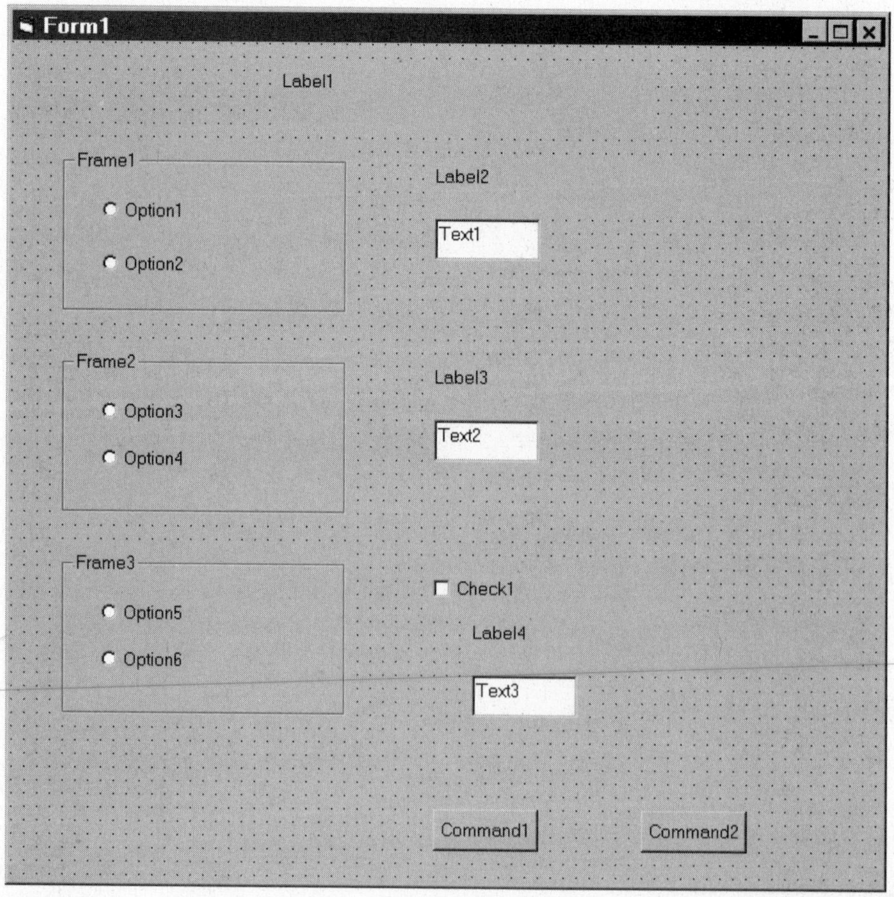

Fig. 4.24

We now assign the following initial values to the control properties listed below. (Note that some of these assignments are repeated from the previous example. The new assignments are italicized.)

Object	Property	Value
Form1	Caption	"Temperature Conversion"
Label1	Caption	"Temperature Conversion"
	Font	MS Sans Serif, 12-point
Label2	Caption	"Enter original temperature in degrees Fahrenheit"
Label3	Caption	"Equivalent temperature in degrees Celsius"
Label4	*Caption*	*"Absolute temperature in degrees Kelvin"*
Option1	Caption	"Fahrenheit to Celsius"
	Value	True
Option2	Caption	"Celsius to Fahrenheit"
Option3	*Caption*	*"Full precision"*
	Value	*True*
Option4	*Caption*	*"Nearest integer"*
Option5	*Caption*	*"Large font"*
	Value	*True*
Option6	*Caption*	*"Small font"*
Frame1	*Caption*	*"Conversion type"*
Frame2	*Caption*	*"Precision"*
Frame3	*Caption*	*"Font size"*
Check1	*Caption*	*"Display absolute temperature"*
Text1	Text	(blank)
Text2	Text	(blank)
Text3	*Text*	*(blank)*
Command1	Caption	"Go"
Command2	Caption	"End"

Fig. 4.25 shows the resulting appearance of the Form Design Window.

We now add the event procedures. Each of the first two option buttons (Fahrenheit to Celsius and Celsius to Fahrenheit) will have an event procedure associated with it, as in the previous example. Now, however, each event procedure will specify *three* labels rather than two – the additional label indicating the units for the absolute temperature (degrees Kelvin or degrees Rankine).

The event procedure associated with the first command button (Go) calculates and formats the equivalent temperature and the corresponding absolute temperature. Note that the absolute temperature is assigned to the temporary string variable T. Then at the end of the event procedure, Text3.Text (which is actually displayed) is either assigned the string represented by T, or an empty (blank) string, depending on whether or not the absolute temperature is displayed. In other words, if the check box has been checked, so that Check1.Value = 1, then the string represented by T is assigned to Text3.Text, and the absolute temperature (along with its accompanying label, Label4.Caption) will appear on the form. If the check box has not been checked, however, then Check1.Value will equal 0, and an empty (blank) string will be assigned to Text3.Text. In this case, the accompanying label (Label4.Caption) also will not appear.

The event procedures are shown beneath Fig. 4.25.

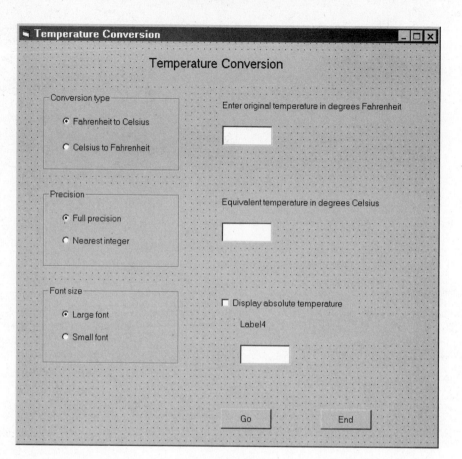

Fig. 4.25

```
Private Sub Option1_Click()
    If (Option1.Value = True) Then
        Label2.Caption = "Enter original temperature in degrees Fahrenheit"
        Text1.Text = ""

        Label3.Caption = "Equivalent temperature in degrees Celsius"
        Text2.Text = ""

        Label4.Caption = "Absolute temperature in degrees Kelvin"
        Text3.Text = ""
    End If
End Sub

Private Sub Option2_Click()
    If (Option2.Value = True) Then
        Label2.Caption = "Enter original temperature in degrees Celsius"
        Text1.Text = ""

        Label3.Caption = "Equivalent temperature in degrees Fahrenheit"
        Text2.Text = ""

        Label4.Caption = "Absolute temperature in degrees Rankine"
        Text3.Text = ""
    End If
End Sub
```

```vb
Private Sub Command1_Click()
    Dim TempIn As Double, TempOut As Double, AbsTemp As Double, T As String

    TempIn = Val(Text1.Text)

    If (Option1 = True) Then
        TempOut = (5 / 9) * (TempIn - 32)
        AbsTemp = TempOut + 273.15
    Else
        TempOut = 1.8 * TempIn + 32
        AbsTemp = TempOut + 459.67
    End If

    Text2.Text = Str(TempOut)
    T = Str(AbsTemp)
    If (Option4.Value = True) Then
        Text2.Text = Str(Format(TempOut, "#."))
        T = Str(Format(AbsTemp, "#."))
    End If

    Text2.FontSize = 8
    Text3.FontSize = 8
    If (Option5.Value = True) Then
        Text2.FontSize = 12
        Text3.FontSize = 12
    End If

    If (Check1.Value = 1) Then
        Label4.Visible = True
        Text3.Text = T
    ElseIf (Check1.Value = 0) Then
        Label4.Visible = False
        Text3.Text = ""
    End If
End Sub


Private Sub Command2_Click()
    End
End Sub
```

Fig. 4.26 shows a conversion of 40 degrees Fahrenheit to 4.4444 degrees Celsius and 277.59 degrees Kelvin (absolute). Note that the results are displayed in full precision, using large (12-point) fonts.

In Fig. 4.27, we see the result of converting 28 degrees Celsius to 82 degrees Fahrenheit. In this case, the absolute temperature is not requested (the check box is unselected, the text box is blank, and the accompanying label is not shown). Also, the converted temperature is shown in a small (8-point) font, rounded to the nearest integer.

4.11 SELECTING FROM A LIST (LIST BOXES AND COMBO BOXES)

A *list box* offers another approach to selecting among several different alternatives. Each alternative can be identified as a single entry within the list. When the program is executed, clicking on a list entry will cause the value of the *list index* to be assigned to the ListIndex property. (The list index is an integer whose value ranges from 0 to $n-1$, where n is the number of entries within the list. Thus, the first item will correspond to index number 0, the second will correspond to index number 1, and so on.) An If-Then-Else block or a Select Case structure can then be used to carry out the desired action.

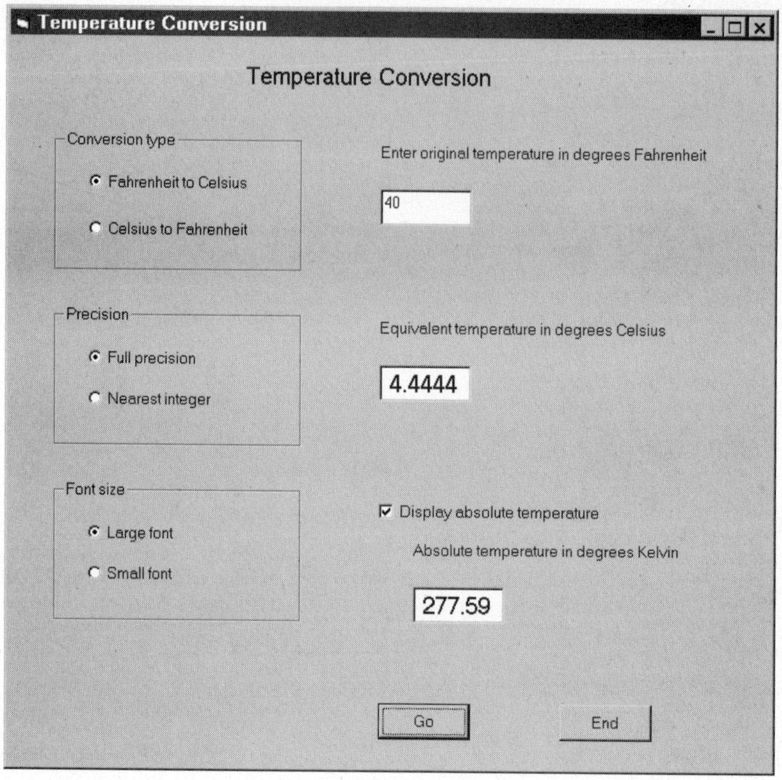

Fig. 4.26

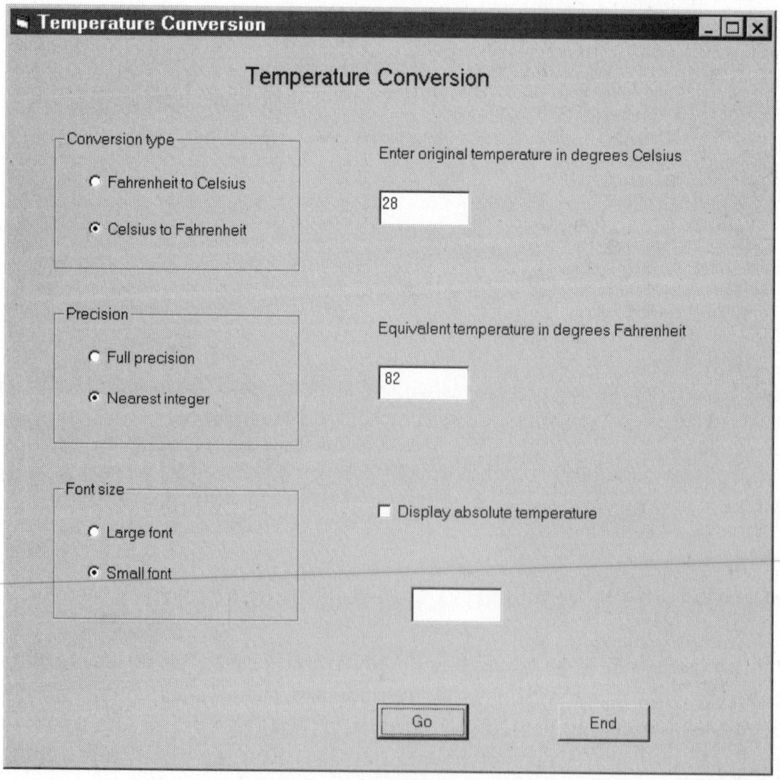

Fig. 4.27

Closely associated with a list box is the *combo box*, which is a single control combining a text box and a list box. The list box component behaves as any other list box (see below). The text box component can be used either to enter an input string or to display an output string (e.g., a label or a heading for the list box), as described in Sec. 4.7.

Initial list entries can be entered as strings in the same manner as other control properties. (Press Ctrl-Enter at the end of each list entry, in order to drop down to the next line.) In addition, list entries can be changed (i.e., reassigned) or added during program execution using the AddItem method or the List function; e.g.,

```
List1.AddItem("Red")
List1.AddItem("White")
List1.AddItem("Blue")
etc.
```

or

```
List1.List(0) = "Red"
List1.List(1) = "White"
List1.List(2) = "Blue"
etc.
```

Typically, these list modification instructions will appear within a Form_Load() event procedure.

The ListCount and ListIndex properties are also useful in many situations. ListCount represents the number of entries within the list (beginning with 1, not 0). It is often used as a stopping condition for a looping structure; e.g.,

```
For Count = 0 To (ListCount − 1)
    . . . . .
Next Count
```

ListIndex represents the index value of the most recently selected list entry (The value corresponding to the first entry is 0, not 1). The use of ListIndex often provides a convenient expression for a Select Case structure; e.g.,

```
Select Case ListIndex

Case 0          'First entry
    . . . . .

Case 1          'Second entry
    . . . . .

    . . . . .   'Last entry

End Select
```

Neither ListCount nor ListIndex can be assigned an initial value. Hence, neither property appears in the Properties Window during the initial program design.

EXAMPLE 4.9 SELECTING FROM A LIST (MULTILINGUAL HELLO REVISITED)

Let us return to the situation described in Example 4.6, in which we display the greeting "Hello" in one of several different languages. In this example, we will use a combo box to display the choice of languages, and a text box to display the appropriate greeting. (There are other ways to accomplish the same thing; for example, a text box to display the choice of languages, and a label to display the greeting.) Since the selection will be made from a combo box (or from a text box, if we had so chosen), only one greeting will be displayed at any one time. Fig. 4.28 shows the preliminary Form Design Window layout.

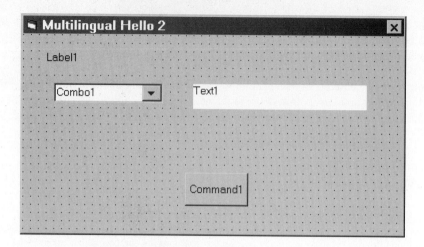

Fig. 4.28

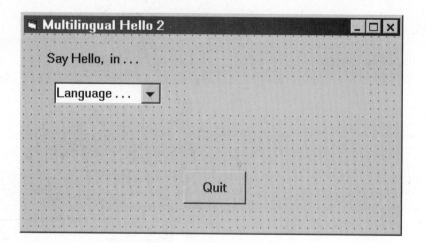

Fig. 4.29

Once the preliminary layout has been completed, we assign the following initial values to the properties:

Object	Property	Value
Form1	Caption	"Multilingual Hello 2"
Label1	Caption	"Say Hello, in . . ."
	Font	MS Sans Serif, 10-point
Combo1	Text	"Language . . ."
	List	"French" (press Control-Enter after each list entry)
		"German"
		"Hawaiian"
		"Hebrew"
		"Italian"
		"Japanese"
		"Spanish"
	Font	MS Sans Serif, 10-point

Object	Property	Value
Text1	Text	(blank)
	BackColor	Gray
	BorderStyle	0 – None
	Font	MS Sans Serif, 14-point
Command1	Caption	"Quit"
	Font	MS Sans Serif, 10-point

Fig. 4.29 shows the appearance of the Form Design Window after assigning these property values.

In order to complete this project, we must associate an event procedures with a combo box click event, and another event procedure with the command button. For the combo box click event, we will use a Select Case structure, based upon the value returned by the ListIndex property when the user clicks on one of the combo box list entries. (We could also have used a series of If-Then-Else structures instead.)

The command button event procedure is very simple, consisting only of the End command inserted between the opening Sub and the closing End Sub statements.

The two event procedures are shown below.

```
Private Sub Combo1_Click()
    Select Case Combo1.ListIndex

    Case 0
        Text1.Text = "Bonjour"

    Case 1
        Text1.Text = "Guten Tag"

    Case 2
        Text1.Text = "Aloha"

    Case 3
        Text1.Text = "Shalom"

    Case 4
        Text1.Text = "Buon Giorno"

    Case 5
        Text1.Text = "Konichihua"

    Case 6
        Text1.Text = "Buenos Dias"
    End Select
End Sub

Private Sub Command1_Click()
    End
End Sub
```

When the program is executed, the combo box shows the title Language . . . in the text-box area. The list of languages can be seen in the drop-down window by clicking on the adjacent down-arrow (see Fig. 4.30). When the user clicks on one of these entries, the corresponding greeting appears within the text box, to the right of the drop-down window.

Fig. 4.31 shows what happens when the user selects German from the list in the drop-down window. Thus, we see that the "hello" greeting in German is "Guten Tag."

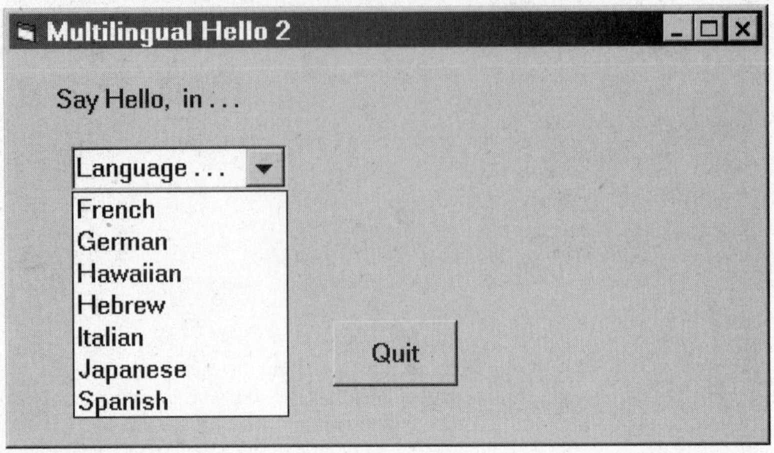

Fig. 4.30

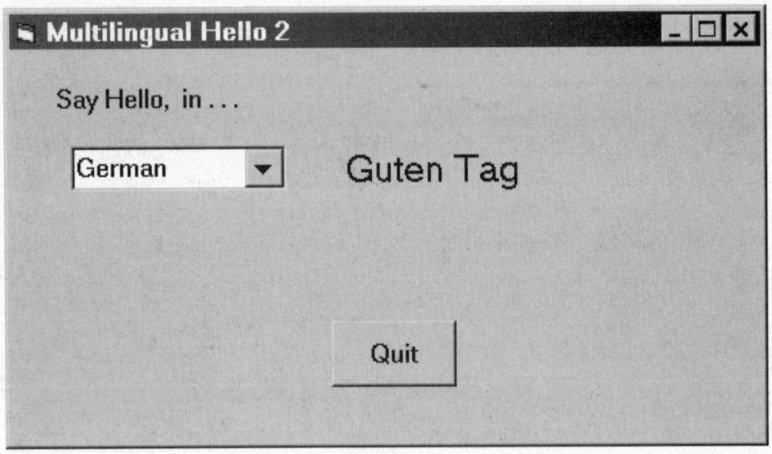

Fig. 4.31

4.12 ASSIGNING PROPERTIES COLLECTIVELY (THE With BLOCK)

When assigning values to several properties within the same object at run time, it is often convenient to do so using a With block. This construct allows the object name to be specified only once, followed by each of the property assignments. The use of With blocks is logically more concise than individual, independent property assignments. It may also be computationally more efficient, particularly if the property references involve several layers (e.g., *form.object.property*).

The general form of the With block is

```
With object name
        .property 1 = . . . . .
        .property 2 = . . . . .
        . . . . .
        .property n = . . . . .
End With
```

Note the period (.) preceding each property specification.

EXAMPLE 4.10 ASSIGNING PROPERTIES USING WITH BLOCKS

Let us again consider the Multilingual Hello program presented in Example 4.9. In this example we will assign only the form caption at design time. The remaining property values will be assigned using With blocks at run time, when the program execution begins.

We begin with the form shown in Fig. 4.32, which is similar to Fig. 4.28 in Example 4.9.

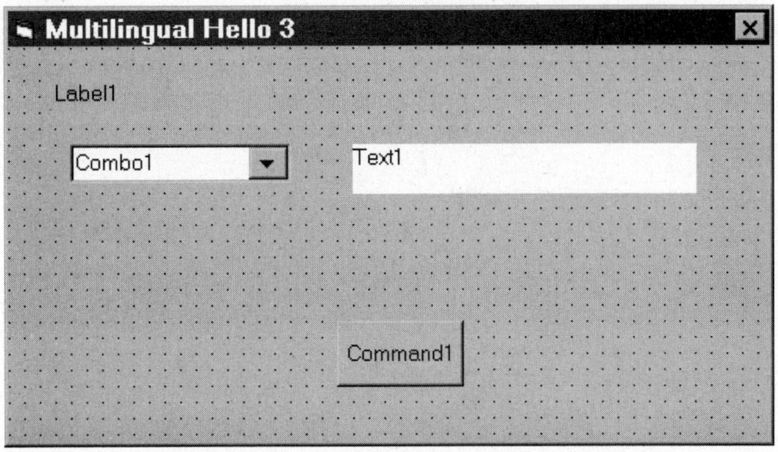

Fig. 4.32

Note that the form has been assigned a caption (Multilingual Hello 3), but the control objects have not been assigned specific property values.

We now add a new event procedure (Form_Load) and modify the two existing event procedures (Combo1_Click and Command1_Click) as follows:

```
Private Sub Form_Load()
    With Label1
        .Caption = "Say Hello, in . . ."
        .Font.Size = 10
    End With

    With Combo1
        .List(0) = "French"
        .List(1) = "German"
        .List(2) = "Hawaiian"
        .List(3) = "Hebrew"
        .List(4) = "Italian"
        .List(5) = "Japanese"
        .List(6) = "Spanish"
        .Text = "Language . . ."
        .Font.Size = 10
    End With

    With Text1
        .Text = ""
        .BackColor = &H8000000A      'Gray
        .BorderStyle = 0
        .Font.Size = 14
    End With                    (Continues on next page)
```

```
        With Command1
            .Caption = "Quit"
            .Font.Size = 10
        End With
    End Sub

    Private Sub Combo1_Click()
        With Text1
            Select Case Combo1.ListIndex
            Case 0
                .Text = "Bonjour"
            Case 1
                .Text = "Guten Tag"
            Case 2
                .Text = "Aloha"
            Case 3
                .Text = "Shalom"
            Case 4
                .Text = "Buon Giorno"
            Case 5
                .Text = "Konichihua"
            Case 6
                .Text = "Buenos Dias"
            End Select
        End With
    End Sub

    Private Sub Command1_Click()
        End
    End Sub
```

Note that the objects Label1, Combo1, Text1 and Command1 are assigned their initial property values within event procedure Form_Load. A separate With block is used for each object; hence, Form_Load contains four different With blocks. Note the embedded Select Case structure within the With block.

The text within the text box control is then reassigned the proper string (the actual greeting) within Combo1_Click. This occurs at run time, when the user clicks on an entry within the combo box.

Execution of the program results in the same behavior as shown in Example 4.9 (see Figs. 4.30 and 4.31).

4.13 GENERATING ERROR MESSAGES (THE MsgBox FUNCTION)

Most comprehensive projects include *error traps*, which detect inappropriate input data or improper conditions that arise during the course of the computation. Some examples are detecting a negative value for an input parameter that is required to be positive, and trapping an attempt to calculate the square root of a negative number. Such conditions can usually be detected using If-Then or If-Then-Else. When an error of this type has been detected, an *error message* is usually displayed and the computation is either suspended or terminated. The error message informs the user that an error has occurred, and may suggest that the user take corrective action.

The MsgBox function offers a convenient way to display error messages, as well as other types of information that may be useful during the course of the computation. This function is written as a single executable statement; i.e.,

MsgBox(*string*)

where *string* represents the error message, in the form of a string (either a string constant or a string variable) that is provided by the programmer. When the error message is encountered, it will generate a message such as that shown in Fig. 4.33. The message disappears when the user clicks on Ok.

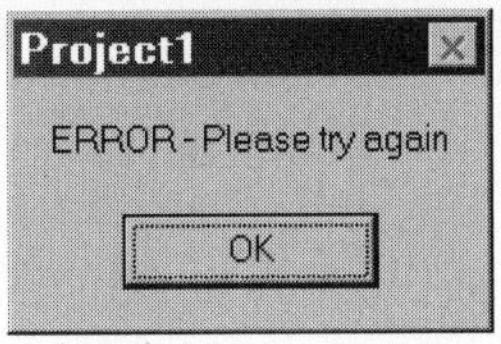

Fig. 4.33 A typical error message

The MsgBox function also allows other display options, including multiple command buttons and a provision for subsequent action that is dependent on the selection of a command button (see Sec. 5.7).

EXAMPLE 4.11 CALCULATING FACTORIALS

The *factorial* of n is defined as $n! = 1 \times 2 \times 3 \times \ldots \times n$. Thus, $2! = 1 \times 2 = 2$; $3! = 1 \times 2 \times 3 = 6$; $4! = 1 \times 2 \times 3 \times 4 = 24$; and so on. Note that n must be a positive integer. Also, note that $n!$ may be a very large number, even for modest values of n (for example, $10! = 3,628,800$). Factorials are used in certain mathematical applications, such as determining how many different ways n objects can be arranged.

A factorial can easily be calculated using a loop structure. For example, in Visual Basic, we can write

```
Dim Factorial As Long, i As Integer, n As Integer

Factorial = 1
For i = 1 To n
    Factorial = Factorial * i
Next i
```

This segment of code assumes that the value of n is known. While progressing through the loop, the value of i will increase from 1 to n. Thus, when first entering the loop, Factorial will have a value of 1. After the first pass, Factorial will again have a value of 1. After the second pass, Factorial $= 1 \times 2 = 2$; after the third pass, Factorial $= 1 \times 2 \times 3 = 6$; and so on, until Factorial $= 1 \times 2 \times 3 = \ldots \times n = n!$ after the last pass.

Now let us build a Visual Basic program that will calculate the factorial of a given positive integer, n. We will include an error trap for non-positive values of n.

The initial layout of the Form Design Window is shown in Fig 4.34.

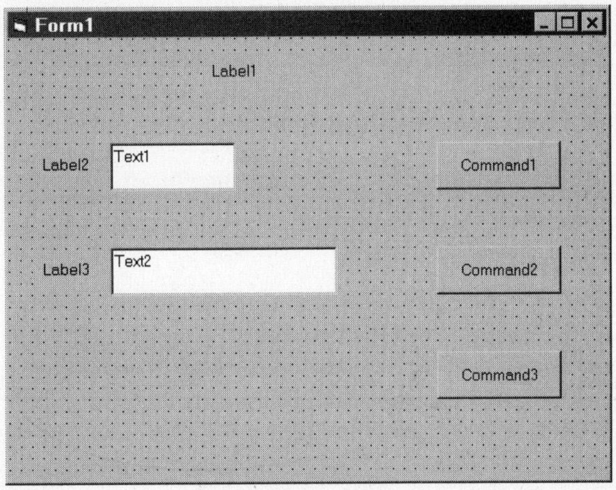

Fig. 4.34

To customize this window, we assign the following initial values to the control properties:

Object	Property	Value
Form1	Caption	"Factorials"
Label1	Caption	"Calculate the factorial of n"
	Font	MS Sans Serif, 12-point
Label2	Caption	"n = "
	Font	MS Sans Serif, 10-point
Label3	Caption	"n! = "
	Font	MS Sans Serif, 10-point
Text1	Text	(blank)
	Font	MS Sans Serif, 10-point
Text2	Text	(blank)
	Font	MS Sans Serif, 10-point
Command1	Caption	"Go"
	Font	MS Sans Serif, 10-point
Command2	Caption	"Clear"
	Font	MS Sans Serif, 10-point
Command3	Caption	"Quit"
	Font	MS Sans Serif, 10-point

Here are the event procedures corresponding to the command buttons.

```
Private Sub Command1_Click()
    Dim Factorial As Long, i As Integer, n As Integer

    n = Val(Text1.Text)
    If n < 1 Then
        Beep
        MsgBox ("ERROR - Please try again")
    Else
        Factorial = 1
        For i = 1 To n
            Factorial = Factorial * i
        Next i
        Text2.Text = Str(Factorial)
    End If
End Sub

Private Sub Command2_Click()
    Text1.Text = ""
    Text2.Text = ""
End Sub

Private Sub Command3_Click()
    End
End Sub
```

Note that the value of n is entered in the first text box and then converted to an integer. We then encounter an error trap in the form of an If-Then-Else block, to determine if n is a positive integer, as required. If n is *not* a positive integer, the com-

puter will beep and generate the message ERROR – Please try again. However, if *n is* a positive integer, the computer enters a loop to determine the value of *n*!, using the logic described on the previous page. The value of *n*! is then converted to
a string and displayed in the second text box.

   When the program is first executed, the screen appears as shown in Fig. 4.35. The user may then enter a value for *n* in
the first text box and click on the Go button. If the value of *n* is a positive integer, the corresponding value of *n*! will be
displayed, as shown in Fig. 4.36. If the value entered for *n* is *not* a positive integer, an error message will be generated, as
shown in Fig. 4.37.

   Clicking on the Clear button will restore the display to that shown in Fig. 4.35. Similarly, clicking on the Quit button
will terminate the computation.

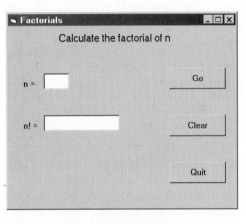

Fig. 4.35

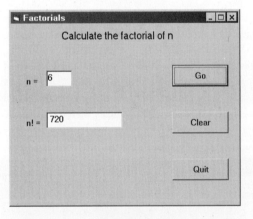

Fig. 4.36

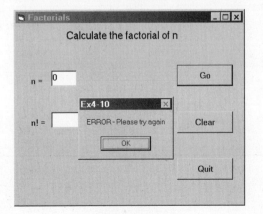

Fig. 4.37

4.14 CREATING TIMED EVENTS (THE TIMER CONTROL)

Applications involving timed events, such as a digital clock or a stopwatch, make use of the timer control (see Fig. 4.1). Like other controls, the timer is placed in the Form Design Window at design time. Its location and appearance are unimportant, because the timer itself does not appear when the program is executed. The values assigned to certain timer properties are critical, however, since they govern the functioning of the timed events.

Of primary importance is the Interval property. This property can be assigned an integer value ranging from 0 to 65,535. A zero value disables the timer. Positive values represent the number of milliseconds between timed events. Thus, a value of 1 represents an interval of one millisecond (one thousandth of a second); 1000 represents a one-second interval; and 60,000 represents one-minute interval. The actual interval may be longer, however, because the frequency of timed events cannot exceed 18.2 per second (which corresponds to a minimum Interval value of 54.9). Furthermore, the interval may be longer if the system is relatively busy (i.e., if substantial computation is taking place within the interval).

In addition, the Enabled property must be assigned a value of True in order to activate the timer. Setting Enabled to False disables the timer. This property may be assigned at design time and/or during program execution.

EXAMPLE 4.12 TIMED EVENTS (A METRONOME)

To illustrate the use of timed events, let us use the timer control to create a metronome. As you are probably aware, a metronome is an instrument used by musicians to maintain a specified tempo (i.e., a specified interval between beats). Commercial metronomes produce a distinct sound (a "beep"), sometimes accompanied by a flashing light, to represent each beat.

In this example we will use two flashing circles to represent the beat, because of the lengthy (and uncontrollable) sound produced by the Visual Basic Beep command. One circle will always be highlighted (shown in bright red) while the other will be shown in the gray background color. The red-gray combination will alternate at the specified tempo. We will restrict the tempo to values falling within the interval 40–220 beats per minute, as most music falls within this interval.

We begin with the Form Design Window shown in Fig. 4.38. Note that clock enclosed by the square at the center of the Form Design Window. This is the timer control, whose name is Timer1. The left rectangle is Shape1, and the right rectangle is Shape2. These rectangles will be converted to circles, which will display the tempo by alternating in color. The command buttons will start and stop the metronome, and end the computation. The text box will specify the tempo.

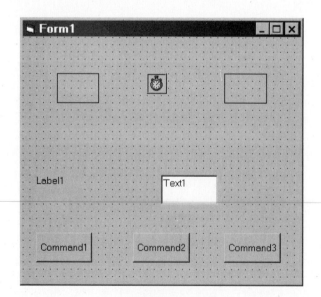

Fig. 4.38

We now resize the label, the text box and the command buttons, and assign the following initial values to the control properties. The results are shown in Fig. 4.39.

Object	Property	Value
Form1	Caption	"Metronome"
Shape1	Shape	3 (Circle)
	FillColor	Red
	FillStyle	1 (Transparent – default value)
Shape2	Shape	3 (Circle)
	FillColor	Red
	FillStyle	1 (Transparent – default value)
Timer	Enabled	False
Label1	Caption	"Tempo (40-220):"
	Font	MS Sans Serif, 10-point
Text1	Caption	(none)
	Font	MS Sans Serif, 10-point
Command1	Caption	"Go"
	Font	MS Sans Serif, 10-point
Command2	Caption	"Stop"
	Font	MS Sans Serif, 10-point
Command3	Caption	"End"
	Font	MS Sans Serif, 10-point

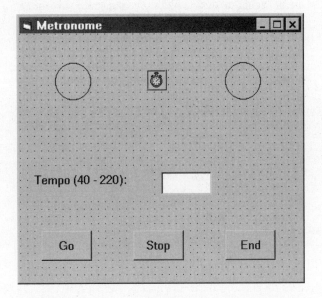

Fig. 4.39

The next step is the creation of appropriate event procedures for the timer and the command buttons. The event procedure corresponding to the timer will consist of an If-Then-Else block that controls the alternating color display within the circles. Thus, if the FillStyle property of the leftmost circle (Shape1) is assigned a value of zero (indicating a transparent object, which will appear gray), then its value is set to 1 and the value of Shape2.FillStyle is set to 0. This will cause the left circle to appear red and the right circle to appear gray. Otherwise, Shape1.FillStyle is assigned a value of 0 and

Shape2.FillStyle is set to 1, causing the left circle to appear gray and the right circle to appear red. This test will be carried out at the beginning of every interval, resulting in the colors alternating between circles from one interval to the next. Notice that the timer interval setting is *not* set within this event procedure.

The Go button activates the metronome. Hence, Command1_Click converts the value entered in the text box to a number and assigned to the variable Tempo. This is followed by an If-Then-Else block that tests to see if the entered value is out or range (less than 40 beats per minute or greater than 220 beats per minute). If so, an error message appears, the text box is cleared, and the user if offered another opportunity to enter a valid value. Otherwise, the timer interval is determined (in terms of the number of milliseconds per interval), and the timer is enabled.

The Stop button allows the user to stop the metronome, set another tempo and restart. Hence, Command2_Click clears the text box and disables the timer. On the other hand, the End button is used to terminate the computation. Hence, Command3_Click contains only an End statement.

Here are the various event procedures.

```
Private Sub Timer1_Timer()
    'Beep
    If (Shape1.FillStyle = 0) Then     'left circle is gray - change to red
        Shape1.FillStyle = 1
        Shape2.FillStyle = 0
    Else                               'left circle is red - change to gray
        Shape1.FillStyle = 0
        Shape2.FillStyle = 1
    End If
End Sub


Private Sub Command1_Click()
    Dim Tempo As Single

    Tempo = Val(Text1.Text)
    If (Tempo < 40 Or Tempo > 220) Then     'Tempo out of range
        Beep
        Text1.Text = ""
        MsgBox ("Tempo out of Range - Please Try Again")
        Exit Sub
    End If
    Timer1.Interval = 60 * (1000 / Tempo)
    Timer1.Enabled = True
End Sub

Private Sub Command2_Click()
    Text1.Text = ""
    Timer1.Enabled = False
End Sub

Private Sub Command3_Click()
    End
End Sub
```

When the program is executed, the circles will alternate in color every half second (120 beats per minute). The action is initiated by entering the value 120 in the text box and then clicking on the Go button, as shown in Fig. 4.40.

4.15 SCROLL BARS

Scroll bars can be used to view a large document by moving the visible window (scrolling) vertically or horizontally. They can also be used to select a particular value within a specified range, or to select a specific item from a list. Visual Basic supports both horizontal and vertical scroll bars. They both work the same way.

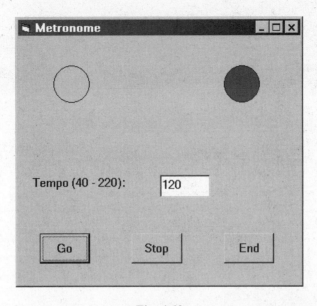

Fig. 4.40

A scroll bar consists of a slide area enclosed by an outward-pointing arrow button at each end, as illustrated in Fig. 4.41. The slide area contains a button (called the "thumb") that can be dragged within the slide area. The location of the thumb within the slide area determines the portion of the document being viewed, the value being selected, etc. Thus, in a horizontal scroll bar, dragging the thumb to the leftmost portion of the slide area permits the leftmost portion of a document to be viewed, or the lowest value to be selected within a range, and so on.

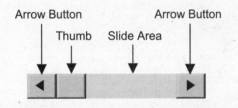

Fig. 4.41 A Horizontal Scroll Bar

There are two other ways to move the thumb within a scroll bar. You can click on the empty slide area, on either side of the thumb. Or you can click on an arrow button at the end of the scroll bar. Each click will produce an incremental movement in the indicated direction. Clicking on the slide area usually results in greater movement than clicking on an arrow button. The magnitudes of the various movements will be determined by the values assigned to certain scroll bar properties.

The most important properties associated with scroll bars are Min, Max, SmallChange and LargeChange. Min and Max represent integer values corresponding to the minimum and maximum thumb locations within the slide area. The defaults are Min = 0 and Max = 32767, though these values can be altered at design time or while the program is executing. The values assigned to Min and Max must always fall within the interval 0 to 32767, and Min must always be assigned a value less than Max.

SmallChange and LargeChange indicate the size of the incremental movements when you click on the arrow buttons or the empty slide area, respectively. Each has a default value of 1, and each can be reassigned a value between 1 and 32767. The larger the value, the greater the movement resulting from a single click. Typically, SmallChange is assigned a smaller value than LargeChange, though this need not always be true. (If you assign SmallChange a value greater than that assigned to LargeChange, a click on an arrow button will result in a larger change than a click on the empty slide area.)

EXAMPLE 4.13 USING SCROLL BARS (THE METRONOME REVISITED)

In this example we again consider the metronome that was originally presented in Example 4.12. Now, however, we will use a horizontal scroll bar rather than a text box to specify the tempo. Fig. 4.42 shows the initial control layout. Comparing this figure with Fig. 4.38, we see that the label has been raised, and the horizontal scroll bar, named HScroll1, has been placed in the location formerly occupied by the text box.

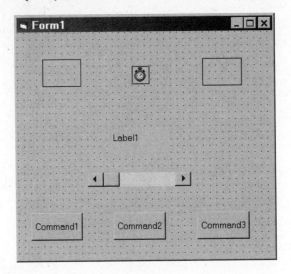

Fig. 4.42

We now assign the following initial values to the control properties.

Object	Property	Value
Form1	Caption	"Metronome"
Shape1	Shape	3 (Circle)
	FillColor	Red
	FillStyle	1 (Transparent – default value)
Shape2	Shape	3 (Circle)
	FillColor	Red
	FillStyle	1 (Transparent – default value)
Timer	Enabled	False
Label1	Caption	(none)
	Font	MS Sans Serif, 10-point
HScroll1	Min	40
	Max	220
	SmallChange	1
	LargeChange	10
	Value	40
Command1	Caption	"Go"
	Font	MS Sans Serif, 10-point
Command2	Caption	"Stop"
	Font	MS Sans Serif, 10-point
Command3	Caption	"End"
	Font	MS Sans Serif, 10-point

Note that the initial values assigned to HScroll1.Min (40) and HScroll1.Max (220) define the lower and upper limits for the tempo.

The resulting Form Design Window is shown in Fig. 4.43.

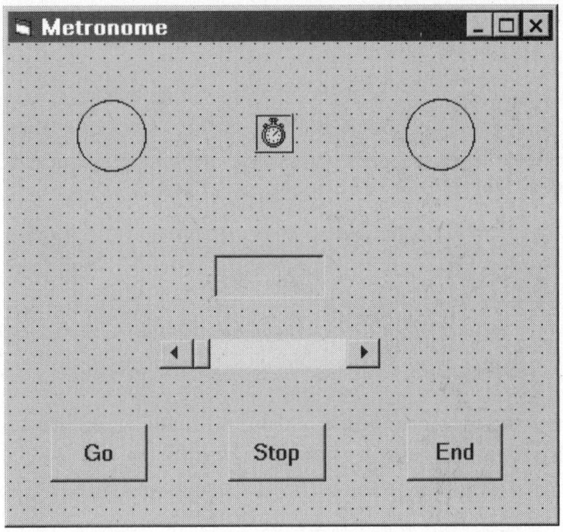

Fig. 4.43

The required event procedures are shown below. The first event procedure, Form_Load, causes the initial tempo (as specified by Hscroll1.Value) to be displayed on the form as Label1. The second event procedure, Hscroll1_Change, resets the tempo shown as Label1 whenever the user clicks on the horizontal scroll bar. The next event procedure, Timer1_Timer, alternates the flashing circles in exactly the same manner as in the previous example.

Command1_Click is now simpler, because we no longer need to provide an error trap for tempos that are out of range. The horizontal scroll bar does this for us, with the values assigned to HScroll1.Min and HScroll1.Max. Hence Command1_Click now accepts the tempo directly from the current value of HScroll1.Value, then determines a value for the timer interval and enables the timer.

The remaining two event procedures, Command2_Click and Command3_Click, are similar to their counterparts in the earlier example.

```
Private Sub Form_Load()
    Label1.Caption = Str(HScroll1.Value)
End Sub


Private Sub HScroll1_Change()
    Label1.Caption = Str(HScroll1.Value)
End Sub


Private Sub Timer1_Timer()
    'Beep
    If (Shape1.FillStyle = 0) Then     'left circle is gray – change to red
        Shape1.FillStyle = 1
        Shape2.FillStyle = 0
    Else                               'left circle is red – change to gray
        Shape1.FillStyle = 0
        Shape2.FillStyle = 1
    End If
End Sub
```

(Continues on next page)

```
Private Sub Command1_Click()
    Dim Tempo As Single

    Tempo = HScroll1.Value
    Timer1.Interval = 60 * (1000 / Tempo)
    Timer1.Enabled = True
End Sub

Private Sub Command2_Click()
    Timer1.Enabled = False
End Sub

Private Sub Command3_Click()
        End
End Sub
```

When the program is executed, the user will specify a tempo with the horizontal scroll bar. Clicking on the Go button then results in the flashing display illustrated in Fig. 4.44. At any time the user may click on the Stop button, reset the tempo, and again click on Go, thus restarting the metronome at a different tempo. Clicking on the End button will terminate the computation.

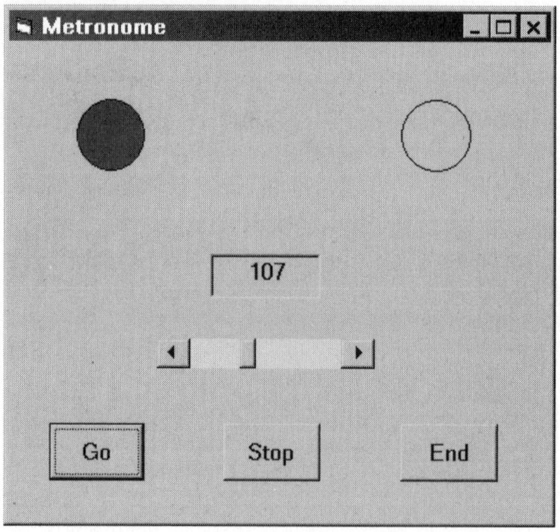

Fig. 4.44

Review Questions

4.1   What is the purpose of the Visual Basic toolbox?

4.2   What is the purpose of each of the following Visual Basic tools?

(*a*)	Check box	(*g*)	Label
(*b*)	Combo box	(*h*)	List box
(*c*)	Command button	(*i*)	Option button
(*d*)	Horizontal scroll bar	(*j*)	Picture box
(*e*)	Frame	(*k*)	Text box
(*f*)	Image box	(*l*)	Vertical scroll bar

4.3   Describe two different methods for adding a control to the Form Design Window.

4.4   How is a control relocated within the Form Design Window?

4.5   How is a control resized within the Form Design Window?

4.6   How is a control removed from the Form Design Window?

4.7   Describe, in general terms, the default naming system used with Visual Basic controls within a Form Design Window.

4.8   What is the recommended procedure for overriding the default naming system used with Visual Basic controls?

4.9   Under what conditions is it generally advisable to override the default naming system used with Visual Basic controls?

4.10 How are values assigned to Visual Basic control properties at design time?

4.11 How are values assigned to Visual Basic control properties during run time?

4.12 What is an event procedure? How does an event procedure begin and end?

4.13 What is the relationship between an event procedure and a command button?

4.14 Can event procedures be associated with Visual Basic controls other than command buttons?

4.15 How is an event procedure created, viewed or edited?

4.16 How do labels and text boxes differ from each other?

4.17 How are numerical values entered and displayed in text boxes?

4.18 How do check boxes and option buttons differ from each other?

4.19 How is a check box disabled (i.e., "grayed out")?

4.20 Can an option button be disabled (i.e., "grayed out")?

4.21 What is the purpose of a frame? How does the inclusion of frames affect groups of option buttons?

4.22 Can check boxes be placed in a frame?

4.23 How do list boxes and combo boxes differ from each other?

4.24 How are new items added to a list or combo box?

4.25 What is the purpose of the ListIndex property? Which controls support this property? How might it be used?

4.26 What is the purpose of the ListCount property? How might it be used?

4.27 What is the purpose of the With block? What advantages are provided by its use?

4.28 What is the purpose of the MsgBox function? How is this function used within a Visual Basic program?

4.29 For what types of applications is the timer control intended?

4.30 When using a timer control, what is the purpose of the Interval property? What restrictions apply to its use?

4.31 When using a timer control, how is the Enabled property used to start and stop the timer?

4.32 Suggest three different uses for a scroll bar.

4.33 Describe the components of a scroll bar. How can each component be used to make a selection?

4.34 When using a scroll bar, what is the purpose of the Min and Max properties?

4.35 When using a scroll bar, what is the purpose of the SmallChange and the LargeChange properties? To which scroll bar component does each property apply?

Programming Problems

4.36 Re-create the project shown in Example 4.3 on your own computer. Verify that the program executes correctly. Then change the project in the following ways:

(*a*) Change the label captions to Current Date: and Current Time:.

(*b*) Change the background colors of the form and the text boxes. (Choose your own colors).

(*c*) Change the command button captions to Execute and Quit.

(*d*) Raise the lower label and the lower text box so that they are closer to the upper label and text box.

(*e*) Move the command buttons to the bottom of the form and align them horizontally.

(*f*) Resize the form and rearrange the controls relative to one another so that the form has an overall pleasing appearance.

(*g*) Access the on-line help for the format function (select Index/Format function from the Help menu). Then experiment with other date and time formats, in order to display the date and time differently.

4.37 Modify the project shown in Example 4.3 so that it uses four labels, rather than two labels and two text boxes. *Hint*: Assign appropriate string values to Label2.Caption and Label4.Caption during program execution. In addition, change the appearance of the output data (i.e., change the format of the current date and time) as you see fit.

4.38 Modify the project shown in Example 4.3 so that either the day and date or the time are shown (but not both). *Hint*: Use two option buttons.

4.39 Modify the project shown in Example 4.3 so that the day and date are always shown, but the time is displayed only as a user-selected option. *Hint*: Use a check box to select the time display.

4.40 Modify the project shown in Example 4.3 so that it displays your name, street address and city instead of the current day and date, and time. *Hint*: Replace the assignment statements that access the format function with string assignments. For example, if you are Santa Claus and a third text box has been introduced to display the city, you might write

```
Text1.Text = "Santa Claus"
Text2.Text = "One Main Street"
Text3.Text = "North Pole"
```

Experiment with the project so that it runs correctly and has a pleasing appearance.

4.41 Alter the project shown in Example 4.4 so that the user enters the the date in the form mm/dd/yy (see Example 2.21), and the computer displays the date in the day/date format used in Example 4.3.

4.42 Modify the project shown in Example 4.5 so that the coins are entered in reverse-order (i.e., first half-dollars, then quarters, etc., with pennies last). Execute the program to assure that it runs correctly.

4.43 Modify the project shown in Example 4.5 so that it adds up the money spent in the several different expense categories (in dollars) rather than adding up the number of pennies, nickels, dimes, etc. The permissible expense categories are:

(*a*)   Food   (*d*)   Car payment

(*b*)   Rent   (*e*)   Entertainment

(*c*)   Transportation   (*f*)   Savings

Enter the amount of money spent for each category as a separate input item. Display the total for the first three categories and the total for all six categories as separate items. Label each input and output quantity appropriately. Execute the program to assure that it runs correctly, using values of your own choosing.

4.44 Modify the project shown in Example 4.6 so that a separate command button is used for each language. (In other words, use a command button in place of each check box.) In addition, include a command button to clear the display, and another command button to quit (hence, a total of nine command buttons – one for each of the seven languages, plus the Clear and Quit buttons).

4.45 Modify the project shown in Example 4.6 so that the two option buttons are replaced by command buttons (hence, a total of four command buttons – one for each conversion type, plus Go and End).

4.46 Create a Visual Basic project that will allow the user to enter a positive integer and determine whether it is even or odd. In addition, include an option that will determine whether or not the given integer is a prime number. Display a message indicating whether the number is even or odd, and another message (in the event the prime-number option is selected) that indicates whether or not the number is a prime.

Note that an integer is even if it can be divided by 2 without any remainder. This can be determined by evaluating the expression n/Mod(2), where n represents the given integer.

Furthermore, an integer n is a prime number if it *cannot* be evenly divided (leaving no fractional remainder) by *any* integer ranging from 2 to $\sqrt{n}$. In other words, an integer is a prime number only if *all* of the quotients n/2, n/3, . . ., Int(Sqr(n)) include a fractional remainder. This can be determined by evaluating the expression n/Mod(d) within a loop, where the divisor d varies from 2 to Int(Sqr(n)). (Note that d = 2 during the first pass through the loop, d = 3 during the second pass, and so on, until d = Int(Sqr(n)) during the last pass.)

4.47 Create a Visual Basic project to determine the sum of the first n positive integers (that is, determine the sum $1 + 2 + 3 + \ldots + n$). Specify n as an input parameter, via an appropriately labeled text box. Use a loop structure to calculate the sum. Display the sum in a separate text box, with an appropriate label.

4.48 Modify the Visual Basic project created in Prob. 4.47 to compute the sum of the integers ranging from n_1 to n_2, where $n_1 < n_2$. Include provisions for carrying out the computation in any of the following ways:

(*a*)   Sum *all* of the integers ranging from n_1 to n_2.

(*b*)   Sum only the even integers within the interval defined by n_1 and n_2.

(*c*)   Sum only the odd integers within the interval defined by n_1 and n_2.

Enter the values of n_1 and n_2 in separate text boxes. Generate an error message if the condition $n_1 < n_2$ is not satisfied. Use option buttons to accommodate the three different choices. In each case, use an appropriate loop to calculate the sum. Display the sum in its own text box. Label all input and output.

4.49 The *mean* (or *arithmetic average*) of a list of n numbers is defined as

$$\bar{x} = (x_1 + x_2 + \cdots + x_n)/n$$

where $\bar{x}$ represents the mean.

Create a Visual Basic project to determine $\bar{x}$, where the values of n and x_1, x_2, etc., are entered as input parameters. Use a single looping structure to enter the x-values and to determine $\bar{x}$ (remember that $\bar{x}$ is a cumulative *sum*, not a cumulative *product*).

4.50 A pizza shop is planning to offer on-line purchasing. Pizzas can be purchased in three different sizes. The cost is $10 for a small pizza (plain, with cheese and tomato sauce), $12 for medium and $15 for large. The following toppings are available: mushrooms, pepperoni, sausage, onions, green peppers, black olives, and shrimp. Each topping is an additional $1 for a small pizza, $1.50 for a medium pizza and $2.25 for a large pizza. In addition, customers can order a "supreme," with everything on it, for $15 (small), $20 (medium), and $27 (large).

   Create a Visual Basic project for this purpose. Allow the customer to specify the size, and the choice of individual toppings. In addition, include an option to order a "supreme" for each of the three sizes. (Disable the individual topping selections if a "supreme" is chosen.) Display the cost of the pizza, the state tax (assuming a rate of 6 percent), and the total cost as separate data items. Test the project, using numerical values of your own choosing.

4.51 Create a Visual Basic project that will allow the user to select the name of a country from a list and then display the corresponding capital, and vice versa. For simplicity, restrict the project to the following countries and their corresponding capitals.

Canada	Ottawa
England	London
France	Paris
Germany	Berlin
India	New Delhi
Italy	Rome
Japan	Tokyo
Mexico	Mexico City
People's Republic of China	Beijing
Russia	Moscow
Spain	Madrid
United States	Washington, D.C.

4.52 Create a Visual Basic project that will either convert U.S. dollars into a foreign currency, or convert a foreign currency into U.S. dollars. The foreign currencies and their U.S. dollar equivalents are:

1 U.S. dollar =	0.6	British pounds
	1.4	Canadian dollars
	2.3	Dutch guilders
	6.8	French francs
	2.0	German marks
	2000	Italian lira
	100	Japanese yen
	9.5	Mexican pesos
	1.6	Swiss francs

   Your project should include two option buttons within a frame, to select either U.S. to foreign conversion or foreign to U.S. conversion. Nine additional option buttons should be placed within another frame, to select the particular foreign currency. Use a text box to specify a given amount of money in the source currency, and another text box to display the equivalent amount of money in the target currency. Include an appropriate set of labels for each conversion type.

4.53 Extend the project written for Prob. 4.52 so that any currency can be converted to any other currency. For simplicity, restrict the currencies to the ten countries (including the U.S.) listed in Prob. 4.52.

4.54 Create a Visual Basic project to solve for the real roots of the quadratic equation

$$ax^2 + bx + c = 0$$

using the well-known quadratic formulas

$$x_1 = \frac{-b + \sqrt{b^2 - 4ac}}{2a} \qquad x_2 = \frac{-b - \sqrt{b^2 - 4ac}}{2a}$$

where x_1 and x_2 represent the desired real roots. (Recall that these formulas are valid only if $b^2 > 4ac$).

Design the program so that the values of a, b and c are entered into separate (labeled) text boxes. Then test to determine if $b^2 > 4ac$, as required. If so, calculate the values of x_1 and x_2, and display them in separate (labeled) text boxes. If b^2 does not exceed $4ac$, display an error message, instructing the user to enter new values for a, b and c.

4.55 Suppose you deposit P dollars in a savings account for n years. If the money earns interest at the rate of i percent per year, compounded annually, then after n years, the original sum of money will have increased to

$$F = P(1 + 0.01i)^n$$

where F represents the final accumulation.

Usually, however, the interest is compounded more often than once a year, even though the interest rate (i) is stated on an annual basis. Thus, if the interest is compounded quarterly, then

$$F = P(1 + 0.01i/4)^{4n}$$

where i is the annual interest rate (expressed as a percentage), and n is still the number of years (not the number of quarters).

Similarly, if the interest is compounded monthly, then

$$F = P(1 + 0.01i/12)^{12n}$$

Moreover, if the interest is compounded daily, then

$$F = P(1 + 0.01i/365)^{365n}$$

These results can be generalized into the following single equation:

$$F = P(1 + 0.01i/c)^{cn}$$

where c takes on the following values:

    Annual compounding: $c = 1$
    Quarterly compounding: $c = 4$
    Monthly compounding: $c = 12$
    Daily compounding: $c = 365$

Create a Visual Basic project to determine the future value of a deposit (F), given P, i and n as input values. Enter each of the input values via a text box (with an accompanying label). Include four option buttons to specify the frequency of compounding. Display the final result in a separate text box.

4.56 Create a Visual Basic project that utilizes the timer control to display a digital clock. To do so, you may use either of the following two strategies:

  (*a*) Assign the Format function with the Now argument (see Example 4.3) to a label caption within the timer event procedure.

  (*b*) Assign the Time function to the label caption within the timer event procedure.

4.57 Create a Visual Basic stop watch that utilizes the timer control. Include command buttons to start and stop the timing. *Hint*: Assign the current value of Now to the user-defined variable StartTime at the beginning of the process. Then display the difference between Now and StartTime at the end of the process.

4.58 Create a Visual Basic alarm clock that utilizes the timer control. Use option buttons to turn the alarm on and off. Specify the wake-up time using one of the following two controls:

  (*a*) A text box
  (*b*) A scroll bar

Chapter 5

Menus and Dialog Boxes

5.1 BUILDING DROP-DOWN MENUS

Drop-down menus represent another important class of components in the user interface, complementing, and in some cases replacing, the Visual Basic controls described in Chap. 4. A drop-down menu will descend from the menu heading (i.e., the name displayed in the main Menu Bar) when the user clicks on the menu heading.

EXAMPLE 5.1 BUILDING DROP-DOWN MENUS

Fig. 5.1 shows a main Menu Bar with three menu names: Continents, Oceans and Seas. Clicking on Continents causes the corresponding drop-down menu to appear, as shown in the figure. Dragging the mouse over one of the items within the drop-down menu will then cause that item to be highlighted.

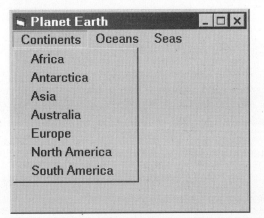

Fig. 5.1 A drop-down menu

To create a drop-down menu, click on the Menu Editor button in the Toolbar (see Fig. 5.2), or select Menu Editor from the Tools menu. Note that the Menu Editor is *not* accessible from the Visual Basic Toolbox.

Menu Editor Button

Fig. 5.2 The Standard Toolbar

The Menu Editor will then appear, as shown in Fig. 5.3. The check boxes labeled Enabled and Visible should be selected, as shown in the figure.

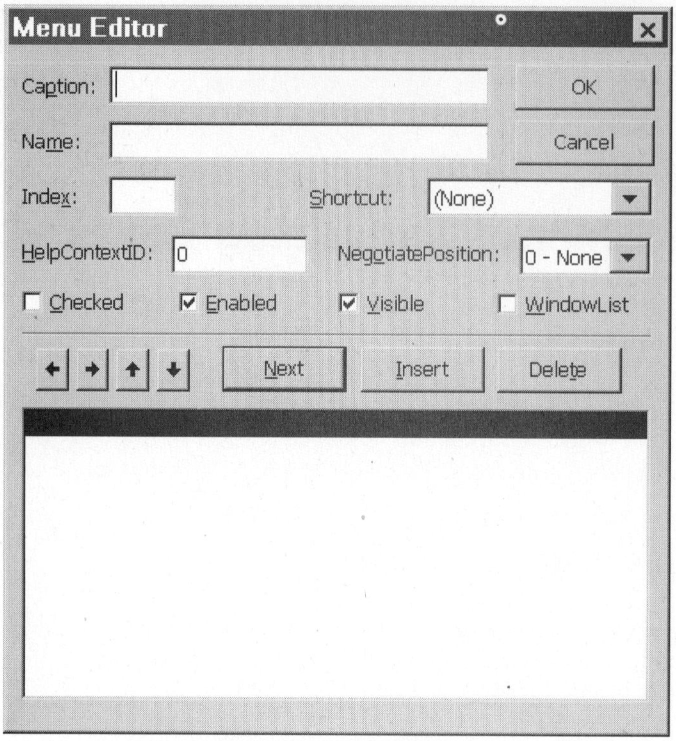

Fig. 5.3 The Menu Editor

You then enter identifiers for the Caption and Name for each menu item. (The Caption is actually the screen name of the item, as it appears in the Menu Bar or within the drop-down menu. The Name is used only in Visual Basic code – it is not displayed when the application is running.) The Caption will appear in the large area at the bottom of the Menu Editor as well as within the Caption field. You may either press the Enter key or click on the Next button after the information has been entered for each menu item.

All of the menu components must be entered, in the following order:

1. The first menu heading (i.e., the screen name for the first menu, which appears in the menu bar).

2. The corresponding menu items for the first menu.

3. The second menu heading.

4. The corresponding menu items for the second menu.

and so on. (The order of the components can be altered after they have been entered if they are not correct initially.)

The menu headings must be flush left within each line. Items that appear *within* each menu must be indented one level, as indicated by four ellipses preceding each item. The indentation is accomplished using the right-arrow button. Click once to indent one level (four ellipses). The opposite action, i.e., moving an indented item to the left, is accomplished with the left-arrow button.

The relative ordering of each menu component can be altered using the up- and down-arrow buttons. Thus, to move an entry ahead of the two preceding entries, highlight the entry to be moved and click on the up-arrow button twice. In addition, a menu component can be inserted by highlighting the item that will appear *below* the insertion, and clicking on the Insert button. Similarly, a menu component can be deleted by highlighting the component and clicking on the Delete button.

Remember that it is the *indentation pattern* that distinguishes the menu heading from the corresponding items in the drop-down menu. Also, it is the *order* of the entries that distinguishes one set of menu components from another. (This may sound more complicated than it really is, as shown in the following example.)

EXAMPLE 5.2 USING DROP-DOWN MENUS (GEOGRAPHY)

Fig. 5.4 shows the appearance of the Menu Editor for the application shown in Fig. 5.1. The first menu heading (i.e., menu name, as shown on the screen) is highlighted. Note that the Caption is Continents, and the Name is mnuContinents (note the prefix mnu to identify the menu item, as recommended by Microsoft and discussed in Sec. 4.4). Remember that the Name does not appear on the screen; it is used as a menu item identifier in Visual Basic program statements.

Many (but not all) of the menu items are shown in the large area at the bottom of the Menu Editor. (Note the vertical slide bar, which provides access to all of the menu items.) The indentation defines the menu items that are grouped beneath each heading. Note the four ellipses (. . . .) preceding each indented item. Pressing the right-arrow key for each menu item causes the ellipses to appear automatically.

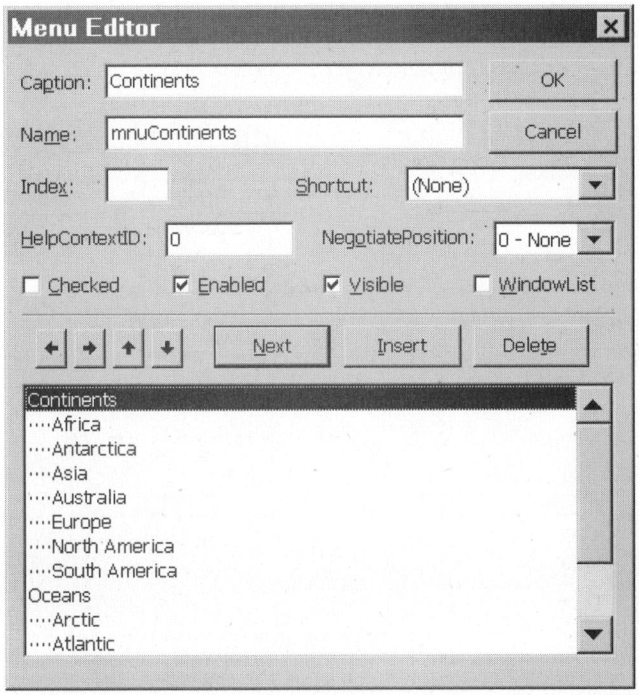

Fig. 5.4

The complete list of menu items (captions and names) is shown below.

Caption	Name
Continents	mnuContinents
....Africa	mnuAfrica
....Antarctica	mnuAntarctica
....Asia	mnuAsia
....Australia	mnuAustralia
....Europe	mnuEurope
....North America	mnuNorthAmerica
....South America	mnuSouthAmerica
Oceans	mnuOceans
....Arctic	mnuArctic
....Atlantic	mnuAtlantic
....Indian	mnuIndian
....Pacific	mnuPacific

(*Continues on next page*)

Caption	Name
Seas	mnuSeas
....Baltic	mnuBaltic
....Bering	mnuBering
....Black	mnuBlack
....Caribbean	mnuCaribbean
....Mediterranean	mnuMediterranean
....Persian Gulf	mnuPersianGulf
....Red	mnuRed
....South China	mnuSouthChina

Execution of this program results in the availability of three drop-down menus. The first drop-down menu is shown in Fig. 5.1. Figs. 5.5(*a*) and (*b*) show the second and third drop-down menus.

Fig. 5.5(*a*)   **Fig. 5.5(*b*)**

Event procedures can be defined for each of the drop-down menu items. Typically, a click-type event procedure is associated with each menu item (but not the menu headings). To do so, simply double-click on each menu item within the Form Design Window, thus accessing the Code Editor Window. Then enter the appropriate instructions between the first (Sub) and last (End Sub) statements, as explained in Chap. 4.

5.2 ACCESSING A MENU FROM THE KEYBOARD

A keyboard *access character* can be defined for each menu item. This allows the user to view a drop-down menu by pressing Alt and the access key for the menu heading, rather than clicking on the menu heading. In addition, once the drop-down menu is shown, the user may select a menu item by pressing its access key (without Alt) rather than clicking on the menu item.

To define an access character, use the Menu Editor to place an ampersand (&) in front of the desired character within each menu item caption (i.e., within each screen name). The access character will then be underlined when the associated menu item is shown. Note that *a drop-down menu must actually be visible on the screen for its access characters to be active.*

The first letter within the caption is often selected as the access character, but this need not be the case, particularly if the use of first letters would result in duplicate access characters among the labels or within a menu. In other words, each of the menu headings must have a unique access character. Similarly, each menu item *within a menu* must have a unique access character, though the same access character may be used (once) in each of two or more menus.

In addition to access characters, we can also define *keyboard shortcuts* for some or all of the menu items within a drop-down menu. A keyboard shortcut is typically a function key, or a Ctrl-key combination or a Shift-key combination. Unlike an access character, which requires that a drop-down menu be displayed before it can be used, a keyboard shortcut can access a menu item directly *without* first activating the drop-down menu. Thus, a keyboard shortcut can be used to select a menu item directly from a window, saving several keystrokes or mouse clicks.

Keyboard shortcuts are selected directly from the Shortcut field within the Menu Editor. Clicking on the down-arrow within this field displays the available choices. The keyboard shortcuts must be unique; that is, if a menu item (including menu headings) has an associated keyboard shortcut, it must be different from all other keyboard shortcuts. Remember, however, that keyboard shortcuts are not required; typically, they are defined only for the more commonly used menu items.

EXAMPLE 5.3 USING MENU ENHANCEMENTS (GEOGRAPHY REVISITED)

Let us now enhance the project shown in the last two examples by adding some additional controls, and by defining event procedures for the menu items. In addition, we will define an access character for each menu item, and, for illustrative purposes, a keyboard shortcut for some of the menu items.

Specifically, we will add a label and a text box to the form, and we will display the area of a geographical feature (a continent, ocean or sea) within the text box if the feature is selected from a menu. In addition, we will add two command buttons, one to clear the text box, and the other to terminate the computation.

The form design window is shown in Fig. 5.6. Note that the first letter of each menu heading is now underlined, indicating that it is a menu access character. Also, note the label Area (square miles): corresponding to Label1, the empty text box for Text1, and the command buttons labeled Clear (Command1) and Quit (Command2).

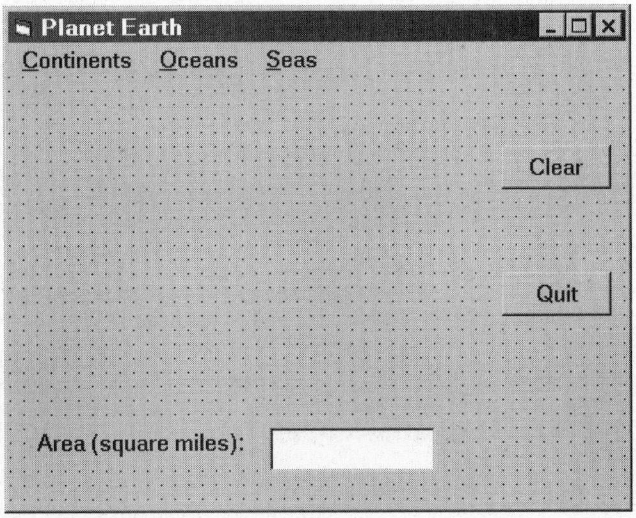

Fig. 5.6

The menu items have been modified to add access characters, as shown below (note the added ampersands).

```
&Continents
....&Africa
....An&tarctica
....As&ia
....A&ustralia
....&Europe
....&North America
....&South America
```
(*Continues on next page*)

```
&Oceans
....&Arctic
....A&tlantic
....&Indian
....&Pacific
&Seas
....&Baltic
....B&ering
....B&lack
....&Caribbean
....&Mediterranean
....&Persian Gulf
....&Red
....&South China
```

In addition, the four menu items listed under Oceans have keyboard shortcuts associated with them. Fig. 5.7 shows the menu editor, with Arctic as the active menu item listed under Oceans. Note that the key combination Ctrl+A has been selected as the keyboard shortcut for this menu item.

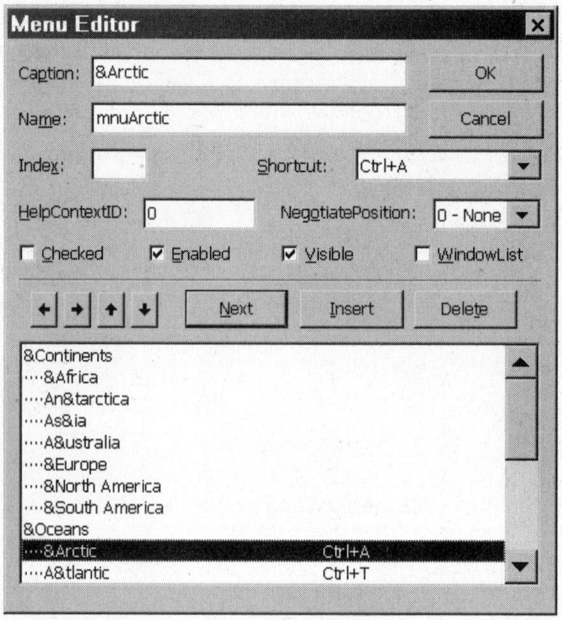

Fig. 5.7

In order to accommodate the new executable features (i.e., the display of the area of each geographical feature) associated with the text box and the two command buttons, we add the following click-type event procedures:

```
Private Sub Command1_Click()
    Text1.Text = ""
End Sub

Private Sub Command2_Click()
    End
End Sub
```

(*Continues on next page*)

```
Private Sub mnuAfrica_Click()
   Text1.Text = "11,700,000"
End Sub

Private Sub mnuAntarctica_Click()
   Text1.Text = "5,400,000"
End Sub

Private Sub mnuArctic_Click()
   Text1 = "5,100,000"
End Sub

Private Sub mnuAsia_Click()
   Text1 = "17,300,000"
End Sub

Private Sub mnuAtlantic_Click()
   Text1.Text = "33,400,000"
End Sub

Private Sub mnuAustralia_Click()
   Text1.Text = "2,900,000"
End Sub

Private Sub mnuBaltic_Click()
   Text1.Text = "148,000"
End Sub

Private Sub mnuBering_Click()
   Text1.Text = "873,000"
End Sub

Private Sub mnuBlack_Click()
   Text1.Text = "196,000"
End Sub

Private Sub mnuCaribbean_Click()
   Text1.Text = "971,000"
End Sub

Private Sub mnuEurope_Click()
   Text1.Text = "3,800,000"
End Sub

Private Sub mnuIndian_Click()
   Text1.Text = "28,400,000"
End Sub

Private Sub mnuMediterranean_Click()
   Text1.Text = "969,000"
End Sub

Private Sub mnuNorthAmerica_Click()
   Text1.Text = "9,400,000"
End Sub
```

(Continues on next page)

```
    Private Sub mnuPacific_Click()
        Text1.Text = "64,200,000"
    End Sub

    Private Sub mnuPersianGulf_Click()
        Text1.Text = "89,000"
    End Sub

    Private Sub mnuRed_Click()
        Text1.Text = "175,000"
    End Sub

    Private Sub mnuSouthAmerica_Click()
        Text1.Text = "6,900,000"
    End Sub

    Private Sub mnuSouthChina_Click()
        Text1.Text = "1,150,000"
    End Sub
```

When the program is executed, the area corresponding to any of the menu items can be displayed in any of three possible ways: by clicking on the appropriate menu heading and then clicking on the desired menu item, by using the access characters instead of the mouse, or by use of the keyboard shortcut, if available. For example, when the program is executed, the Oceans menu appears as shown in Fig. 5.8. Thus, the area of the Arctic ocean can be displayed by clicking on Oceans and then Arctic, by pressing Alt-O followed by A, or by pressing Ctrl-A directly from the main window. The resulting display, shown in Fig. 5.9, is the same in each case.

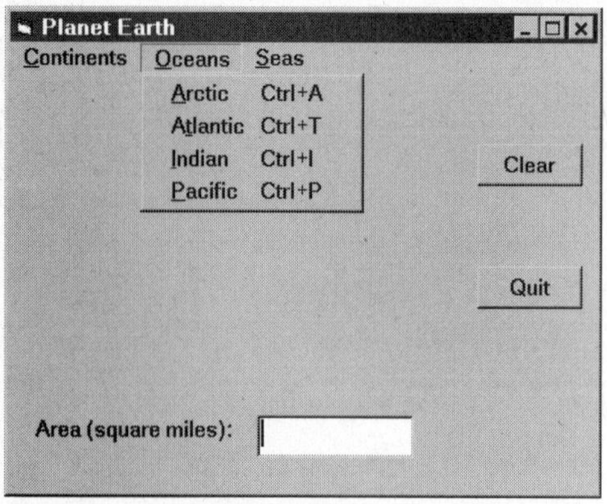

Fig. 5.8

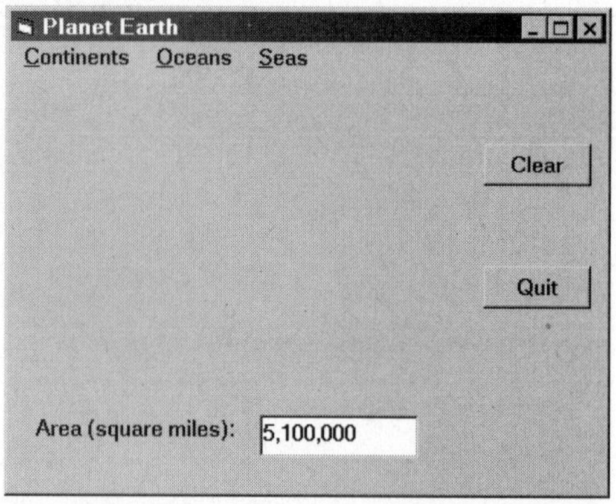

Fig. 5.9

The process can be continued for other menu items as long as desired. Moreover, the display area can be cleared at any time by pressing the Clear button. Also, the program execution can be ended by pressing the Quit button.

5.3 MENU ENHANCEMENTS

The menu editor includes other features that permit various menu item enhancements. For example, a check mark (✓) can be assigned to a menu item, indicating the on-off status of the menu item. Selecting the box labeled Checked will cause the menu item to be checked initially (see Fig. 5.3, 5.4 or 5.7). Its status can then be changed (i.e., the check mark can be removed and later displayed) under program control when the program is executing.

Another useful feature is the ability to deactivate a menu item by deselecting the Enabled box (see Fig. 5.3). The menu item will then appear "grayed out" within the menu, and it will not respond to mouse clicks, keyboard access characters or keyboard shortcuts. In addition, a menu item may be made invisible (and inactive) by deselecting the Visible box (see Fig. 5.3). Both of these features can later be changed under program control.

Finally, the items within a menu can be grouped together by introducing separators at various locations within a menu. Each separator is a menu item consisting only of a single dash (minus sign). Note that each separator must follow the same rules of indentation as its surrounding menu items.

EXAMPLE 5.4　MORE MENU ENHANCEMENTS (GEOGRAPHY REVISITED)

Returning to the Geography project shown in Examples 5.2 and 5.3, suppose we rearrange the list of continents into geographical groupings, with separators between each group. We will also disable Oceans, make Seas invisible, and place a check mark next to Africa (listed under Continents). In addition, we will add check boxes to the main window so that Oceans can be enabled and Seas can be made visible. Finally, we will add the Visual Basic code required by the check boxes, and to toggle the Africa check mark on and off.

In order to rearrange the list of continents and introduce separators, the Continents menu items in the Menu Editor must appear as shown below. Note the separators following Europe, South America and Australia.

```
&Continents
....&Africa
....As&ia
....&Europe
    -
....&North America
....&South America
    -
....A&ustralia
    -
....An&tarctica
```

The remaining menu items will appear in the same order as in Example 5.3.

Figures 5.10(*a*), (*b*) and (*c*) show the Menu Editor settings for the three menu items. Note the status of the check boxes in each figure (for each of the menu items).

Fig. 5.11 shows the form design window after the new controls (Check1 and Check2) have been added. Notice that Oceans now appears "grayed out," and Seas does not appear on the menu bar at all.

We must now add the following two event procedures so that the check box controls will function properly.

```
Private Sub Check1_Click()              Private Sub Check2_Click()
    If Check1.Value = 1 Then                If Check2.Value = 1 Then
        mnuOceans.Enabled = True               mnuSeas.Visible = True
    Else                                    Else
        mnuOceans.Enabled = False              mnuSeas.Visible = False
    End If                                  End If
End Sub                                  End Sub
```

Notice the reference to the menu item properties mnuOceans.Enabled and mnuSeas.Visible in the above event procedures.

In addition, we must modify the event procedure mnuAfrica_Click() to toggle the check mark on and off. Here is the modified event procedure.

```
Private Sub mnuAfrica_Click()
    If mnuAfrica.Checked = True Then
        mnuAfrica.Checked = False
    Else
        mnuAfrica.Checked = True
    End If
    Text1.Text = "11,700,000"
End Sub
```

Notice the reference to the menu item property mnuAfrica.Checked.

Fig. 5.10(*a*)

Fig. 5.10(*b*)

Fig. 5.10(*c*)

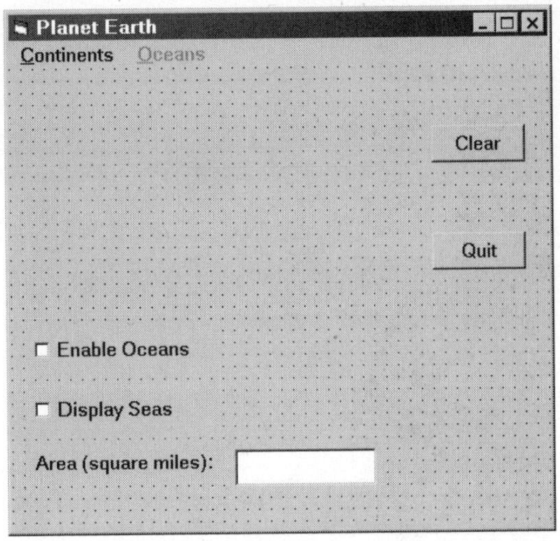

Fig. 5.11

When the program is executed, the window will initially appear as shown in Fig. 5.12(*a*). Clicking on the Enable Oceans check box will cause the Oceans label to become active, as shown in Fig. 5.12(*b*). Also, clicking on the Display Seas check box will allow the Seas label to become visible.

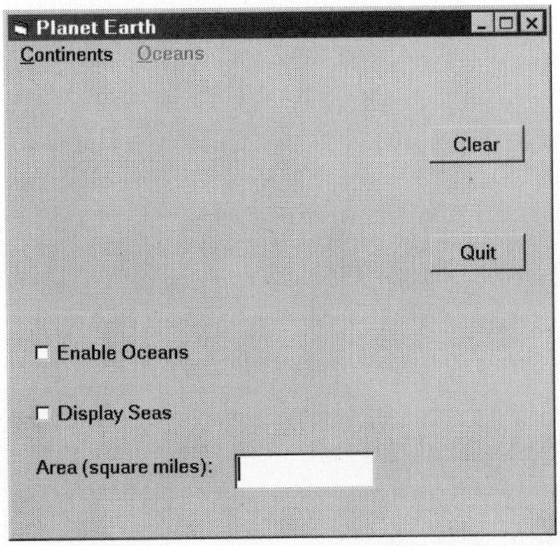

Fig. 5.12(*a*)

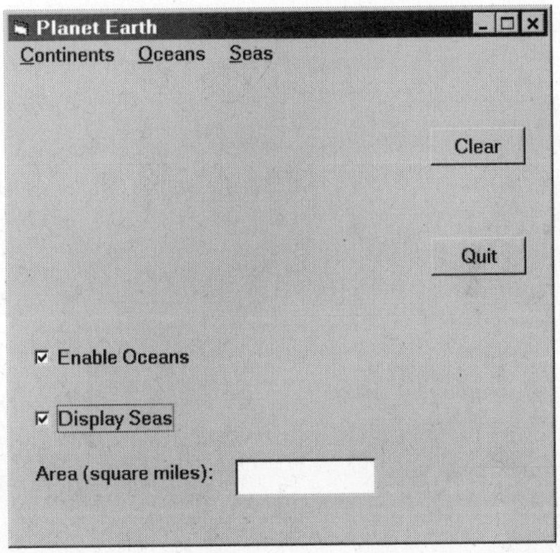

Fig. 5.12(*b*)

Now suppose we click on Continents. The drop-down menu appears as in Fig. 5.13(*a*), with a check mark in front of Africa. If we then click on Africa, the corresponding area will be displayed, as shown in Fig. 5.13(*b*). Now if we again click on Continents, the drop-down menu will again appear but now the check mark preceding Africa will not appear, having been toggled off. If this cycle (Continents/Africa) is repeated, the check mark will alternately reappear, then disappear, etc.

5.4 SUBMENUS

A menu item may have a *submenu* associated with it. Placing the mouse over the menu item (or pressing the access character, keyboard shortcut, etc.) will cause the corresponding submenu to be displayed adjacent to the parent menu item, as shown in Fig. 5.14. The submenu items may be assigned the same properties (e.g., access characters, keyboard shortcuts, check marks, deactivation, etc.) as any other menu item.

The use of submenus allows menu selections to be arranged in a logical, hierarchical manner.

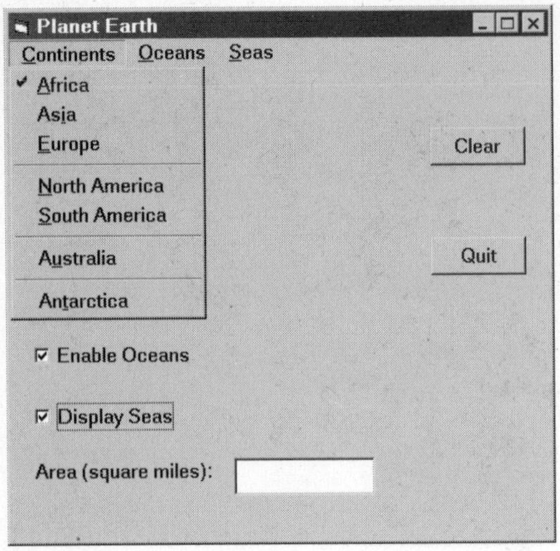

Fig. 5.13(*a*)

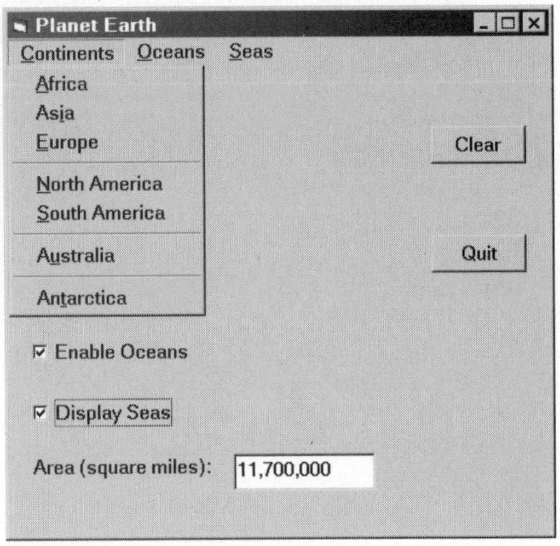

Fig. 5.13(*b*)

To create a submenu, simply indent the submenu items beneath the parent menu item within the Menu Editor. When the program is executed, each menu item having a submenu will be identified by a right-pointing arrow at its edge, as illustrated in the following example.

EXAMPLE 5.5 USING SUBMENUS (GEOGRAPHY REVISITED)

In this example we will modify the program presented in Example 5.3 so that there is only one menu heading, Geography. This menu will contain three menu items, Continents, Oceans and Seas. Each of these menu items will have its own submenu, as shown in Fig. 5.14. Thus, the program will offer the same features as in Example 5.3, though the menu entries will be arranged differently.

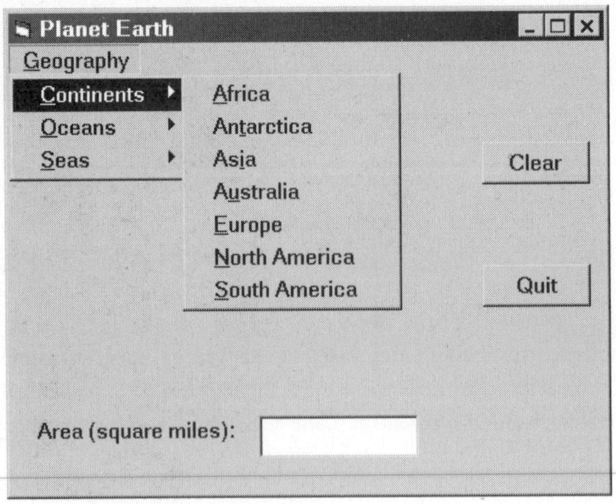

Fig. 5.14

To carry out this modification, we will alter the list of menu items within the Menu Editor, adding the overall heading Geography at the top of the list, and then indenting all of the remaining menu items by one level. The modified list will appear as follows:

```
&Geography
....&Continents
........&Africa
........An&tarctica
........As&ia
........A&ustralia
........&Europe
........&North America
........&South America
....&Oceans
........&Arctic
........A&tlantic
........&Indian
........&Pacific
....&Seas
........&Baltic
........B&ering
........B&lack
........&Caribbean
........&Mediterranean
........&Persian Gulf
........&Red
........&South China
```

Note that Continents, Oceans and Seas are indented under Geography, and their respective subentries are indented one additional level. Also, note that Geography will utilize its first letter (G) as a keyboard character.

Fig. 5.14 shows the Continents submenu that may be viewed during program execution. Figures 5.15(*a*) and 5.15(*b*) show the two additional submenus.

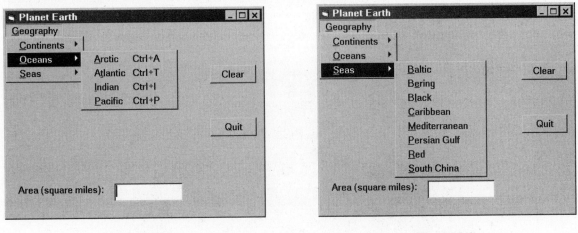

Fig. 5.15(*a*)   **Fig. 5.15(*b*)**

5.5 POP-UP MENUS

Another frequently used menu type is the *pop-up* menu. A pop-up menu can appear anywhere within a form, usually in response to clicking the right mouse button. Normally, the upper left corner of the pop-up menu appears at the location of the mouse click, though the position of the pop-up menu can be altered by specifying some additional parameters (see Visual Basic's online help for more information on this topic).

A pop-up menu is created via the Menu Editor in the same manner as a drop-down menu, except that the main menu item is not visible (i.e., the Visible feature is unchecked). An event procedure must then be entered into the Code Editor so that the pop-up menu appears in response to the mouse click. The general form of the event procedure (assuming a right mouse click) is shown in Fig. 5.16. All of the components of this event procedure have a predefined meaning and must be entered as shown. (The undefined underscore, which represents the caption for the first pop-down menu item, is supplied by the programmer.) Note that the first and last lines are generated automatically by the Code Editor, provided the correct object name (Form) is selected in the upper left portion of the Code Editor, and the correct action (MouseDown) is selected in the upper right.

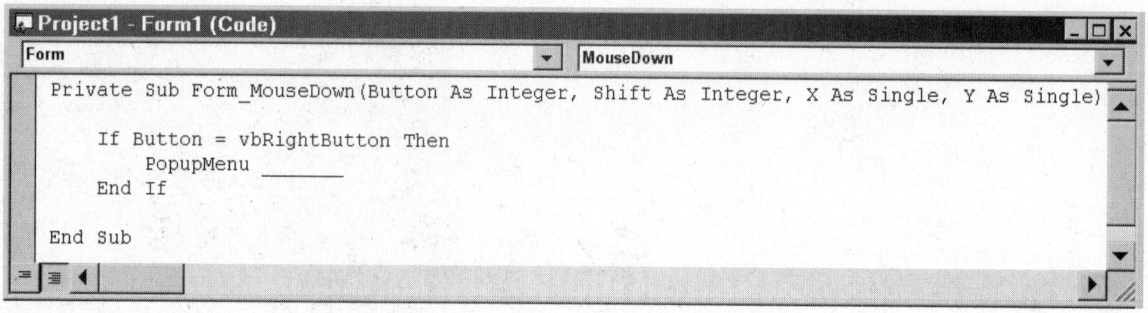

```
Project1 - Form1 (Code)                                                    _ □ ×
Form                                ▼    MouseDown                                ▼

  Private Sub Form_MouseDown(Button As Integer, Shift As Integer, X As Single, Y As Single)

      If Button = vbRightButton Then
          PopupMenu _____
      End If

  End Sub
```

Fig. 5.16

The action specified by each pop-up menu item must be entered into the Code Editor as a separate event procedure, as before. Thus, one event procedure is required to display the pop-up menu, and an additional event procedure is required for each of the various actions taken in response to the pop-up menu selections.

EXAMPLE 5.6 USING A POP-UP MENU

Let us create a program that initially displays a gray-colored form containing a circle with a gray center (i.e., without any distinctive fill color). The program will include a pull-down menu allowing the user to change the circle's fill color to red, green or blue, and to clear the fill color (thus restoring the original gray color). The program will include two objects: a shape (the circle), and a command button, used to end the computation. The initial form is shown in Fig. 5.17.

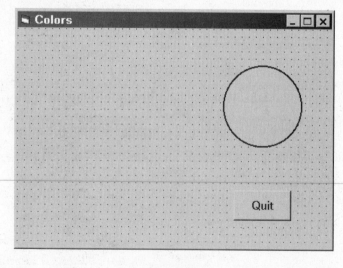

Fig. 5.17

In order to achieve this appearance, the objects have been assigned the following properties:

Object	Property	Value
Form1	Caption	"Colors"
Command1	Caption	"Quit"
	Font	MS Sans Serif, 10-point
Shape	Shape	3 – Circle
	BorderWidth	2
	FillStyle	0 – Solid
	FillColor	Gray

Fig. 5.18 shows the Menu Editor, with the entries required to change the color within the circle. Notice the caption (Colors) and the name (mnuColor) assigned to the first menu item. Also, note the use of separators between the menu items.

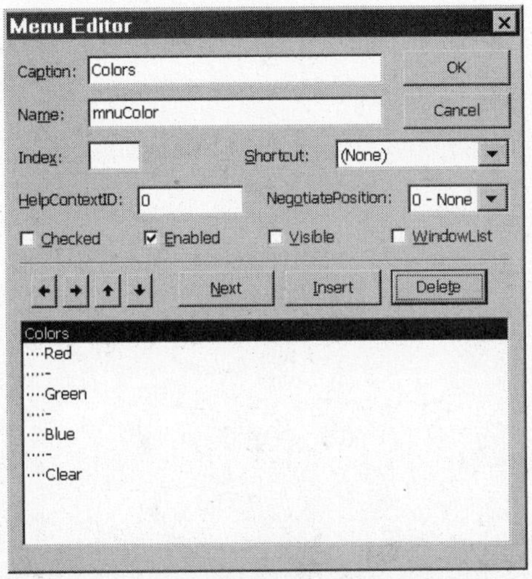

Fig. 5.18

In order to display the menu and bring about the desired color changes in response to the menu selections, we must add the following event procedures via the Code Editor Window.

```
Private Sub Form_MouseDown(Button As Integer, Shift As Integer, X As Single, Y As
Single)
    If Button = vbRightButton Then
        PopupMenu mnuColor
    End If
End Sub

Private Sub RedColor_Click()
    Shape1.FillColor = vbRed
End Sub

Private Sub GreenColor_Click()
    Shape1.FillColor = vbGreen
End Sub

Private Sub BlueColor_Click()
    Shape1.FillColor = vbBlue
End Sub
```

(*Continues on next page*)

```
Private Sub ClearColor_Click()
    Shape1.FillColor = vbMenuBar      'Gray
End Sub

Private Sub Command1_Click()
    End
End Sub
```

We have already explained that the first of these event procedures causes the pop-up menu to appear in response to clicking the right mouse button. All of the components in this event procedure are reserved words with a predefined meaning, except for mnuColor, which is the name of the first menu item (see Fig. 5.18).

The next four event procedures (RedColor, GreenColor, Blue Color, and ClearColor) assign the desired fill colors to the circle (Shape1.FillColor). Within these event procedures, the identifiers vbRed, vbGreen, vbBlue and vbMenuBar are predefined Visual Basic constants that represent the colors red, green, blue and medium gray, respectively.

When the program is executed, the form originally appears as shown in Fig. 5.19.

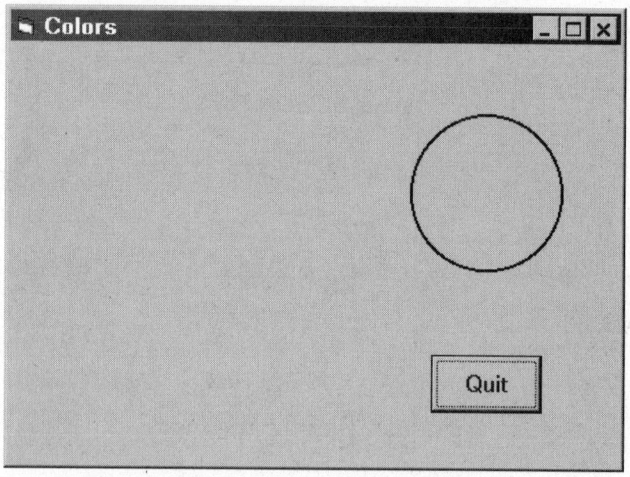

Fig. 5.19

Clicking the right mouse button then causes the pop-up menu to appear, as in Fig. 5.20.

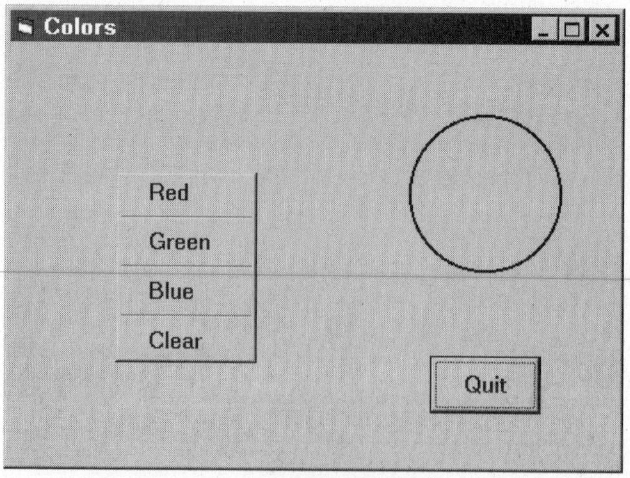

Fig. 5.20

Selecting one of the menu items then alters the fill color of the circle, as shown in Fig. 5.21. Note that the original gray color can be restored by selecting Clear.

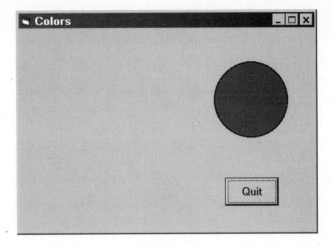

Fig. 5.21

5.6 DIALOG BOXES

A *dialog box* is used to exchange information between the program and the user. It is a separate form that is generally accessed in response to a selection from a menu or a list. Dialog boxes typically contain common controls (e.g., labels, text boxes, option buttons, check boxes, and command buttons) to enter or display information. In addition, the dialog box features must be accessible from other forms (i.e., from "primary" or "parent" forms), and the information entered into the dialog box by the user must be recognizable within these forms.

A "secondary" form (e.g., a dialog box) can be *added* to an active project via the Load command; i.e.,

Load *form*

For example, the command

Load Form2

will cause the form named Form2 to be loaded into the currently active project.

Similarly, a form can be *removed* from an active project, thus freeing up memory, via the Unload command; i.e.,

Unload *form*

For example,

Unload Form2

Thus, the form named Form2 will be unloaded (removed) from the currently active project. As a result, references to the object named Form2 will no longer be recognized within the currently active project.

Loading a form into an active project does not in itself cause the form to be visible. To make the form visible, we use the Show method; i.e.,

form.Show

(Recall that a *method* is similar to a property. Whereas properties represent values associated with objects, however, methods carry out actions on objects.) For example,

Form2.Show

This causes the form named Form2 to become visible within the currently active project. Moreover, Form2 will be the currently active form, and it will be displayed on top of any other visible forms.

If the form.Show method is followed by a 1; e.g.,

> Form2.Show 1

the new form will be displayed as a *modal* form. That is, the form will remain in place, preventing the activation of any other forms, until the user disposes of the form by accepting it (e.g., by clicking OK), or rejecting it (e.g., by clicking Cancel).

The Hide method is directly analogous but opposite to the Show method. Thus, the command

> Form2.Hide

causes Form2 to no longer be visible within the currently active project. This command does *not* cause Form2 to be *unloaded* from the project.

Recall that we refer to a property (or method) associated with an object in a single-form project as

> *object name.property*

For example,

> Text1.Text

When working with multiform projects, however, it is often necessary to refer to a property (or method) of an object in a different form. To do so, we precede the object name with the form name; i.e.,

> *form name.object name.property*

For example,

> Form2.Text1.Text

Of course, the placement of these references is determined by the program logic.

EXAMPLE 5.7 USING DIALOG BOXES (MULTILINGUAL HELLO REVISITED)

We now present a version of the Multilingual Hello program, originally shown in Examples 4.6 and 4.9. The current version will make use of drop-down menus and dialog boxes, and will require four different forms (a primary form, two dialog boxes that accept input from the user, and a dialog box showing the results).

Fig. 5.22(*a*)   Fig. 5.22(*b*)

When the program is executed, the primary form will show a menu bar with two entries: Languages and Display. The primary form and the accompanying Languages menu is shown in Fig. 5.22(*a*). Fig. 5.22(*b*) shows the primary form and the accompanying Display menu.

The ellipses (three dots) following the menu items Color... and Font... in the Display menu indicate that the user must provide additional information within a dialog box before each of the menu items can complete its task. The ellipses are not added automatically; rather, they are typed by the programmer at the end of the menu item's caption.

When the user clicks on one of the language selections, a dialog box (i.e., a secondary form) will appear showing the appropriate "Hello" greeting. For example, Fig. 5.23(*a*) shows the dialog box resulting from the selection of French within the Languages menu.

Fig. 5.23(*a*)

Fig. 5.23(*b*)

The Display menu results in two different dialog boxes that allow the user to alter the appearance of the greeting. The first dialog box (Color...) allows the user to change the color of the text and the background, as shown in Fig. 5.24(*a*). The second dialog box (Font...), shown in Fig. 5.24(*b*), allows the user to change the size of the text in the "Hello" greeting. For example, Fig. 5.23(*b*) shows the appearance of the greeting when the text is shown in a blue, 12-point font against a gray background. (Unfortunately, the printed page does not show the blue color convincingly, though it really is there.)

Fig. 5.24(*a*)

Fig. 5.24(*b*)

Now let's see how this project is created. Fig. 5.25 shows the Form Design Window for the primary form, which has the caption International Hello and is named Form1.

The Menu Editor accompanying Form1 is shown in Fig. 5.26. Note that the window in the bottom portion of the Menu Editor lists the menu items in both menus shown in Form1. Each menu item has an associated event procedure. These event procedures control the entire project; they are the key to understanding how the project works.

International Hello
Language
Display
Quit

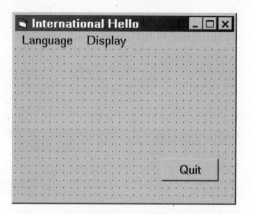

Fig. 5.25

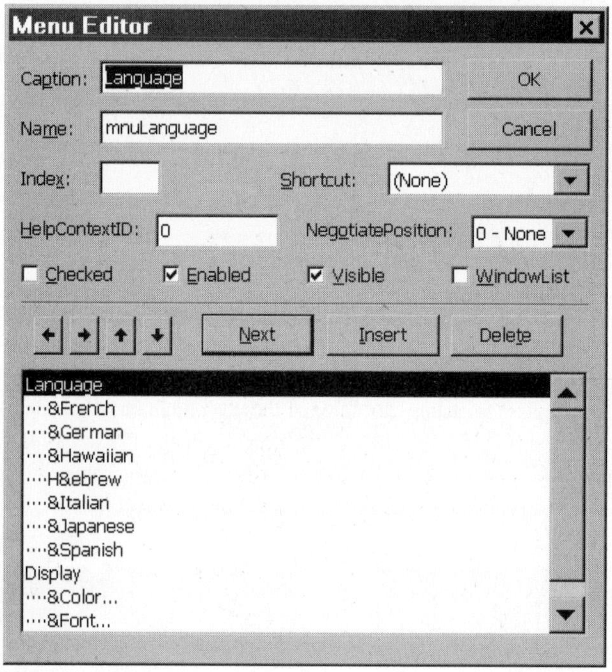

Menu Editor
Caption:
Language
OK
Name:
mnuLanguage
Cancel
Index:
Shortcut:
(None)
HelpContextID:
0
NegotiatePosition:
0 - None
Checked
Enabled
Visible
WindowList
Next
Insert
Delete
Language
····&French
····&German
····&Hawaiian
····H&ebrew
····&Italian
····&Japanese
····&Spanish
Display
····&Color...
····&Font...

Fig. 5.26

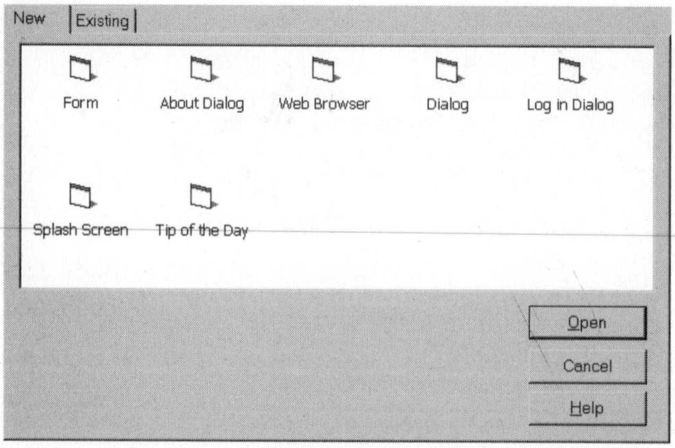

New
Existing
Form
About Dialog
Web Browser
Dialog
Log in Dialog
Splash Screen
Tip of the Day
Open
Cancel
Help

Fig. 5.27

We now add a secondary form to the project. This form will be used as a dialog box to display the desired result, such as the results shown in Figs. 5.23(*a*) and 5.23(*b*). To do so, we choose Add Form/New from the Visual Basic Project menu. This results in the Visual Basic dialog box shown in Fig. 5.27. We then select Form from this dialog box. An empty secondary form will then appear in its own Form Design Window, superimposed over the primary form.

In order to utilize the secondary form as a dialog box, we add a label, a text box, and a command button, as shown in Fig. 5.28(*a*). If we then alter the captions and the font size, we obtain the dialog box shown in Fig. 5.28(*b*).

Fig. 5.28(*a*)

Fig. 5.28(*b*)

We now consider the relationship between the primary and secondary forms (Form1 and Form2). The secondary form will appear when we click on one of the menu items listed in the primary form under Language. The link is the event procedure associated with the language selection in the primary form. Thus, each event procedure must generate the appropriate label and text box message in the secondary form, and then cause the secondary form to become visible.

Here are the event procedures associated with the Language menu items in the primary form:

```
Private Sub mnuFrench_Click()
    Form2.Label1.Caption = "Hello in French is..."
    Form2.Text1.Text = "Bonjour"
    Form2.Show
End Sub

Private Sub mnuGerman_Click()
    Form2.Label1.Caption = "Hello in German is..."
    Form2.Text1.Text = "Guten Tag"
    Form2.Show
End Sub

Private Sub mnuHawaiian_Click()
    Form2.Label1.Caption = "Hello in Hawaiian is..."
    Form2.Text1.Text = "Aloha"
    Form2.Show
End Sub

Private Sub mnuHebrew_Click()
    Form2.Label1.Caption = "Hello in Hebrew is..."
    Form2.Text1.Text = "Shalom"
    Form2.Show
End Sub
```

(*Continues on next page*)

```
    Private Sub mnuItalian_Click()
        Form2.Label1.Caption = "Hello in Italian is..."
        Form2.Text1.Text = "Buon Giorno"
        Form2.Show
    End Sub

    Private Sub mnuJapanese_Click()
        Form2.Label1.Caption = "Hello in Japanese is..."
        Form2.Text1.Text = "Konichihua"
        Form2.Show
    End Sub

    Private Sub mnuSpanish_Click()
        Form2.Label1.Caption = "Hello in Spanish is..."
        Form2.Text1.Text = "Buenos Dias"
        Form2.Show
    End Sub
```

Each event procedure assigns a label and a text string for the secondary form, and then displays the secondary form. The net result is a display such as that shown in Fig. 5.23.

Note that these event procedures are associated with the primary form but refer to objects in the secondary form; hence, the two assignment statements in each event procedure are preceded with the form name (e.g., Form2.Label2.Caption = . . .).

The secondary form also includes an event procedure, associated with its command button (Close). This event procedure simply hides the form; i.e.,

```
    Private Sub Command1_Click()
        Form2.Hide
    End Sub
```

Thus, clicking on the Close button causes the secondary form to disappear from view.

Now let us turn our attention to the second of the two menus (i.e., the Display menu) in the primary form, and the corresponding two dialog boxes. We need to add two additional forms to the project. To do so, we again choose Add Form/New from the Visual Basic Project menu, resulting in the Visual Basic dialog box shown in Fig. 5.27. We could select Form from this dialog box, as we did before, but let's select Dialog instead. This selection results in a new form which already contains two command buttons, labeled OK and Cancel (see Fig. 5.29). In all other respects, this form is the same as that resulting from the Form selection, which we had chosen earlier. We will click on the Dialog selection twice, thus adding the two desired dialog boxes.

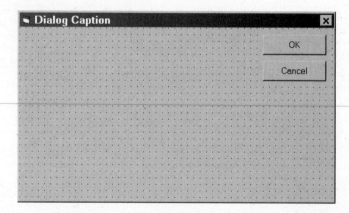

Fig. 5.29

We now add two frames to the first dialog box (one to select the text color, the other for the background color), with three option buttons within each frame. Fig. 5.30(*a*) shows the Form Design Window, after adding the appropriate captions.

The second dialog box is similar to the first, though it contains only one frame, which selects the font size. Its Form Design Window is shown in Fig. 5.30(*b*).

Now let's consider the relationship between the primary form and these two dialog boxes. The Display menu in the primary form has the following two event procedures associated with it.

```
Private Sub mnuColor_Click()
    Dialog1.Show
End Sub
Private Sub mnuFont_Click()
    Dialog2.Show
End Sub
```

The first event procedure causes the Colors dialog box to be displayed when the user selects Color from the Display menu. Similarly, the second event procedure causes the Fonts dialog box to be displayed when the user selects Font from the Display menu.

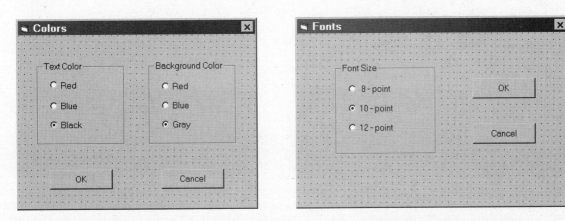

Fig. 5.30(*a*)　　　　　　　　　　　　　　　　**Fig. 5.30(*b*)**

The actions taken by the Colors dialog box are controlled by the following event procedures, associated with the OK and Cancel buttons. (Recall that the identifiers vbRed, vbBlue, vbBlack and vbMenuBar are predefined Visual Basic constants that represent the colors red, blue, black and gray, respectively.)

```
Private Sub OKButton_Click()
    If Option1.Value = True Then
        Form2.Label1.ForeColor = vbRed
        Form2.Text1.ForeColor = vbRed
    ElseIf Option2.Value = True Then
        Form2.Label1.ForeColor = vbBlue
        Form2.Text1.ForeColor = vbBlue
    ElseIf Option3.Value = True Then
        Form2.Label1.ForeColor = vbBlack
        Form2.Text1.ForeColor = vbBlack
    End If
```

(*Continues on next page*)

```
        If Option4.Value = True Then
            Form2.BackColor = vbRed
            Form2.Label1.BackColor = vbRed
        ElseIf Option5.Value = True Then
            Form2.BackColor = vbBlue
            Form2.Label1.BackColor = vbBlue
        ElseIf Option6.Value = True Then
            Form2.BackColor = vbMenuBar   'Gray
            Form2.Label1.BackColor = vbMenuBar
        End If
        Dialog1.Hide
    End Sub

    Private Sub CancelButton_Click()
        Dialog1.Hide
    End Sub
```

The Fonts dialog box works the same way as the Colors dialog box. Here are the event procedures associated with the OK and Cancel buttons.

```
    Private Sub OKButton_Click()
        If Option1.Value = True Then
            Form2.Label1.FontSize = 8
            Form2.Text1.FontSize = 8
        ElseIf Option2.Value = True Then
            Form2.Label1.FontSize = 10
            Form2.Text1.FontSize = 10
        ElseIf Option3.Value = True Then
            Form2.Label1.FontSize = 12
            Form2.Text1.FontSize = 12
        End If
        Dialog2.Hide
    End Sub

    Private Sub CancelButton_Click()
        Dialog2.Hide
    End Sub
```

Finally, the primary form includes the following two additional event procedures.

```
    Private Sub Form1_Load()
        Load Form2
        Load Dialog1
        Load Dialog2
    End Sub

    Private Sub Command1_Click()
        End
    End Sub
```

The first event procedure causes the three dialog boxes to be loaded into the computer's memory (but not displayed) when the application begins. The second event procedure simply ends the computation.

Execution of the program produces results similar to those shown at the beginning of the example [see Figs. 5.22(*a*) and (*b*), 5.23(*a*) and (*b*), and 5.24(*a*) and (*b*)].

5.7 MORE ABOUT THE MsgBox FUNCTION

We first discussed the MsgBox function in Sec. 4.13, where we used it to create error messages. The form generated by this function is actually a type of dialog box which displays a given output string and one or more command buttons (e.g., OK), and returns a positive integer whose value depends on the action taken by the user. (In this situation, the user action consists of clicking on one of the available command buttons.)

The choice of command buttons is determined by a nonnegative integer that is included in the function reference. In general terms, the function reference may be written as

integer variable = MsgBox(*string, integer, title*)

The value of the *integer* argument (default 0) defines the command buttons that appear within the dialog box. Also, *title* represents a string that will appear in the message box's title bar. It's default value (if not included as an explicit argument) will be the project name.

The function's *return value* (a positive integer whose value depends on the particular command button selected by the user) is assigned to the *integer variable* shown on the left of the equal sign. Note that the integer argument and the return value are two different entities.

Some of the more commonly used *integer* arguments and their resulting MsgBox command buttons are summarized below.

Integer Argument	*Resulting Command Buttons*
0	OK
1	OK, Cancel
2	Abort, Retry, Ignore
3	Yes, No, Cancel
4	Yes, No
5	Retry, Cancel

The value returned by the MsgBox function will depend upon the particular command button selected by the user during program execution. The possible values are summarized below.

Command Button	*Return Value*
OK	1
Cancel	2
Abort	3
Retry	4
Ignore	5
Yes	6
No	7

EXAMPLE 5.8

Consider the Visual Basic code segment shown below. Initially, the variables CustomerName and AcctNo are assigned null values, and a value of 7 is assigned to the integer variable Verify. Assigning this value to Verify causes the Do-Loop structure to continue to execute repeatedly, until Verify is assigned a different value within the loop.

Meaningful values are assigned to the input variables during each pass through the loop. (Let us disregard the details of where these values originate.) The message box shown in Fig. 5.31 is then displayed. Notice the three command buttons (Yes, No and Cancel), as determined by the second argument (3) in the MsgBox function access. Also, notice the message box title (Sample Message Box) in the title bar, as specified by the third argument in the MsgBox function access.

```
Dim CustomerName As String, AcctNo As Integer, Verify As Integer

'Initialize the input variables
CustomerName = ""
AcctNo = 0

Do
    'Enter customer's name
    . . . . .
    CustomerName = . . .    'assign a customer name

    'Enter customer's account number
    . . . . .
    AcctNo = . . .             'assign an account number

    Verify = MsgBox("Is this correct?", 3, "Sample Message Box")    'Yes, No, Cancel

Loop While Verify = 7

If Verify = 2 Then
    'reset the input variables
    CustomerName = ""
    AcctNo = 0
End If
```

Fig. 5.31

The value returned by the message box determines what happens next. It the user clicks on the Yes button, the MsgBox function will return a value of 6. Hence, Verify will be assigned the value 6 and the looping action will end.

On the other hand, if the user clicks on the No button, the MsgBox function will return a value of 7 and the looping action will continue. New values will therefore be assigned to CustomerName and AcctNo, and the message box will again be displayed. This looping action will continue until the user clicks on Yes, indicating satisfaction with the current values of CustomerName and AcctNo, or else clicks on Cancel, which terminates the looping action.

If the user clicks on Cancel, the MsgBox function will return a value of 2. This will cause the computation to end. The If-Then block will then reset the input variables CustomerName and AcctNo to their original null values, thus cancelling the assignments made within the loop.

The appearance of the message box can be adjusted with additional argument values. In addition, a message box can be associated with online help. Consult the Visual Basic online help for more information on these topics.

5.8 THE InputBox FUNCTION

The InputBox function is similar to the MsgBox function. However, this function is primarily intended to display a dialog box that accepts an *input* string, whereas the MsgBox function is primarily intended to show an *output* string. The dialog box generated by the InputBox function will automatically include a string prompting the user for input, and a text box where the user can enter an input string. It will also include two command buttons – OK and Cancel. Fig. 5.32 shows a typical input box with a prompt and a blank text box, awaiting user input.

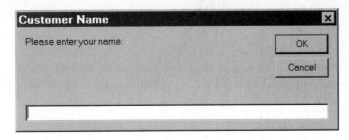

Fig. 5.32

In general terms, the function reference may be written as

string variable = Input Box(*prompt, title, default*)

The first argument (*prompt*) represents a string that appears within the dialog box as a prompt for input. The second argument (*title*) represents a string that will appear in the title bar. It's default value (if not included as an explicit argument) will be the project name. The last argument (*default*) represents a string appearing appearing initially in the input box's text box. The *default* string will be empty if this last argument is not included in the function reference.

When executed, the function will return the string entered by the user, and assign this string to the *string variable* shown on the left of the equal sign.

EXAMPLE 5.9 USING INPUT BOXES

To illustrate the use of the InputBox function, let us expand the application presented in Example 5.8. In particular, let us enter a customer name and account number via input boxes (rather than through text boxes, which is probably the most straightforward way to enter this information). We will develop a complete application that begins with the form shown in Fig. 5.33(*a*) and ends with a form similar to that shown in Fig. 5.33(*b*).

Fig. 5.33(*a*)   **Fig. 5.33(*b*)**

We begin with the Form Design Window shown in Fig. 5.34(*a*) and alter the control properties so that the Form Design Window takes on the appearance shown in Fig. 5.34(*b*). We then add an event procedures for each of the two command buttons.

Consider the first event procedure, which is associated with the Go button. (The second event procedure simply terminates the computation, as should be obvious by now.)

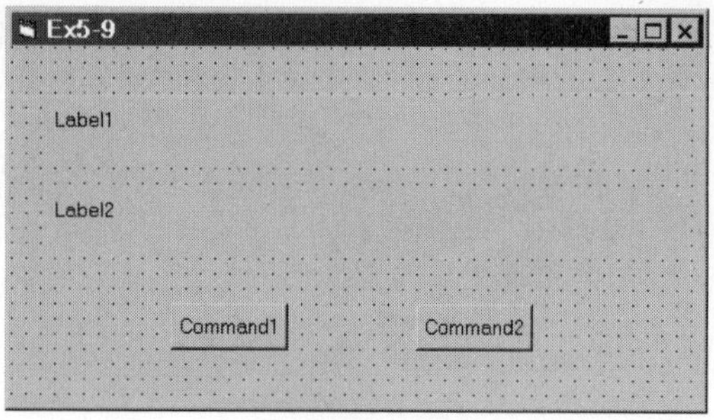

Fig. 5.34(a)

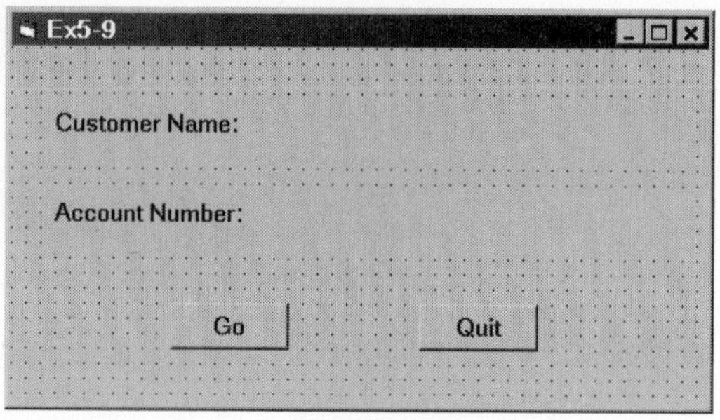

Fig. 5.34(b)

```
Private Sub Command1_Click()
    Dim CustomerName As String, L1 As String, L2 As String
    Dim AcctNo As Integer, Verify As Integer

    L1 = "Customer Name: "
    L2 = "Account Number: "

    Do
        Label1 = L1
        Label2 = L2

        CustomerName = InputBox("Please enter your name:", "Customer Name")
        Label1 = L1 & CustomerName

        AcctNo = Val(InputBox("Please enter your account number:", "Account Number"))
        Label2 = L2 & Str(AcctNo)

        'Process the account

        Verify = MsgBox("Is this correct?", 3, "Verify")
    Loop While Verify = 7

    If Verify = 2 Then
        Label1 = L1
        Label2 = L2
    End If
End Sub

Private Sub Command2_Click()
    End
End Sub
```

When the program is executed the string variables L1 and L2 are assigned the labels Customer Name: and Account Number:, which will later be concatenated with the actual customer name and account number. The program then enters a loop, which will be terminated by an OK or Cancel response from a message box similar to the one in Example 5.8.

Within the loop, an input box is first generated for the customer name. The resulting string, represented by the string variable CustomerName, is then concatenated with L1 to form a complete label for Label1. This process is then repeated for the account number, providing a string which is concatenated with L2 to form a complete label for Label2.

Note that the account number is converted to an integer after being entered through the input box. This permits the account number to be used in any numerical calculations, which are not included within this example (the single remark Process the account refers to the unspecified computational commands.) The numerical account number is then converted back to a string when it is added to Label2.

Each input box allows the user to either accept or reject the string entered. The Cancel feature will most likely not be needed, however, since the user may backspace, etc. to correct the input information before pressing the Enter key. However, if the user should press Cancel rather than OK, an empty string will be returned and included in Label1 or Label2.

Fig. 5.35(*a*)

Fig. 5.35(*b*)

Finally, a message box is generated which allows the user to verify that both input items are correct. We have already discussed the details of this type of dialog box (see Example 5.8).

The program execution begins by displaying the primary form, as shown in Fig. 5.33(*a*). When the user presses the Go button, the input box shown in Fig. 5.35(*a*) appears. The user then enters his/her customer name, as shown in Fig 5.35(*b*), and then presses the OK or the Cancel button. The second input box then appears, requesting the user's account number, as shown in Fig. 5.36.

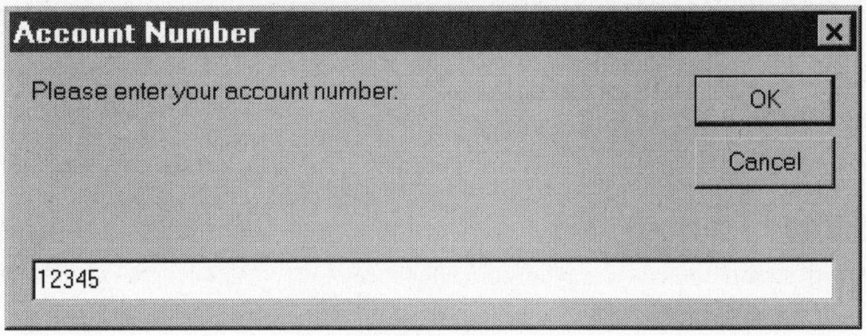

Fig. 5.36

Once the user enters the account number and clicks on the OK button, a message box is displayed, as shown in Fig. 5.37. Clicking on the Yes button then causes the final version of the primary form to appear, as shown in Fig. 5.33(*b*). If the user clicks on the No button, the program responds by again displaying the dialog boxes requesting the customer name and the account number. If the user selects Cancel, the primary form is returned to its original state.

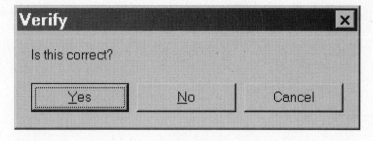

Fig. 5.37

In addition to the features described above, the screen location of the input box can be specified with additional argument values. Also, an input box, like a message box, can be associated with online help. See Visual Basic's online help for more information about these features.

Review Questions

5.1 What is the difference between a drop-down menu and a pop-up menu?

5.2 What is the purpose of the Menu Editor? How is the Menu Editor accessed?

5.3 Within the Menu Editor, what is the purpose of the Enabled check box?

5.4 Within the Menu Editor, what is the purpose of the Visible check box?

5.5 Within the Menu Editor, what is the difference between the Caption and the Name? Are they both required?

5.6 Describe the order in which the various menu items are entered into the Menu Editor.

5.7 Within the Menu Editor, what is the reason for indentation within the list of menu items? How is this indentation carried out? How is it reversed?

5.8 How is a menu item inserted into the Menu Editor's list of menu items? How is a menu item deleted? How is the relative location of a menu item changed?

5.9 What is a keyboard access character? How is an access character associated with a menu item?

5.10 Can two menu items within the same menu have the same keyboard access character?

5.11 Can a menu item within one menu have the same keyboard access character as a menu item within another menu?

5.12 What is a keyboard shortcut? How do keyboard shortcuts differ from keyboard access characters? How is a keyboard shortcut associated with a menu item? (Compare with Question 5.9.)

5.13 Can a menu item within one menu have the same keyboard shortcut as a menu item within another menu? (Compare with Question 5.11.)

5.14 What is indicated by a check mark shown next to a menu item? How is a check mark displayed initially? How is a check mark later added or removed, during program execution?

5.15 How is a menu item initially deactivated? How is a menu item later activated or deactivated, during program execution?

5.16 How is a separator included within a list of menu items? Must separators be indented? How are separators moved relative to surrounding menu items?

5.17 What is the purpose of a submenu? How is a submenu created within the Menu Editor? How is the presence of a submenu identified during program execution?

5.18 How is a pop-up menu created? How is it activated?

5.19 How can a pop-up menu be made to appear in response to some action other than a right mouse click?

5.20 What is the purpose of a dialog box?

5.21 How is a secondary form added to an active project? How is it removed?

5.22 How is a secondary form made visible once it has been loaded? How is it hidden?

5.23 What is a modal form? How can a form be displayed as a modal form once it has been loaded?

5.24 When writing Visual Basic code, how do you refer to the property of an object that resides within a different form?

5.25 What is the purpose of the MsgBox function? What is the general form of a MsgBox function access?

5.26 A message box generated by the MsgBox function may have various command buttons, depending on how the function is accessed. How is the choice of command buttons specified in the function access?

5.27 When the user clicks on a command button within a message box, how is the particular command button selection identified? In what way is this information useful?

5.28 What is the purpose of the *title* argument in a MsgBox function access? How does the *title* argument differ from the *string* argument?

5.29 What is the purpose of the InputBox function? How does the InputBox function differ from the MsgBox function?

5.30 What is the general form of an InputBox function access?

5.31 What additional arguments may be included in a MsgBox function access? What additional arguments may be included in an InputBox function access? What do these additional arguments represent?

Programming Problems

5.32 Re-create the Geography project shown in Example 5.5 using a pop-up menu. Retain the listing of Continents, Oceans and Seas as primary menu items, as in Example 5.5. Add a keyboard shortcut for each of the primary menu items.

5.33 Re-create the Geography project shown in Example 5.5 using a pop-up menu, as in Prob. 5.32. Now, however, create dialog boxes containing options buttons in place of the submenus. Thus, you should create one dialog box allowing the user to select a continent, another to select an ocean, and a third to select a sea. Be sure to include appropriate command buttons within each dialog box.

5.34 Expand Prob. 5.33 so that multiple objects can be selected from each dialog box. In other words, allow the user to select two or more continents, two or more oceans, etc. To do so, use check boxes rather than option buttons for each group of objects. Display the corresponding area for each object selected. (*Suggestion*: Place a combo box within each dialog box.)

5.35 Re-create the project shown in Example 4.3 (current date and time) using a drop-down menu. Label the main menu selection View. Within this menu, label the individual menu items Date and Time. Include keyboard access characters and keyboard shortcuts for each menu item.

5.36 Repeat Prob. 5.35 using a pop-up menu instead of a drop-down menu.

5.37 Re-create the "piggy bank" problem shown in Example 4.5 so that it uses a menu and dialog boxes. Label the main menu selection Money, and include the following two menu items: Number of Coins, and Dollar Amount. For the first menu selection (Number of Coins), create a dialog box that allows the user to enter the number of pennies, nickels, dimes, etc., as in Example 4.5. Provide a check box for each type of coin. Include a Go button, but omit the Clear button.

For the second menu selection (Dollar Amount), create a separate dialog box that allows the user to enter the *dollar amount* in pennies, in nickels, in dimes, etc. Again, provide a check box for each type of coin, and include a Go button.

The Go button within each dialog box should display a new dialog box containing the appropriate text boxes, so that the user may enter data. The user should then press a command button labeled Total within this dialog box, to display the total amount of money (see Prob. 4.43). Use a message box to display the actual total amount.

5.38 Modify the "multilingual hello" program in Example 4.6 so that a menu labeled Languages is displayed when the program is executed. Within Languages, each menu item will correspond to a different language. Clicking on a menu item will then display a message box containing the appropriate greeting in the chosen language. Include an appropriate title that identifies the language.

5.39 Expand the temperature conversion program shown in Example 4.7 so that it can convert between Celsius, Fahrenheit, Kelvin and Rankin degrees (i.e., from any one temperature to any other). Let us refer to the given temperature (i.e., the given system of units) as the "source" temperature, and the desired temperature (i.e., the desired system of units) as the "target" temperature.

The program should include a main menu, labeled Temperature, which includes four menu items – one for each system of units. Each of these menu items will represent a source unit. Hence, it should have its own submenu, which shows the three possible target units for that source unit. For example, the first menu item under Temperature might be Celsius, and the corresponding submenu items might be To Fahrenheit, To Kelvin, and To Rankine. Selection of a submenu item should then result in a dialog box that accepts the source temperature and, after clicking on a Go button, displays the resulting target temperature.

Recall that $°F = 1.8°C$, $°K = °C + 273.15$, and $°R = °F + 459.67$.

5.40 Create a Visual Basic project to determine the sum of the integers ranging from n_1 to n_2, where $n_1 < n_2$. Specify n_1 and n_2 as input parameters. Allow the computation to be carried out in any of the following ways:

(*a*)   Sum *all* of the integers ranging from n_1 to n_2.

(*b*)   Sum only the even integers within the interval defined by n_1 and n_2.

(*c*)   Sum only the odd integers within the interval defined by n_1 and n_2.

Use a menu to determine which integers will be summed. In each case, use an appropriate loop to calculate the sum. Display the sum in a separate text box, with an appropriate label. (see Probs. 4.47 and 4.48). Generate an error message if the condition $n_1 < n_2$ is not satisfied.

5.41 Create a Visual Basic project that will allow the user to select the name of a country from a list and then display the corresponding capital, and vice versa. Use a menu to determine which task will be carried out (i.e., select the country and display the capital, or select the capital and display the country). Attach an a appropriate dialog box to each of the menu items.

Restrict the project to the following countries and their corresponding capitals, as in Prob. 4.51.

Canada	Ottawa
England	London
France	Paris
Germany	Berlin
India	New Delhi
Italy	Rome
Japan	Tokyo
Mexico	Mexico City
People's Republic of China	Beijing
Russia	Moscow
Spain	Madrid
United States	Washington, D.C.

5.42 Create a Visual Basic project that will either convert U.S. dollars into a foreign currency or convert a foreign currency into U.S. dollars, as in Prob. 4.52. Use a menu to determine which type of conversion will be carried out (i.e., U.S. to foreign, or foreign to U.S.). Attach an appropriate dialog box to each of the menu selections.

The foreign currencies and their U.S. dollar equivalents are:

1 U.S. dollar = 0.6 British pounds
1.4 Canadian dollars
2.3 Dutch guilders
6.8 French francs
2.0 German marks
2000 Italian lira
100 Japanese yen
9.5 Mexican pesos
1.6 Swiss francs

Your project should include two option buttons within a frame, to select either U.S. to foreign conversion or foreign to U.S. conversion. Nine additional option buttons should be placed within another frame to select the particular foreign currency. Use a text box to specify a given amount of money in the source currency, and another text box to display the equivalent amount of money in the target currency. Include an appropriate set of labels for each conversion type.

5.43 In Prob. 4.55 we considered the following problem: Deposit P dollars in a savings account for n years. If the money earns interest at the rate of i percent per year, compounded annually, then after n years, the original sum of money will have increased to F, where

$$F = P(1 + 0.01i)^n \qquad \text{for annual compounding}$$

$$F = P(1 + 0.01i/4)^{4n} \qquad \text{for quarterly compounding}$$

$$F = P(1 + 0.01i/12)^{12n} \qquad \text{for monthly compounding}$$

$$F = P(1 + 0.01i/365)^{365n} \qquad \text{for daily compounding}$$

(*Note*: In all of these expressions, i is the *annual* interest rate, expressed as a percentage, and n is the number of *years*.)

Recall that these results can be generalized into the following single equation:

$$F = P(1 + 0.01i/c)^{cn}$$

where c takes on the following values:

Annual compounding: $c = 1$

Quarterly compounding: $c = 4$

Monthly compounding: $c = 12$

Daily compounding: $c = 365$

Create a Visual Basic project to determine the future value of a deposit (F), given P, r and n as input values, using a menu to select the frequency of compounding. Enter each of the input values into an appropriate dialog box. Display the final result in a separate message box. Test the program using input values of your own choosing.

Chapter 6

Debugging and Executing a New Project

By now we have learned enough about Visual Basic to create complete Visual Basic projects. We therefore pause briefly from our coverage of new features and devote some attention to the methods used to detect and correct the different types of errors that can occur in improperly written programs. We will also show how a project can be compiled into an executable package that can be executed independently of the Visual Basic development system.

6.1 SYNTACTIC ERRORS

Many different kinds of errors can arise when creating and executing a new Visual Basic project. For example, *syntactic errors* (also called *compilation errors*) occur when Visual Basic commands are written improperly. Syntactic errors are relatively easy to fix, since the Visual Basic development system does a good job of flagging these errors. When a syntactic error is detected, the offending statement is highlighted within the Code Editor Window, and the nature of the error is explained (often in cryptic terms) within a message box.

EXAMPLE 6.1 SYNTACTIC ERRORS

Let's once again consider the "piggy bank" problem originally presented in Example 4.5. Recall the single Visual Basic command associated with the Go command button:

```
Text6.Text = 0.01 * Val(Text1.Text) + 0.05 * Val(Text2.Text) + 0.1 * Val(Text3.Text) +
             0.25 * Val(Text4.Text) + 0.5 * Val(Text5.Text)
```

Now suppose that the right parenthesis at the end of the command had inadvertently been omitted; i.e.,

```
Text6.Text = 0.01 * Val(Text1.Text) + 0.05 * Val(Text2.Text) + 0.1 * Val(Text3.Text) +
             0.25 * Val(Text4.Text) + 0.5 * Val(Text5.Text
```

An attempt to run this program will result in a syntactic error message, as shown in Fig. 6.1.

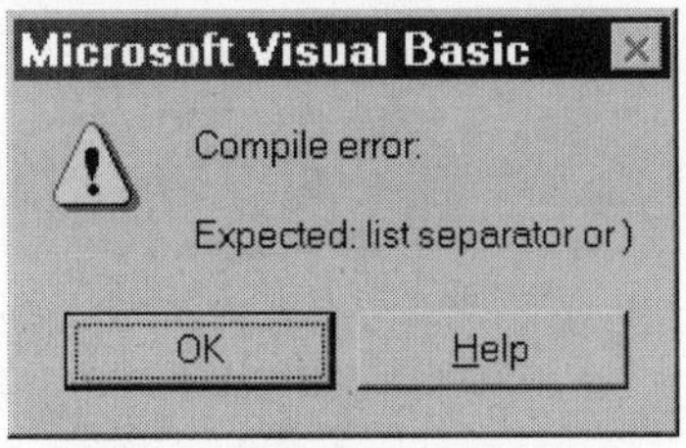

Fig. 6.1 A syntactic error message

Notice the error message

Compile error:

Expected: list separator or)

This message indicates the missing right parenthesis. Also, the command containing the error is highlighted in red within the Code Edit Window, as indicated in Fig. 6.2. (The highlighting is not apparent in Fig. 6.2 because of the inability to display colors.) When the missing right parenthesis is restored, the highlighting disappears and the program compiles normally.

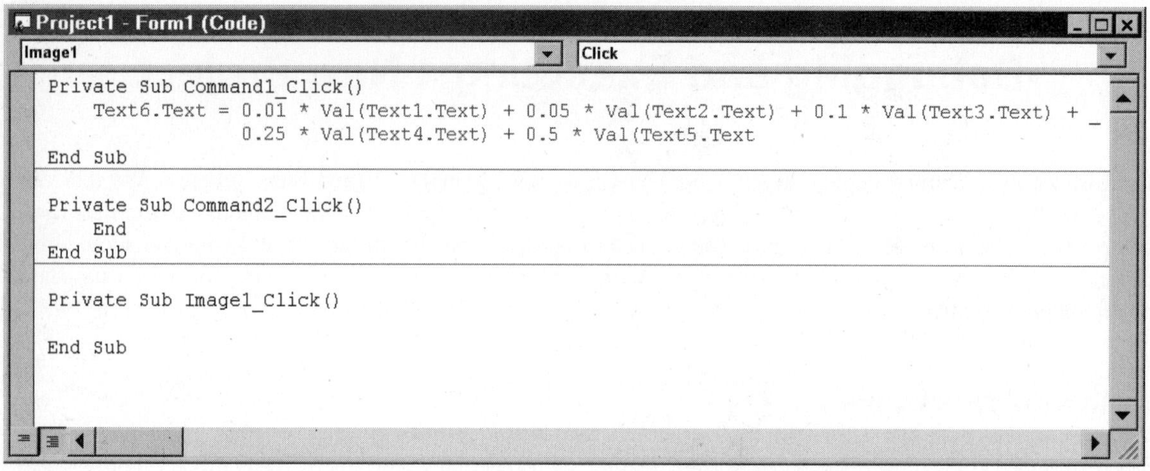

```
Project1 - Form1 (Code)                                                    _ □ X

Image1                                      ▼    Click                         ▼

    Private Sub Command1_Click()
        Text6.Text = 0.01 * Val(Text1.Text) + 0.05 * Val(Text2.Text) + 0.1 * Val(Text3.Text) + _
                     0.25 * Val(Text4.Text) + 0.5 * Val(Text5.Text
    End Sub

    Private Sub Command2_Click()
        End
    End Sub

    Private Sub Image1_Click()

    End Sub
```

Fig. 6.2 The Code Edit Window, highlighting a statement containing a syntactic error

6.2 LOGICAL ERRORS

Errors may also occur during program execution. Many execution errors are caused by faulty program logic (e.g., dividing by zero or attempting to take the square root of a negative number). Hence, they are often referred to as *logical errors*. Some logical errors cause the program to "crash" during execution (i.e., the execution abruptly terminates and an error message is generated). Other logical errors allow the program to execute in a normal manner, but produce results that are incorrect.

If a logical error results in a system crash, a message is produced indicating the reason for the crash, as shown in Fig. 6.3. Also, the location of the error is flagged within the Code Window, as shown in Fig. 6.4, if the Debug option is selected within the message box. (The offending statement is highlighted in yellow in Fig. 6.4. Also, the arrow in the left margin identifies the location of the error.)

```
Microsoft Visual Basic

Run-time error '6':

Overflow




    Continue        End         Debug         Help
```

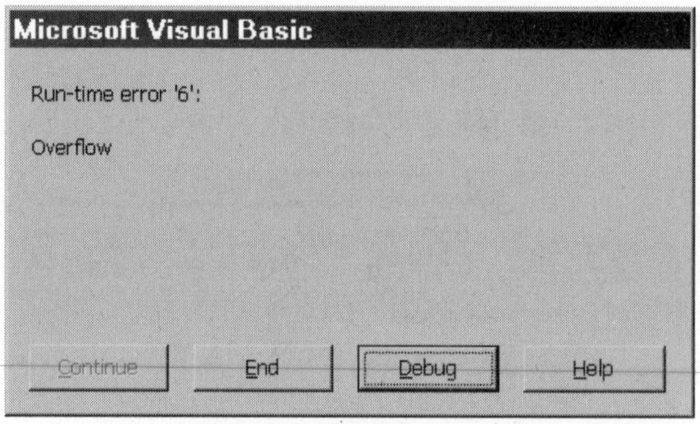

Fig. 6.3 A run-time error message

Though the reason for the error (Overflow) is not immediately apparent, inspection of Figs. 6.3 and 6.4 suggests that the overflow condition is caused by a division by zero. This should provide the programmer with some insight into the cause of the errror. (In this case, the variable r is undefined; hence its value is zero. The denominator therefore has a value of zero, and the attempt to divide by zero results in an overflow.)

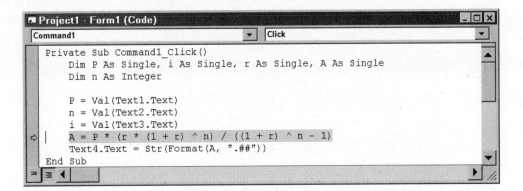

Fig. 6.4

Logical errors that produce incorrect results without a system crash can be very difficult to find. However, the Visual Basic *debugger* contains features that can assist you in locating the source of the errors. These features include *stepping* through a program, one instruction at a time (so that you can "look around" after executing each instruction); setting *breakpoints*, which cause the execution of a program to be suspended; and defining *watch values*, which display the current values of specific variables or expressions.

Visual Basic allows you to access its debugging features three different ways: via the Debug menu on the main menu bar, through certain function keys, or through the Debug toolbar, as illustrated in Fig. 6.5. (The Debug toolbar can be displayed by selecting Toolbars/Debug from the View menu.)

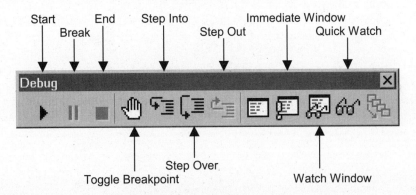

Fig. 6.5 The Debug Toolbar

The general strategy is to place a breakpoint near (preferably, slightly ahead of) the suspected source of error. Then execute the program in the normal fashion, until the breakpoint is encountered. Now define one or more watch values and step through the program, one instruction at a time. By observing the watch values as you step through the program, you can usually identify where the error is located. Once the location of the error is known, the source of the error can usually be identified.

6.3 SETTING BREAKPOINTS

There are several different ways to set a breakpoint. The first step is to examine the program listing within the Code Editor Window and identify the statement where the break point will be located. Then select the statement, or simply click anywhere within the statement, and set the breakpoint in any of the following ways:

1. Select Toggle Breakpoint from the Debug menu.

2. Click on the Toggle Breakpoint button within the Debug toolbar (see Fig. 6.5).

3. On an Intel-based computer, press function key F9.

Once the breakpoint has been set, the statement will be clearly highlighted, as shown in Fig. 6.6. Observe the dark circle to the left of the selected statement, in addition to the heavy highlighting.

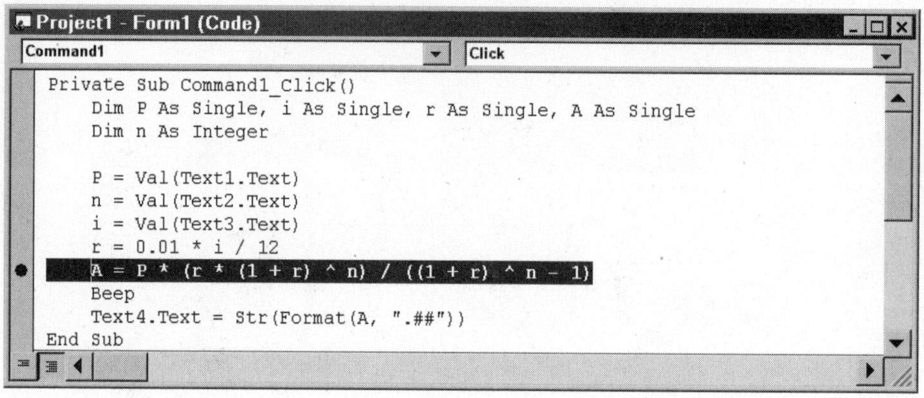

Fig. 6.6

Note that the breakpoint is set *ahead* of the selected statement. That is, the break in the program execution will occur just *before* the selected statement is executed. Also, note that the breakpoint is removed the same way it is set; i.e., by selecting Toggle Breakpoint from the Debug menu, by clicking on the Toggle Breakpoint button on the Debug toolbar, or by pressing function key F9. Thus, the breakpoint feature is referred to as a *toggle* (i.e., the breakpoint is alternatively enabled and disabled during successive selections).

If a program contains several different breakpoints, it may be convenient to remove all of them at once. To do so, simply select Clear All Breakpoints from the Debug menu, of press function keys Ctrl-Shift-F9 simultaneously.

You may also define a "temporary" breakpoint by clicking on any point within a statement, and then either selecting Run to Cursor from the Debug menu or pressing function keys Ctrl-F8. The program may then be executed up to the temporary breakpoint. You can then define appropriate watch values and step through the remainder of the program, one instruction at a time. Unlike a regular breakpoint, however, which remains in place until it is toggled off, the temporary breakpoint becomes inactive after one program execution.

6.4 DEFINING WATCH VALUES

Watch values are the current values of certain variables or expressions that are displayed at breakpoints. Visual Basic supports three different types of watch values: ordinary watch values, *quick watch* values, and *immediate* watch values. Of these, ordinary watch values are generally the most useful, because they remain active as you step through a program on a line-by-line basis. If a particular command causes a variable or expression to change its value, the change is seen as it happens. Thus, unusual or unexpected values can be associated with specific commands within the code listing.

Watch values are displayed in a separate *Watches* window. To open the Watches window, select Watch Window from the View menu, or click on the Watch Window button on the Debug toolbar. The Watches window will then appear at the bottom of the screen, as shown in Fig. 6.7. You may then define watch values by adding specific variables or expressions to the Watches window. This may be accomplished in any of the following ways:

1. Select Add Watch... from the Debug menu and then enter the required information in the Add Watch dialog box, as shown in Fig. 6.8.

2. Right-click on the Watches window, select Add Watch..., and then enter the required information in the Add Watch dialog box (the same dialog box shown in Fig. 6.8.)

3. Highlight an expression in the Code Editor Window and select Add Watch... from the Debug menu. The highlighted expression will then in the Add Watch dialog box (see Fig. 6.8).

4. Highlight an expression in the Code Editor Window. Then right-click and select Add Watch... The highlighted expression will appear automatically in the Add Watch dialog box (see Fig. 6.8).

As you step through a program beyond a breakpoint (see Sec. 6.5 below), the current value of each watch value will be displayed within the Watches window. Thus, you can see the watch values change as you progress through through each line of the program, as shown in Fig. 6.9.

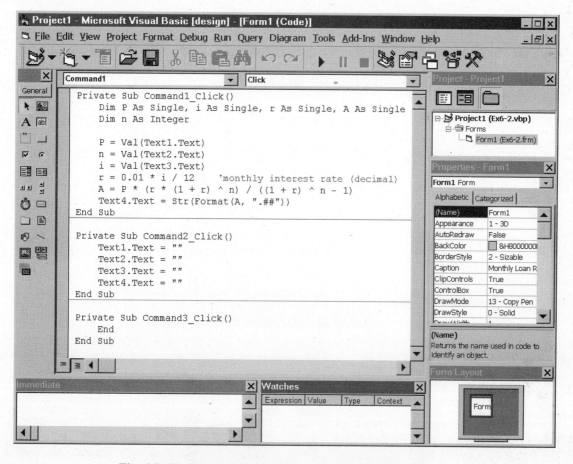

Fig. 6.7 The VB environment, showing the Watches window

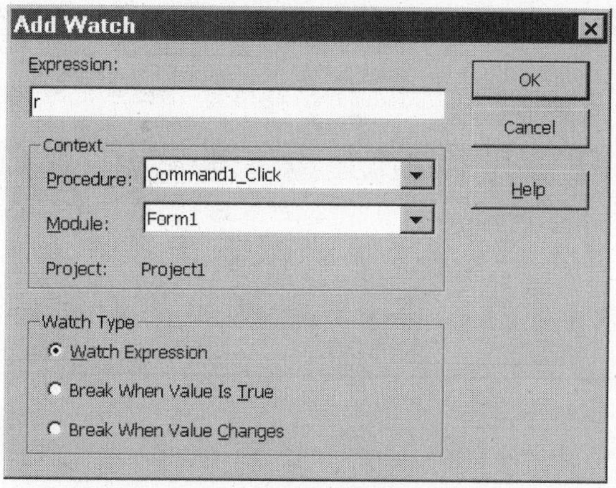

Fig. 6.8 The Add Watch dialog box

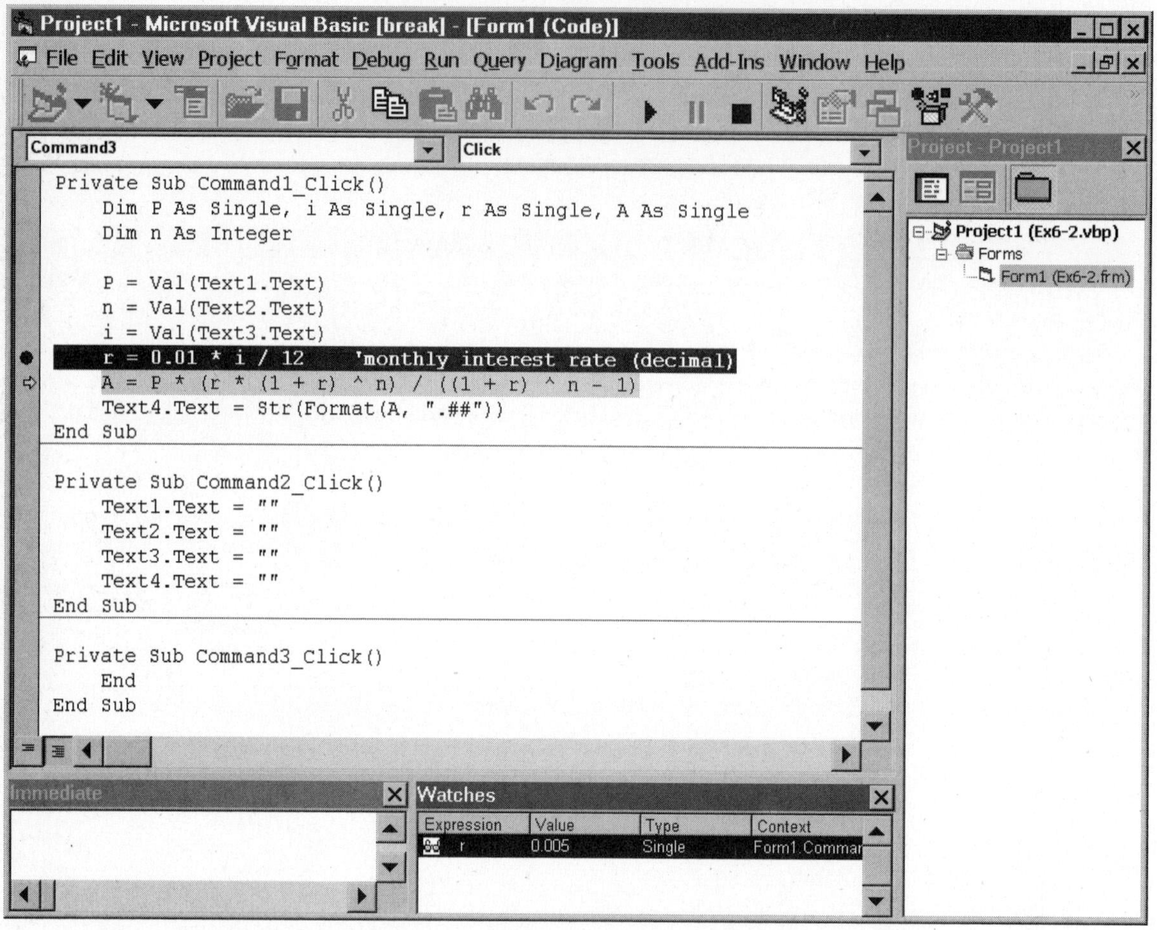

Fig. 6.9 The Watches window appears automatically when the watch variable r is added

Existing watch variables and expressions can easily be edited or removed by right-clicking within the Watches window and then selecting Edit Watch... or Delete Watch. Editing or deletion of watch values can also be carried out by selecting Edit Watch... from the Debug menu and then supplying the appropriate information to the Edit Watch dialog box, as shown in Fig. 6.10.

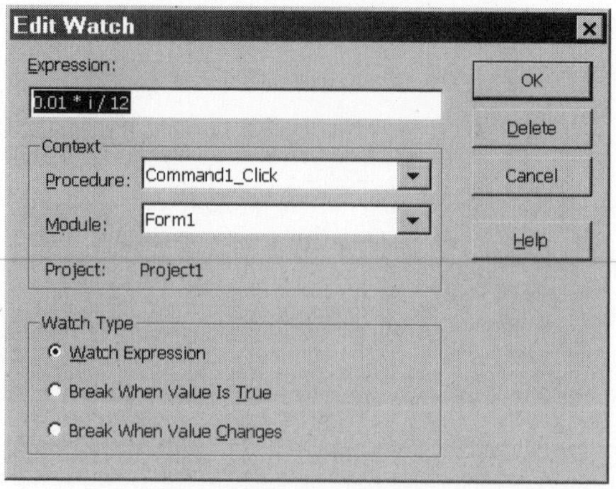

Fig. 6.10 The Edit Watch dialog box

Now suppose your program has executed up to a breakpoint, and you would like to know the current value of a variable or expression that has not been previously defined as a watch value. This can easily be accomplished by highlighting the variable or expression, and then calling upon Visual Basic's *Quick Watch* feature. To access quick watch, do any of the following:

1. Select Quick Watch... from the Debug menu.

2. Press function keys Shift-F9 simultaneously.

3. Click on the Quick Watch button within the Debug toolbar (see Fig. 6.5).

The current value of the selected variable or expression will then appear within the Quick Watch dialog box, as shown in Fig. 6.11.

Once the Quick Watch dialog box is displayed, it must be removed before stepping can be initiated. Thus, quick watch values are not updated as you step through the program. However, you can convert a quick watch variable or expression to an ordinary watch value by clicking on the Add button within the Quick Watch dialog box (see Fig. 6.11).

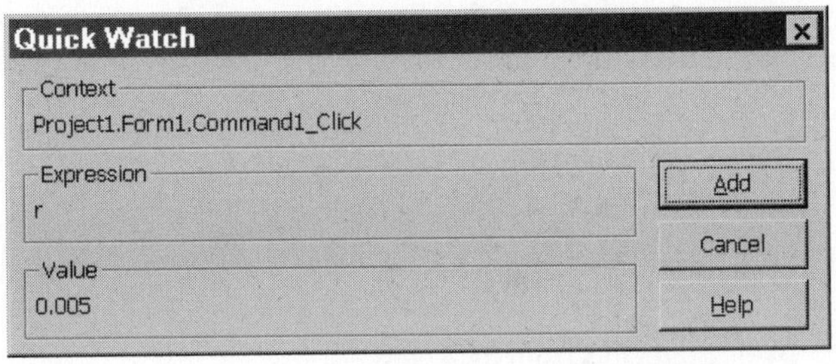

Fig. 6.11 The Quick Watch dialog box

Another way to determine the current value of a variable or expression at a break point is to enter the variable/expression into the Immediate window. To do so, type a question mark (?), followed by the variable or expression. The current value will then be displayed immediately. For example, to determine the value of the variable r at a break point (after r has been assigned a value), simply type

        ?r

into the Immediate window. The current value will then be displayed within the Immediate window, as shown in Fig. 6.12.

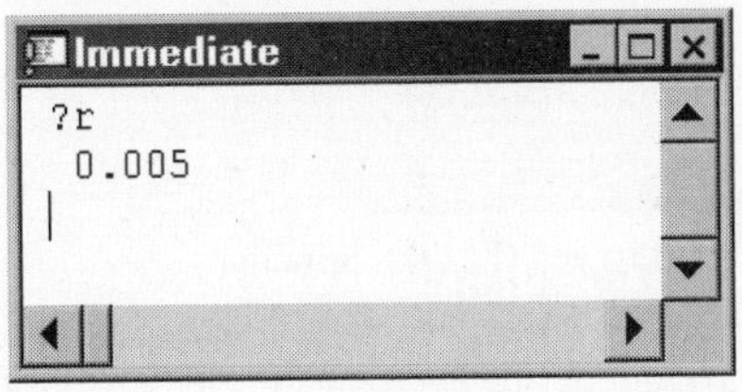

Fig. 6.12 The Immediate window

The Immediate window is usually displayed automatically within the Visual Basic environment (note the lower left corner of Figs. 6.7 or 6.9). If it is not present, however, it may be displayed in any of the following ways:

1. Select Immediate Window from the View menu.

2. Press function keys Ctrl+G simultaneously.

3. Click on the Immediate Window button within the Debug toolbar.

Note that immediate values, like quick watch values, are not updated as you progress through the program on a step-by-step basis. The Immediate window remains visible, however, showing the value of the variable or expression when the variable/expression was last typed into the Immediate window.

6.5 STEPPING THROUGH A PROGRAM

The line-by-line stepping can be initiated either from the beginning of the program or from a breakpoint. There are actually three different types of stepping: Step Into, Step Over, and Step Out. Each is discussed below.

1. Step Into results in line-by-line stepping within the current procedure, and any subordinate procedures that are accessed by the current procedure (see Chap. 7 for more information about procedures). This is the most common choice for simple programs.

2. Step Over results in line-by-line stepping within the current procedure, but it bypasses stepping through any subordinate procedures that are accessed along the way (see Chap. 7). The subordinate procedures are executed, however, so that any final values resulting from the subordinate procedures are in effect as the stepping continues beyond the procedure access. Step Over may be selected instead of Step Into if a subordinate procedure is very lengthy (e.g., includes loops), or is believed to produce no useful debugging information.

3. Step Out results in execution of all remaining statements within the current procedure, and then pauses at the first statement following the procedure access in the parent routine.

To carry out the actual line-by-line (statement-by-statement) stepping, do any of the following for each desired step:

1. Select Step Into (or Step Over, Step Out) from the Debug menu.

2. Press function key F8 to Step Into (or Shift+F8 to Step Over, Ctrl+Shift+F8 to Step Out).

3. Click on the Step Into button (or the Step Over or Step Out button) on the Debug toolbar (see Fig. 6.5).

Whenever a step is taken, the statement to be executed next will be highlighted within the Code Edit window, with a right-pointing arrow in the left margin, as shown in Fig. 6.9.

EXAMPLE 6.2 STEPPING THROUGH A PROGRAM

Suppose we wish to determine the monthly cost of a loan, given the amount of the loan, the annual interest rate (expressed as a percentage), and the length of the loan (i.e., the number of months to repay the loan). Calculations of this type are used to determine the cost of car loans, home mortgages, etc. To do so, we must evaluate the formula

$$A = P \frac{r(1+r)^n}{(1+r)^n - 1}$$

where A = the amount of each monthly payment

P = the amount of money originally borrowed (i.e., the principal)

r = the monthly interest rate, expressed as a decimal

n = the number of monthly payments to repay the loan (i.e., the length of the loan)

The monthly interest rate, r, is determined from the annual interest rate, i, as

$$r = 0.01i / 12$$

Note that this equation involves both a conversion from an annual interest rate to a monthly interest rate (hence, the division by 12), and a conversion from a percentage to a decimal value (hence, the factor 0.01).

The formula can be simplified somewhat by writing

$$A = Prf / (f - 1)$$

where

$$f = (1 + r)^n$$

A Visual Basic program has been written to carry out this calculation. The program accepts the values of P, n and i within separate text boxes, and then displays the calculated value of A within another text box. The Form Design Window is shown in Fig. 6.13.

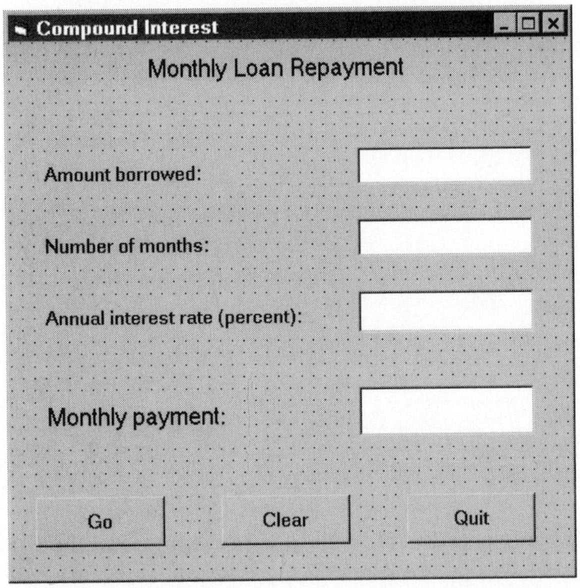

Fig. 6.13 The Form Design Window

The corresponding Visual Basic code is shown in the Code Editor Window in Fig. 6.14.

```
Project1 - Form1 (Code)
Command1                    Click

Private Sub Command1_Click()
    Dim P As Single, i As Single, r As Single, A As Single
    Dim f As Single, n As Integer

    P = Val(Text1.Text)
    n = Val(Text2.Text)
    i = Val(Text3.Text)
    r = 0.01 * i / 12      'monthly interest rate (decimal)
    f = (1 + r) ^ n
    A = P * r * f / f - 1
    Text4.Text = Str(Format(A, ".##"))
End Sub

Private Sub Command2_Click()
    Text1.Text = ""
    Text2.Text = ""
    Text3.Text = ""
    Text4.Text = ""
End Sub

Private Sub Command3_Click()
    End
End Sub
```

Fig. 6.14 The Code Editor Window

Now suppose we want to borrow \$10,000 for 48 months at an annual interest rate of 9.5 percent, compounded monthly. Hence, $P = 10,000$, $n = 48$ and $i = 9.5$. Entering these values into their respective text boxes and clicking on the Go button, we obtain a monthly payment of \$78.17, as shown in Fig. 6.15. This result is clearly incorrect, since 48 payments of \$78.17 each returns only \$3752.16 to the lender – obviously much less than the original \$10,000 loan, not to mention the interest that is also due.

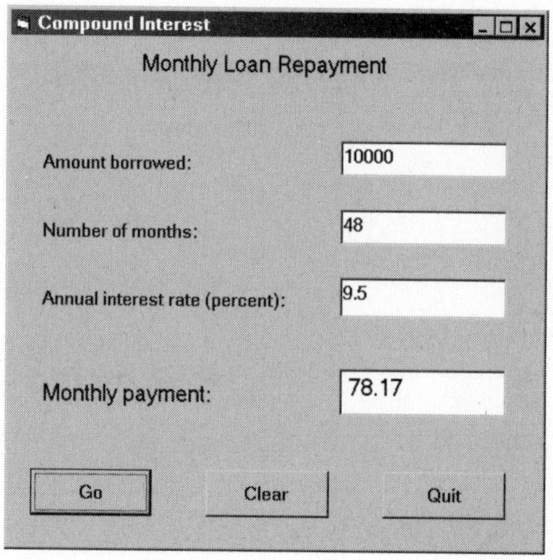

Fig. 6.15

This error appears to be the result of faulty program logic. Hence, we will use the Visual Basic debugger to assist us in locating the source of the error. We first set a breakpoint at the statement

```
r = 0.01 * i / 12
```

as shown in Fig. 6.16. Note that the location of this breakpoint has been selected carefully so that it follows the entry of all input data, but precedes any internal calculations.

Next, we select the variables P, n, i, r, f and A as watch values. These variables are listed (in alphabetical order) within the Watches window at the bottom of Fig. 6.16. Initially, we see the message <out of context> for the value of each variable, since the program has not been executed.

We are now ready to run the program and initiate the debugging process. Hence, we enter the three given values (i.e., $P = 10000$, $n = 48$ and $i = 9.5$), as shown in Fig. 6.16, and then click on the Go button. The program then executes up to the breakpoint, as shown in Fig. 6.17. By examining the values in the Watches window, we verify that the input data have been entered correctly, but the calculated values of A, f and r are zero (because they have not been assigned values within the program). Note that the location of the breakpoint and the highlight indicating the location of the next executable statement coincide. (The location of the next executable statement can be identified in this case by the right-pointing arrow in the left margin, and the lighter color highlight.)

We now take one step forward, by pressing function key F8 (to initiate Step Into). The result can be seen in Fig. 6.18. Now the watch value for r has changed from 0 to approximately 0.00792 (more precisely, 0.007916667). This value can easily be verified as being correct, since $0.01 \times 9.5 / 12 = 0.007916667$. The two remaining values for A and f are still zero, since these variables have not been assigned any values. Note that the location of the breakpoint is unchanged, as it should be, but the highlight indicating the next executable statement has moved down one line as a result of the step.

Let us now step forward once more. Fig. 6.19 shows the results of this step. The watch value for f has now changed from 0 to 1.460098, and the remaining watch values are unchanged. A simple hand calculation (using a calculator) indicates that the value assigned to f is correct. Notice that the highlight indicating the next executable statement has again moved down one line, as a result of this latest step.

Another step forward results in the watch value 78.17 being assigned to the variable A, as shown in Fig. 6.20. We have already noted that this value is incorrect. Since all of the previously calculated watch values are correct, however, we conclude that the error must be in the calculation of A. Closer inspection of this statement reveals a missing pair of parentheses in the denominator.

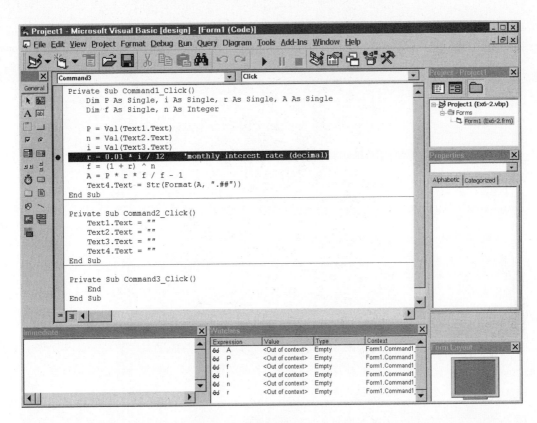

Fig. 6.16

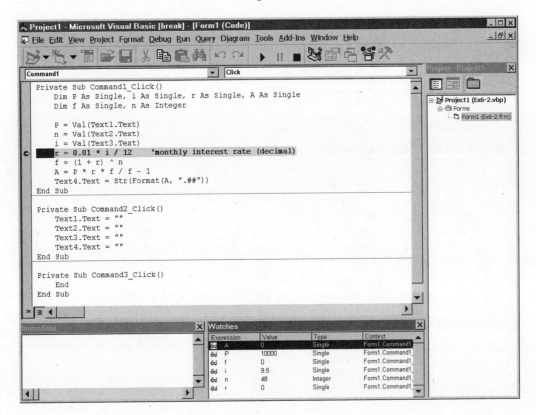

Fig. 6.17

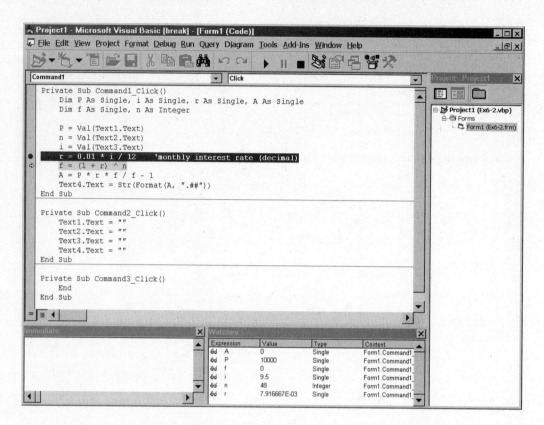

Fig. 6.18

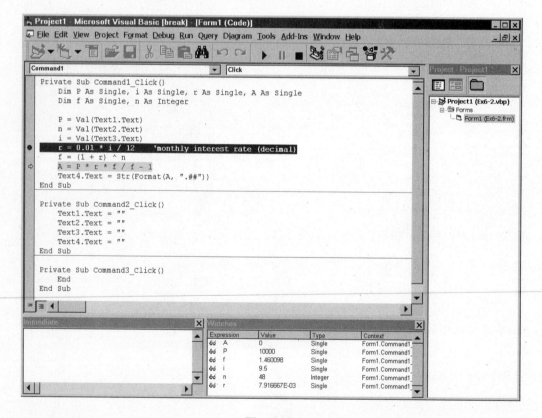

Fig. 6.19

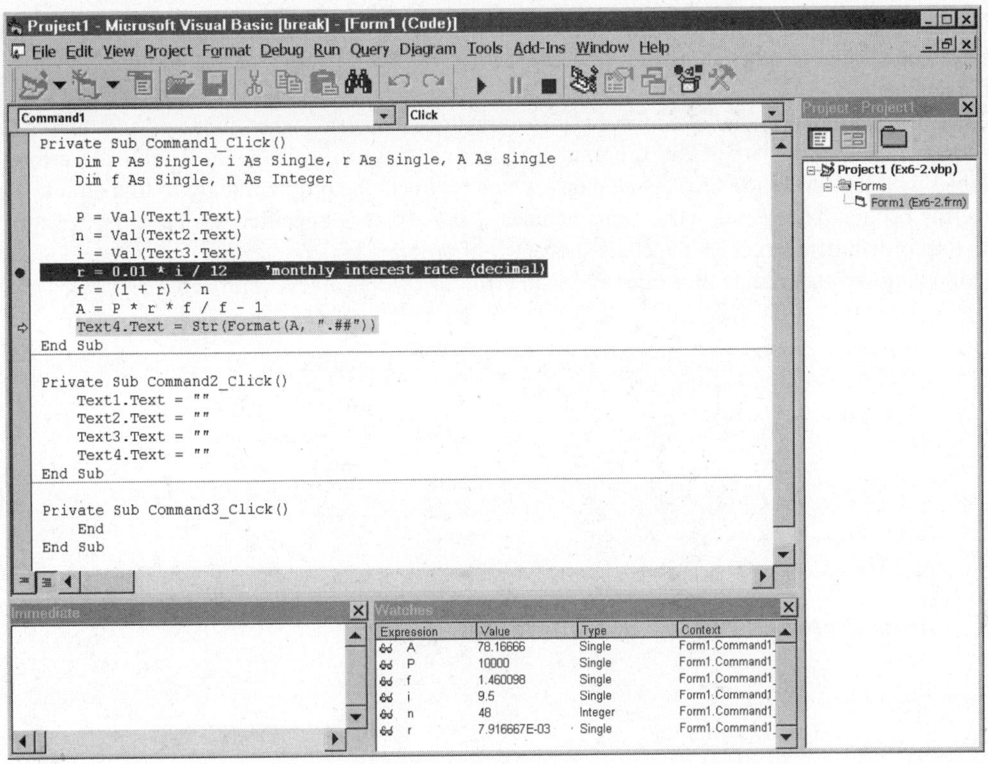
Project1 - Microsoft Visual Basic [break] - [Form1 (Code)]
File Edit View Project Format Debug Run Query Diagram Tools Add-Ins Window Help
Command1
Click
Private Sub Command1_Click()
Dim P As Single, i As Single, r As Single, A As Single
Dim f As Single, n As Integer
P = Val(Text1.Text)
n = Val(Text2.Text)
i = Val(Text3.Text)
r = 0.01 * i / 12 'monthly interest rate (decimal)
f = (1 + r) ^ n
A = P * r * f / f - 1
Text4.Text = Str(Format(A, ".##"))
End Sub
Private Sub Command2_Click()
Text1.Text = ""
Text2.Text = ""
Text3.Text = ""
Text4.Text = ""
End Sub
Private Sub Command3_Click()
End
End Sub
Project - Project1
Project1 (Ex6-2.vbp)
Forms
Form1 (Ex6-2.frm)
Immediate
Watches
Expression Value Type Context
A 78.16666 Single Form1.Command1
P 10000 Single Form1.Command1
f 1.460098 Single Form1.Command1
i 9.5 Single Form1.Command1
n 48 Integer Form1.Command1
r 7.916667E-03 Single Form1.Command1

Fig. 6.20

The successive watch values leads us to conclude that the assignment statement for `A` should be written

```
A = P * r * f / (f - 1)
```

rather than

```
A = P * r * f / f - 1
```

as it is currently written. After making this correction and rerunning this problem, we obtain a correct value of `A` = 251.23 as a final result. In other words, a loan of $10,000 at 9.5 percent annual interest requires a repayment schedule of $251.23 per month for 48 months.

Note that we were able to identify the location and then the source of this error through the use of stepping and watch values within the Visual Basic debugger.

6.6 USER-INDUCED ERRORS

User-induced errors are the result of mistakes made by the user when the program is executing (e.g., entering numbers that are out of range, or entering nonnumerical characters when a numerical value is expected). Errors of this type can usually be anticipated and "trapped" by one or more `If-Then-Else` blocks. However, it may be more convenient to use an *error handler* routine to trap the error and then take appropriate remedial action. The use of error handlers is described in the next section.

6.7 ERROR HANDLERS

An error handler is a series of Visual Basic statements that is intended to recognize an error when it occurs (i.e., to "trap" an error) and then provide appropriate corrective action. The nature of the corrective action depends on the type of error encountered. In some situations, the user can re-enter input data that will prevent the error from occurring. In other situations, the error can simply be bypassed, or the source of the error can be corrected automatically.

When writing an error handler, we must be able to recognize an error when it occurs and then redirect the program logic to a special part of the program that is written specifically to deal with the error. This is accomplished with the On Error-GoTo statement, which redirects the program logic to to a remote statement when an error occurs. The remote statement includes a *label* that is specified within the On Error-GoTo statement, thus providing a target for the continuing flow of program logic.

The following skeletal outline illustrates a typical error trap within an event procedure.

```
Private Sub procedure name

    On Error GoTo label

    . . . . .

    Exit Sub

label:
    remote statement      'Begin error trap

    . . . . .

    Resume

End Sub
```

The On Error-GoTo statement directs the program logic to the remote statement with the specified *label* (the first statement in the error trap routine) in the event that an error is detected during the program execution. This statement and the succeeding statements, through and including Resume, are then executed. (Presumably, these statements will provide whatever actions are required to correct the error.)

The Resume statement can be written in several different ways. If it is written simply as Resume, as in the above skeletal outline, it returns the program logic to the statement that originally caused the error. This works well if the source of the error has been corrected within the error trap. You can also write the Resume statement as Resume Next or Resume *return label*. Resume Next causes the program logic to be returned to the statement immediately following the one that caused the error. Resume *return label* causes the program logic to be returned to the remote statement with the specified *return label*. (Note that this labeled statement is *not* the beginning of the error trap. Thus, there are two different labeled statements – one to initiate the error trap, and the other to serve as a return point once the error-trap routine has been completed.)

Error trapping within a program can be disabled by a special form of the On Error-GoTo statement; namely,

```
On Error GoTo 0
```

This feature is useful if you want to activate error trapping in one part of a program, and then disable it in another part.

Returning to the previous skeletal outline, now suppose that an error is *not* detected during program execution. The program logic will then continue sequentially, as usual, until the Exit Sub statement is encountered. The Exit Sub statement directs the program logic out of the event procedure, thus avoiding the error trap.

Note that the Resume and Exit Sub statements are not always needed within an error handler. Or one may be required, but not the other. The program logic will dictate whether or not these statements will be included.

Visual Basic associates an integer error code with each type of execution error. Thus, an error handler can process an error code (by means of an `If-Then-Else` block or a `Select Case` structure), and take appropriate corrective action. The complete list of error codes is extensive, including some that refer to error types that have not yet been discussed in this book. A representative list error codes that refer to some common execution errors is given in Table 6.1. Note the brief nature of the error messages.

Table 6.1 Some Representative Error Codes

Error Code	Corresponding Error Message
3	Return without GoSub
5	Invalid procedure call or argument
6	Overflow
7	Out of memory
9	Subscript out of range
11	Division by zero
13	Type mismatch
14	Out of string space
16	Expression too complex
17	Can't perform requested operation
18	User interrupt occurred
20	Resume without error
35	Sub, Function or Property not defined
51	Internal error
57	Device I/O error
61	Disk full
68	Device unavailable
70	Permission denied
91	Object variable or With block variable not set
92	For loop not initialized
93	Invalid pattern string
94	Invalid use of Null

EXAMPLE 6.3 AN ERROR HANDLER

A student has written a Visual Basic program to determine the real roots of the quadratic equation

$$ax^2 + bx + c = 0$$

using the well-known formulas

$$x_1 = \frac{-b + \sqrt{b^2 - 4ac}}{2a}, \qquad x_2 = \frac{-b - \sqrt{b^2 - 4ac}}{2a}$$

These formulas are valid only when $a > 0$ (to avoid division by zero) and $b^2 > 4ac$ (to avoid attempting to take the square root of a negative number). The Form Design Window is shown in Fig. 6.21.

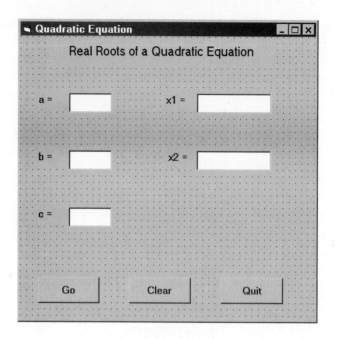

Fig. 6.21

Fig. 6.22 shows the corresponding Visual Basic code in the Code Editor Window. Note that the code does not include any provisions to test for improper input conditions; i.e., $a = 0$, or $b^2 \leq 4ac$.

```
Project1 - Form1 (Code)

Command1                              Click

    Private Sub Command1_Click()
        Dim a, b, c, d, x1, x2

        a = Val(Text1.Text)
        b = Val(Text2.Text)
        c = Val(Text3.Text)

        d = (b ^ 2 - 4 * a * c)

        x1 = (-b + Sqr(d)) / (2 * a)
        x2 = (-b - Sqr(d)) / (2 * a)


        Text4.Text = Str(x1)
        Text5.Text = Str(x2)
    End Sub

    Private Sub Command2_Click()
        Text1.Text = ""
        Text2.Text = ""
        Text3.Text = ""
        Text4.Text = ""
        Text5.Text = ""
    End Sub

    Private Sub Command3_Click()
        End
    End Sub
```

Fig. 6.22

When this program is executed with a dataset that satisfies the required conditions, such as $a = 2$, $b = 5$ and $c = 3$, it displays the correct calculated values $x_1 = -1$ and $x_2 = -1.5$, as shown in Fig. 6.23. However, if the program is executed with a dataset that violates the condition $b^2 > 4ac$, such as $a = 5$, $b = 2$, $c = 3$, an error message is generated, as shown in Fig. 6.24, and the program stops. The user may then either terminate the computation or enter the debugger.

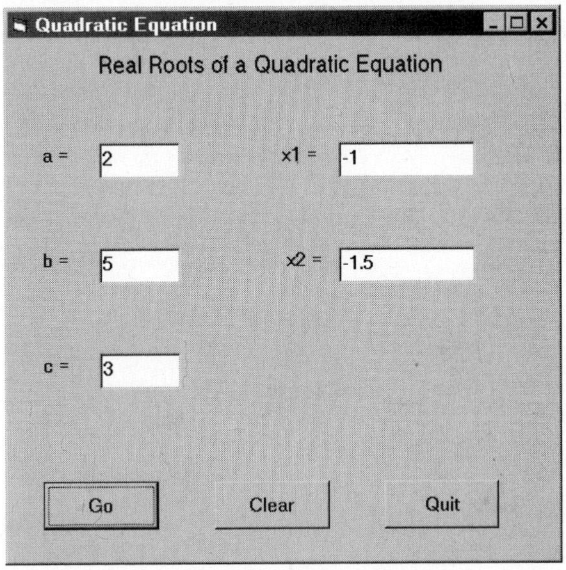

Fig. 6.23

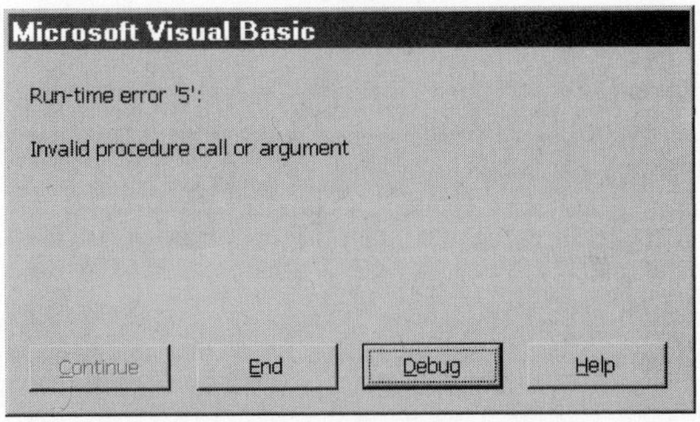

Fig. 6.24

Similarly, if the program is executed with $a = 0$, $b = 2$, and $c = 3$, we obtain the error message shown in Fig. 6.25.

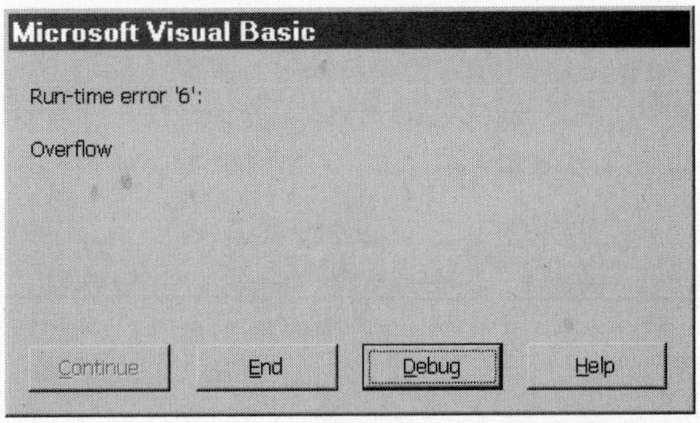

Fig. 6.25

To remedy these conditions, the student has added an error handler to event procedure `Command1_Click()` that tests for each of the two error conditions. When activated, the error handler displays a more descriptive error message and clears the input data fields, thus allowing the user to enter another dataset without first shutting down the program. The corrected Visual Basic code is shown below.

```
Private Sub Command1_Click()
    Dim a, b, c, d, x1, x2

    On Error GoTo ErrorMessage

    a = Val(Text1.Text)
    b = Val(Text2.Text)
    c = Val(Text3.Text)

    d = (b ^ 2 - 4 * a * c)        'calculate discriminant

    x1 = (-b + Sqr(d)) / (2 * a)
    x2 = (-b - Sqr(d)) / (2 * a)

    Text4.Text = Str(x1)
    Text5.Text = Str(x2)

    Exit Sub

ErrorMessage:
    If Err.Number = 5 Then
        MsgBox ("Negative discriminant (b^2 < 4ac):  Re-enter input data")
    ElseIf (Err.Number = 6 Or Err.Number = 11)Then
        MsgBox ("Division by zero (a = 0):  Re-enter input data")
    End If
    Resume ClearInput

ClearInput:
    Text1.Text = ""
    Text2.Text = ""
    Text3.Text = ""

End Sub

Private Sub Command2_Click()
    Text1.Text = ""
    Text2.Text = ""
    Text3.Text = ""
    Text4.Text = ""
    Text5.Text = ""
End Sub

Private Sub Command3_Click()
    End
End Sub
```

If an error is encountered during program execution, the `OnError GoTo ErrorMessage` statement directs the program logic to the error handler, whose first statement is identified by the label `ErrorMessage:` (Note that the colon is a part of the label.) The error handler routine continues through the `Resume ClearInput` statement. If a type-5 error is encountered (because $b^2 < 4ac$), the error message shown in Fig. 6.26 is displayed. (Note that the test is based upon the value assigned to the `Number` property of the system-defined error object `Err`.)

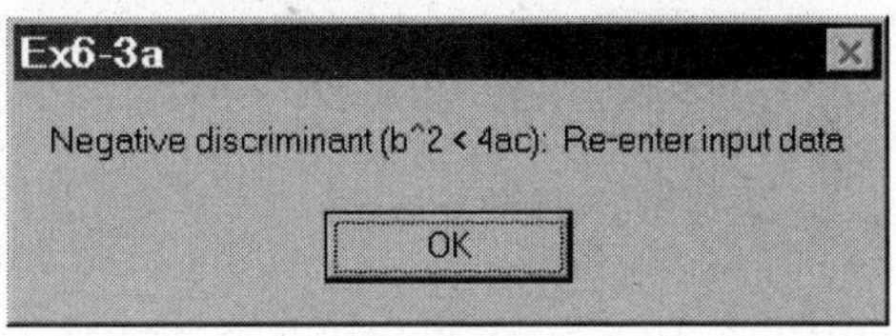

Fig. 6.26

Clicking on OK causes the input data fields to be cleared, so that a new dataset may be entered without shutting down and then restarting the program.

If the user specifies $a = 0$ but $b > 0$ as input parameters, the program will experience a division by zero when attempting to calculate the values of x_1 and x_2. Visual Basic recognizes this particular calculation as an overflow rather than an explicit division by zero, because the numerator and denominator are expressions rather than single quantities. Thus, to be on the safe side, the error trap tests for both conditions – an overflow (`Err.Number = 6`), and an explicit division by zero (`Err.Number = 11`). In either case, the error message shown in Fig. 6.27 is displayed. The input data fields will be cleared when the user clicks on OK, as with the type-5 error.

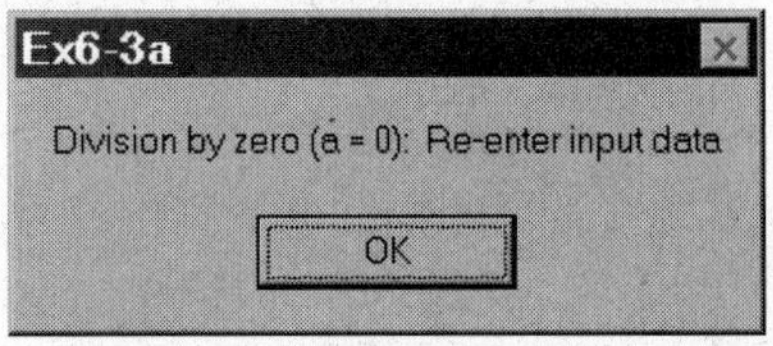

Fig. 6.27

Returning to the Visual Basic code, notice that the error handler ends with the `Resume ClearInput` statement. This statement not really necessary in this case, since the program logic would automatically drop down into the succeeding statements that clear the input data upon completion of the error handler. However, it is good programming practice to include the `Resume ClearInput` statement, since some intervening statements (between the error handler and the clear input statements) may be added at some future time. Hence, it is included here as a matter of good programming practice.

Notice also that the error handler does not account for the situation $b^2 = 4ac$. (as, for example, is encountered when $a = 2$, $b = 4$, and $c = 2$). This condition does not produce a computational error, but does result in identical values of x_1 and x_2, since there is only one real root when $b^2 = 4ac$. The code can easily be modified to recognize this situation and display an appropriate message. This modification is left to the reader as a programming exercise (see Prob. 6.54).

6.8 GENERATING A STAND-ALONE EXECUTABLE PROGRAM

Once your program has been debugged, you may want to generate a separate, stand-alone version. Stand-alone programs are convenient because they can be run independently of the Visual Basic development system, and they can easily be transported from one computer to another. On the other hand, they cannot be edited, and the interactive debugger is not available in the event of an execution error.

Generating a stand-alone executable program is easily carried out. Simply select Make from the File menu within the Visual Basic environment. Then provide the name of the executable file (typically, the same name as the source file) and click the OK button. This will result in a new file with the given name and the extension .exe. The new file, *name*.exe, can then be moved out of the Visual Basic system or moved to a different computer, and then executed on its own.

EXAMPLE 6.4 GENERATING A STAND-ALONE EXECUTABLE PROGRAM

Suppose we wish to generate an independent, stand-alone version of the quadratic equation program presented in Example 6.3. We will save this program with the name QuadraticEqns.exe.

To accomplish this, we open the desired project within the Visual Basic Environment and then select Make Ex6.3 from the File menu, as shown in Fig. 6.28. Note that the default file name is Ex6-3.exe, which is taken from the name of the current Visual Basic project (Ex6-3.vbp).

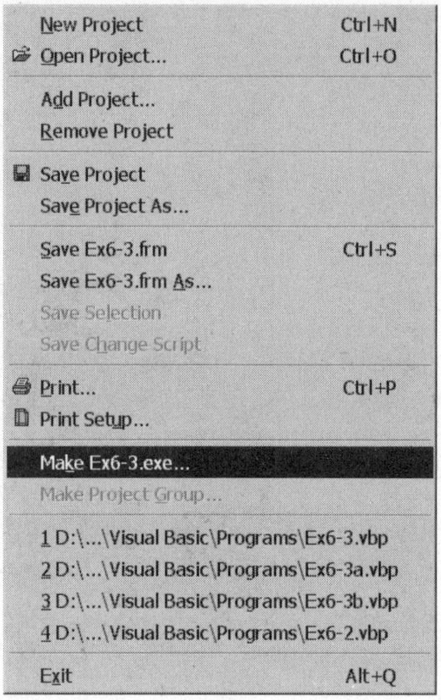

Fig. 6.28

When we click on the Make selection, We obtain the dialog box shown in Fig. 6.29. This dialog box allows us to specify a file name and a location for the new file. The file name can now be changed from Ex6-3.exe to QuadraticEqns.exe, as shown in Fig. 6.30.

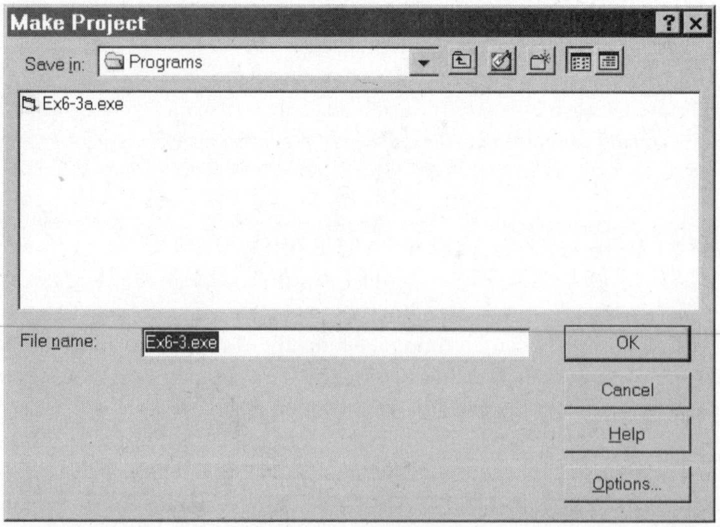

Fig. 6.29

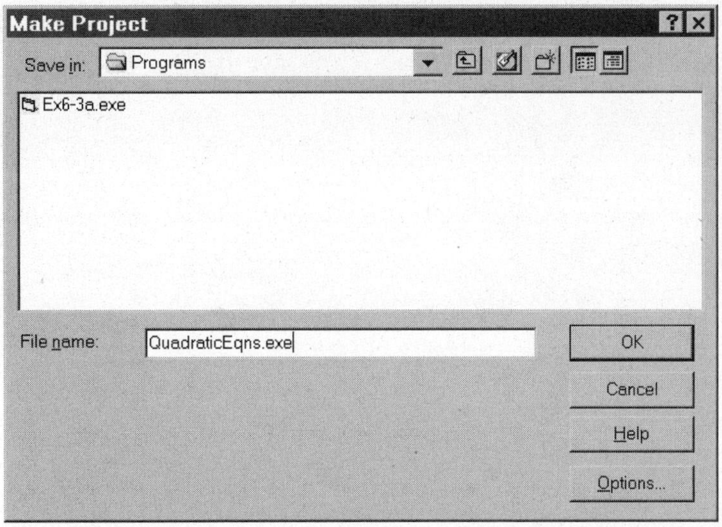

Fig. 6.30

Clicking on the OK button results in the creation of the stand-alone executable file QuadraticEqns.exe, located in the Programs folder.

It should be noted that the creation of this stand-alone executable results in the single file QuadraticEqns.exe being created from the three files (Ex6-3.frm, Ex6-3.vbp and Ex6-3.vbw) that originally comprised the project. However, the new file is substantially larger than the combined size of the original three files. (The exact file sizes will vary from one computer system to another.)

Review Questions

6.1 What is a syntactic error? When do syntactic errors occur? What happens when a syntactic error is detected?

6.2 Cite another commonly used name for a syntactic error.

6.3 What is a logical error? When are logical errors detected? How do logical errors differ from syntactic errors?

6.4 Cite another commonly used name for a logical error.

6.5 What happens when a logical error results in a system crash?

6.6 What happens when a logical error occurs during program execution but allows the program to execute normally, without crashing? How is the occurrence of a logical error recognized under these conditions?

6.7 Describe three different ways to access the Visual Basic debugger.

6.8 Describe the general strategy that is used to locate and identify the source of a logical error.

6.9 What is a breakpoint? Where are breakpoints typically located within a Visual Basic program? How are breakpoints identified when viewing the program listing?

6.10 Describe three different methods for setting a breakpoint within a Visual Basic program.

6.11 Suppose a break in the program execution occurs at a breakpoint. Does the break occur before or after the statement containing the breakpoint has been executed?

6.12 Describe three different ways to remove a breakpoint.

6.13 Suppose a program contains several different breakpoints. How can all of the breakpoints be removed at once?

6.14 What is a "temporary" breakpoint? How is a temporary breakpoint set? How does a temporary breakpoint differ from an ordinary breakpoint?

6.15 What is a watch value?

6.16 What is the difference between an ordinary watch value, a quick watch value, and an immediate watch value? Where does each type of watch value appear?

6.17 How is the Watches window opened within the Visual Basic environment?

6.18 Describe four different ways to add a variable or expression to the Watches window.

6.19 What happens to the existing watch values as you step through a program?

6.20 How is a watch value edited? How is a watch value removed?

6.21 In what way is the quick watch feature useful when debugging a program that already has several watch values defined?

6.22 Describe three different ways to access the quick watch feature.

6.23 How does a quick watch value differ from an ordinary watch value?

6.24 How is a quick watch value converted to an ordinary watch value? Why might you want to do this?

6.25 What type of information can be obtained from the Immediate window at a break point? How is this information obtained?

6.26 Describe three different ways to display the Immediate window if it is not already shown.

6.27 What is the difference between Step Into, Step Over, and Step Out? When would each be used?

6.28 Describe three different ways to step through a program beyond a breakpoint using Step Into.

6.29 Describe three different ways to step through a program beyond a breakpoint using Step Over.

6.30 Describe three different ways to step through a program beyond a breakpoint using Step Out.

6.31 When stepping through a program, how can you tell which statement is about to be executed?

6.32 What is a user-induced error? How do user-induced errors differ from syntactic errors and logical errors?

6.33 What is an error handler?

6.34 What is the purpose of the On Error-GoTo statement?

6.35 What is a label? Within a given statement, how can a label be identified?

6.36 What is the purpose of the Resume statement?

6.37 Describe three different forms of the Resume statement. What is the purpose of each?

6.38 What is the purpose of the On Error GoTo 0 statement?

6.39 What is the purpose of the Exit Sub statement?

6.40 Are Resume and Exit Sub required in all programs that include an error handler? Explain.

6.41 What are error codes? How can error codes be used within an error handler?

6.42 What are the advantages to a stand-alone executable program? What are the disadvantages?

6.43 Describe the process used to generate a stand-alone executable program from Visual Basic source files.

6.44 How are the name and location of a stand-alone executable program specified?

Programming Problems

6.45 Re-create the project shown in Example 6.2 on your own computer. Experiment with the choice of breakpoints and watch values. Request quick watch and immediate watch values at breakpoints. Then step through the program and observe what happens as you move from one instruction to another.

6.46 Add an error handler to the project created in the preceding problem. Include tests for overflows and division by zero.

6.47 Suppose you save A dollars a month for n years. If the annual interest rate (expressed as a percentage) is i and the interest is compounded monthly, how much money will you accumulate at the end of the n years?

This question can be answered by direct evaluation of the following formula:

$$F = A\frac{(1+r)^{12n} - 1}{r}$$

where r represents the monthly interest rate, expressed as a decimal. Hence,

$$r = 0.01i / 12$$

as in Example 6.2.

Using Example 6.2 as a guide, create a Visual Basic project to solve this problem. Include an error handler that tests for overflows and division by zero. Test the program with the following test values:

(a) $A = \$100$, $i = 6$ percent per year, $n = 10$ years.

(b) $A = \$100$, $i = 0$ percent per year, $n = 10$ years.

Use the debugger to set breakpoints and watch values. Then step through the program to observe what happens when using data set (b).

6.48 Modify the Visual Basic project shown in Example 4.8 (extended temperature conversion) so that the input temperatures are confined to the following intervals:

(a) Given temperature in Fahrenheit degrees: $°F \geq -459.67$

(b) Given temperature in Celsius degrees: $°C \geq -273.15$

Add an error handler that utilizes If-Then blocks to trap inappropriate input temperatures. Test the error handler by entering data that fall outside of the acceptable ranges. In addition, verify that the program is working correctly by stepping through the program with valid input temperatures.

6.49 Modify the Visual Basic project shown in Example 4.11 (calculating factorials) in the following ways:

(a) Declare factorial to be an integer variable rather than a long integer variable.

(b) Step through the program for the case n = 10.

(c) Add an error handler that utilizes an On Error-GoTo statement to test for an overflow condition.

(d) Restore factorial to be a long integer variable, as in the given example.

(e) Step through the program for the case n = 10. Compare with the results obtained in part (b).

6.50 Repeat Prob. 4.46 (even/odd/prime numbers) with the following modifications:

(a) Add an error handler for nonpositive values of n (i.e., for n ≤ 0).

(b) Step through the prime-number part of the program, to gain insight into the program logic. Test the program for each of the following input values:

(i)   n = 10 (not a prime number)

(ii)   n = 13 (prime number)

6.51 Repeat Prob. 4.48 (sum of integers from n_1 to n_2, where $n_2 > n_1$). Add an error handler to prevent the user from entering a value of n_2 that does not exceed n_1. Step through the program to verify that the program executes correctly for all three options.

6.52 Create a Visual Basic project to evaluate the polynomial

$$y = [(x-1)/x] + [(x-1)/x]^2/2 + [(x-1)/x]^3/3 + [(x-1)/x]^4/4 + [(x-1)/x]^5/5$$

for positive values of x (i.e., x > 0). Include an error handler to prevent inappropriate values of x from being entered. Step through the program to verify that it is working correctly.

6.53 Create a complete Visual Basic project for each of the following problems. Be sure that all of the calculated results are labeled clearly. Include provisions for clearing the input data and repeating the calculations. In addition, include error traps to prevent execution errors and inappropriate input data.

(a) Calculate the volume and area of a sphere using the expressions

$$V = 4\pi r^3/3, \quad A = 4\pi r^2$$

where r > 0 is the radius of the sphere.

(b) The pressure, volume and temperature of a mass of air are related by the expression

$$PV = 0.37m(T + 460)$$

where   P = pressure, pounds per square inch

V = volume, cubic feet

m = mass of air, pounds

T = temperature, °F

Determine the mass of air when the pressure, volume and temperature are given. Note that P, V and m must exceed zero. In addition, restrict T to values that are not less than −50°F.

Test the project by determining the answer to the following problem: An automobile tire contains 2 cubic feet of air. If the tire is inflated to 28 pounds per square inch at room temperature (68°F), how much air is in the tire?

(c) If a, b and c represent the three sides of a triangle (a > 0, b > 0 and c > 0), then the area of the triangle is

$$A = [\, s\,(s-a)\,(s-b)\,(s-c)\,]^{\,1/2}$$

where $s = (a + b + c)\,/\,2$. Also, the radius of the *largest inscribed* circle is given by

$$r_i = A/s$$

and the radius of the *smallest circumscribed* circle is

$$r_c = abc\,/\,(4A)$$

Calculate the area of the triangle, the area of the largest inscribed circle and the area of the smallest circumscribed circle for each of the following sets of data:

a:	11.88	5.55	10.00	13.75	12.00	20.42	7.17	173.67
b:	8.06	4.54	10.00	9.89	8.00	27.24	2.97	87.38
c:	12.75	7.56	10.00	11.42	12.00	31.59	6.66	139.01

(*d*)   The increase in population of a bacteria culture with time is directly proportional to the size of the population. Thus the larger the population, the faster the bacteria will increase in number. Mathematically the population at any time can be expressed as

$$P = P_0[1 + ct + (ct)^2/2 + (ct)^3/6 + \ldots + (ct)^n/n!]$$

where t = time in hours beyond a reference time

   P_0 = bacteria population at the reference time

   P = bacteria population at time t

   c = an experimental constant

   n = indicates the number of terms in the series (specifically, n is one less than the number of terms in the series; e.g., if $n = 2$, there will be three terms in the series.)

(*i*)   Calculate the population multiplication factor (P/P_0) at 2, 5, 10, 20 and 50 hours beyond the reference time, assuming c=0.0289. Include the first 5 terms of the series (i.e., let $n = 4$). Based upon these calculations, describe, in general terms, how the the population multiplication factor varies with time. *Hint*: To avoid unnecessary calculations, make use of the relationship $n! = n \times (n-1)!$

(*ii*)   Calculate the population multiplication factor (P/P_0) at 50 hours beyond the reference time, assuming $c = 0.0289$ and $n = 10$.

(*iii*)   Calculate the population multiplication factor (P/P_0) at 50 hours beyond the reference time, assuming $c = 0.0289$ and $n = 20$.

Based upon the results of parts (*i*), (*ii*) and (*iii*), describe, in general terms, the sensitivity of the population multiplication factor to n.

6.54   Modify the program shown in Example 6.3 to accommodate the special situation that occurs when $b^2 = 4ac$, resulting in a single real root for the quadratic equation

$$ax^2 + bx + c = 0$$

Display a message indicating that there is only one real root, along with the value of the root.

Chapter 7

Procedures

7.1 MODULES AND PROCEDURES

Large projects are much more manageable if they broken up into *modules*, each of which contains portions of the code comprising the entire project. Visual Basic supports several types of modules, each of which is stored as a separate file. *Form modules* contain declarations, event procedures and various support information for their respective forms and controls. Form modules are stored as files identified by the extension .frm. Whenever you add a new form to a project and then save the form, a separate form module (i.e., a new .frm file) is created. A new form can be created by selecting Add Form from Visual Basic's Project menu. This results in a new form design window, within you may add the required code.

A project may also include a *standard module*. Standard modules contain declarations and procedures that can be accessed by other modules. Standard modules are stored as files with the extension .bas. A standard module can be created by selecting Add Module from Visual Basic's Project menu. This results in a new code editor window, within which you may add the necessary declarations and procedures.

Visual Basic also supports other types of modules, including *class modules* (extension .cls), whose characteristics are beyond the scope of our present discussion.

A *procedure* (including an event procedure) is a self-contained group of Visual Basic commands that can be accessed from a remote location within a Visual Basic program. The procedure then carries out some specific action. Information can be freely transferred between the "calling" location (i.e., the command which accesses the procedure) and the procedure itself. Thus, it is possible to transfer information to a procedure, process that information within the procedure, and then transfer a result back to the calling location. Note, however, that not all procedures require an information transfer – some merely carry out an action without any information interchange.

Large modules are customarily decomposed into multiple procedures, for several reasons. First, the use of procedures eliminates redundancy (that is, the repeated programming of the same group of instructions at different places within a program). Secondly, it enhances the clarity of a program by allowing the program to be broken down into relatively small, logically concise components. And finally, the use of independent procedures allows programmers to develop their own libraries of frequently used routines.

Visual Basic supports three types of procedures – *Sub* procedures (sometimes referred to simply as *subroutines*), *Function* procedures (also called *functions*), and *Property* procedures. Sub and function procedures are commonly used in beginning and intermediate level programs. Hence, our focus in this chapter will be on sub and function procedures. The *shell* (beginning and ending statements) for a new sub or function procedure can be added to a project by selecting Add Procedure... from the Tools menu.

7.2 SUB PROCEDURES (SUBROUTINES)

In its simplest form, a sub procedure is written as

```
Sub procedure name (arguments)
    . . . . .
    statements
    . . . . .
End Sub
```

168

The *procedure name* must follow the same naming convention used with variables (see Sec. 2.3). In addition, a procedure name cannot be identical to a constant or variable name within the same module.

The list of *arguments* is optional. Arguments represent information that is transferred into the procedure from the calling statement. Each argument is written as a variable declaration; i.e.,

> *argument name* As *data type*

The data type can be omitted if the argument is a variant.

Multiple arguments must be separated by commas. If arguments are not present, an empty pair of parentheses must appear in the Sub statement.

EXAMPLE 7.1 DEFINING A SUB PROCEDURE

Here is a sub procedure that determines the smallest of two numbers.

```
Sub Smallest(a, b)
    Dim Min
    If (a < b) Then
        Min = a
        MsgBox "a is smaller (a = " & Str(Min) & ")"
    ElseIf (a > b) Then
        Min = b
        MsgBox "b is smaller (b = " & Str(Min) & ")"
    Else
        Min = a
        MsgBox "Both values are equal (a, b = " & Str(Min) & ")"
    End If
End Sub
```

This procedure has two arguments, a and b. Both are variants. The procedure compares the values of the arguments, determines which is smaller, and then displays the value of the smaller argument in a message box.

Note that the variable Min is a variant that is defined locally within the procedure. It represents the smallest value among the arguments. This variable is not required in this example (we could simply use a or b instead). However, it is a good idea to include this variable, in case the procedure should be expanded to process the minimum value in some manner without altering the given values of the arguments.

Also, note that we could also have included explicit data typing in the first two lines; i.e.,

```
Sub Smallest(a As Variant, b As Variant)
    Dim Min As Variant
```

or, if we choose a different data type,

```
Sub Smallest(a As Single, b As Single)
    Dim Min As Single
```

etc., if we wished.

A sub procedure can be accessed from elsewhere within the module via the Call statement. The Call statement is written

> Call *procedure name* (*arguments*)

The list of arguments in the Call statement must agree with the argument list in the procedure definition. The arguments must agree in *number*, in *order*, and in *data type*. However, the respective names may be different. Thus, if the procedure definition includes three arguments whose data types are single, integer, and string, the Call statement must also contain three arguments whose data types are single, integer, and string, respectively. The names of the arguments within the procedure definition need not, however, be the same as the names of the arguments in the Call statement. For example, the arguments within the procedure definition might be named a, b and c, whereas the corresponding arguments within the Call statement might be called x, y and z.

Here is another way to access a sub procedure.

procedure name   arguments

Note the absence of the keyword Call, and the absence of parentheses.

When the procedure is accessed, the values of the arguments within the calling portion of the program become available to the arguments within the procedure itself. Thus, the values of the arguments are transferred from the calling portion of the program to the procedure. Moreover, if the value of an argument is altered within the procedure, the change will be recognized within the calling portion of the program. (Actually, it is the *addresses* of the arguments that are shared; hence, the *contents* of those addresses can be accessed from either the calling portion of the program or from within the procedure itself.) This type of transfer is called passing by *reference*.

EXAMPLE 7.2 ACCESSING A SUB PROCEDURE (SMALLEST OF TWO NUMBERS)

Here is a complete Visual Basic program that makes use of the sub procedure given in Example 7.1. The program determines the smallest of two numbers and then displays the result. Fig. 7.1 shows the preliminary control layout.

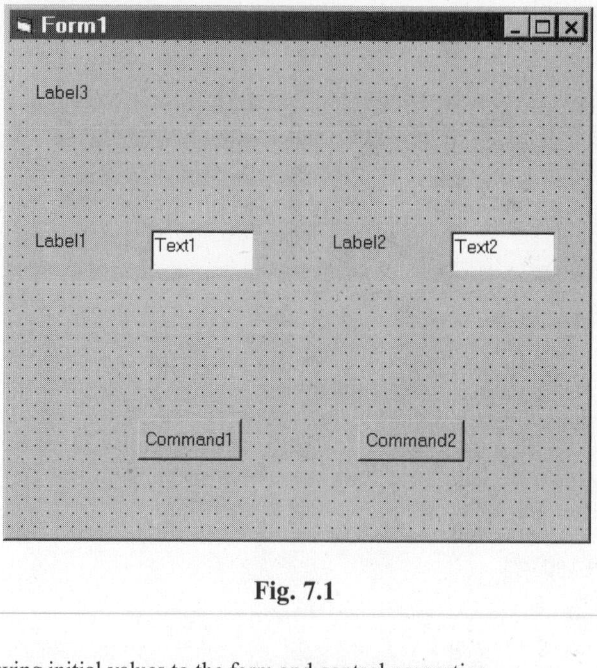

Fig. 7.1

We now assign the following initial values to the form and control properties.

Object	Property	Value
Form1	Caption	"Min of Two Numbers"
Label1	Caption	"a = "
	Font	MS Sans Serif, 10-point

Object	Property	Value
Label2	Caption	"b = "
	Font	MS Sans Serif, 10-point
Label3	Caption	"Determine the Smallest of Two Numbers"
	Font	MS Sans Serif, 12-point
Text1	Caption	(none)
	Font	MS Sans Serif, 10-point
Text2	Caption	(none)
	Font	MS Sans Serif, 10-point
Command1	Caption	"Go"
	Font	MS Sans Serif, 10-point
Command2	Caption	"Quit"
	Font	MS Sans Serif, 10-point

These property assignments result in the form shown in Fig. 7.2.

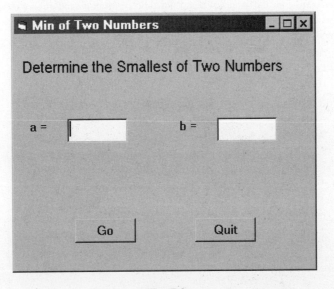

Fig. 7.2

The required procedures (a sub procedure and two event procedures) are shown below.

```
Sub Smallest(a, b)
    Dim Min
    If (a < b) Then
        Min = a
        MsgBox "a is smaller (a = " & Str(Min) & ")"
    ElseIf (a > b) Then
        Min = b
        MsgBox "b is smaller (b = " & Str(Min) & ")"
    Else
        Min = a
        MsgBox "Both values are equal (a, b = " & Str(Min) & ")"
    End If
End Sub
```

```
Private Sub Command1_Click()
    Dim x As Variant, y As Variant

    x = Val(Text1.Text)
    y = Val(Text2.Text)
    Call Smallest(x, y)
    'or:
    'Smallest x, y
End Sub

Private Sub Command2_Click()
    End
End Sub
```

The sub procedure (Smallest) is the same as that shown in Example 7.1.

When the user clicks on the Go button, event procedure Command1_Click() is activated. This causes the two values entered in the text boxes to be converted to numerical values and assigned to the variants x and y, respectively. These values are then transferred to the sub procedure Smallest when the sub procedure is accessed via the Call statement. Within Smallest, the arguments (i.e., the values of x and y within the event procedure) are referred to as a and b. The sub procedure then determines which argument represents the smallest value and displays an appropriate message indicating the result.

Fig. 7.3 shows what happens when the program is executed. Here the user has entered the values 5 and 3 for a and b, respectively. The message shown in Fig. 7.4 is generated when the user clicks on the Go button.

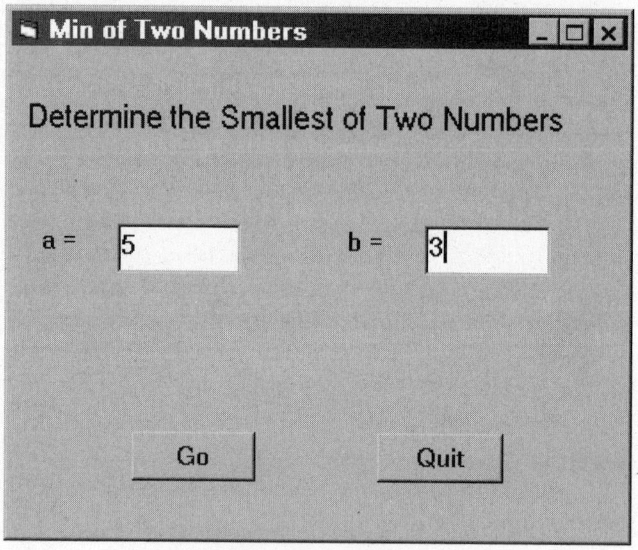

Fig. 7.3

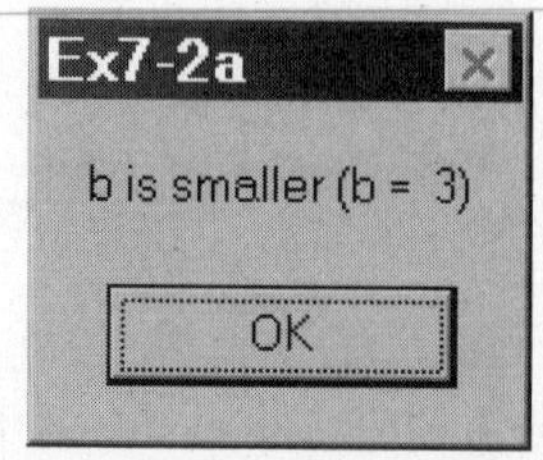

Fig. 7.4

When passing an argument by reference, the argument name may be preceded by the reserved word `ByRef` within the procedure definition; i.e.,

> `ByRef` *argument name* `As` *data type*

The `ByRef` designation is not essential, however, because this is the default mode of transfer in Visual Basic.

An argument passed by reference is usually written as a single variable within the calling statement. It may be possible, however, to write an argument as an *expression* within the calling statement and still pass its value to a procedure by reference (most programming languages do not allow expressions to be passed by reference). This works because the expression is assigned its own address, which is accessible from within the procedure. Note, however, that information cannot be transferred back to the calling portion of the program when the calling argument is written as an expression (see below).

Arguments can also be passed to a procedure by *value*. In this case, the value assigned to each argument in the calling statement (rather than the argument's address) is passed directly to the corresponding argument within the procedure. This is strictly a one-way transfer; that is, the argument values are transferred *from* the calling statement *to* the procedure. If any of these values is altered within the procedure, the new value will *not* be transferred back to the calling statement. Passing arguments by value can be useful, however, since the arguments in the calling statement can always be written as expressions rather than single variables.

In order to pass an argument by value, the argument name within the procedure must be preceded by the reserved word `ByVal`; i.e.,

> `ByVal` *argument name* `As` *data type*

If a procedure includes multiple arguments, some may be passed by reference and others by value.

EXAMPLE 7.3 SMALLEST OF THREE NUMBERS

Let us now modify the program presented in Example 7.3 to find the smallest of *three* numbers by repeatedly using a variation of the sub procedure `Smallest` introduced earlier. Our strategy will be to enter three numbers, a, b and c, via text boxes, then call `Smallest` to determine the smaller of the first two values (a and b). This value (called min) will be returned to the calling portion of the program. Then `Smallest` will be called again, this time receiving the values for c and min, and returning the lesser of these. The returned value will again be called min, overwriting the previous value.

This example further illustrates the manner in which information is passed back and forth between a calling program and a sub procedure. Each time the procedure is accessed, it will accept two numbers from the calling statement and return one (the smaller value) via a transfer by reference. The two input values can be transferred either by value or by reference; we will transfer by value, simply to illustrate the technique. The preliminary control layout is shown in Fig. 7.5.

We now assign the following initial values to the form and control properties.

Object	Property	Value
Form1	Caption	"Min of Three Numbers"
Label1	Caption	"a = "
	Font	MS Sans Serif, 10-point
Label2	Caption	"b = "
	Font	MS Sans Serif, 10-point
Label3	Caption	"c = "
	Font	MS Sans Serif, 10-point
Label4	Caption	"Min = "
	Font	MS Sans Serif, 10-point

(*Continues on next page*)

Object	Property	Value
Label5	Caption	"Determine the Smallest of Three Numbers"
	Font	MS Sans Serif, 12-point
Text1	Caption	(none)
	Font	MS Sans Serif, 10-point
Text2	Caption	(none)
	Font	MS Sans Serif, 10-point
Text3	Caption	(none)
	Font	MS Sans Serif, 10-point
Text4	Caption	(none)
	Font	MS Sans Serif, 10-point
Command1	Caption	"Go"
	Font	MS Sans Serif, 10-point
Command2	Caption	"Clear"
	Font	MS Sans Serif, 10-point
Command3	Caption	"Quit"
	Font	MS Sans Serif, 10-point

These assignments result in the Form Design Window shown in Fig. 7.6.

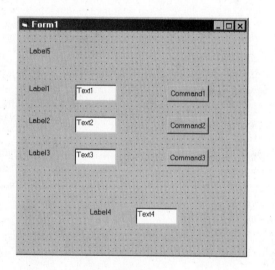

Fig. 7.5

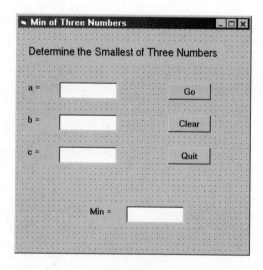

Fig. 7.6

Here are the corresponding procedures.

```
Sub Smallest(ByVal a, ByVal b, ByRef c)
    If (a < b) Then
        c = a
    Else
        c = b
    End If
End Sub
```

```
Private Sub Command1_Click()
    Dim x, y, z, min

    x = Val(Text1.Text)
    y = Val(Text2.Text)
    z = Val(Text3.Text)
    Call Smallest(x, y, min)
    Call Smallest(z, min, min)
    Text4.Text = Str(min)
End Sub

Private Sub Command2_Click()
    Text1.Text = ""
    Text2.Text = ""
    Text3.Text = ""
    Text4.Text = ""
End Sub

Private Sub Command3_Click()
    End
End Sub
```

Now suppose that we execute the program using the values a = 3, b = 4 and c = 2, as shown in Fig. 7.7. The first call to sub procedure Smallest from event procedure Command1 will transfer the values x = 3 and y = 4 to the procedure, returning the value 3, which will temporarily be assigned to min. (Note that the three input values are referred to as x, y and z within Command1, simply to illustrate the flexibility that is permitted when naming arguments.) The second call to Smallest will then transfer the values z = 2 and min = 3, returning the value 2, which will be assigned to min, replacing the earlier value.

Clicking on the Go button produces the result shown in Fig. 7.8.

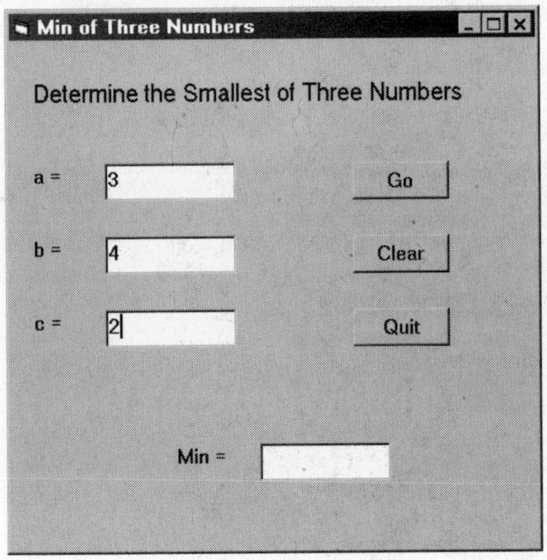

Fig. 7.7

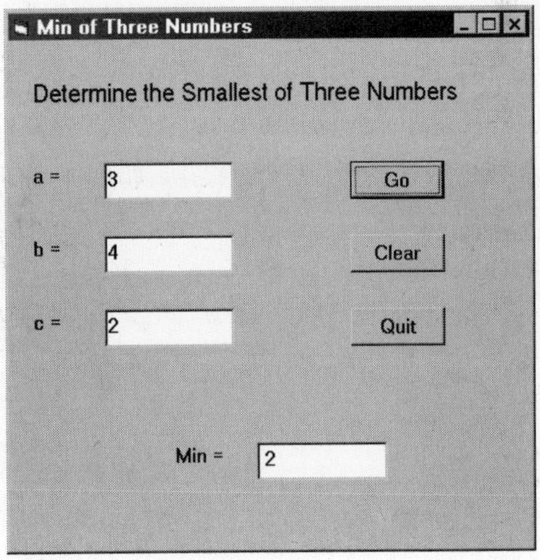

Fig. 7.8

7.3 EVENT PROCEDURES

Event procedures should be quite familiar by now, as we have been using them throughout this book. An event procedure is a special type of sub procedure. It is accessed by some specific action, such as clicking on an object, rather than by the Call statement or by referring to the procedure name. The particular action associated with each event procedure is selected from the upper-right drop-down menu within the Code Editor Window. The object name and the activating event collectively make up the event procedure name. Thus, Command1_Click(). is the name of an event procedure that is activated by clicking on command button Command1.

Like any other sub procedure, arguments may be used to transfer information into an event procedure. An empty pair of parentheses must follow the procedure name if arguments are not present.

EXAMPLE 7.4 DEFINING AN EVENT PROCEDURE

Returning to the project presented in Example 7.3, suppose we double click on command button Command1 within the Form Design Window, as shown in Fig. 7.5. The Code Editor Window will then be displayed, as shown in Fig. 7.9.

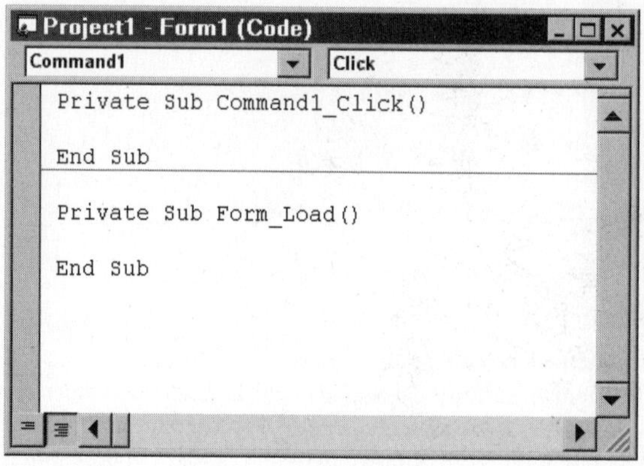

Fig. 7.9

The object in this case is Command1 and the desired action is a mouse click, as indicated by the two menu selections at the top of Fig. 7.9. If a different action is desired, it can be selected by clicking on the down arrow in the upper right window and then selecting from the resulting menu, as shown in Fig. 7.10.

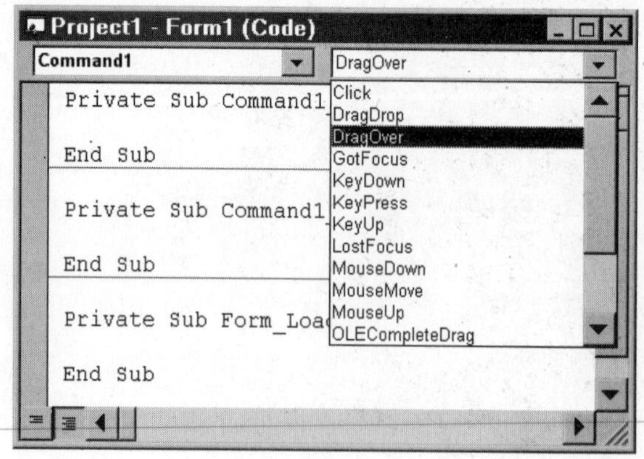

Fig. 7.10

Once the object and the action have been selected, the first and last lines of the event procedure are generated automatically within the Code Editor Window, as shown in Figs. 7.9 and 7.10. The user must then provide the remaining Visual Basic statements, thus completing the event procedure.

The term Private appearing in the first line determines the *scope* of the event procedure; i.e., the portion of the program in which the event procedure is recognized. We will discuss this further later in this chapter (see Sec. 7.5).

The complete event procedure `Command1_Click()`, originally shown in Example 7.3, is shown within the Code Editor Window in Fig. 7.11. The reader is again reminded that the indented statements are provided by the programmer. Note that this event procedure accesses the sub procedure `Smallest` twice.

```
Project1 - Form1 (Code)                       _ □ ×
Command1              ▼    Click                        ▼
    Private Sub Command1_Click()                       ▲
        Dim x, y, z, min

        x = Val(Text1.Text)
        y = Val(Text2.Text)
        z = Val(Text3.Text)
        Call Smallest(x, y, min)
        Call Smallest(z, min, min)
        Text4.Text = Str(min)

    End Sub                                             ▼
```

Fig. 7.11

7.4 FUNCTION PROCEDURES

A function procedure is similar to a sub procedure, with one important difference: a function is intended to return a single data item, just as a library function returns a single data item. Each function name therefore represents a data item, and has a data type associated with it. Within a function definition, the function name must be assigned the value to be returned, as though the function name were an ordinary variable.

In its simplest form, a function procedure is written as

> Function *procedure name* (*arguments*) As *data type*
>
> . . . . .
> *statements*
> . . . . .
> *procedure name* = ...
> . . . . .
> End Function

As with a sub procedure, the list of *arguments* is optional. Arguments represent information that is transferred into the procedure from the calling statement. Each argument is written as a variable declaration; i.e.,

> *argument name* As *data type*

Remember that the data type can be omitted if the argument is a variant.

Multiple arguments must be separated by commas. If arguments are not present, an empty pair of parentheses must appear in the `Function` statement.

The *data type* designation in the `Function` statement refers to the data item being returned. This designation is not essential – the returned data item will be considered to be a variant if the designation is not included.

Notice that the procedure name is assigned a value at some point within the procedure (multiple assignments are permitted, in accordance with the required program logic). This is the value being returned by the function. Thus, within a function, the procedure name is used as though it were an ordinary variable. (Contrast this with a sub procedure, where the procedure name does *not* represent a data item.)

EXAMPLE 7.5 DEFINING A FUNCTION PROCEDURE

Here is a function procedure that determines the factorial of a positive integer quantity. The function is based upon logic similar to that given in Example 4.11.

```
Function Factorial(n As Integer) As Long
    Dim i As Integer

    If n < 1 Then
        Beep
        MsgBox ("ERROR - Please try again")
    Else
        Factorial = 1
        For i = 1 To n
            Factorial = Factorial * i
        Next i
    End If
End Function
```

This procedure has one integer argument, n, which represents the value whose factorial will be determined. Thus, the value of n is transferred into the procedure, and its factorial is returned as a long integer. Note that the factorial is referred to by the function name, `Factorial`. Notice also that the function name (`Factorial`) is assigned a value at two different places within the procedure, as required by the program logic.

A function procedure is accessed in the same manner as a library function, by writing the function name and its required arguments as an expression. Thus, the function name (and its arguments) can be assigned to another variable, etc. The list of arguments in the function access must agree with the argument list in the function definition in *number*, in *order* and in *data type*. As with sub procedures, however, the names of the arguments in the function access may be different than the argument names used in the function definition.

EXAMPLE 7.6 ACCESSING A FUNCTION PROCEDURE

Let us now consider a complete Visual Basic program that determines the factorial of a positive integer n. The program will use the function procedure presented in the last example.

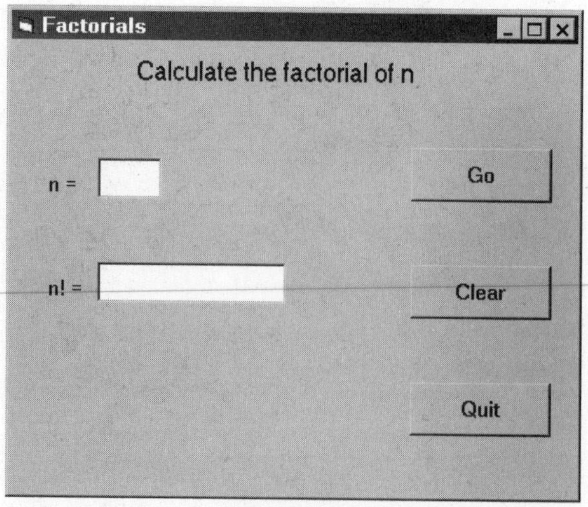

Fig. 7.12

The layout of the form design window, shown in Fig. 7.12, is identical to that given in Example 4.11. However, the code is different, as shown below.

```
Function Factorial(n As Integer) As Long
    Dim i As Integer

    If n < 1 Then
        Beep
        MsgBox ("ERROR - Please try again")
    Else
        Factorial = 1
        For i = 1 To n
            Factorial = Factorial * i
        Next i
    End If
End Function

Private Sub Command1_Click()
    Dim n As Integer, nFact As Long

    n = Val(Text1.Text)
    nFact = Factorial(n)
    Text2.Text = Str(nFact)
End Sub

Private Sub Command2_Click()
    Text1.Text = ""
    Text2.Text = ""
End Sub

Private Sub Command3_Click()
    End
End Sub
```

Note the manner in which the function procedure Factorial is accessed within event procedure Command1_Click; i.e.,

```
nFact = Factorial(n)
```

Thus, the value of n is transferred into Factorial as an argument. The factorial of n is then returned by the function and assigned to the long integer variable nFact. The value of nFact is then converted to a string and displayed within text box Text2.

In the above code, two separate statements are used to access Factorial and to display its returned value; i.e.,

```
nFact = Factorial(n)
Text2.Text = Str(nFact)
```

This was done in order to clarify the program logic. The two statements can be combined, however, by simply writing

```
Text2.Text = Str(Factorial(n))
```

When executed, this program behaves in the same manner as the program shown in Example 4.11. The result obtained with a representative value of n = 11 is shown in Fig. 7.13.

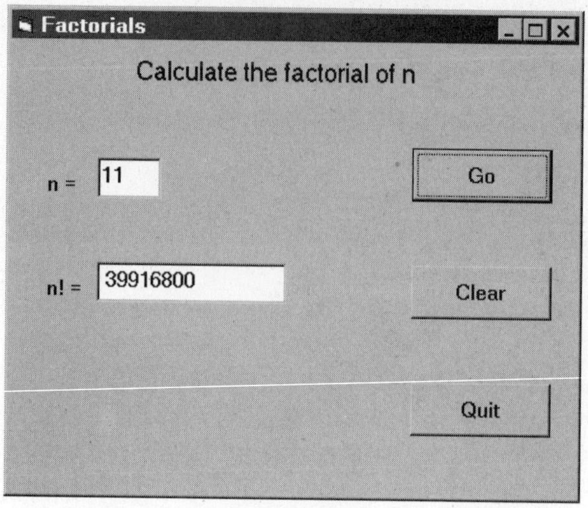

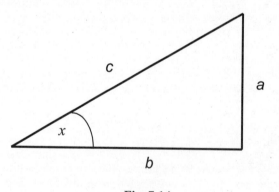

Fig. 7.13

A function reference may appear within a more complex expression, as though the function name were an ordinary variable. However, any required arguments must follow the function name, enclosed in parentheses and separated by commas.

EXAMPLE 7.7 CALCULATING THE SINE OF AN ANGLE

In trigonometry, the *sine* of an angle within a right triangle is the value obtained when the side opposite the angle is divided by the hypoteneuse. Thus, in Fig. 7.14, the sine of the angle x is the quotient a/c. This quantity, usually written as $\sin(x)$, is used in numerous scientific and technical applications, many of which do not involve geometry. (Note that the angle x is expressed in *radians*, where 2π radians $= 360°$.)

Fig. 7.14

The numerical value of $\sin(x)$ can easily be determined using the Visual Basic sin function, provided x (in radians) is given as an argument. However, the value of $\sin(x)$ can also be approximated by the series

$$\sin(x) = x - \frac{x^3}{3!} + \frac{x^5}{5!} - \frac{x^7}{7!} + \cdots = \sum_{i=1}^{n} (-1)^{(i+1)} \frac{x^{2i-1}}{(2i-1)!}$$

The accuracy of this approximation increases as the number of terms in the series (n) increases. In principle, the summation results in an exact answer when n becomes infinite. As a practical matter, the summation is usually sufficiently accurate for modestly large values of n (say, $n = 5$ or $n = 6$).

In this example we will develop a Visual Basic program that evaluates sin(*x*) using the first *n* terms of the series expansion, and then compares this value with the more accurate value returned from the Visual Basic sin function. The values of *x* (in degrees) and *n* will be input values. When evaluating the series expansion, we will make use of the Factorial function procedure presented in the last two examples.

The preliminary control layout is shown in Fig. 7.15, followed by the initial property assignments.

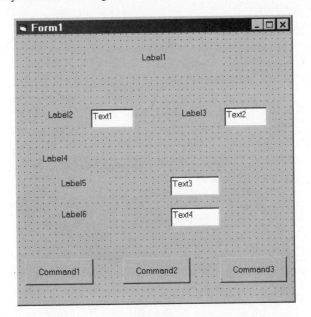

Fig. 7.15

Object	Property	Value
Form1	Caption	"Sine of x"
Label1	Caption	"Series approximation for sin(x)"
	Font	MS Sans Serif, 12-point
Label2	Caption	"x = "
	Font	MS Sans Serif, 10-point
Label3	Caption	"n = "
	Font	MS Sans Serif, 10-point
Label4	Caption	"Sin (x):"
	Font	MS Sans Serif, 10-point
Label5	Caption	"Series approximation:"
	Font	MS Sans Serif, 10-point
Label6	Caption	"Correct value:"
	Font	MS Sans Serif, 10-point
Text1	Caption	(none)
	Font	MS Sans Serif, 10-point
Text2	Caption	(none)
	Font	MS Sans Serif, 10-point
Text3	Caption	(none)
	Font	MS Sans Serif, 10-point

(*Continues on next page*)

Object	Property	Value
Text4	Caption	(none)
	Font	MS Sans Serif, 10-point
Command1	Caption	"Go"
	Font	MS Sans Serif, 10-point
Command2	Caption	"Clear"
	Font	MS Sans Serif, 10-point
Command3	Caption	"Quit"
	Font	MS Sans Serif, 10-point

These assignments result in the final Form Design Window shown in Fig. 7.16.

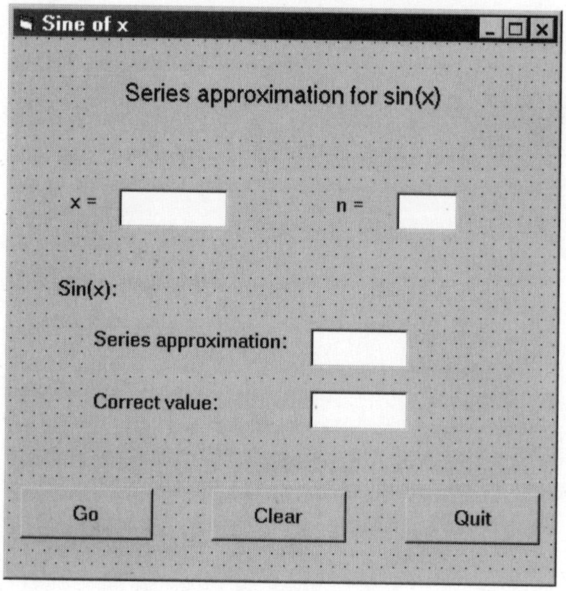

Fig. 7.16

The required procedures are shown below. Notice that the first procedure is the function procedure `Factorial`, which is repeated from the previous two examples. Also, note that `Factorial` is accessed as a part of an expression within the event procedure `Command1_Click`.

```
Function Factorial(n As Integer) As Long
    Dim i As Integer

    If n < 1 Then
        Beep
        MsgBox ("ERROR - Please try again")
    Else
        Factorial = 1
        For i = 1 To n
            Factorial = Factorial * i
        Next i
    End If
End Function
```

```
Private Sub Command1_Click()
    Const Pi As Single = 3.1415927
    Dim n As Integer, i As Integer
    Dim Angle As Single, Rad As Single, Approx As Single, Exact As Single
    Dim Sum As Single, C As Single

    Angle = Val(Text1.Text)
    Rad = 2 * Pi * Angle / 360          'convert angle to radians
    n = Val(Text2.Text)

    Sum = 0
    C = 1
    For i = 1 To n
        Sum = Sum + C * Rad ^ (2 * i - 1) / Factorial(2 * i - 1)
        C = -C                          'reverse sign for next member in series
    Next i
    Approx = Sum
    Exact = Sin(Rad)                    'library function
    Text3.Text = Str(Approx)
    Text4.Text = Str(Exact)
End Sub

Private Sub Command2_Click()
    Text1.Text = ""
    Text2.Text = ""
    Text3.Text = ""
    Text4.Text = ""
End Sub

Private Sub Command3_Click()
    End
End Sub
```

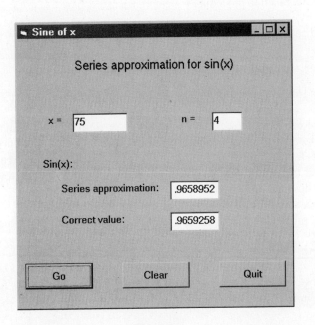

Fig. 7.17

When event procedure Command1_Click is first entered, the angle is changed from degrees to radians using the formula

$$r = 2\pi d/360$$

where r = the angle in radians
$\quad\quad\quad d$ = the angle in degrees

The evaluation of the series expansion is then carried out in a For–Next loop. Note that the series includes a coefficient C whose value alternates between +1 and −1. This computational shortcut has the same effect as raising −1 to various powers within the loop (as shown in the series expansion), thus avoiding some unnecessary multiplication.

When the program is executed, it displays the value of sin(x) as determined by the first n terms of the series, and the correct value of sin(x) as determined by the Visual Basic library function. Some representative results are shown in Fig. 7.17, where sin(75°) is determined as 0.9658952 using the first four terms of the series expansion, and 0.9659258 using the Visual Basic library function. Note that the results agree to four significant figures; i.e., sin(75°) = 0.9659 using either method.

You may wish to experiment with this program by specifying the same angle and trying different values of n. Or, by investigating the accuracy of the approximation for a given value of n when the angle is varied.

7.5 SCOPE

Scope refers to the portion of a program within which a procedure definition (or a variable or named constant definition) is recognized. The scope of a sub procedure is determined by the identifier `Public` or `Private`, which precedes the procedure name; e.g.,

`Public Sub` *procedure name (arguments)*

or

`Private Sub` *procedure name (arguments)*

Similarly, the scope of a function procedure is determined as

`Public Function` *procedure name (arguments)* `As` *data type*

or

`Private Function` *procedure name (arguments)* `As` *data type*

A `Public` procedure can be accessed from *any* module or form within a program, whereas a `Private` procedure will be recognized only within the module or form within which it is defined. The default is `Public`. Hence, if a programmer-defined procedure does not include a `Public/Private` specification (as in the examples presented earlier in this chapter), it is assumed to be `Public`. Note, however, that event procedures automatically include the designation `Private` when they are created.

When a `Public` procedure is accessed from a module or form other than the module or form containing the module definition, the procedure name must be preceded by the form name containing the definition; e.g.,

`Call` *form name.procedure name (arguments)*

for a sub procedure access. Function procedures are accessed similarly, with the form name containing the function definition preceding the function name; e.g.,

variable = form name. function name (arguments)

Variables and named constants that are defined within a procedure are local to that procedure. However, variables and named constants can also be declared within a module, external to any procedures defined within the module. Such variables (or named constants) can be declared `Public` or `Private`; e.g.,

> `Private` *variable name* `As` *data type*

or

> `Public` *variable name* `As` *data type*

In the first example (`Private`), the variable will be recognized anywhere within the module in which it is declared, but not in other modules. If a different (local) variable with the same name is declared *within* a procedure, then the local variable can be referenced within the procedure simply by its name. The (global) variable declared outside of the procedure can also be referenced within the procedure, by prefixing its name with the form name; e.g.,

> *form name.variable name*

EXAMPLE 7.8

Here is a skeletal outline of a module containing both a global and a local variable having the same name.

```
Private Factor As Integer

Private Sub Sample()
    Dim Factor As Integer
    . . . . .
    Form1.Factor = 3        'assign 3 to the global variable
    Form2 = 6               'assign 6 to the local variable
    . . . . .
End Sub
```

Note that the use of multiple variables having the same name is generally not recommended.

If a variable is declared to be `Public` within a module, then the variable will be recognized anywhere within the entire project. The variable can be referenced within the module in which it is declared simply by its name (unless it is referenced within a procedure containing a local variable with the same name, as described previously). To reference the variable within other modules, it must be preceded by its form name.

EXAMPLE 7.9

Now consider two different modules that contain public variables. The following skeletal outline illustrates how these variables can be utilized within each module.

Form Module 1	*Form Module 2*

```
Public Red                    Public Green

Private Sub FirstSub()        Private Sub SecondSub()
    . . . . .                     . . . . .
    Red = 3                       Form1.Red = 7
    'or Form1.Red = 3             Green = 2
    Form2.Green = 6               'or Form2.Green = 2
End Sub                       End Sub
```

Once the actions defined within a procedure have been completed and control is returned to the remote access point, the values assigned to the local variables within the procedure are not retained. There are situations, however, in which it may be desirable for a local variable to retain its value between procedure calls. This can be accomplished by declaring the variable to be `Static`; e.g.,

> `Static` *variable name* `As` *data type*

Note that `Static` is used in place of `Dim`.

All of the variables within a procedure can be made to retain their values by declaring the entire procedure to be `Static`; for example,

> `Private Static Sub` *procedure name* (*arguments*)

> `Public Static Function` *procedure name* (*arguments*) `As` *data type*

and so on. In these examples, note that `Static` appears in addition to `Private` or `Public`.

Sometimes the program logic requires that a procedure be exited if some logical condition is satisfied, without executing all of the instructions within the procedure. This can be accomplished with an `Exit Sub` or `Exit Function` statement; e.g.,

```
Private Sub procedure name (arguments)
    . . . . .
    If (logical condition) Then
        Exit Sub
    Else
        . . . . .
    End If
End Sub
```

Function procedures operate in the same manner, except that `Exit Function` replaces `Exit Sub`.

EXAMPLE 7.10 SHOOTING CRAPS

Craps is a popular dice game in which you throw a pair of dice one or more times until you either win or lose. The game can be simulated on a computer by substituting the generation of random numbers for the actual throwing of the dice.

There are two ways to win in craps. You can throw the dice once and obtain a score of either 7 or 11; or you can obtain a 4, 5, 6, 8, 9 or 10 on the first throw and then repeat the same score on a subsequent throw before obtaining a 7. Similarly, there are two ways to lose. You can throw the dice once and obtain a 2, 3 or 12; or you can obtain a 4, 5, 6, 8, 9 or 10 on the first throw and then obtain a 7 on a subsequent throw before repeating your original score.

We will develop the game interactively in Visual Basic, so that one throw of the dice will be simulated each time you click on a command button. A text box will indicate the outcome of each throw. At the end of each game, the cumulative number of wins and losses will be displayed. A command button will allow you to play again if you wish.

Our program will require a random number generator that produces uniformly distributed integers between 1 and 6. (By *uniformly distributed*, we mean that any integer between 1 and 6 is just as likely to occur as any other integer within this range.) To do so, we will make use of the `Rnd` library function, which generates *fractional* random numbers that are uniformly distributed between 0 and 1. We will also utilize the `Randomize` function, which is used to initialize the random number generator.

Now let us see how we can convert these random numbers into something that simulates throwing a pair of dice. We can generate a random *integer*, uniformly distributed between 0 and 5, by writing `Int(6 * Rnd)`. Hence, to obtain a random integer that is uniformly distributed between 1 and 6, we simply add 1 to this expression; that is, we write `1 + Int(6 * Rnd)`. The value returned by this expression will represent the result of throwing a single die. To simulate throwing a pair of dice, we repeat the random number generation; that is, we evaluate the above expression twice, once for each die. (Remember that *each reference to* Rnd *will return a different random value.*) The strategy fits very naturally into the Visual Basic function procedure ThrowDice presented below.

```
Public Function ThrowDice() As Integer
    Dim d1 As Integer, d2 As Integer

    d1 = 1 + Int(6 * Rnd)      'first die
    d2 = 1 + Int(6 * Rnd)      'second die
    ThrowDice = d1 + d2
End Function
```

This function will return a randomly generated integer quantity whose value varies between 2 and 12 each time it is accessed. (Note that the sum of the two random integers will *not* be uniformly distributed, even though the values assigned to d1 and d2 are.)

In order to incorporate this function into an interactive game, we will utilize two different forms – one that shows the cumulative number of wins and losses and initiates a new game or terminates the computation, and a second form that shows the history of each individual game (see Fig. 7.18. The preliminary control layouts are shown in Figs. 7.18(*a*) and 7.18(*b*).

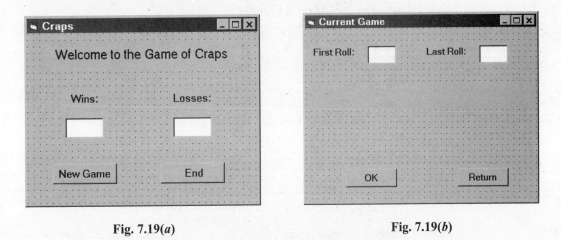

Fig. 7.18(*a*)   Fig. 7.18(*b*)

Our goal will be to transform the appearance of these forms into the forms shown in Figs. 7.19(*a*) and (*b*).

Fig. 7.19(*a*)   Fig. 7.19(*b*)

To do so, we will assign the following initial values to the control and form properties.

Object	Property	Value
Form1	Caption	"Craps"
Form1.Label1	Caption	"Welcome to the Game of Craps"
	Font	MS Sans Serif, 12-point
	Alignment	2 - Center
Form1.Label2	Caption	"Wins:"
	Font	MS Sans Serif, 10-point
	Alignment	2 - Center
Form1.Label3	Caption	"Losses:"
	Font	MS Sans Serif, 10-point
	Alignment	2 - Center
Form1.Text1	Caption	(none)
	Font	MS Sans Serif, 10-point
	Alignment	2 - Center
Form1.Text2	Caption	(none)
	Font	MS Sans Serif, 10-point
	Alignment	2 - Center
Form1.Command1	Caption	"New Game"
	Font	MS Sans Serif, 10-point
Form1.Command2	Caption	"End"
	Font	MS Sans Serif, 10-point
	Alignment	2 - Center
Form2	Caption	"Current Game"
Form2.Label1	Caption	"First Roll:"
	Font	MS Sans Serif, 10-point
	Alignment	2 - Center
Form2.Label2	Caption	"Last Roll:"
	Font	MS Sans Serif, 10-point
	Alignment	2 - Center
Form2.Label3	Caption	(none)
	Font	MS Sans Serif, 12-point
	Alignment	2 - Center
Form2.Text1	Caption	(none)
	Font	MS Sans Serif, 10-point
	Alignment	2 - Center
Form2.Text2	Caption	(none)
	Font	MS Sans Serif, 10-point
	Alignment	2 - Center
Form2.Command1	Caption	"OK"
	Font	MS Sans Serif, 10-point
Form2.Command2	Caption	"Return"
	Font	MS Sans Serif, 10-point
	Alignment	2 - Center

The required declarations and procedures for Form1 are shown next.

```
        Public FirstScore As Integer, NextScore As Integer
        Public Wins As Integer, Losses As Integer

        Public Function ThrowDice() As Integer
            Dim d1 As Integer, d2 As Integer

            d1 = 1 + Int(6 * Rnd)      'first die
            d2 = 1 + Int(6 * Rnd)      'second die
            ThrowDice = d1 + d2
        End Function

        Private Sub Form_Load()
            Wins = 0
            Losses = 0
            Text1.Text = "0"
            Text2.Text = "0"
            Randomize
        End Sub

        Private Sub Command1_Click()
            FirstScore = ThrowDice()
            Form2.Label2.Enabled = False
            Form2.Text2.Enabled = False
            Form2.Command1.Enabled = False
            Form2.Command2.Enabled = True
            Form2.Text1.Text = Str(FirstScore)
            Form2.Text2.Text = ""
            If (FirstScore = 7 Or FirstScore = 11) Then
                Form2.Label3.Caption = "Congratulations! You Win on the First Throw"
                Wins = Wins + 1
            ElseIf (FirstScore = 2 Or FirstScore = 3 Or FirstScore = 12) Then
                Form2.Label3.Caption = "Sorry, You Lose on the First Throw"
                Losses = Losses + 1
            Else
                Form2.Label3.Caption = "Please Throw the Dice Again"
                Form2.Label2.Enabled = True
                Form2.Text2.Enabled = True
                Form2.Command1.Enabled = True
                Form2.Command2.Enabled = False
            End If
            Form2.Show
        End Sub

        Private Sub Command2_Click()
            End
        End Sub
```

The code begins by declaring FirstScore, NextScore, Wins and Losses as public integer variables. Hence, these variables can be accessed anywhere within the project. Following the declarations, we see the definition of function ThrowDice, which we already discussed.

The remaining code comprises three event procedures – Form1_Load, Command1_Click and Command2_Click. The first of these, Form1_Load, simply sets the initial number of wins and losses to zero, and initializes the random number generator.

The second event procedure, `Command1_Click`, is more complicated. It first rolls the dice once, and then initializes a number of controls within Form2. the `If-ElseIf-Else` structure contains appropriate assignments for an initial win within each game, and an initial loss within each game. In the event that the first roll of the dice does not result in either a win or a loss, the controls within Form2 are reset, in preparation for additional rolls of the dice. Then the result of the initial roll is displayed in Form2.

Finally, the last event procedure, `Command2_Click`, simply ends the computation.

Now let us turn our attention to the event procedures associated with Form2, as shown below.

```
Private Sub Command1_Click()
    NextScore = Form1.ThrowDice()
    Text2.Text = Str(NextScore)

    If (NextScore = Form1.FirstScore) Then
        Label3.Caption = "You Win"
        Form1.Wins = Form1.Wins + 1
        Command1.Enabled = False
        Command2.Enabled = True
    ElseIf (NextScore = 7) Then
        Label3.Caption = "You Lose"
        Form1.Losses = Form1.Losses + 1
        Command1.Enabled = False
        Command2.Enabled = True
    End If

End Sub

Private Sub Command2_Click()
    Form1.Text1 = Str(Form1.Wins)
    Form1.Text2 = Str(Form1.Losses)
    Form2.Hide
End Sub
```

Within Form2, command button `Command1` will be active only if additional rolls of the dice are required (because the first roll resulted in neither a win nor a loss). `Command1_Click` simulates one additional roll of the dice. If this roll results in a win, the wins counter is incremented, an appropriate message is displayed, `Command1` is disabled, and `Command2` is enabled. And if the additional roll results in a loss, the losses counter is incremented, a message is displayed, `Command1` is disabled, and `Command2` is enabled. On the other hand, if the additional roll results in neither a win nor a loss, nothing happens, because another roll of the dice will be required. Hence, `Command1` remains enabled and `Command2` remains disabled.

Unfortunately, the logic within the code is not as clear as it might be, because of the numerous statements that either enable or disable certain controls (specifically, Label2, Text2, and the two command buttons) within Form2. This situation can be remedied somewhat by introducing four additional sub procedures that enable or disable the Form2 controls. We can also add a sub procedure to carry out the initial assignments within Form1. Here is the modified code, with the additional procedures (called `Initialize`, `SetButtons`, `ResetButtons`, `SetLastRoll` and `ResetLastRoll`) added to the Form1 code.

Form1

```
Public FirstScore As Integer, NextScore As Integer
Public Wins As Integer, Losses As Integer
```

(Continues on next page)

```
Private Sub Initialize()
    Wins = 0
    Losses = 0
    Text1.Text = "0"
    Text2.Text = "0"
    Randomize
End Sub

Public Sub SetButtons()
    Form2.Command1.Enabled = False
    Form2.Command2.Enabled = True
End Sub

Public Sub ResetButtons()
    Form2.Command1.Enabled = True
    Form2.Command2.Enabled = False
End Sub

Private Sub SetLastRoll()
    Form2.Label2.Enabled = False
    Form2.Text2.Enabled = False
End Sub

Private Sub ResetLastRoll()
    Form2.Label2.Enabled = True
    Form2.Text2.Enabled = True
End Sub

Public Function ThrowDice() As Integer
    Dim d1 As Integer, d2 As Integer

    d1 = 1 + Int(6 * Rnd)
    d2 = 1 + Int(6 * Rnd)
    ThrowDice = d1 + d2
End Function

Private Sub Form_Load()
    Initialize
End Sub

Private Sub Command1_Click()
    FirstScore = ThrowDice()
    SetLastRoll
    SetButtons
    Form2.Text1.Text = Str(FirstScore)
    Form2.Text2.Text = ""
    If (FirstScore = 7 Or FirstScore = 11) Then
        Form2.Label3.Caption = "Congratulations! You Win on the First Throw"
        Wins = Wins + 1
    ElseIf (FirstScore = 2 Or FirstScore = 3 Or FirstScore = 12) Then
        Form2.Label3.Caption = "Sorry, You Lose on the First Throw"
        Losses = Losses + 1
```

(Continues on next page)

```
        Else
            Form2.Label3.Caption = "Please Throw the Dice Again"
            ResetLastRoll
            ResetButtons
        End If
        Form2.Show
    End Sub


Private Sub Command2_Click()
    End
End Sub
```

Form2

```
Private Sub Command1_Click()
    NextScore = Form1.ThrowDice()
    Text2.Text = Str(NextScore)

    If (NextScore = Form1.FirstScore) Then
        Label3.Caption = "You Win"
        Form1.Wins = Form1.Wins + 1
        Form1.SetButtons
    ElseIf (NextScore = 7) Then
        Label3.Caption = "You Lose"
        Form1.Losses = Form1.Losses + 1
        Form1.SetButtons
    End If

End Sub


Private Sub Command2_Click()
    Form1.Text1 = Str(Form1.Wins)
    Form1.Text2 = Str(Form1.Losses)
    Form2.Hide
End Sub
```

Finally, it may be desirable to place the global declarations (FirstScore, NextScore, Wins and Losses), the function procedure (ThrowDice), and the sub procedures (Initialize, SetButtons, ResetButtons, SetLastRoll and ResetLastRoll) within a separate module. Here is the code based upon this modification.

Module1

```
Public FirstScore As Integer, NextScore As Integer
Public Wins As Integer, Losses As Integer


Public Function ThrowDice() As Integer
    Dim d1 As Integer, d2 As Integer

    d1 = 1 + Int(6 * Rnd)
    d2 = 1 + Int(6 * Rnd)
    ThrowDice = d1 + d2
End Function
```

```
    Public Sub SetButtons()
        Form2.Command1.Enabled = False
        Form2.Command2.Enabled = True
    End Sub

    Public Sub ResetButtons()
        Form2.Command1.Enabled = True
        Form2.Command2.Enabled = False
    End Sub

    Public Sub SetLastRoll()
        Form2.Label2.Enabled = False
        Form2.Text2.Enabled = False
    End Sub

    Public Sub ResetLastRoll()
        Form2.Label2.Enabled = True
        Form2.Text2.Enabled = True
    End Sub

    Public Sub Initialize()
        Wins = 0
        Losses = 0
        Form1.Text1.Text = "0"
        Form1.Text2.Text = "0"
        Randomize
    End Sub
```

Form1

```
    Private Sub Form_Load()
        Initialize
    End Sub

    Private Sub Command1_Click()
        FirstScore = ThrowDice()
        SetLastRoll
        SetButtons
        Form2.Text1.Text = Str(FirstScore)
        Form2.Text2.Text = ""
        If (FirstScore = 7 Or FirstScore = 11) Then
            Form2.Label3.Caption = "Congratulations! You Win on the First Throw"
            Wins = Wins + 1
        ElseIf (FirstScore = 2 Or FirstScore = 3 Or FirstScore = 12) Then
            Form2.Label3.Caption = "Sorry, You Lose on the First Throw"
            Losses = Losses + 1
        Else
            Form2.Label3.Caption = "Please Throw the Dice Again"
            ResetLastRoll
            ResetButtons
        End If
        Form2.Show
    End Sub
```

```
Private Sub Command2_Click()
    End
End Sub
```

Form2

```
Private Sub Command1_Click()
    NextScore = ThrowDice()
    Text2.Text = Str(NextScore)

    If (NextScore = FirstScore) Then
        Label3.Caption = "You Win"
        Wins = Wins + 1
        SetButtons
    ElseIf (NextScore = 7) Then
        Label3.Caption = "You Lose"
        Losses = Losses + 1
        SetButtons
    End If

End Sub

Private Sub Command2_Click()
    Form1.Text1 = Str(Wins)
    Form1.Text2 = Str(Losses)
    Form2.Hide
End Sub
```

Notice that the declarations and procedure definitions within Module1 are all Public, so that they can be accessed within both Form1 and Form2. Also, note that the references to the various procedures are written somewhat differently in this version of the code, since the procedure definitions and the procedure references are contained in different modules.

Fig. 7.20 shows the opening dialog box when the program is executed. Clicking on New Game will result in another dialog box, similar to that shown in Fig. 7.21. (Fig. 7.21 shows the dialog box that results from winning on the first throw. Other dialog boxes are similar.) Note that the only choice shown in Fig. 7.21 is to return to the opening dialog box, since this particular game has ended with a win. Also, note that the "last roll" (i.e., the roll following the first roll) box is disabled, since this particular game required only one roll of the dice.

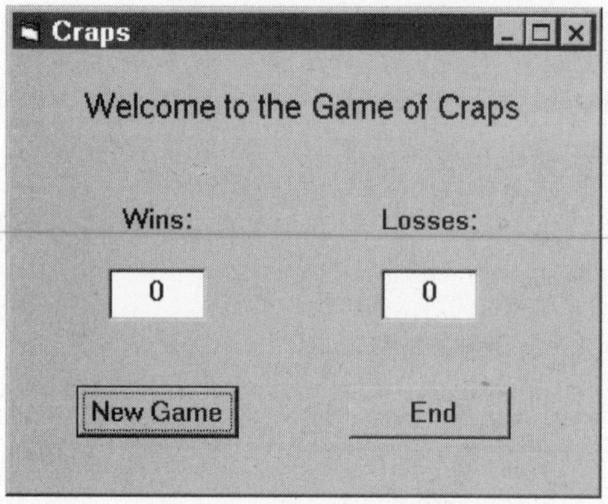

Fig. 7.20

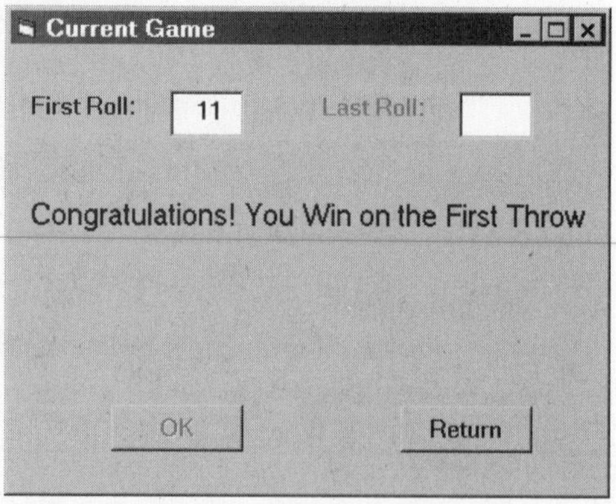

Fig. 7.21

If the first roll of the dice results in neither a win nor a loss, a succession of dialog boxes similar to that shown in Fig. 7.22 will appear until a win or a loss is finally encountered, as shown in Fig. 7.23. While the game is in progress, the only choice shown in Fig. 7.22 is OK (meaning throw the dice again). This continues until the game has ended.

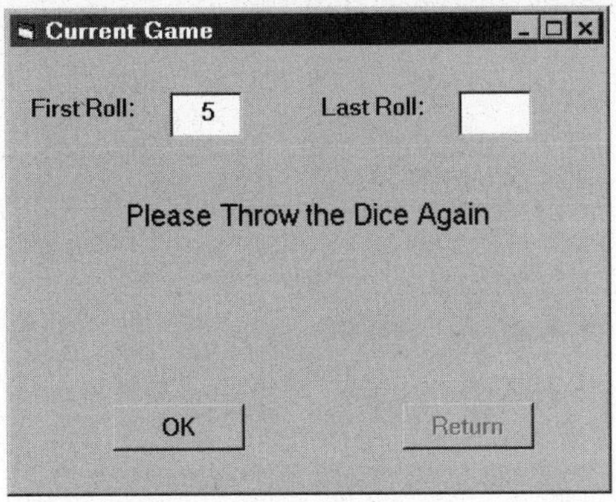

Fig. 7.22 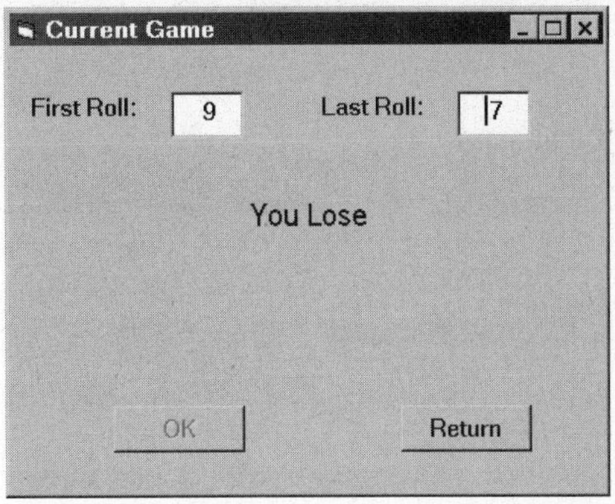　　　　　　　　　　　　　　　　**Fig. 7.23**

Once the game has ended, the OK button is disabled and the Return button becomes active, as shown in Fig. 7.23. (Note that the message has changed, indicating a win or a loss.) When the user clicks on the Return button, the original dialog box will reappear showing the current number of wins and losses, as shown in Fig. 7.24.

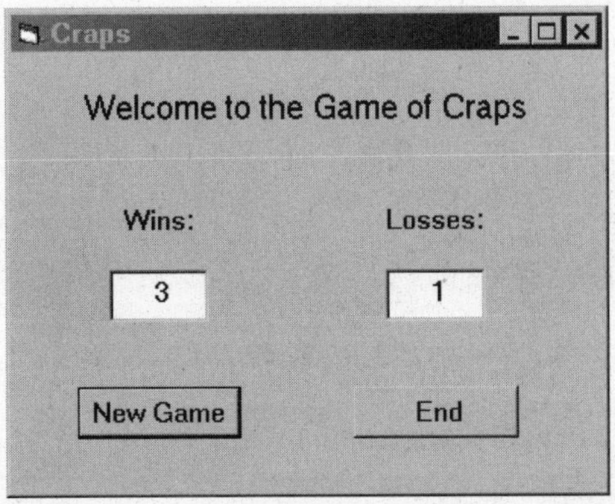

Fig. 7.24

All three versions of this project produce the same output, as shown in Figs. 7.20 through 7.24. Hence, the coding style is transparent to the user, as expected. From a programmer's perspective, however, it is instructive to compare all three versions of the code, particularly the global declarations, the procedure definitions, and the procedure references. There are subtle differences in the use of Public and Private declarations, and in the manner in which the procedures and global variables are accessed in various places within the code.

7.6 OPTIONAL ARGUMENTS

When accessing a procedure, the passing of one or more arguments can be made optional. To do so, each optional argument declaration within the first line of the procedure definition must be preceded by the keyword Optional. For example, if a sub procedure is defined with one mandatory argument and one optional argument, the first line of the procedure declaration will be

Sub *procedure name* (*argument1* As *data type1*, Optional *argument2* As *data type2*)

(The declaration could, of course, begin with the keyword `Private` or the keyword `Public`, as discussed in Sec. 7.5.) Function procedures are defined in the same manner. Optional arguments must always follow mandatory arguments in the argument list.

A default value may be specified for each optional argument, by writing

Optional *argument* As *data type* = *value*

The default value will be assigned to the argument if an actual argument value is not provided in the procedure reference.

EXAMPLE 7.11

Here is a skeletal outline showing a function procedure that utilizes an optional argument.

```
Private Function Sample(x As Integer, Optional y As Integer = 999) As Integer

    Sample = x ^ 2

    If (y = 999) Then       'bypass remaining calculations
        Exit Function
    Else                     'modify result using optional argument
        Sample = x ^ 2 + y ^ 2
    EndIf
End Function
```

Note that the second argument, y, is optional and is assigned a default value of 999.

If this function is accessed with only one argument, e.g.,

```
n = Sample(3)
```

it will return a value of 9. However, if the function is accessed with two arguments, e.g.,

```
n = Sample(3, 4)
```

it will return a value of 25.

Here is a sub version of the same procedure.

```
Private Sub Sample(x As Integer, z As Integer, Optional y As Integer = 999)

    z = x ^ 2

    If (y = 999) Then       'bypass remaining calculations
        Exit Function
    Else                     'modify result using optional argument
        z = x ^ 2 + y ^ 2
    EndIf
End Function
```

Note that the optional argument (y) appears at the end of the list of arguments, as required.

If this procedure is accessed as

```
Sample(3, 0)
```

it will assign a value of 9 to the second argument (z). But if the procedure access is written as

        Sample(3, 0, 4)

then the second argument will be assigned a value of 25.

Review Questions

7.1 What is a module in Visual Basic? How do form modules differ from general modules?

7.2 What is the difference between a module and a procedure?

7.3 Name three significant advantages to the use of procedures.

7.4 What is the difference between a sub procedure and an event procedure?

7.5 What is the difference between a sub procedure and a function procedure?

7.6 How are sub procedures named? Does a sub procedure name represent a data item?

7.7 What is the purpose of arguments? Are arguments required in every procedure?

7.8 How are arguments written within the first line of a procedure definition?

7.9 Summarize the rules for writing the first and last lines of a sub procedure.

7.10 Cite two different ways to access a sub procedure.

7.11 Describe the correspondence that is required between the arguments in a procedure access and the arguments that appear in a procedure definition.

7.12 What is meant by passing an argument by reference?

7.13 What is meant by passing an argument by value? How does this differ from passing an argument by reference?

7.14 What type of argument passing (i.e., by reference or by value) does Visual Basic employ as a default?

7.15 Within the first line of a procedure definition, how can you specify that an argument will be passed by reference? How can you specify that it will be passed by value?

7.16 Can a single procedure include some arguments that are passed by reference and other arguments that are passed by value?

7.17 Can arguments be utilized within an event procedure?

7.18 When defining an event procedure, how can the event type be associated with the procedure code?

7.19 How are function procedures named? Does a function procedure name represent a data item? Compare with the rules that apply to the naming of sub procedures.

7.20 Summarize the rules for writing the first and last lines of a function procedure. Compare with the rules that apply to sub procedures.

7.21 Why would a function procedure name be assigned a value? Can a sub procedure name be assigned a value?

7.22 Can a function procedure name be assigned a value at more than one location within a function procedure?

7.23 How is a function procedure accessed? Compare with the methods used to access a sub procedure.

7.24 What is meant by the scope of a procedure? How is the scope of a procedure affected by use of the keywords `Public` and `Private` in the first line of the procedure definition?

7.25 What is meant by the scope of a variable? How is the scope of a variable affected by use of the keywords Public and Private in the variable declaration?

7.26 How can a variable within a procedure be made to retain its assigned value after the procedure has been executed and control is returned to the calling portion of the program?

7.27 How can all varibles within a procedure be made to retain their assigned values after the procedure has been executed and control is returned to the calling portion of the program? Compare with the answer to the preceding question.

7.28 How can control be transferred out of a procedure without executing all of the instructions within the procedure?

7.29 When accessing a procedure, how can the passing of one or more arguments be made optional?

7.30 Where must optional arguments be placed within a procedure definition, relative to required arguments?

7.31 How is an optional argument assigned a default value within a procedure definition?

Problems

7.32 Write a function procedure for each of the situations described below.

  (*a*) Evaluate the algebraic formula

$$p = \log (t^2 - a) \quad \text{if } t^2 > a$$

$$p = \log (t^2) \quad \text{if } t^2 \leq a$$

  (*b*) Suppose that L1 and L2 each represent a single letter. Construct a single string containing the two letters, arranged in alphabetical order.

  (*c*) Calculate the average of two random numbers, each having a value between *a* and *b*.

  (*d*) Examine the sign of the number represented by the variable X. If the value of X is negative, return the string Negative; if the value of X is positive, return the string Positive; and if the value of X is zero, return the string Zero.

  (*e*) Suppose Word represents a string that is a multiletter word. Examine each of the letters and return the letter that comes first in the alphabet. *Hint*: Use the Len function to determine the word length, and the Mid function to examine each individual character.

7.33   Each of the situations described below requires a reference to one of the functions defined in Prob. 7.32. Write an appropriate statement, or a sequence of statements, in each case.

(*a*)   Assign a value to *q*, where *q* is evaluated as

$$\log [(a + b)^2 - c] \qquad \text{if } (a + b)^2 > c,$$

and

$$\log [(a + b)^2] \qquad \text{if } (a + b)^2 \le c \qquad \text{[see Prob. 7.32(}a\text{)].}$$

(*b*)   Suppose LC1 and LC2 each represent a lowercase letter. Form an uppercase string consisting of the two letters, arranged in alphabetical order [see Prob. 7.32(*b*)].

(*c*)   Determine the average of two random numbers, each having a value between 1 and 10. Assign this result to V1. Then determine the average of two additional random numbers, each bounded between 1 and 10. Assign this result to V2. Then determine the average of V1 and V2 [see Prob. 7.32(*c*)].

(*d*)   Repeat problem (*c*) using only one expression to obtain the final average. (*Note*: In this case, the variables V1 and V2 will not be required.)

(*e*)   Determine the average of two random numbers, each having a value between −1 and 1. Then determine whether the resulting average is positive, negative, or zero. Display an appropriate message box indicating the result [see Probs. 7.32(*c*) and (*d*)].

7.34   Write a sub procedure for each of the situations described below.

(*a*)   Examine the sign of the number represented by the variable X. If the value of X is negative, return the string Negative; if the value is positive, return the string Positive; and if the value is zero, return the string Zero [compare with Prob. 7.32(*d*)].

(*b*)   Suppose a, b, c and d all represent integer arguments. If d is assigned a value of 1, rearrange the values of a, b and c into ascending order. If d = 2, rearrange a, b and c in descending order. And if d is assigned any other value, return values of 0 for a, b and c.

(*c*)   Suppose a, b, c and d all represent real, single-precision arguments. Evaluate each of the following formulas:

$$c = \sqrt{a^2 + b^2}\ , \qquad d = \sqrt{ab}$$

7.35   Each of the situations described below requires a reference to one of the procedures defined in Prob. 7.34. Write an appropriate statement, or a sequence of statements, in each case.

(*a*)   Generate a random value bounded between −1 and 1, and determine its sign. Then display a message box indicating Negative, Positive or Zero [see Prob. 7.34(*a*)].

(*b*)   Access the sub procedure written in Prob. 7.34(*b*) two different ways.

(*c*)   Assign two positive, single-precision values to a and b, and access the sub procedure written in Prob. 7.34(*c*), returning values for c and d. Then access the procedure again, supplying these values of c and d. (This will return two new values for c and d.)

7.36 Determine the result of each of the following program segments.

   (*a*)
```
Function Fix(Message As String) As String
    Fix = "'" + Message + "'"
End Function

. . . . .
Message = "Hello, There!"
Text = Fix(Message)
```

   (*b*)
```
Function Square(y As Single) As Single
    Square = y ^ 2 + 2 * y + 3
End Function

. . . . .
x = 2
z = Square(x)
```

   (*c*)
```
Function Square(y As Single) As Single
    Square = y ^ 2 + 2 * y + 3
End Function

. . . . .
x = 2
z = Square(Square(x))
. . . . .
```

   (*d*)
```
Function frm(a As Single, b As Single, c As Single, y As Single)As Single
    If (a < 2) Then
        Formula = a * y ^ 3 - b * y + c / y
    Else
        Formula = a * y ^ 2 + b * y + c
    End If
End Function

. . . . .
z = frm(3, 4, 5, 2)
. . . . .
```

   (*e*)
```
Function Scramble(Message As String) As String
    Dim NewStr As String, c As String, i As Integer, n As Integer

    NewStr = ""
    n = Len(Message)
    For i = 1 To n
        c = Mid(Message, i, 1)
        NewStr = NewStr & Chr(Asc(c) + 1)
    Next i
    Scramble = NewStr
End Function

. . . . .
Message = "Hello, There!"
Message = Scramble(Message)
. . . . .
```

```
(f)  Sub Change(Message As String)
         Dim a As String, b As String, n As Integer, i As Integer

         n = Len(Message)
         a = ""
         For i = 1 To n
             b = Mid(Message, i, 1)
             If (b >= "A" And b <= "Z") Then
                 a = a + Lcase(b)
             ElseIf (b >= "a" And b <= "z") Then
                 a = a + Ucase(b)
             Else
                 a = a + b
             End If
         Next i
         Message = a
     End Sub

     Dim Str1 As String, Str2 As String, Str3 As String
     . . . . .
     Str1 = "1600 Pennsylvania Avenue NW, Washington, DC 20500"
     Call Change(Str1)
     Str2 = Str1
     Call change(Str1)
     Str3 = Str1
     . . . . .

(g)  Sub Sum(Total As Integer, n2 As Integer, Optional n1 As Integer = 1)
         Dim i As Integer

         Total = 0
         For i = n1 to n2
             Total = Total + i
         Next i
     End Sub

     Dim First As Integer, Second As Integer, Total As Integer
     . . . . .
     Call Sum(Total, 6)
     First = Total
     . . . . .
     Sum Total, 6, 3
     Second = Total
     . . . . .
```

Programming Problems

7.37 Rewrite the program shown in Example 7.3 so that it utilizes a function procedure rather than a sub procedure. Execute the program to verify that it is written correctly.

7.38 Rewrite the program shown in Example 7.6 so that it utilizes a sub procedure rather than a function procedure to determine the factorial. Which type of procedure is best suited to this particular problem?

7.39   Rewrite the program shown in Example 7.7 so that it utilizes the sub procedure written for Prob. 7.38. Execute the program to verify that it is written correctly.

7.40   Modify the program shown in Example 7.10 (shooting craps) so that the function procedure ThrowDice is replaced by a sub procedure.

7.41   Redesign the program shown in Example 7.10 so that a *sequence* of craps games will be simulated automatically and noninteractively. Enter the total number of games as an input quantity. Execute the program to simulate 1000 successive craps games. Use the results to estimate the probability of coming out ahead when playing multiple games of craps. (This value, expressed as a decimal, is the total number of wins divided by the total number of games played. If the probability exceeds 0.5, it favors the player; otherwise, it favors the house.)

7.42   Modify each of the following examples presented in previous chapters so that it utilizes one or more programmer-defined sub or function procedures.

   (*a*)   The piggy bank program shown in Example 4.5.

   (*b*)   The multilingual "hello" program shown in Example 4.6.

   (*c*)   The temperature conversion program shown in Example 4.7.

   (*d*)   The modified temperature conversion program shown in Example 4.8.

   (*e*)   The metronome program shown in Example 4.12.

   (*f*)   The geography program shown in Example 5.4.

   (*g*)   The modified multilingual "hello" program shown in Example 5.7.

   (*h*)   The loan program shown in Example 6.2 (using the corrected version of the code).

   (*i*)   The program to determine the real roots of a quadratic equation shown in Example 6.3.

7.43   Write a complete Visual Basic program for each of the following problems that were originally described in earlier chapters. Include one or more sub procedures and/or function procedures in each program.

   (*a*)   Enter a positive integer and determine whether it is even or odd, and whether or not it is a prime number (see Prob. 4.46).

   (*b*)   Calculate the arithmetic average of a list of *n* numbers (see Prob. 4.49).

   (*c*)   Determine the capital of a country, or select a capital and determine the corresponding country (see Prob. 4.51).

   (*d*)   Convert between U.S. and foreign currencies (see Prob. 4.52).

   (*e*)   Calculate the amount of money that accumulates in a savings account after *n* years (see Prob. 4.55).

   (*f*)   Repeat Prob. 7.43(*e*) using the single, generalized compound interest formula discussed in Prob. 5.43.

(g) Solve the compound interest problem described in Prob. 6.47 (accumulating monthly deposits). Include a provision for either of the following features:

    (i) Determine the accumulation (F) resulting from fixed monthly payments (A) for n years.

    (ii) Determine the monthly payment (A) required to accumulate a specified amount (F) after n years.

(h) Evaluate the polynomial given in Prob. 6.52. Generalize the polynomial so that it can be evaluated using the first n terms, where n is a specified input parameter.

(i) Evaluate the area of a triangle, the radius of the largest inscribed circle, and the radius of the smallest circumscribed circle, using the formulas provided in Prob. 6.53(c).

(j) Determine the increase in the population of a bacterial culture, using the series expansion given in Prob. 6.53(d). Express the population increase in terms of the ratio P/P_0. Enter the values for c, n and t as input parameters.

Chapter 8

Arrays

8.1 ARRAY CHARACTERISTICS

Many applications require the processing of multiple data items that have common characteristics, such as a set of numerical data items represented by $x_1, x_2, \ldots, x_n$. In such situations, it is often convenient to place the data items into an *array*, where they will all share the same name (e.g., x). The data items that make up an array can be any data type, though they must all be the same data type. (An exception is the variant-type array, where each data item may be of a different data type. However, the use of variant-type arrays is generally considered a poor programming practice.)

Each individual array element (i.e., each individual data item) is referred to by specifying the array name followed by one or more *subscripts*, enclosed in parentheses. Each subscript is expressed as an integer quantity, beginning with 0. Thus, in the *n*-element array x, the array elements are x(0), x(1), ..., x(n – 1).

The number of subscripts determines the *dimensionality* of the array. For example, x(i) refers to the i*th* element in a one-dimensional array x. It is helpful to think of a one-dimensional array as a *list*, as illustrated in Fig. 8.1. (Note that Element 1 corresponds to subscript value 0, Element 2 corresponds to subscript 1, etc.)

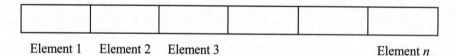

Element 1   Element 2   Element 3   Element *n*

Fig. 8.1 A one-dimensional array

Similarly, y(i, j) refers to an element in the two-dimensional array y. Think of a two-dimensional array as a *table*, where i refers to the row number and j refers to the column number, as illustrated in Fig. 8.2.

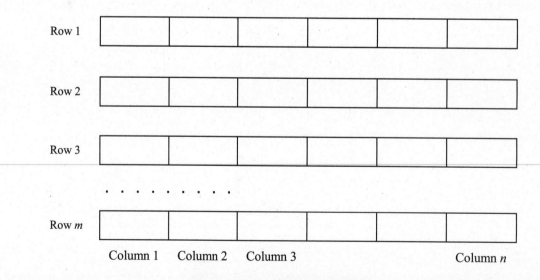

Fig. 8.2 A two-dimensional array

Higher-dimensional arrays, such as the three-dimensional array $z(i, j, k)$, are formed by specifying additional subscripts in the same manner. Note, however, that multidimensional arrays can quickly become very large, and hence require vast amounts of storage. You should therefore avoid the temptation to define multidimensional arrays that are unnecessarily large.

8.2 ARRAY DECLARATIONS

An array must be declared before it can appear within an executable statement. The `Dim` statement is used for this purpose. This statement defines the *dimensionality* (i.e., the number of subscripts), the *size* (range of each subscript), the *data type* and the *scope* of an array (see Chap. 7). Within the `Dim` statement, each array name must be followed by one or more integer constants, enclosed in parentheses. If several integer constants are present (indicating a multidimensional array), they must be separated by commas.

To declare an array within a procedure, the `Dim` statement is generally written as

> `Dim` *array name* (*subscript 1 upper limit, subscript 2 upper limit, etc.*) `As` *data type*

Within a module (but outside of a procedure), array declarations are written as

> `Private` *array name* (*subscript 1 upper limit, subscript 2 upper limit, etc.*) `As` *data type*

or

> `Public` *array name* (*subscript 1 upper limit, subscript 2 upper limit, etc.*) `As` *data type*

as discussed in Chap. 7 (see Sec. 7.5).

Each subscript normally ranges from 0 to the specified *upper limit*. Thus, the `Dim` statement

> `Dim c(10) As Integer`

defines an eleven-element integer array consisting of the data items $c(0)$, $c(1)$, $c(2)$, . . ., $c(10)$. However, the specification of a different lower limit can also be included within a `Dim` statement (or a `Public` or `Private` statement). In this case, the general form of the `Dim` statement is

> `Dim` *array name* (*subscript 1 lower limit* `To` *subscript 1 upper limit,*
> *subscript 2 lower limit* `To` *subscript 2 upper limit, etc.*) `As` *data type*

`Public` and `Private` statements are written in the same manner.

EXAMPLE 8.1

A Visual Basic module includes the following array declarations.

> `DIM Customers(200) As String, Net(100) As Single, Sales(1 To 50, 1 To 100) As Single`

This statement defines Customers to be a one-dimensional string array containing 201 elements, ranging from `Customers(0)` to `Customers(200)`. Similarly, `Net` is a one-dimensional, single-precision array containing 101 elements, and `Sales` is a two-dimensional, single-precision array containing 5,000 elements (i.e., 50 rows and 100 columns; $50 \times 100 = 5{,}000$).

In some applications, it is more natural to use arrays whose subscripts begin at 1 rather than 0. Thus, a one-dimensional, *n*-element array will range from 1 to *n* rather than 0 to *n* — a more natural selection for many programmers. The `Option Base` statement allows the lower limit for all arrays within a module to be changed to 1. This statement is written simply as

```
Option Base 1
```

`Option Base` must appear at the module level (not within a procedure), and it must precede any array declarations within the module.

EXAMPLE 8.2

A Visual Basic module includes the following array declarations.

```
Option Base 1
DIM Customers(200) As String, Net(100) As Single, Sales(50, 100) As Single
```

This statement defines `Customers` to be a one-dimensional string array containing 200 elements, ranging from `Customers(1)` to `Customers(200)`. Similarly, `Net` is a one-dimensional, single-precision array containing 100 elements, and `Sales` is a two-dimensional, single-precision array containing 5,000 elements. (Compare with Example 8.1.)

In Visual Basic, the elements of a numeric array are initialized to 0 when the array is declared. The elements of a string array are initialized as empty strings.

The elements of an array may be a user-defined data type rather than a standard data type. This is handled in the same manner as ordinary variables, as explained in Chap. 2 (see Sec. 2.4).

In general terms, the data type definition is written as

```
Type data type name
      member name 1 As data type 1
      member name 2 As data type 2
      . . . . . .
End Type
```

The array declarations can then be written as

`Dim` *array name* (*subscript 1 lower limit* `To` *subscript 1 upper limit,*
                         subscript 2 lower limit `To` *subscript 2 upper limit, etc.*) `As` *user-defined data type*

EXAMPLE 8.3

Here is a typical user-defined data type, similar to that shown in Example 2.7. Now, however, we will declare two arrays whose elements are of this type. Arrays of this type might be useful in a customer billing application.

```
Type Customer
      CustomerName As String
      AcctNo As Integer
      Balance As Single
End Type
```

Once the data type has been defined, we can declare one or more variables of this data type, as follows.

```
Dim OldCustomer(100) As Customer, NewCustomer(100) As Customer
```

8.3 PROCESSING ARRAY ELEMENTS (SUBSCRIPTED VARIABLES)

The individual elements within an array are called *subscripted variables*. Subscripted variables can be utilized within a program in the same manner as ordinary variables.

A subscripted variable can be accessed by writing the array name, followed by the value of the subscript enclosed in parentheses. Multidimensional array elements require the specification of multiple subscripts, separated by commas. The subscripts must be integer valued and they must fall within the range specified by the corresponding array declaration.

A subscript can be written as a constant, a variable or a numeric expression. Noninteger values will automatically be rounded, as required. If the value of a subscript is out of range (i.e., too large or too small), execution of the program will be suspended and an error message will appear.

EXAMPLE 8.4

All of the subscripted variable assignments shown below are written correctly.

```
Dim Names(10) As String, Values(10, 20) As Single, k(10) As Integer
Dim a As Single, b As Single, m As Integer, n As Integer
. . . . .
Names(3) = "Aaron"                     values(8, 5) = 5.5
Names(i) = "Susan"                     values(m, n) = -3.2
Names(k(i)) = "Martin"                 values(m - 1, n + 3) = m + n
Names(2 * a - b) = "Gail"              values(a + b, a - b) = 3 * a
Names(sqr(a ^ 2 + b ^ 2)) = "Sharon"   values(abs(a + b), abs(a - b)) = a + b
```

Some of the subscripts may not be integer valued as written. In such cases, the noninteger values will automatically be rounded. Suppose, for example, the numeric expression (2 * a - b) has a value of 4.2. Then the subscripted variable Names(2 * a - b) will be interpreted as Names(4). Similarly, if (2 * a - b) has a value of 4.7, then the subscripted variable Names(2 * a - b) will be interpreted as Names(5).

Within a user-defined array, the individual components (members) of a subscripted variable can be accessed as

   array name (*subscript*) . *member name*

These components can be used in the same manner as ordinary variables. Thus, they can appear within expressions, and they can be assigned values (see Secs. 2.5 and 2.10).

EXAMPLE 8.5

Consider the user-defined data type and the accompanying arrays, first introduced in Example 8.3; i.e.,

```
Type Customer
    CustomerName As String
    AcctNo As Integer
    Balance As Single
End Type

Dim OldCustomer(100) As Customer, NewCustomer(100) As Customer
Dim i As Integer, j As Integer
```

We can assign values to the members of the subscripted variables in the following manner.

```
OldCustomer(5).CustomerName = "Smith"      NewCustomer(2).CustomerName = "Jones"

OldCustomer(i).AcctNo = 1215               NewCustomer(j).AcctNo = 1610

OldCustomer(i + 3).Balance = 44.75         NewCustomer(i + j).Balance = 187.32
```

and so on.

EXAMPLE 8.6 MULTILINGUAL HELLO USING AN ARRAY

Here is a variation of Example 4.9, in which the user selects a language from a combo box and an appropriate "hello" greeting is displayed within a text box. In Example 4.9 we used a Select Case structure to place the proper greeting in the text box. Now we will simplify the code by placing the greetings in an array, and then assigning the proper array element to the text box.

Recapping from Example 4.9, Fig. 8.3 shows the preliminary Form Design Window layout. Fig. 8.4 shows the Form Design Window after assigning the initial property values listed below.

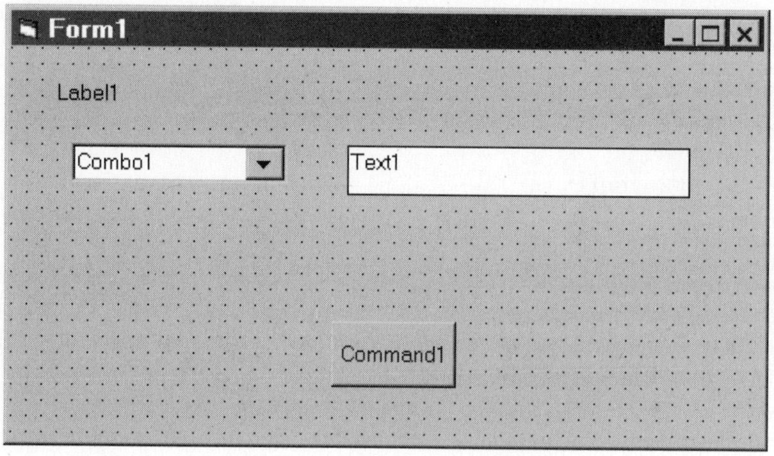

Fig. 8.3

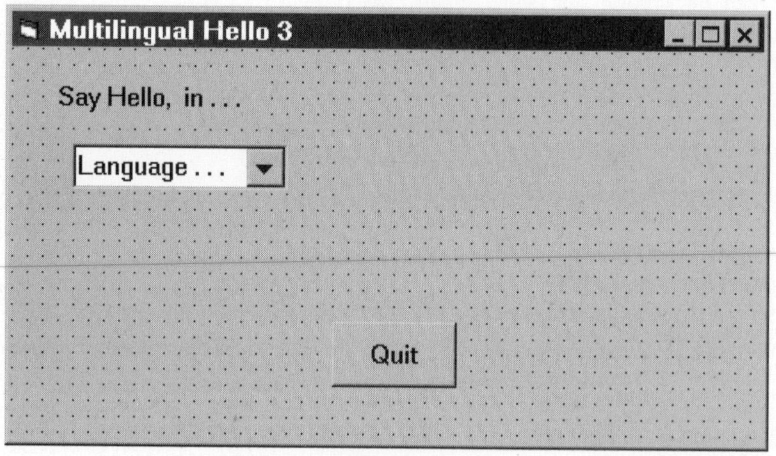

Fig. 8.4

Object	Property	Value
Form1	Caption	"Multilingual Hello 3"
Label1	Caption	"Say Hello, in . . ."
	Font	MS Sans Serif, 10-point
Combo1	Text	"Language . . ."
	List	"French" (press Control-Enter after each list entry)
		"German"
		"Hawaiian"
		"Hebrew"
		"Italian"
		"Japanese"
		"Spanish"
	Font	MS Sans Serif, 10-point
Text1	Text	(blank)
	BackColor	Gray
	BorderStyle	0 – None
	Font	MS Sans Serif, 14-point
Command1	Caption	"Quit"
	Font	MS Sans Serif, 10-point

Now consider the event procedure associated with the combo box.

```
Private Sub Combo1_Click()
    Dim Hello(6) As String

    'assign the array elements
    Hello(0) = "Bonjour"
    Hello(1) = "Guten Tag"
    Hello(2) = "Aloha"
    Hello(3) = "Shalom"
    Hello(4) = "Buon Giorno"
    Hello(5) = "Konichihua"
    Hello(6) = "Buenos Dias"

    'assign one array element to the text box
    Text1.Text = Hello(Combo1.ListIndex)
End Sub
```

This procedure first assigns the appropriate greetings to the array elements. The appropriate array element is then assigned to Text1.Text, as determined by the value of Combo1.ListIndex. (Note that the value assigned to Combo1.ListIndex is determined at run time, when the user clicks on an entry within the combo box.)

It is interesting to compare this event procedure with the corresponding event procedure shown in Example 4.9. The present version is shorter and logically more straightforward, since the Select Case structure is not required. In general, the degree of simplification obtained by using arrays increases with the complexity of the code.

The command button is used to end the computation. Hence, its event procedure is very simple, as shown below.

```
Private Sub Command1_Click()
    End
End Sub
```

When the program is executed, the combo box appears, showing the title Language . . . in the text-box area, as shown in Fig. 8.5. The user may then click on the downward-pointing arrow, resulting in the list of languages shown in Fig. 8.6. When the user selects one of these entries, the corresponding greeting appears within the text box, to the right of the drop-down window.

Fig. 8.7 shows what happens when the user selects Italian from the list in the drop-down window. Thus, we see that the "hello" greeting in Italian is "Buon Giorno."

Fig. 8.5

Fig. 8.6

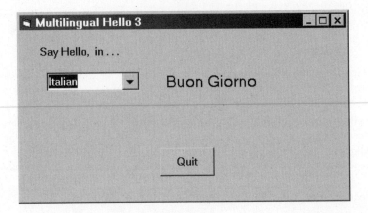

Fig. 8.7

Before leaving this example, we present another way to write the event procedures. In principle, this method is more efficient, since the array elements are assigned their string values only once, when the form is loaded. As a practical matter, however, either version of the code will behave in the same manner.

```vb
Dim Hello(6) As String

Private Sub Form_Load()
    'initialize the array elements
    Hello(0) = "Bonjour"
    Hello(1) = "Guten Tag"
    Hello(2) = "Aloha"
    Hello(3) = "Shalom"
    Hello(4) = "Buon Giorno"
    Hello(5) = "Konichihua"
    Hello(6) = "Buenos Dias"
End Sub

Private Sub Combo1_Click()
    Text1.Text = Hello(Combo1.ListIndex)
End Sub

Private Sub Command1_Click()
    End
End Sub
```

8.4 PASSING ARRAYS TO PROCEDURES

Arrays can be passed to procedures as arguments, in much the same manner as ordinary variables are passed as arguments. If an argument is an array, however, an empty pair of parentheses must follow the array name. This requirement must be satisfied in both the procedure access and the first line of the procedure definition, as illustrated in the following example.

EXAMPLE 8.7 PASSING AN ENTIRE ARRAY TO A PROCEDURE

Here is a skeletal structure of a Visual Basic program that passes an entire array to a sub procedure. The first n elements are then assigned numerical values within the procedure.

Note that the array is called x in the calling portion of the program, and v within the procedure. This is permissible, as long as the array arguments are of the same size and the same data type, and they appear in the same relative location within each argument list.

```vb
Dim x(10) As Integer, n As Integer
. . . . .
n = . . . . .
Call Setup(x(), n)        'procedure reference
'or Setup x(), n

Private Sub Setup(v() As Integer, n As Integer)        'procedure definition
    Dim i As Integer
    For i = 0 to n
        v(i) = i ^ 2
    Next i
End Sub
```

Since the array elements are passed by reference, the values assigned to the array elements within the procedure will be recognized elsewhere within the program (e.g., in the calling portion of the program).

Individual array elements (i.e., subscripted variables) may also be passed to procedures as arguments. Subscripted variables are written in the normal manner when they appear as arguments within a procedure reference. The corresponding arguments in the first line of the procedure definition may be either subscripted variables or ordinary variables, depending on the program logic.

EXAMPLE 8.8 PASSING ARRAY ELEMENTS TO A PROCEDURE

This example illustrates how subscripted variables are passed to a procedure as arguments. In this case, we will assign single-precision values to the array elements 1 through 100 within the calling portion of the program. We then pass two consecutive array elements to the procedure, which returns the square root of the sum of their squares. This value is assigned to the first array element (i.e., array element $x(0)$).

```
Dim x(100) As Single, i As Integer, n As Integer

For i = 1 To 100
    x(i) = i                          'assign values to the array elements
Next i
. . . . .
n = . . . . .                         'assign a value to n
x(0) = Hypotenuse(x(n), x(n + 1))     'function reference
. . . . .

Private Function Hypotenuse(a As Single, b As Single) As Single   'function definition
    Hypotenuse = Sqr(a ^ 2 + b ^ 2)
End Function
```

If n is assigned a value of 3, what value will be assigned to $x(0)$?

In the next example we see a complete Visual Basic project that passes both an entire array and a single array element as arguments.

EXAMPLE 8.9 SMALLEST OF TWO NUMBERS

In Example 7.2 we saw a complete Visual Basic program allowing the user to enter two numbers. The program determined the smaller of the two and displayed the result within a message box. Here is a variation of that program in which we utilize a three-element, one-dimensional array x to hold the numbers. We will place the two input values in elements $x(1)$ and $x(2)$, and then "tag" the smaller value by placing it in $x(0)$, which we will then send to a message box.

The user interface will be unchanged from Example 7.2. Hence, the control layout will be identical to that shown in Figs. 7.1 and 7.2. Here is the new source code.

```
Dim x(2) As Single

Private Sub Command1_Click()
    x(1) = Val(Text1.Text)
    x(2) = Val(Text2.Text)
    Call Smallest(x())
End Sub
```

(*Continues on next page*)

```
        Private Sub Command2_Click()
            End
        End Sub


        Sub Smallest(x() As Single)
            Dim Text As String

            If (x(1) < x(2)) Then
                x(0) = x(1)
                Text = "a is smaller (a = "
            ElseIf (x(1) > x(2)) Then
                x(0) = x(2)
                Text = "b is smaller (b = "
            Else
                x(0) = x(1)
                Text = "Both values are equal (a, b = "
            End If
            Call Message(Text, x(0))
        End Sub


        Sub Message(Text As String, Value As Single)
            Dim LineOut As String

            LineOut = Text & Str(Value) & ")"
            MsgBox LineOut
        End Sub
```

Note that the entire array x is passed to the sub procedure Smallest from Command1_Click. Within Smallest, the smaller of the two values is determined and assigned to x(0). Finally, the value of x(0), together with an appropriate message, are passed to sub procedure Message.

Within Message, the message and the value of x(0) are combined into a single string. This string is then displayed within a message box.

When the program is executed, it behaves in exactly the same manner as the earlier program shown in Example 7.2. Figs.s 7.3 and 7.4 show representative output.

EXAMPLE 8.10 SORTING A LIST OF NUMBERS

Here is a more comprehensive example, based upon the well-known problem of sorting a list of numbers into ascending (or descending) order. Let us generate ten random numbers (using the RND library function, as explained in Example 7.10) and store them in a single-precision array, x. We will then rearrange the array so that the elements are sorted from smallest to largest. The program will be written so that unnecessary storage is not required. Therefore, the program will contain only one array, and the rearrangement will be carried out one element at a time.

The rearrangement will begin by scanning the first n elements of x for the smallest number. This value will then be interchanged with the first number in x, thus placing the smallest number at the top of the list. Next the remaining $(n-1)$ numbers will be scanned for the smallest, which will be exchanged with the second number. Then the remaining $(n-2)$ numbers will be scanned for the smallest, which will be interchanged with the third number, and so on, until the entire array has been rearranged. Note that a complete rearrangement will require a total of $(n-1)$ passes through the array, though the length of each scan will become progressively smaller with each successive pass.

In order to find the smallest number within each pass (i.e., within the ith pass), we sequentially compare the starting number x(i), with each successive number in the array, x(j), where j > i. If x(j) is smaller than x(i), we interchange the two numbers; otherwise, we leave the two numbers in their original positions. Once this procedure has been applied to the entire array, the ith number will be smaller than any of the subsequent numbers. This process is carried out $(n-1)$ times, for $i = 1, 2, \ldots, n-1$.

The only remaining question is how the two numbers are actually interchanged. To carry out the interchange, we first assign the value of $x(i)$ to a temporary variable, Temp, for future reference. Then we assign the current value of $x(j)$ to $x(i)$. Finally, we assign the original value of $x(i)$, which is now assigned to Temp, to $x(j)$. The interchange of the two numbers is now complete.

The following programmer-defined sub procedure (Sort_Array) carries out this strategy for an n-element array x.

```
Private Sub Sort_Array(x() As Single, n As Integer)
    Dim Temp As Single
    Dim i As Integer, j As Integer

    For i = 0 To n - 1
        For j = i + 1 To n
            If (x(j) < x(i)) Then
                Temp = x(i)
                x(i) = x(j)
                x(j) = Temp
            End If
        Next j
    Next i
End Sub
```

To display the results, we create a form containing a label, two combo boxes, and three command buttons, as shown in Fig. 8.8. One combo box will be used to display the list of random numbers, in the order they were generated. The other will display the sorted list of numbers. The three command buttons will generate and sort the list, clear the list, and end the computation, respectively.

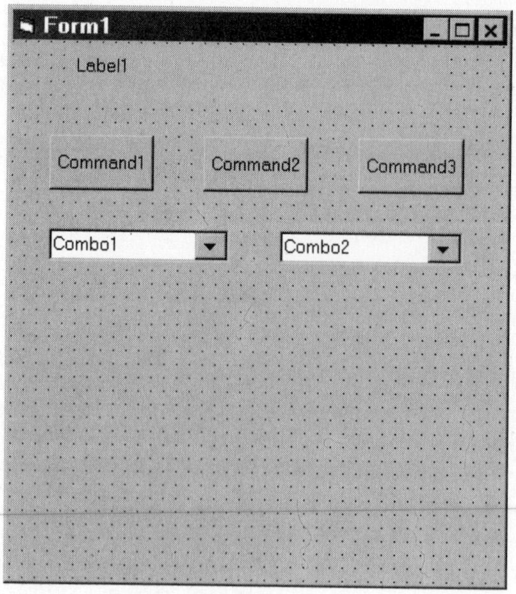

Fig. 8.8

We now consider the corresponding event procedures. In contrast to our customary practice, we will assign initial values to the control properties at run time, when the form is first loaded. Event procedure Form_Load contains the property assignments.

```
Private Sub Form_Load()
    Form1.Caption = "Random Number Sort"

    Label1.Caption = "Sorting Random Numbers"
    Label1.FontSize = 12
    Label1.Alignment = 2    'Center

    Command1.Caption = "Go"
    Command1.FontSize = 10

    Command2.Caption = "Clear"
    Command2.FontSize = 10

    Command3.Caption = "End"
    Command3.FontSize = 10

    Combo1.FontSize = 10
    Combo1.Visible = False

    Combo2.FontSize = 10
    Combo2.Visible = False
End Sub
```

Event procedure Command1_Click does most of the actual computation. In particular, this procedure initializes the random number generator, generates the random numbers, assigns them to the array elements and copies the array elements to Combo1, carries out the sort, and then copies the sorted array elements to Combo2.

Command2_Click clears the combo boxes by assigning empty strings to the list elements, and Command3_Click ends the computation. Here are the remaining event procedures.

```
Private Sub Command1_Click()
    Dim x(10) As Single, Temp As Single
    Dim Index As Integer, SubIndex As Integer

    Randomize

    'Generate the random array elements and copy into Combo1
    For Index = 0 To 9
        x(Index) = Rnd
        Combo1.List(Index) = Str(x(Index))
    Next Index
    Combo1.Text = "Random List"

    'Sort the array
    Call Sort_Array(x(), 9)

    'Copy the sorted array elements into Combo2
    For Index = 0 To 9
        Combo2.List(Index) = Str(x(Index))
    Next Index
    Combo2.Text = "Sorted List"

    Combo1.Visible = True
    Combo2.Visible = True
End Sub
```

```
Private Sub Command2_Click()
    Dim Index As Integer

    For Index = 0 To 9
        Combo1.List(Index) = ""
        Combo2.List(Index) = ""
    Next Index
End Sub

Private Sub Command3_Click()
    End
End Sub
```

When the program is executed, we first see the form shown in Fig. 8.9. If we then click on the Go button, the combo boxes become visible, as shown in Fig. 8.10. Clicking on either of the downward-pointing arrows then results in the accompanying list being displayed, as shown in Figs. 8.11 (a) and (b).

Fig. 8.9

Fig. 8.10

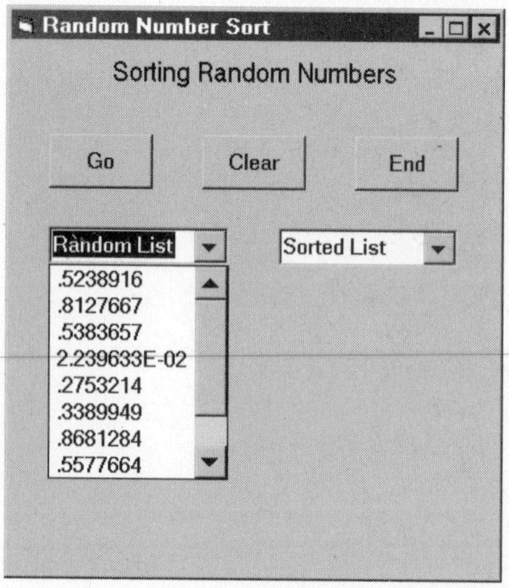

Fig. 8.11 (a)

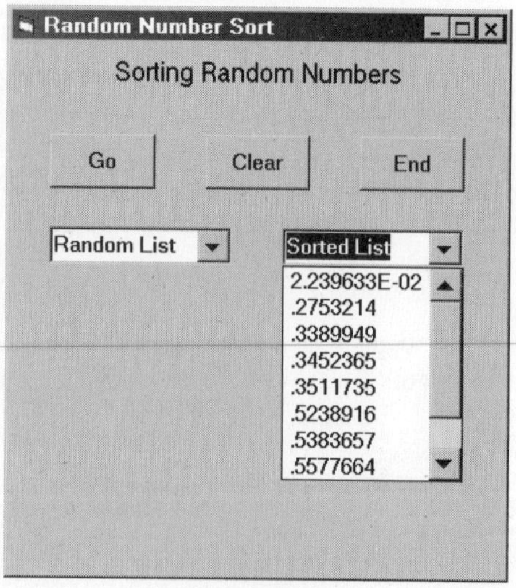

Fig. 8.11(b)

Multidimensional arrays are declared and processed in much the same manner as one-dimensional arrays. The following example illustrates the use of multidimensional arrays.

EXAMPLE 8.11 DEVIATIONS ABOUT AN AVERAGE

In this example we will enter a list of n numbers and calculate their average, using the well-known formula

$$average = (x_1 + x_2 + \cdots + x_n) / n$$

where x_1, x_2, x_3, etc., represent the individual numbers.

We will then calculate the *deviation* of each number about the average, where the deviation is determined as

$$d_i = x_i - average$$

for $i = 1, 2, 3, \ldots, n$. The deviations tell us by how much each number differs from the average (either above, when the deviation is positive, or below, when the deviation is negative).

In order to compute the deviations, we must save the individual x-values until after the average has been calculated. We will therefore save the x-values within an array. We will also save the deviations so that they can be displayed at a later time, along with the original x-values. Hence, we will utilize a single two-dimensional array, with n rows and two columns. The first column will contain the x-values, and the second column will contain the corresponding deviations.

We could display the results in two combo boxes if we wished, as in the last example. Instead, however, let us display the results using the Print statement, which was discussed in Sec. 2.11. This allows us to display the data in adjacent columns, where they can easily be compared. The use of the Print statement also provides a concise, convenient way to label the calculated results at the end.

We begin with the preliminary layout shown in Fig. 8.12. The three command buttons will again represent the Go button (which will carry out all of the calculations), the Clear button and the End button, as in the last example. The right portion of the form remains empty, in order to provide space for the final results.

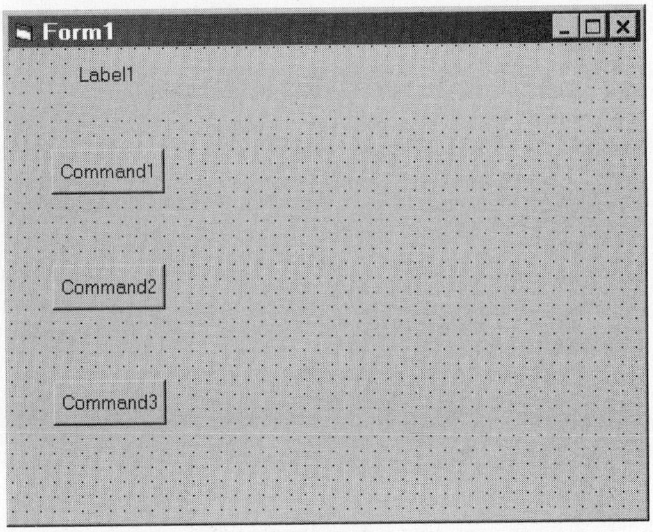

Fig. 8.12

Let us again assign the initial values to the control properties within event procedure Form_Load, as in the last example. The event procedure, and its accompanying declarations, are shown below. Notice that the array declaration restricts us to no more than 10 data points. Also, note that command button Command2 (the Clear button) is initially disabled, to prevent the user from attempting to clear an array that does not contain any data.

```
Option Base 1
Dim x(10, 2) As Double, i As Integer, n As Integer

Private Sub Form_Load()
    Form1.Caption = "Deviations About an Average"

    Label1.Caption = "Deviations About an Average"
    Label1.FontSize = 12
    Label1.Alignment = 2      'Center

    Command1.Caption = "Go"
    Command1.FontSize = 10

    Command2.Caption = "Clear"
    Command2.FontSize = 10
    Command2.Enabled = False

    Command3.Caption = "End"
    Command3.FontSize = 10
End Sub
```

We now turn our attention to command button Command1, which enters the data, calculates and average and a set of deviations, and displays the results. We also determine the sum of the deviations within Command1, as a check (the deviations should sum to zero if the calculations are carried out correctly). Here is event procedure Command1_Click.

```
Private Sub Command1_Click()
    Dim Prompt As String
    Dim Sum As Double, Average As Double

    n = Val(InputBox("How many values?"))
    If (n > 10) Then
        MsgBox ("ERROR - n cannot exceed 10.  Please try again.")
        Exit Sub
    End If

    'Calculate the Average
    Sum = 0
    For i = 1 To n
        Prompt = "Please enter a value for i = " & Str(i)
        x(i, 1) = Val(InputBox(Prompt))
        Sum = Sum + x(i, 1)
    Next i
    Average = Sum / n
    Command2.Enabled = True

    'Calculate the Deviations About the Average
    Sum = 0
    For i = 1 To n
        x(i, 2) = x(i, 1) - Average
        Sum = Sum + x(i, 2)
    Next i
```

(Continues on next page)

```
        'Display the Results
        Print
        Print
        Print
        Print
        Print , , "Values", "Deviations"
        Print
        For i = 1 To n
            Print , , x(i, 1), x(i, 2)
        Next I
        Print
        Print , , "Average = "; Average
        Print
        Print , , "Sum of Deviations = "; Sum
    End Sub
```

Notice that the input data are provided through input boxes. The user is first prompted for the number of *x*-values. An error trap prevents the user from specifying a value greater than 10, because of the array size restriction. This is followed by a loop that enters each *x*-value, places each value in the first column of the array, and computes a cumulative sum. The average is then determined, after the loop has been completed. Note that command button Command2 is also enabled at this point, since *n* different *x*-values have now been provided.

Once the average has been determined, another loop appears in which the deviations are calculated and placed in the second column of the array. The deviations are also summed, as a check on the computational accuracy.

Finally, the results are displayed on the form with a series of Print statements. Notice that two commas follow the keyword Print in each of the non-empty Print statements. The commas force the data to be displayed on the right side of the form, beyond the command buttons.

Here are the two remaining event procedures. The Cls (clear screen) statement in Command2_Click clears the printed display within the form. We then use a double loop to clear out the array elements. Note that the outer loop is used to process each row, and the inner loop processes both columns for a given row. Finally, the Clear button is again disabled, awaiting the next set of data.

```
    Private Sub Command2_Click()
        'Clear the Form
        Cls

        'Clear the Array
        If (n <= 10) Then
            For i = 1 To n
                For j = 1 To 2
                    x(i, j) = 0
                Next j
            Next i
        End If

        Command2.Enabled = False
    End Sub


    Private Sub Command3_Click()
        End
    End Sub
```

Now suppose we wish to execute the program for the following six x-values:

$$x_1 = \quad 3 \qquad x_4 = \quad 4.4$$
$$x_2 = -2 \qquad x_5 = \quad 3.5$$
$$x_3 = 12 \qquad x_6 = -0.8$$

When the program is executed, we see the form shown in Fig. 8.13. If we then click on the Go button, we see the input box shown in Fig. 8.14. In this case, the user has provided a value of $n = 6$, indicating that six x-values will be provided. Clicking on OK then generates six different input boxes, each prompting for an x-value. Fig. 8.15 shows the first of the input boxes. The value is entered by clicking on the OK button.

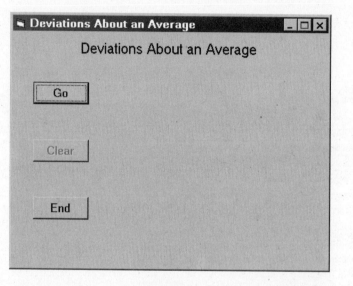

Fig. 8.13

Fig. 8.14

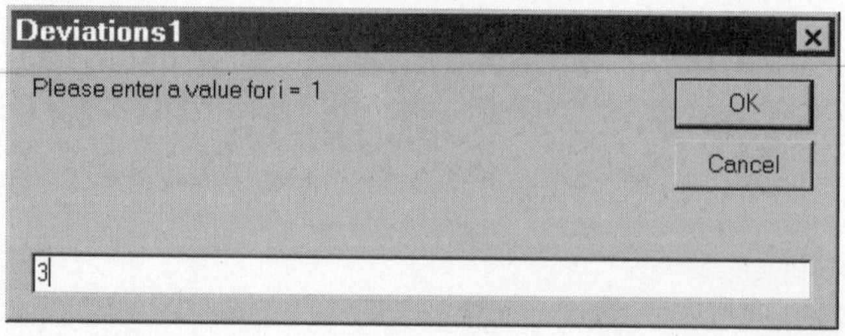

Fig. 8.15

When all six values have been entered, the *x*-values, the average and the list of deviations are calculated and displayed, as shown in Fig. 8.16. Note that the sum of the deviations is approximately 2.66×10^{-15}, a value that is very close to zero but not identically zero because of numerical roundoff and truncation.

Clicking on the Clear button restores the form to its starting condition, as shown in Fig. 8.13. A new set of data may then be entered. And, of course, clicking on the End button simply terminates the computation.

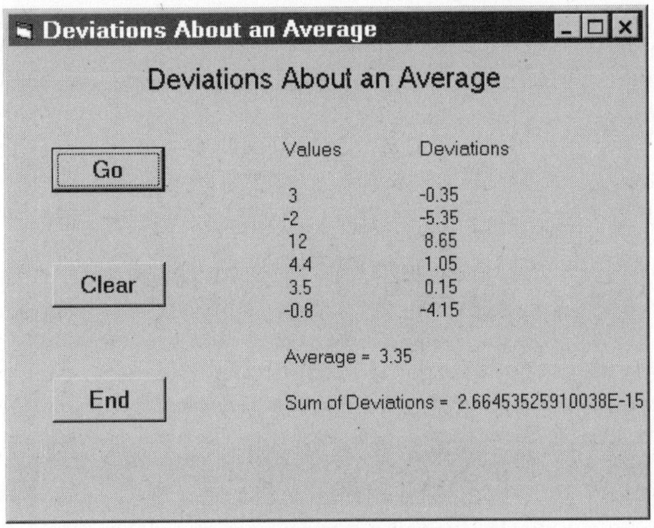

Fig. 8.16

8.5 DYNAMIC ARRAYS

A *dynamic array* is an array whose size can be changed at various places within a program. To declare a dynamic array, we use the Dim statement, followed by the array name and an *empty* pair of parentheses; i.e.,

       Dim *array name* ( ) As *data type*

Within a module but outside of a procedure, we can also use either the Private or the Public statement; i.e.,

       Private *array name* ( ) As *data type*

or

       Public *array name* ( ) As *data type*

To specify the actual array size, we use the ReDim statement; i.e.,

       ReDim *array name* (*subscript 1 upper limit, subscript 2 upper limit, etc.*)

Lower limits may also appear within the ReDim statement; i.e.,

       ReDim *array name* (*subscript 1 lower limit* To *subscript 1 upper limit,*
                      subscript 2 lower limit To *subscript 2 upper limit, etc.*) As *data type*

Unlike the Dim statement, integer variables or expressions may be used to represent the subscript limits.

The ReDim statement need not immediately follow the Dim statement; it can (and usually does) appear at some later point within the program. Moreover, it may appear more than once, allowing the array to be resized each time it appears.

EXAMPLE 8.12

Here is a skeletal outline of a procedure that utilizes a dynamic array.

```
Sub Sample()
    Dim x()As Integer, n As Integer
    . . . . .
    ReDim x(10)
    . . . . .
    ReDim x(30)
    . . . . .
    n = . . . . .
    ReDim x(n)
    . . . . .
End Sub
```

Within the `Dim` statement, we see that x is declared as a dynamic array, because of the empty parentheses. We then dimension x to be a 20-element array. Subsequently, the size of x is again altered, first as a 30-element array, and then as an n-element array. In the last case, the value assigned to the integer variable n will determine the array size.

When a numerical array is redimensioned, the values previously assigned to the array elements will be reset to zero. Similarly, when a string array is redimensioned, the strings previously assigned to the array elements will replaced by empty strings. However, the previously assigned values will be retained if the `ReDim` statement includes the keyword `Preserve`; i.e.,

> `ReDim Preserve` *array name* (*subscript 1 upper limit, subscript 2 upper limit, etc.*)

When the `Preserve` feature is utilized, *only the upper limit of the last subscript can be altered*; i.e., you cannot alter the *lower* limit of the last subscript, nor can you alter any of the other subscripts.

EXAMPLE 8.13

In this skeletal outline, we make use of the `Preserve` feature within a `ReDim` statement.

```
Sub Sample()
    Dim x()As Integer, j as Integer
    . . . . .
    ReDim x(10)
    For j = 1 To 10
        x(j) = j ^ 2
    Next j
    . . . . .
    ReDim Preserve x(12)
    . . . . .
End Sub
```

The `For-Next` loop assigns a value to each of the ten array elements. The last `ReDim` statement causes two additional elements to be added to the array, while preserving the ten previously assigned values. Without including `Preserve` in the `ReDim` statement, the first ten array elements would have been reset to zero.

EXAMPLE 8.14 DEVIATIONS ABOUT AN AVERAGE USING DYNAMIC ARRAYS

In Example 8.11 we presented a Visual Basic project that enters a series of numbers, calculates their average and then determines the deviation of each number about the average. We now modify this project to use dynamic arrays.

The use of dynamic arrays enhances the generality of the project in several ways. First, the project is no longer restricted to processing ten or fewer numbers. Moreover, the code is simplified in two ways – an error trap for values of n greater than 10 is no longer required, nor is a double loop required to clear the array.

The modified code is shown below. The new `Dim` statement and the two required `ReDim` statements are italicized. Also, note that `Format` functions have been added to several of the `Print` statements.

```
Option Base 1
Dim x() As Double, i As Integer, n As Integer

Private Sub Form_Load()
    Form1.Caption = "Deviations About an Average"

    Label1.Caption = "Deviations About an Average"
    Label1.FontSize = 12
    Label1.Alignment = 2      'Center

    Command1.Caption = "Go"
    Command1.FontSize = 10

    Command2.Caption = "Clear"
    Command2.FontSize = 10
    Command2.Enabled = False

    Command3.Caption = "End"
    Command3.FontSize = 10
End Sub

Private Sub Command1_Click()
    Dim Prompt As String
    Dim Sum As Double, Average As Double

    n = Val(InputBox("How many values?"))
    ReDim x(n, 2)
    Command2.Enabled = True

    'Calculate the Average
    Sum = 0
    For i = 1 To n
        Prompt = "Please enter a value for i = " & Str(i)
        x(i, 1) = Val(InputBox(Prompt))
        Sum = Sum + x(i, 1)
    Next i
    Average = Sum / n

    'Calculate the Deviations About the Average
    Sum = 0
    For i = 1 To n
        x(i, 2) = x(i, 1) - Average
        Sum = Sum + x(i, 2)
    Next I
```

(Continues on next page)

```
        'Display the Results
        Print
        Print
        Print
        Print
        Print , , "Values", "Deviations"
        Print
        For i = 1 To n
            Print , , Format(x(i, 1), "###.#"), Format(x(i, 2), "##.##")
        Next i
        Print
        Print , , "Average = "; Format(Average, "###.#")
        Print
        Print , , "Sum of Deviations = "; Format(Sum, "Scientific")
End Sub

Private Sub Command2_Click()
        'Clear the Form
        Cls
        ReDim x(n, 2)
        Command2.Enabled = False
End Sub

Private Sub Command3_Click()
        End
End Sub
```

Note that the code is smaller than in Example 8.11, since an If-Then-Else block has been removed from event procedure Command1_Click and a double loop has been removed from event procedure Command2_Click.

When the program is executed, it behaves in exactly the same manner as the program presented in Example 8.11, except that we can now process larger lists of numbers. Fig. 8.17 shows the results obtained when processing the exam scores for twelve students.

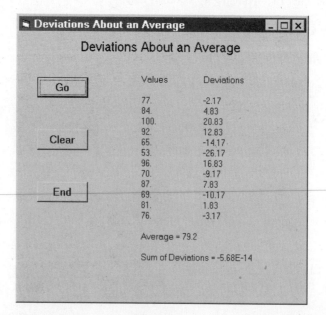

Fig. 8.17

8.6 ARRAY-RELATED FUNCTIONS

Visual Basic includes several array-related library functions, as summarized in Table 8.1 below. These functions are rarely needed in simple programs, but they can be very useful in more complex programs, where it may be necessary to create arrays or to determine array properties during program execution.

Table 8.1 Array-Related Library Functions

Function	Application	Description
Array	`Dim x As Variant` `x = Array(3, 0.2, "OK")`	Creates a variant-type array. The arguments represent array elements. For example, x is a 3-element array containing an integer value (x(0) = 3), a single-precision value (x(1) = 0.2), and a string (x(2) = "OK").

IsArray	`If IsArray(x) Then`
	`    MsgBox "Array Defined"`
	`Else`
	`    MsgBox "Array Undefined"`
		Returns a True/False value that is True if the argument is an array, and False otherwise.

LBound	`Dim x(3 To 10)` `y = LBound(x)`	Returns the subscript lower limit of the array argument.
	`Dim c(3 To 10, 5 To 20)` `y = LBound(c, 2)`	If the array is multidimensional, LBound returns the lower limit of the subscript indicated by its second argument.
UBound	`Dim x(3 To 10)` `y = UBound(x)`	Returns the subscript upper limit of the array argument.
	`Dim c(3 To 10, 5 To 20)` `y = UBound(c, 2)`	If the array is multidimensional, UBound returns the upper limit of the subscript indicated by its second argument.

EXAMPLE 8.15

Here is a Visual Basic code segment that illustrates the use of the array-related library functions Array, IsArray, LBound and UBound.

```
Dim x As Variant, x1 As Variant, x2 As Variant, x3 As Variant, x4 As Variant
Dim i1 As Integer, i2 As Integer
x = Array(3, 0.2, "OK")
    . . . . .
If IsArray(x) Then      'is x an array?
    i1 = LBound(x)
    i2 = UBound(x)
    x1 = x(LBound(x))
    x2 = x(UBound(x))
    x3 = x(LBound(x) + 1)
    x4 = x(UBound(x) − 2)
End If
```

When executed, this code segment will result in the following assignments:

i1 = 0	(array lower bound)	x2 = "OK"	(last array element)
i2 = 2	(array upper bound)	x3 = 0.2	(second array element)
x1 = 3	(first array element)	x4 = 3	(first array element)

8.7 CONTROL ARRAYS

Multiple controls of the same type can be grouped into an array, in the same manner as a collection of data items. Such a grouping is known as a *control array*. Under certain conditions, the control array elements may share a common event procedure, using an index (i.e., a subscript value) to distinguish one control from another. Control arrays are created at design time (i.e., at the time controls are added to the Form Design Window). Additional control array elements can also be added and later deleted at run time (when the program is executed).

A control array can be created by placing a control within the Form Design Window and assigning a value of 0 to its Index property. Then copy and paste the control, resulting in a new control with the same name (but an index value of 1) in the upper left corner of the Form Design Window. You may then drag the new control to its desired location within the Form Design Window. This process may be repeated as many times as you wish. Each repetition will result in a new control (i.e., a new element) within the control array. *Remember that all of the control array elements will share the same name, but are distinguishable by the value of their index.* The captions will also be the same, when the control array is created in this manner.

EXAMPLE 8.16

Suppose we wish to create a two-element control array whose elements are check boxes. Let us begin with an empty form, and then add one check box in the normal manner. When the check box is first added, it will be named Check1 and its caption will also be Check1. Fig. 8.18 shows the location of Check1 within the Form Design Window. When Check1 is first created, its Index property will be unassigned.

Now let us assign the value 0 to the Index property within the Properties Window, as shown in Fig. 8.19. This will result in Check1 automatically being referred to as the array element Check1(0), as shown at the top of the Properties Window (see Fig. 8.19). We then right-click on Check1 and select Copy, then right-click on the form and select Paste. Another check box, also named Check1 and having the caption Check1, will then appear in the upper left-hand corner of the Form, as shown in Fig. 8.20(*a*). We can then drag the new check box to its desired location, beneath the original check box, as shown in Fig. 8.20(*b*).

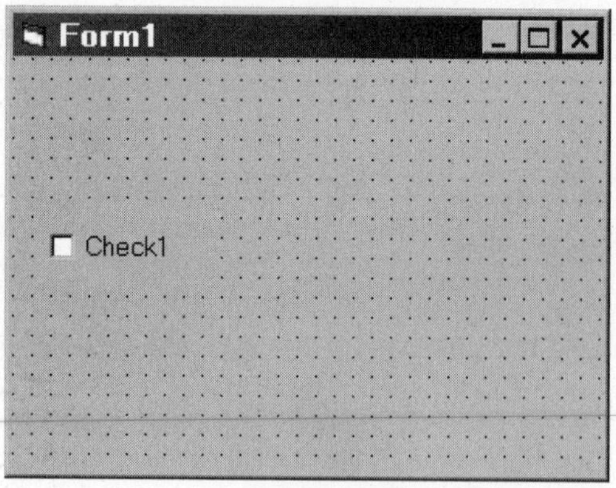

Fig. 8.18 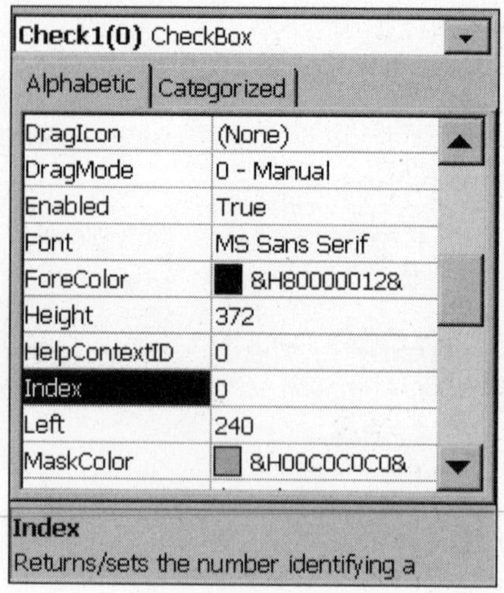   Fig. 8.19

Note that both check boxes have the same label and the same caption (Check1). However, the first check box will be referred to as Check1(0) and the second check box will be referred to as Check(1), since both check boxes are members of a control array.

Fig. 8.20(*a*)   **Fig. 8.20(*b*)**

Another way to create a control array is to place a control in the Form Design Window in the usual manner, and then place a second control of the same type in the Form Design Window. If you rename the second control so that its name is the same as the first control, a dialog box will appear, allowing you to create a control array if you wish. Again, all of the array elements will have the same name, but a different index value.

When the array elements are created in this manner, their captions will be different, unless you decide to change them so that they are all alike.

EXAMPLE 8.17

We now extend the form developed in Example 8.16 by adding a second control array, consisting of two labels. Let us create the new control array differently, however, as described above. We begin by placing a label control in the form, as shown in Fig. 8.21(*a*). We then add a second form beneath it, as shown in Fig. 8.21(*b*). So far, the two labels are unrelated — neither is an array element.

We now create the desired control array be renaming the second label from Label2 to Label1. (Note that we are changing only the control name, not the caption.) Fig. 8.22 shows the Properties Window with the new name. This name change then generates the dialog box shown in Fig. 8.23. Clicking on Yes will then automatically create the array. Its two elements will be referred to as Label1(0) and Label1(1), though both elements will be named simply Label1. So far, the captions remain different. We can change the second caption to Label1 if we wish, resulting in the form shown in Fig. 8.24. Note that the renaming of the second caption from Label2 to Label1 is not required, but it is a good idea if additional control elements will be added via the copy/paste method.

Fig. 8.21(*a*)   **Fig. 8.21(*b*)**

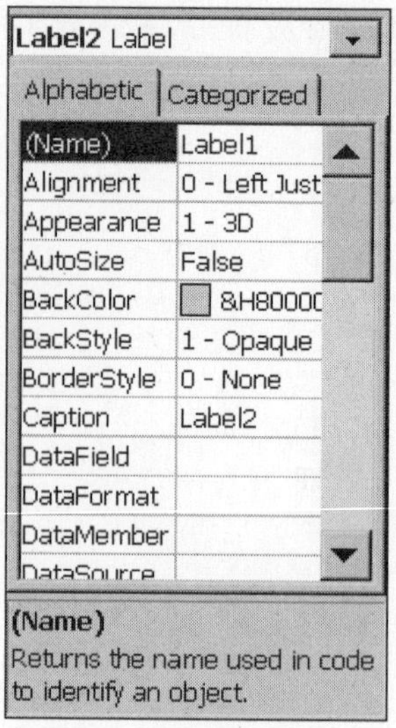

Label2 Label	▼

Alphabetic	Categorized

(Name)	Label1	▲
Alignment	0 - Left Just	
Appearance	1 - 3D	
AutoSize	False	
BackColor	&H80000	
BackStyle	1 - Opaque	
BorderStyle	0 - None	
Caption	Label2	
DataField		
DataFormat		
DataMember		
DataSource		▼

(Name)
Returns the name used in code
to identify an object.

Fig. 8.22

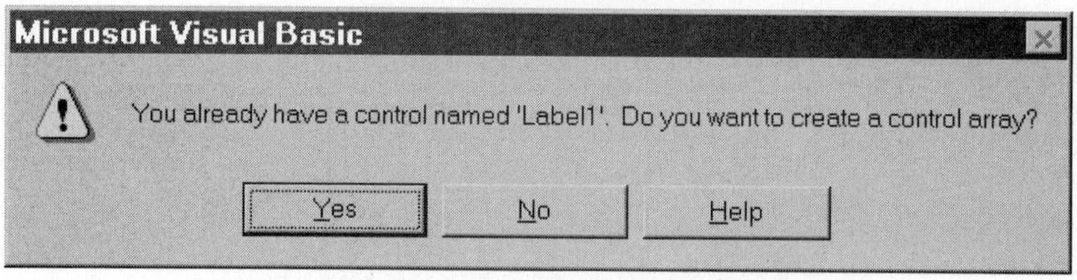

Microsoft Visual Basic   ☒

⚠   You already have a control named 'Label1'. Do you want to create a control array?

[Yes]   [No]   [Help]

Fig. 8.23

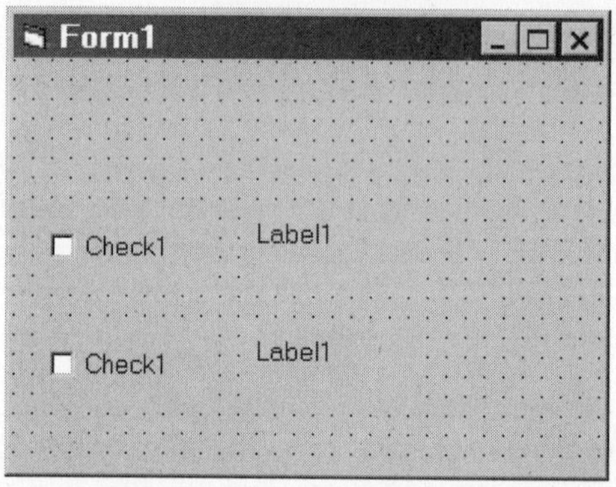

Form1   _ ☐ ☒

☐ Check1   Label1

☐ Check1   Label1

Fig. 8.24

Once a control array has been created, an individual element (i.e., an individual control) is referred to simply by writing the array name followed by the appropriate index (subscript number), enclosed in parentheses; i.e.,

   control array name (*subscript*)

Similarly, a property associated with a control array element is referred to by writing the array name, followed by the appropriate index in parentheses, followed by a period and the property identifier; i.e.,

   control array name (*subscript*).*property*

Thus, it is possible to assign values to control array elements, property values can be tested, etc., within Visual Basic code.

The following example illustrates the use of control arrays within a complete Visual Basic project.

EXAMPLE 8.18 SELECTING MULTIPLE FEATURES USING CONTROL ARRAYS

Example 4.6 presents a Visual Basic project that allows the user to select one or more languages and then display an appropriate "hello" greeting for each of the selected languages. The project contains multiple check boxes and multiple labels. The individual controls within each control type share common properties (namely, font size and visibility status). Therefore, this project is a good candidate for the use of control arrays.

In this example we will re-create the project originally presented in Example 4.6 using two different control arrays – one consisting of seven check boxes (one for each language), the other consisting of seven labels (each containing an appropriate "hello" message). Hence, we begin by creating the form shown in Fig. 8.25. The two control arrays, called Check1 and Label1, respectively, were created using the method illustrated in Example. 8.17. Initial values will not be assigned to any of the control properties. Instead, these initial property assignments will be made at run time.

In addition to the two control arrays, Fig. 8.25 also shows the placement of an ordinary label (Label2), which will be used as a title, and two command buttons (Command1 and Command2), which will become Go and Quit, respectively. The initial property values for these controls will be assigned at run time, along with the required control array property values.

Now consider the event procedure Form_Load, which follows Fig. 8.25. This procedure begins with a declaration (Count), followed by caption assignments for the individual elements in each of the two control arrays. These assignments are followed by a simple loop that assigns font sizes and visibility status to the control array elements, as required.

Following the control array property assignments, we see a caption assignment for the form, and caption/font size assignments for the remaining controls. In addition, the Alignment property associated with Label2 is assigned a value that will cause the caption to be centered within the label.

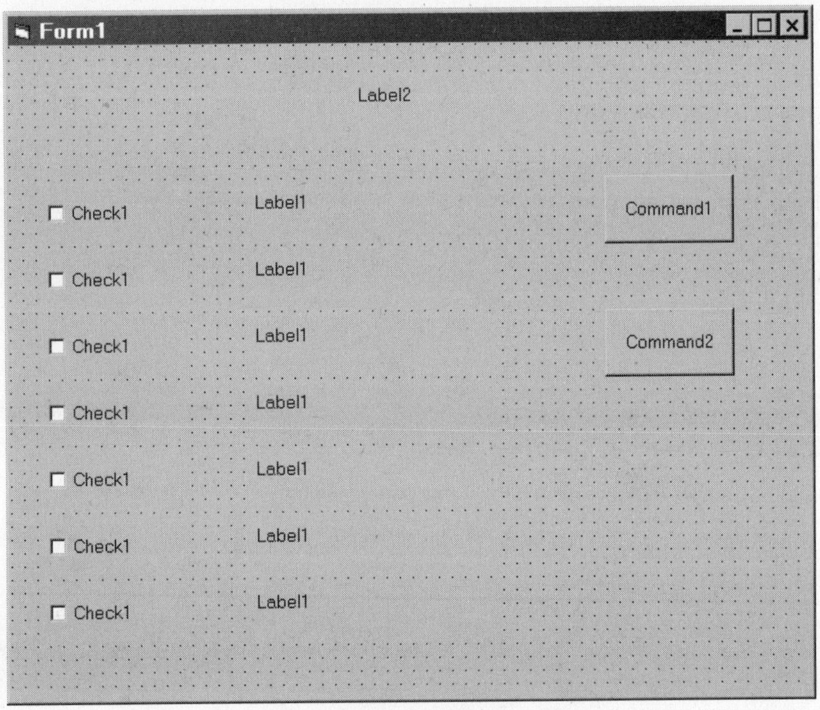

Fig. 8.25

```
Private Sub Form_Load()
    Dim Count As Integer

    chkLanguage(0).Caption = "French"
    chkLanguage(1).Caption = "German"
    chkLanguage(2).Caption = "Hawaiian"
    chkLanguage(3).Caption = "Hebrew"
    chkLanguage(4).Caption = "Italian"
    chkLanguage(5).Caption = "Japanese"
    chkLanguage(6).Caption = "Spanish"

    lblHello(0).Caption = "Bonjour"
    lblHello(1).Caption = "Guten Tag"
    lblHello(2).Caption = "Aloha"
    lblHello(3).Caption = "Shalom"
    lblHello(4).Caption = "Buon Giorno"
    lblHello(5).Caption = "Konichihua"
    lblHello(6).Caption = "Buenos Dias"

    For Count = 0 To 6
        chkLanguage(Count).FontSize = 10
        lblHello(Count).Visible = False
        lblHello(Count).FontSize = 14
    Next Count

    Form1.Caption = "Multilingual Hello"

    Label2.Caption = "Say Hello, in . . ."
    Label2.FontSize = 14
    Label2.Alignment = 2       'Center

    Command1.Caption = "Go"
    Command1.FontSize = 10

    Command2.Caption = "Quit"
    Command2.FontSize = 10
End Sub


Private Sub Command1_Click()
    Dim Count As Integer

    For Count = 0 To 6
        lblHello(Count).Visible = False
        If chkLanguage(Count).Value = 1 Then
            lblHello(Count).Visible = True
        End If
    Next Count
End Sub


Private Sub Command2_Click()
    End
End Sub
```

Now consider event procedure Command1_Click, which corresponds to the Go button. Other than the initial declaration, this event procedure consists of a single loop that examines all of the check boxes and displays the labels whose corresponding boxes have been checked. This is accomplished by resetting the Visible property (initially False) to True. This logic is much simpler than the series of If-Then-Else statements utilized in Example 4.6, thus illustrating the utility of the control arrays.

Execution of the program results in the same behavior as shown in Example 4.6. Fig. 8.26 shows a typical result.

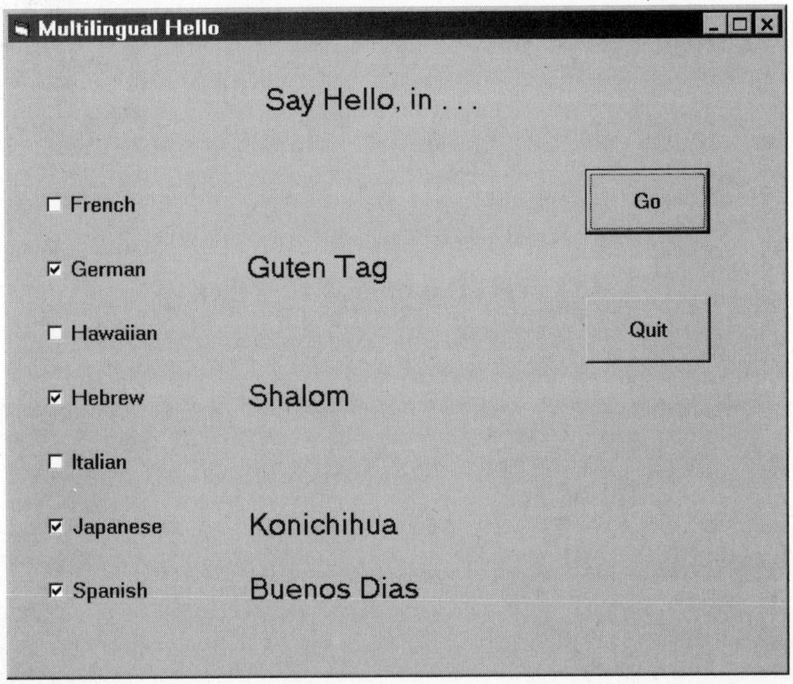

Fig. 8.26

Once a control array has been created, an additional element can be added during run time, using the Load statement; i.e.,

       Load *control array name* (*subscript*)

(Remember that the control array must have been created at design time.) Once a new element has been created, it generally must be moved to the desired location within the frame (via the Move statement). Moreover, certain of its properties must generally be assigned appropriate values.

An element added at run time can later be deleted, using the Unload statement; i.e.,

       Unload *control array name* (*subscript*)

Note, however, that elements created at *design* time *cannot* be deleted at run time.

EXAMPLE 8.19 ADDING AND DELETING CONTROL ARRAY ELEMENTS AT RUN TIME

Now let us extend the Visual Basic project presented in Example 8.18 by including a provision for adding and and later deleting a new control array element at run time. We will also create a new control array consisting of command buttons, and illustrate how the elements of this control array can share a common event procedure.

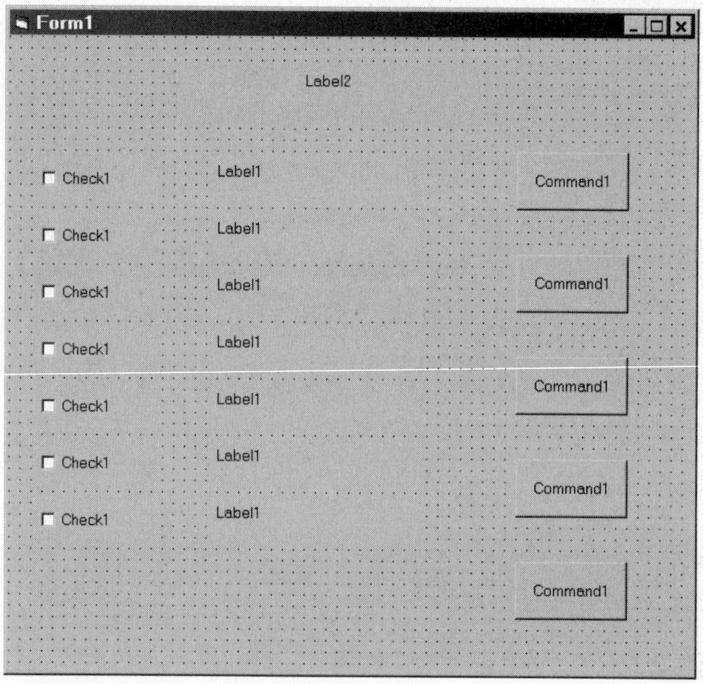

Fig. 8.27

Fig. 8.27 shows the control layout. Comparing this with the control layout used in Example 8.18 (see Fig. 8.25), we see that we are now using five command buttons rather than two. These command buttons will be used to display the appropriate greetings (similar to the Command1 button in Fig. 8.25), clear all check boxes and corresponding greetings, add a new check box and a corresponding greeting, delete the new check box and greeting, and end the computation (as does the Command2 button in Fig. 8.25). The command buttons are now elements of a new control array, which explains why they all appear with the same name.

Notice also that the form has been lengthened, to make room for the additional command buttons, and for the new check box/greeting, which are not shown in Fig. 8.27.

Now let us consider the corresponding event procedures.

```
Dim n As Integer

Private Sub Form_Load()
    Dim Count As Integer, ButtonCount As Integer

    chkLanguage(0).Caption = "French"
    chkLanguage(1).Caption = "German"
    chkLanguage(2).Caption = "Hawaiian"
    chkLanguage(3).Caption = "Hebrew"
    chkLanguage(4).Caption = "Italian"
    chkLanguage(5).Caption = "Japanese"
    chkLanguage(6).Caption = "Spanish"

    lblHello(0).Caption = "Bonjour"
    lblHello(1).Caption = "Guten Tag"
    lblHello(2).Caption = "Aloha"
    lblHello(3).Caption = "Shalom"
```

(Continues on next page)

```
        lblHello(4).Caption = "Buon Giorno"
        lblHello(5).Caption = "Konichihua"
        lblHello(6).Caption = "Buenos Dias"

        Command1(0).Caption = "Go"
        Command1(1).Caption = "Clear"
        Command1(2).Caption = "Add"
        Command1(3).Caption = "Delete"
        Command1(4).Caption = "Quit"

        For ButtonCount = 0 To 4
            Command1(ButtonCount).FontSize = 10
        Next ButtonCount

        n = 6
        For Count = 0 To n
            chkLanguage(Count).FontSize = 10
            lblHello(Count).Visible = False
            lblHello(Count).FontSize = 14
        Next Count

        Form1.Caption = "Multilingual Hello"

        Label2.Caption = "Say Hello, in . . ."
        Label2.FontSize = 14
        Label2.Alignment = 2   'Center
End Sub

Private Sub Command1_Click(Index As Integer)
    Dim Count As Integer

    Select Case Index

    Case 0     'Go
        For Count = 0 To n
            lblHello(Count).Visible = False
            If chkLanguage(Count).Value = 1 Then
                lblHello(Count).Visible = True
            End If
        Next Count

    Case 1     'Clear
        For Count = 0 To n
            chkLanguage(Count).Value = 0
            lblHello(Count).Visible = False
        Next Count

    Case 2     'Add
        n = n + 1
        Load chkLanguage(n)
        chkLanguage(n).Move 360, 5520       'x, y coordinates from upper left
        chkLanguage(n).Caption = "New"
        chkLanguage(n).Visible = True
```

(Continues on next page)

```
        Load lblHello(n)
        lblHello(n).Move 2280, 5520        'x, y coordinates from upper left
        lblHello(n).Caption = "Greetings"

    Case 3      'Delete
        Unload chkLanguage(n)
        Unload lblHello(n)
        n = n - 1

    Case 4      'Quit
        End

    End Select
End Sub
```

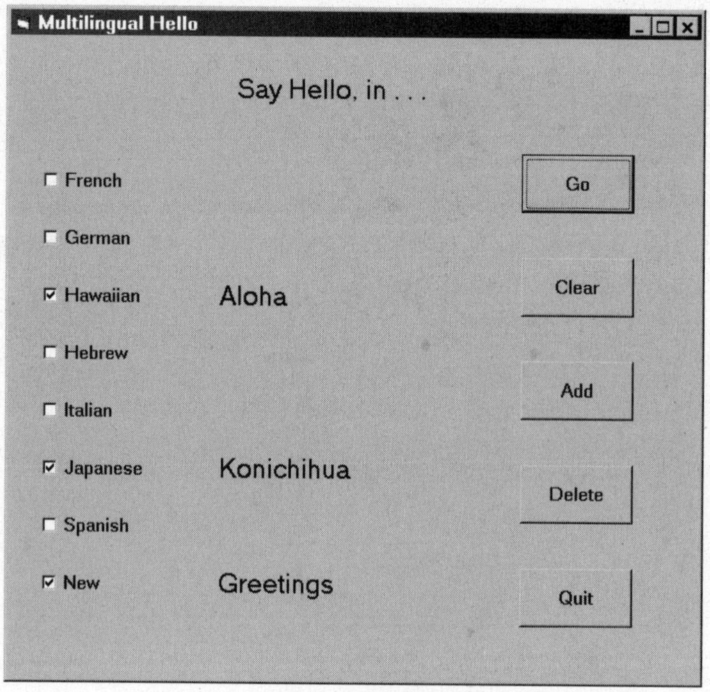

Fig. 8.28

First, note that we now introduce a global variable, n, to represent the number of languages/greetings. This is necessary because this number will change, as a result of adding and later deleting a new entry. We then present a modified version of procedure Form_Load, which assigns initial values to certain properties (namely, captions, font size, visibility status, and alignment) associated with the control array elements.

Following Form_Load we see event procedure Command1_Click, which is activated by clicking on any of the command buttons in control array Command1. Note that the procedure definition includes the argument Index, which indicates which control button has been clicked. Index then serves as a basis for the Select Case structure, which carries out the appropriate action. Thus, if the first button (labeled Go) is clicked (corresponding to Index = 0), the Case 0 instructions will be executed, causing the appropriate greeting to be displayed for each check box that has been checked. Similarly, clicking on the second button (labeled Clear, and corresponding to Index = 1) causes all of the check boxes to be unchecked and the corresponding messages to be hidden; and so on.

Case 2 (Add) requires some additional explanation. This group of commands adds a new entry to the list of languages and the corresponding list of greetings. We first increase the value of n by 1, to accommodate the new entries. We then use the Load command to add an additional element to the control array chkLanguages. The following command (chkLanguage(n).Move) locates the new entry to its desired position beneath the other languages rather than in the upper left-hand corner. This is followed by two additional commands that assign a caption (New) and cause the new array element to be visible. This entire sequence, beginning with the Load command, is then repeated for the new entry in control array lblHello.

Case 3 (Delete) uses the Unload command to delete the new control array elements. (Remember that Unload can be used *only to delete control array elements created at run time*.) The value assigned to n is then adjusted downward to reflect the new array size.

Fig. 8.28 shows the result of first clicking on the Add button, then selecting three check boxes, including New, and then clicking on Go. Clicking on Delete then causes the last entry to disappear, as shown in Fig. 8.29.

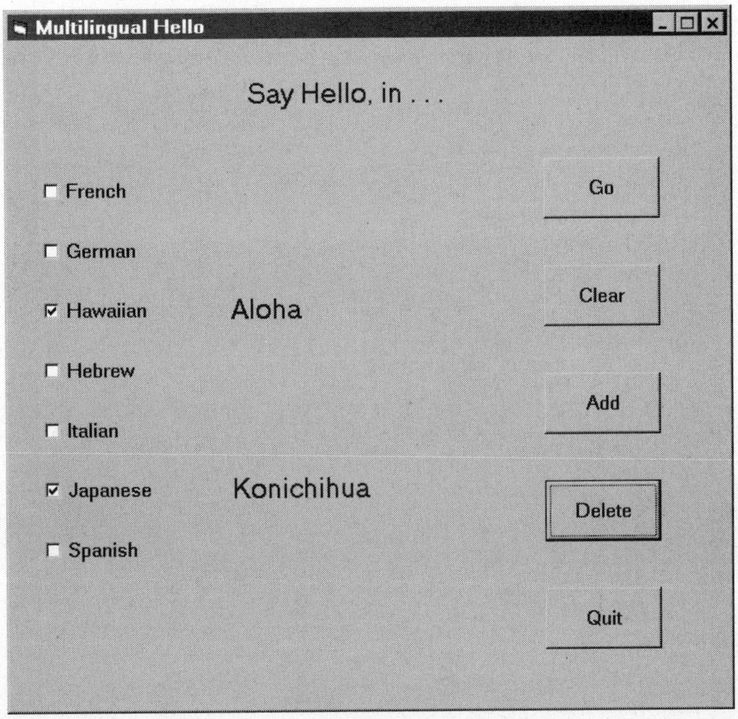

Fig. 8.29

Before leaving this example, we mention that it is somewhat contrived, as it is intended to illustrate the use of a shared event procedure and the use of the Load and Unload statements. In reality, a program that allows the user to add a greeting in a new language would most likely be a bit more sophisticated – in particular, it should include the following features:

1. Ask the user where the new entry will be located (above or below an existing entry in the list of languages).

2. Prompt the user for the new language.

3. Prompt the user for the corresponding greeting. (The location of the greeting can be determined automatically, once the location of the new language is determined.)

4. If the new entry is later deleted, any empty space that might be created by the deletion should be removed by moving all succeeding entries higher up in the list.

Or, carrying this argument one step further, it would be nice to locate the new entry automatically without any user input, based upon its proper location within the alphabetized listing of the languages. We leave these enhancements as exercises for the user.

8.8 LOOPING WITH `For Each-Next`

The `For Each-Next` structure is a convenient looping mechanism when working with arrays, particularly when it is unclear how many elements are in an array (because the program logic may have resulted in the addition or deletion of array elements). In general terms, the `For Each-Next` structure is written as

```
For Each index In array name
    . . . . . . . .
    executable statements
    . . . . . . . .
Next index
```

This structure may be used with either static or dynamic arrays. In either case, the *index* must be a variant.

The `For Each-Next` structure is equivalent to the simplest form of the more commonly used `For To-Next` loop originally discussed in Sec. 3.6; i.e.,

```
For index = value1 To value2
    . . . . . . . .
    executable statements
    . . . . . . . .
Next index
```

However, the `For To-Next` structure requires that *value1* and *value2* be known explicitly, whereas `For Each-Next` does not.

The `For Each-Next` structure is not restricted to arrays. It can also be used with other more advanced Visual Basic objects, though this topic is beyond the scope of our present discussion.

EXAMPLE 8.20

Here is a Visual Basic code segment that sums the elements in an array, using a `For Each-Next` loop.

```
Option Base 1
Dim x() As Integer, Sum As Integer, i As Variant


. . . . .

ReDim x(10)
For i = 1 To 10
    x(i) = i
Next i

Sum = 0
For Each i In x
    Sum = Sum + x(i)
    Print x(i), Sum
Next I
Print
Print "Final Sum = "; Sum
```

Note that x is a dynamic array in this example, to illustrate the technique. An ordinary (static) array could have been used instead.

The elements of x must be assigned values within a conventional `For To-Next` loop (or some other means) prior to entering the `For Each-Next` loop. Thus, we cannot use the simpler code segment

```
Option Base 1
Dim x() As Integer, Sum As Integer, i As Variant



. . . . .


ReDim x(10)
Sum = 0
For Each i In x
    x(i) = i
    Sum = Sum + x(i)
    Print x(i), Sum
Next I
Print
Print "Final Sum = "; Sum
```

The advantage to the For Each-Next structure is that the value of n is not required within the loop structure and hence need not be known explicitly. This feature can be very useful if the number of array elements changes during the program execution, as a result of elements being added or deleted.

Review Questions

8.1   What is an array? In what ways do arrays differ from ordinary variables?

8.2   What condition must be satisfied by all elements within a given array?

8.3   How are individual array elements identified?

8.4   What are subscripted variables? How are they written? What restrictions apply to the values that may be assigned to subscripts?

8.5   What is meant by the dimensionality of an array?

8.6   Suggest a practical way to visualize one-dimensional and two-dimensional arrays.

8.7   When declaring an array, what information is provided the Dim statement? How is the Dim statement written?

8.8   How are the lower and upper bounds of a subscript specified in a Dim statement?

8.9   How can the subscript range of all arrays be specified to begin at 1 rather than 0?

8.10 What value is assigned to all numeric array elements when the array is first declared? What value is assigned to all string arry elements?

8.11 How can an array be declared whose elements are of a user-defined data type?

8.12 How are individual array elements accessed?

8.13 Within a user-defined array, how are individual members of an array element accessed?

8.14 How is an array argument written within the first line of a procedure definition?

8.15 How is an array passed to a procedure as an argument?

8.16 How is an individual array element passed to a procedure as an argument?

8.17 When an array element is passed to a procedure as an element, must the corresponding argument in the procedure definition also be an array element? Explain fully.

8.18 What is a dynamic array? How is a dynamic array declared?

8.19 Once a dynamic array has been declared, how is its size specified? Can a numeric variable or a numeric expression be used for the size specification?

8.20 Can lower subscript limits and upper subscript limits both appear within a dynamic array size specification?

8.21 When a dynamic array is redimensioned, what happens to the values previously assigned to the array elements?

8.22 How can the values previously assigned to the elements of a dynamic array be retained when the array is redimensioned?

8.23 Summarize the purpose of each of the following array-related functions: `Array`, `IsArray`, `LBound`, `UBound`.

8.24 What is a control array? How is a control array created?

8.25 When the elements of a control array share a common event procedure, how is one control distinguished from another within the event procedure?

8.26 Can all of the elements of a control array be assigned the same caption? Can the elements be assigned different captions?

8.27 How are the individual controls within a control array accessed?

8.28 How can a property of a control array element be accessed?

8.29 How is a new control added to a control array during run time? How is an existing control deleted?

8.30 Suppose a control is created as a part of a control array at design time. Can the control be deleted from the array during run time?

8.31 How does the `For Each-Next` structure differ from the more commonly used `For To-Next` structure? What advantage does the `For Each-Next` structure offer?

8.32 Can the `For Each-Next` structure be utilized with dynamic arrays?

8.33 What restriction applies to the index within a `For Each-Next` structure?

Problems

8.34 The following examples each involve references to arrays and/or subscripted variables. Describe the array that is referred to in each situation.

(*a*) `Dim Cost(100) As Single, Items(100, 3) As Integer`

(*b*) `P(i) = P(i) + Q(i, j)`

(c)   `Message(3) = "ERROR CHECK"`

(d)
```
Dim Sum As Double
. . . . .
Sum = 0
For k = 0 To 3
    For j = 0 To 2
        Sum = Sum + Z(k, j)
    Next j
Next k
```

(e)
```
Dim Target As String
. . . . .
Target = . . . . .
. . . . .
If A(5) = Target Then
    MsgBox ("Match Found")
End If
```

8.35   Shown below are several statements or groups of statements involving arrays or array elements. Describe the purpose of each statement or group of statements.

(a)
```
Dim Values(12) As Single
. . . . .
Call Sub1(Values(3))
```

(b)
```
Dim Values(12) As Single
. . . . .
Call Sub1(Values())             (Compare with the previous question)
```

(c)
```
Dim Values(12) As Single
. . . . .
Call Sub1(Values())
. . . . .
ReDim Values(6)
Call Sub1(Values())             (Compare with the previous question)
```

(d)
```
Dim Values(12) As Single
. . . . .
Call Sub1(Values())
. . . . .
ReDim Preserve Values(6)
Call Sub1(Values())             (Compare with the previous question)
```

(e)
```
Dim Values(12) As Single, Index As Integer
. . . . .
For Each Index In Values
    Values(Index) = . . . . .
Next Index
```

(f)
```
For Index = 1 To 6
    Button(Index).FontSize = 12
Next Index
```

8.36 Write one or more statements for each of the following problem situations. Assume that each subscript ranges from 1 to its maximum value (rather than from 0 to its maximum value).

(*a*) Sum the first n elements of the one-dimensional array Costs.

(*b*) Sum all elements in column 3 of the two-dimensional array Values. Assume Values has 60 rows and 20 columns.

(*c*) Sum all elements in row 5 of the two-dimensional array Values described in part (*b*).

(*d*) Sum all elements in the first m rows and the first n columns of the two-dimensional array Values described in part (*b*).

(*e*) Display the first 30 even elements in the one-dimensional string array Names; i.e., display Names(2), Names(4),..., Names(60).

(*f*) Calculate the square root of the sum of the squares of the first 100 odd elements of the one-dimensional array X; i.e., calculate $[X(1)^2 + X(3)^2 + X(5)^2 + ... + X(199)^2]^{1/2}$.

(*g*) Generate the elements of the two-dimensional array H, where each element of H is defined by the formula

$$h_{ij} = 1 / (i + j - 1)$$

Assume that H has 8 rows and 12 columns.

(*h*) Pass the array H generated in the last problem to a sub procedure called Search. Also, show the first line of the procedure definition.

(*i*) A one-dimensional array K has n elements. Display the value of each subscript and each corresponding element for those elements whose values do not exceed Kmax. Display the output in two columns, with the value of the subscript in the first column and the corresponding subscripted variable in the second column. Label each column.

(*j*) A two-dimensional array W has k rows and k columns. Calculate the product of the elements on the main diagonal of W, where the main diagonal runs from upper left to lower right. In other words, calculate W(1, 1) * W(2, 2) * W(3, 3) * . . . * W(k, k).

(*k*) Declare a dynamic, one-dimensional string array called Colors. At some point in the program, specify that Colors will have 20 elements, maintaining any strings that have previously been assigned to Colors.

(*l*) Write a For Each-Next loop that determines the length of each string within Colors (described in the previous problem) and determines which element contains the shortest string. Display the result in a message box. Use the Len function to determine each string length.

(*m*) Loop through all elements of a control array named Labels. Determine how many elements are assigned a 10-point font size.

Programming Problems

8.37   Modify the Visual Basic project shown in Examples 7.2 and 8.9 (smallest of two numbers) to determine either the smallest of two numbers or the largest of two numbers (but not both). Add option buttons so that the user may designate his or her choice. Place the labels in a control array and assign the initial properties at run time. Do the same with the the text boxes, the command buttons and the option buttons.

8.38   Modify the project shown in Example 8.10 (sorting a list of numbers) so that a specified (non-random) list of *n* numbers can be entered via a series of input boxes, as in Example 8.11.

8.39   Extend the project developed for the previous problem (sorting a list of numbers) so that any one of the following four rearrangements can be carried out:

(*a*)   Smallest to largest, by magnitude

(*b*)   Smallest to largest, algebraic (by sign)

(*c*)   Largest to smallest, by magnitude

(*d*)   Largest to smallest, algebraic

Note that the numbers within the list need not necessarily be positive.
   Include a set of option buttons that will allow the user to specify which rearrangement will be used each time the program is executed. Test the program using the following values.

43	−85	−4	65
−83	10	−71	−59
61	−51	−45	−32
14	49	19	23
−94	−34	−50	86

8.40   Write a Visual Basic program that will rearrange a list of names into alphabetical order. To do so, enter the names into a one-dimensional string array, with each element representing one complete name. The list of names can then be alphabetized in the same manner that a list of numbers is rearranged from smallest to largest, as in Example 8.10.
   Use the program to rearrange the following list of names.

Washington	Taylor	Harrison, B.	Kennedy
Adams, J.	Fillmore	McKinley	Johnson, L. B.
Jefferson	Pierce	Roosevelt, T.	Nixon
Madison	Buchanan	Taft	Ford
Monroe	Lincoln	Wilson	Carter
Adams, J. Q.	Johnson, A.	Harding	Reagan
Jackson	Grant	Coolidge	Bush, G. H. W.
Van Buren	Hayes	Hoover	Clinton
Harrison, W. H.	Garfield	Roosevelt, F. D.	Bush, G. W.
Tyler	Arthur	Truman	
Polk	Cleveland	Eisenhower	

8.41   Modify the Visual Basic project shown in Example 8.11 (deviations about an average) so that it utilizes dynamic arrays.

8.42   Modify the Visual Basic project shown in Example 8.11 (deviations about an average) so that the original list of numbers and the list of deviations are each displayed in a separate combo box, as in Example 8.10. Display the average value within a separate text box, accompanied by a label. Do the same for the sum of the deviations.

8.43   Write a Visual Basic program that will generate a list of values of the equation

$$y = 2\,e^{-0.1t}\sin 0.5t$$

for integer values of t ranging from 0 to 60. Place the values in a one-dimensional array. Display the list within a blank portion of the form using the `Print` statement, as in Example 8.11.

8.44   Repeat Problem 8.43, displaying the list of calculated values within a combo box, as in Example 8.10.

8.45   Write a Visual Basic program that will generate a table of $\sin x$, $\cos x$, $\tan x$, $\log_e x$ and e^x. Generate 101 entries for uniformly spaced values of x between 0 and π (i.e., let $x = 0$, $\pi/100$, $2\pi/100$, ... , $99\pi/100$, π). Place the values within a multidimensional array. Include a feature that will display the value of all five functions for any tabulated x-value selected from a text box.

8.46   Write a Visual Basic program that will sum the elements in each row and each column of a table of numbers. Use a multidimensional array to represent the table. Display the sum of each row and the sum of each column. Then calculate the sum of the row sums and the sum of the column sums (they should be equal). Label the sums appropriately.
Test the program using the following table of numbers.

6	0	−12	4	17	21
−8	15	5	5	−18	0
11	3	1	−17	12	7
13	2	13	−9	24	4
−27	−3	0	14	8	−10

8.47   Solve Problem 8.46 by calculating the *product*, rather than the sum, of each row and each column. Then determine the sum of the row products and the sum of the column products (will they be equal?).

8.48   Write a Visual Basic program that will generate a table of compound interest factors, F/P, where

$$F/P = (1 + i / 100)^{n}$$

In this formula F represents the future value of a given sum of money, P represents its present value, i represents the annual interest rate expressed as a percentage, and n represents the number of years.
Use a multidimensional array to represent the table. Let each row in the table correspond to a different value of n, with n ranging from 1 to 20 (hence 20 rows). Let each column represent a different interest rate. Include the following interest rates: 4, 5, 6, 8, 10, 12 and 15 percent (hence a total of seven columns). Be sure to label the rows and columns appropriately.

8.49   Probs. 4.52 and 5.42 present the following list of foreign currencies and their U.S. dollar equivalents.

1 U.S. dollar =	0.6	British pounds
	1.4	Canadian dollars
	2.3	Dutch guilders
	6.8	French francs
	2.0	German marks
	2000	Italian lira
	100	Japanese yen
	9.5	Mexican pesos
	1.6	Swiss francs

Write a Visual Basic program that will accept two different currencies and return the value of the second currency per one unit of the first currency. (For example, if the two currencies are Japanese yen and Mexican pesos, the program will return the number of Mexican pesos equivalent to one Japanese yen.) Use the data given above to carry out the conversions. Utilize a one-dimensional array to represent the foreign currencies. Compare this version of the program with those written for Problems 4.52 and 5.42.

8.50   A group of students earned the following scores for the six examinations taken in a Visual Basic programming course.

Name	Exam Scores (percent)					
Adams	45	80	80	95	55	75
Brown	60	50	70	75	55	80
Davis	40	30	10	45	60	55
Fisher	0	5	5	0	10	5
Hamilton	90	85	100	95	90	90
Jones	95	90	80	95	85	80
Ludwig	35	50	55	65	45	70
Osborne	75	60	75	60	70	80
Prince	85	75	60	85	90	100
Richards	50	60	50	35	65	70
Smith	70	60	75	70	55	75
Thomas	10	25	35	20	30	10
Wolfe	25	40	65	75	85	95
Zorba	65	80	70	100	60	95

Write a Visual Basic program that will accept each student's name and exam scores as input and then determine an average score for each student. Place the names in a one-dimensional array, and place the exam scores, including the student average, in a corresponding multidimensional array. Use a separate dialog box for entering and displaying information for each student.

8.51   Extend the program written for Problem 8.50 so that an overall class average (i.e., the average of the individual student averages) and the deviation of each student's average about the overall class average are determined. Create an additional column within the multidimensional array to hold the deviations about the class average.

Display the class average, followed by the following information for each student:

> student name
>
> individual exam scores
>
> student average
>
> deviation of the student average about the class average.

8.52   Extend the program written for Problem 8.51 to allow for unequal weighting of the individual exam scores. In particular, assume that each of the first four exams contributes 15 percent to the final score, and each of the last two exams contributes 20 percent.

Place the six weighting factors (0.15, 0.15, 0.15, 0.15, 0.20, 0.20) in a separate one-dimensional array. Then determine each student's average as

$$average = f_1 \times exam_1 + f_2 \times exam_2 + \cdots + f_6 \times exam_6$$

where f_1, f_2, etc. represent the weighting factors (expressed as decimals) and $exam_1$, $exam_2$, etc. represent the individual exam scores.

8.53 Problems 4.51 and 5.41 present the following lists of countries and their corresponding capitals.

Canada	Ottawa
England	London
France	Paris
Germany	Berlin
India	New Delhi
Italy	Rome
Japan	Tokyo
Mexico	Mexico City
People's Republic of China	Beijing
Russia	Moscow
Spain	Madrid
United States	Washington

Write a Visual Basic program that will accept the name of a country as input and then display the corresponding capital, and vice versa. Use a two-dimensional array (12 rows, 2 columns) to represent the two lists. Compare this version of the program with those written for Problems 4.51 and 5.41.

8.54 Write a Visual Basic program that calculates the variance, *var*, of a list of numbers two different ways, using the following two formulas:

$$var = [\,(x_1 - avg)^2 + (x_2 - avg)^2 + \cdots + (x_n - avg)^2\,]\,/\,n$$

and

$$var = (x_1^2 + x_2^2 + \cdots + x_n^2)\,/\,n$$

where *avg* is the mean (average) value, calculated as

$$avg = (x_1 + x_2 + \cdots + x_n)\,/\,n$$

and *n* is the number of values in the list.

Use single-precision arithmetic to carry out the calculations. Store the *x*-values in a single-precision array.

Mathematically, the two formulas for *var* can be shown to be identical. When the values of the given numbers are very close together, however, then the value obtained for *var* using the second formula can be considerably in error, particularly when using single-precision arithmetic. The reason for this is that we must calculate the difference between two values that are very nearly equal. Such calculated differences can be highly inaccurate. The first formula for the variance yields much more accurate results under these conditions.

Demonstrate that the above statements are true by calculating the variance of the values given below. (The correct answer is *var* = 0.00339966.)

99.944	100.054	100.059	100.061
100.039	100.066	100.029	100.098
99.960	99.936	100.085	100.038
100.093	99.932	100.079	100.024
99.993	99.913	100.095	100.046

8.55   Repeat Problem 8.54 using double-precision arithmetic, and a double-precision array to store the *x*-values. Compare the results with those obtained in the previous problem.

8.56   Write a Visual Basic program that will encode or decode a line of text. To encode a line of text, proceed as follows.

1.   Enter the line of text and store it as a string.

2.   Enter a positive integer (a *key*), which will be used to form the coded version of the text.

3.   For each character in the string, including blank spaces, carry out the following steps, using the `Mid` and `Asc` library functions.

   (*a*)   Convert the character to its ASCII equivalent.

   (*b*)   Add the key to the ASCII value, thus forming the value of an encoded character.

   (*c*)   Use the `Mod` library function to prevent the value obtained in step (b) from exceeding `Max`, where `Max` represents the highest permissible value in the ASCII code. (If the value obtained in step (*b*) exceeds `Max` we must subtract the largest possible multiple of `Max` from this value, so that the encoded number will always fall between 0 and `Max` and will therefore represent some valid ASCII character.)

   (*d*)   Store the encoded ASCII values in an integer array.

4.   Assemble the encoded ASCII characters into a string, and display the string in a text box.

The procedure is reversed when decoding a line of text. Be certain, however, that the same integer key is used in decoding as was used in encoding.

8.57   Write a Visual Basic program that will allow a person to play a game of tic-tac-toe against the computer. Write the program in such a manner that the computer can be either the first or the second player. If the computer is to be the first player, let the first move be generated randomly. Display the complete status of the game after each move. Have the computer acknowledge a win by either player when it occurs. Include arrays and procedures within the program, as appropriate.

8.58   Write a Visual Basic program that will simulate a game of blackjack between two players. Note that the computer will not be a participant in this game but will simply deal the cards to each player and provide each player with one or more "hits" (additional cards) when requested.

   The cards are dealt in order, first one card to each player, then a second card to each player. Additional hits may then be requested by the first player and then by the second player.

   The object of the game is to obtain 21 points, or as many points as possible without exceeding 21 points. A player is automatically disqualified if his or her hand exceeds 21 points. Face cards count 10 points and an ace can count either 1 point or 11 points. Thus, a player can obtain 21 points with the first two cards (blackjack!) if dealt an ace and either a 10 or a face card. If a player has a relatively low score with the first two cards, he or she may request one or more hits.

   Use a random number generator to simulate the dealing of the cards. Be sure to include a provision that the same card is not dealt more than once. Include arrays and procedures wherever appropriate.

8.59   Roulette is played with a wheel containing 38 different squares along its circumference. Two of these squares, numbered 0 and 00, are green; 18 squares are red, and 18 are black. The red and black squares alternate in color and are numbered 1 through 36 in random order. Each number appears once and only once.

   A small marble is spun within the wheel. Eventually, the marble comes to rest in a groove beneath one of the squares. The game is played by betting on the outcome of each spin in any one of the following ways:

1. By selecting a single red or black square, at 35-to-1 odds. (Thus, if a player were to bet $1.00 and win, he or she would receive a total of $36.00 – the original $1.00 plus an additional $35.00.)

2. By selecting a color (either red or black) at 1-to-1 odds. (Thus, if a player chose red on a $1.00 bet, he or she would receive $2.00 if the marble came to rest beneath any red square.)

3. By selecting either the odd or the even numbers (excluding 0 and 00) at 1-to-1 odds.

4. By selecting either the low 18 or the high 18 numbers at 1-to-1 odds (again, 0 and 00 are excluded).

The player will automatically lose if the marble comes to rest beneath one of the green squares (0 or 00).

Write a Visual Basic program that will simulate a roulette game. Allow the players to bet any way they wish. Then display the outcome of each game, followed by a message indicating whether each player has won or lost. Include arrays and procedures, as appropriate.

8.60 Write a Visual Basic program that will simulate a game of BINGO. Display each letter-number combination as it is drawn. Be sure that no combination is drawn more than once. Remember that each of the letters B-I-N-G-O corresponds to a certain range of numbers, as indicated below.

```
B:     1 – 15
I:    16 – 30
N:    31 – 45
G:    46 – 60
O:    61 – 75
```

Include arrays and procedures within the program, as appropriate.

Chapter 9

Data Files

A *file* is an orderly, self-contained collection of information. Any type of information can be stored within a file. Thus, a file may contain the instructions that comprise a Visual Basic program, it may be a graphical bitmap, it may contain information used to create music, or it may consist of data values (typically, numerical values and strings). This last type of file is commonly known as a *data file*.

Data files offer a convenient means of storing large quantities of information, since the files can be stored on auxiliary storage devices (e.g., a hard drive) and read into the computer as needed. Moreover, individual data items within a data file can easily be read into the computer, updated and written back out to the data file, all under the control of a single program. This chapter is concerned with Visual Basic programs that create and process data files.

9.1 DATA FILE CHARACTERISTICS

Visual Basic recognizes three different types of data files: *sequential files* (also called *text files*), *random access files*, and *binary files* (also called *unformatted files*). Sequential files are the easiest to work with, since they can be created by a text editor or word processor, or by a Visual Basic program. Such files consist of variable-length strings, organized into individual lines of text. Sequential files can be displayed or printed at the operating system level (outside of Visual Basic), and they are easily imported into an application program, such as a word processor or spreadsheet program. In order to access a particular line of text, however, you must start at the beginning of the file and progress through the file sequentially, until the desired line has been located. This process can be very time-consuming when searching through a large file.

Random access files are organized into fixed-length *records*. (A *record* is a set of related data items, such as a name, an address and a telephone number. Each data item within a record fills a *field*). Any record can be accessed directly by specifying the corresponding record number or record location. Thus, it is not necessary to read through the entire file in order to access a particular record. Applications that require direct access to individual records without regard to their order (as, for example, the daily updating of customer accounts as they are received) will therefore execute much faster with direct rather than sequential data files.

Finally, binary files store information as a continuous sequences of bytes. Such files appear unintelligible when printed or displayed on a computer screen, but their contents can be read into or written out of a computer faster than other file types, particularly sequential files.

9.2 ACCESSING AND SAVING A FILE IN VISUAL BASIC: THE COMMON DIALOG CONTROL

Visual Basic includes special tools for opening an existing file, and for saving either a new file or an existing file that has been modified. These tools are included in a group of *common dialog objects* that must be added to the Toolbox before any of these tools can be accessed. To do so, select Components from the Project menu. Then click on the Controls tab and check the box labeled Microsoft Common Dialog Control, as shown in Fig. 9.1.

Once the common dialog control has been activated, the common dialog control icon will appear in the lower right portion of the Toolbox, as shown in Fig. 9.2.

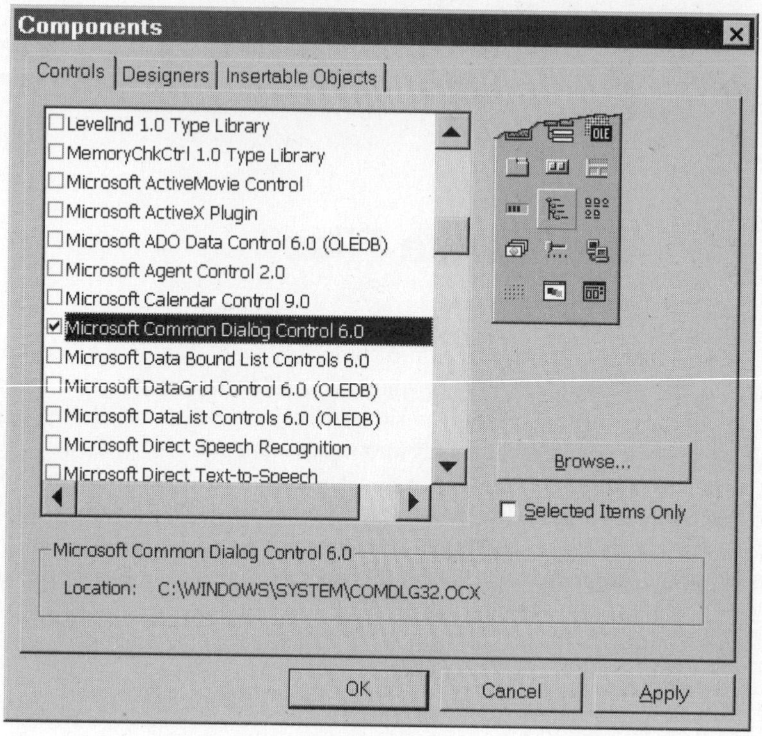

Fig. 9.1 Activating the Common Dialog Control

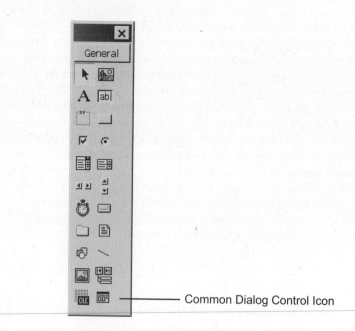

Fig. 9.2 The Toolbox, with the addition of the Common Dialog Control

When developing a Visual Basic project that involves opening a file or saving a file, place the common dialog control within a form, as you would with any other control tool. Unlike most other control tools, however, the common dialog control does not appear within the form when the project is being executed. Therefore, it does not matter where it is placed within the form. Usually, it is located in some out-of-the-way corner where it will not interfere with other controls, as shown in Fig. 9.3.

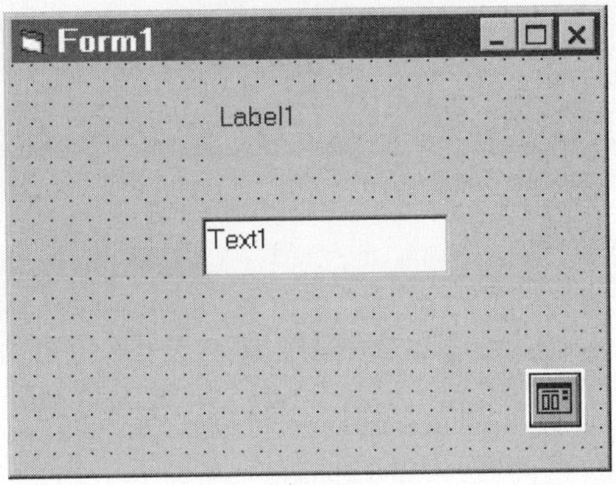

Fig. 9.3

The common dialog control allows an application to easily access existing files or save new files through its common dialog boxes. For example, to access an existing file (i.e., to "open" the file), simply add a statement similar to that shown below at the appropriate place.

```
CommonDialog1.ShowOpen
```

When this statement is encountered during program execution, a dialog box similar to that shown in Fig. 9.4 will appear. The user may then use this dialog box to access a file within the currently active folder, or may maneuver to another folder to access a file. The type of files (i.e., the extension) can be specified within the program by assigning an appropriate string to the CommonDialog1.Filter property; e.g.,

```
CommonDialog1.Filter = "Text files (*.txt)|*.txt"
```

(This particular string assignment restricts the display to text files, though this restriction can be overridden by clicking on the down-arrow at the end of the box labeled Files of type.)

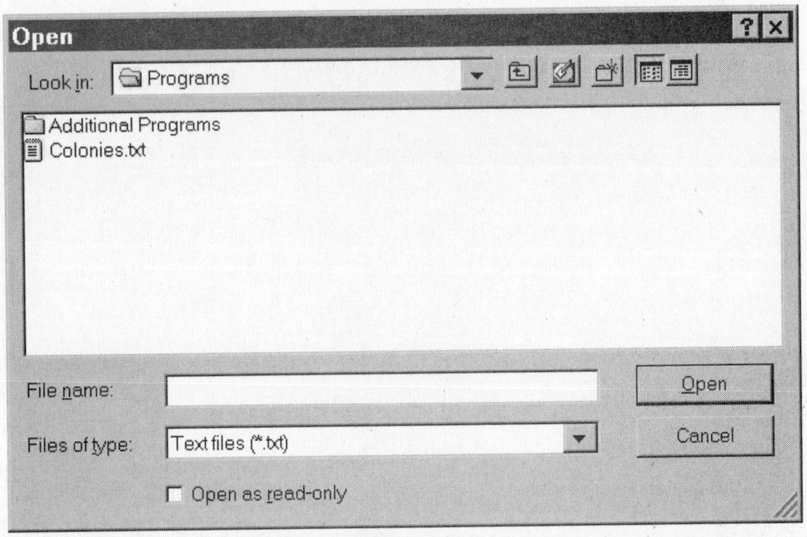

Fig. 9.4 The File Open dialog box

Similarly, to save a file with a specified name, add a statement such as

```
CommonDialog1.ShowSave
```

When the ShowSave statement is encountered, a dialog box resembling that shown in Fig. 9.5 will appear. The user may then use this dialog box to save a file within the currently active folder, or some other folder either above or below the currently active folder. The type of files (i.e., the extension) that can be saved is specified by assigning an appropriate string to the CommonDialog1.Filter property, as shown previously. The file type can be changed by clicking on the down-arrow at the end of the box labeled Save as type.

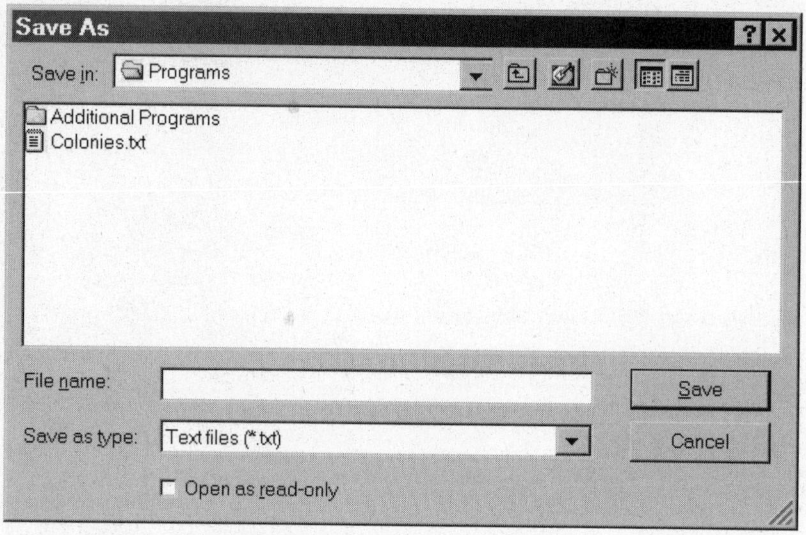

Fig. 9.5 The Save As dialog box

The common dialog control also permits the display of dialog boxes that allow the user to specify printer settings, to select a font, or to select a color. These dialog boxes are not required for accessing or saving data files, though the Print dialog box, shown in Fig. 9.6, is used in many file-related applications. The Print dialog box is generated by including a statement resembling the following at the appropriate place within the code.

```
CommonDialog1.ShowPrint
```

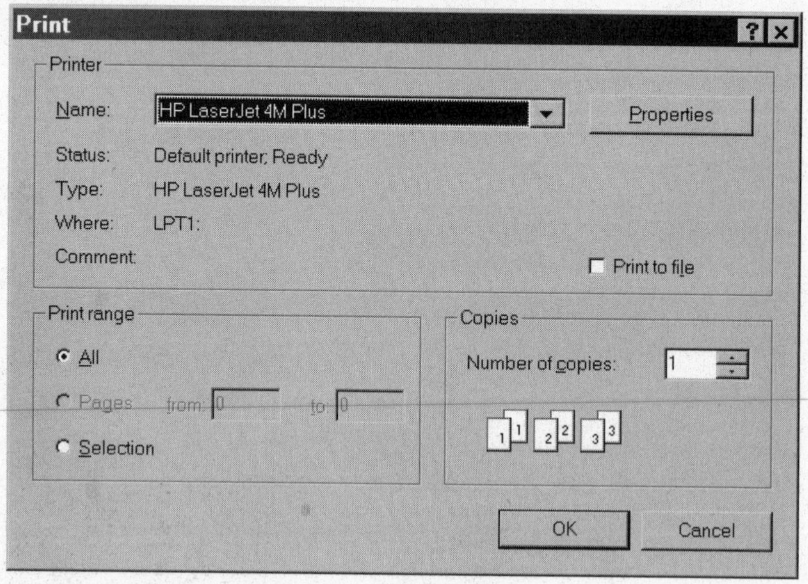

Fig. 9.6 The Print dialog box

9.3 PROCESSING A DATA FILE

All applications involving the use of data files are based upon the same overall sequence of events. Specifically, the following three tasks must be carried out.

1. Open the data file.

2. Process the file, as required by the application.

3. Close the file.

Opening the data file associates a *channel number* (also called a *file number*) with a named data file. It also specifies certain information about the data file, such as the *mode* (Input, Output, Append, Random, or Binary), the *access type* (Read, Write, or ReadWrite) and any *restrictions* (Shared, Lock Read, Lock Write, or Lock ReadWrite). (Do not confuse opening a data file with the process of *retrieving* a data file via the Open dialog box, as described in the last section.)

Processing the data file generally involves reading the data items, modifying the data items, displaying the data items, and then writing the modified data items. There are many variations of this theme, depending upon the particular application.

Closing the data file is a formality that simply deactivates the conditions that were specified when the file was opened. Visual Basic automatically closes all data files at the end of program execution if Close statements are not explicitly included within the program. Good programming practice suggests, however, that all open data files be closed explicitly.

A file can no longer be accessed after it is closed, unless it is later reopened. Note, however, that a file can be reopened in another mode, with another access type, etc., after it has been closed. Some applications require that a file be reopened after it has been closed, as, for example, to read a set of data items after the records have been created or modified by the same program.

EXAMPLE 9.1

Here is a skeletal outline of a Visual Basic procedure that reads data from a sequential file.

```
Private Sub mnuOpen_Click()
    Dim OldFile As String, i As Integer

    CommonDialog1.ShowOpen
    OldFile = CommonDialog1.FileName
    Open OldFile For Input As #1
    i = 0
    Do Until EOF(1)
        . . . . .
        'read each data item from the input file, then process the data item
        'continue until an end-of-file (EOF) condition has been detected on channel #1
        . . . . .
        i = i + 1
    Loop
    Close #1
End Sub
```

The CommonDialog1.ShowOpen command generates the Open dialog box, as shown in Fig. 9.4. The file name entered in this dialog box is then assigned to the string variable OldFile.

The Open statement specifies that the data file is a sequential input file (i.e., an input text file) associated with data channel #1. The Do Until loop then reads data from the input file and updates the data (the details of which are not shown). Each pass through the loop reads and updates one data item. Note that EOF is a library function that returns a True condition once an end-of-file condition has been detected. Hence, the looping action continues until an end-of-file condition is encountered on data channel #1. Finally, the Close statement closes the file associated with data channel #1.

Writing to a sequential file is handled in a similar manner, as outlined below.

```
Private Sub mnuSaveAs_Click()
    Dim NewFile As String, i As Integer, n As Integer

    CommonDialog1.ShowSave
    NewFile = CommonDialog1.FileName
    Open NewFile For Output As #2
    n = . . . . .
    For i = 0 To n

        . . . . .
        'write each data item to the output file on channel #2
        . . . . .

    Next i
    Close #2
End Sub
```

The CommonDialog1.ShowSave command generates the Save As dialog box, similar to that shown in Fig. 9.5. The file name entered in this dialog box is then assigned to the string variable NewFile.

The Open statement specifies that the data file is a sequential output file (i.e., an output text file) associated with data channel #2. The For To-Next loop writes the data to the output file after the data has been processed (the details of which are not shown). Each pass through the loop writes one data item. Note that the value for n is assumed known.

The Close statement then closes the file associated with data channel #2.

It is also possible to write new information at the end of an existing sequential file. To do so, the above outline might be written as

```
Private Sub mnuSaveAs_Click()
    Dim OldFile As String, i As Integer, n As Integer

    CommonDialog1.ShowSave
    OldFile = CommonDialog1.FileName
    Open OldFile For Append As #1
    n = . . . . .
    For i = 0 To n

        . . . . .
        'write each new data item at the end of the existing file on channel #1
        . . . . .

    Next i
    Close #1
End Sub
```

Note the use of the keyword Append (rather than Input or Output) in the Open statement. This is required when appending information to an existing sequential file.

Before leaving this example, we remark that the Open statement is written somewhat differently when working with random or binary files. The details will be discussed later in this chapter.

9.4 SEQUENTIAL DATA FILES (TEXT FILES)

A sequential data file is characterized by the fact that the data is stored sequentially, as plain text (i.e., as ASCII characters). The text is organized into individual lines, with each line ending with ASCII *line feed* (LF) and *carriage return* (CF) characters. Each line of text can contain both numeric constants and strings, in any combination.

When opening a sequential file, the Open statement is generally written in one three ways, depending on whether the file is an input file, an output file, or an append file, as shown in Example 9.1. The three possibilities are

Open *filename* For Input As #*n*

Open *filename* For Output As #*n*

Open *filename* For Append As #*n*

where *n* refers to the channel number (i.e., the file number).

Data items are usually read from a sequential data file via the Input # statement. This statement is written in general terms as

Input #*n*, *data items*

where *n* refers to the channel number and *data items* refers to the list of input data items, separated by commas. The input data items are typically variables, array elements, control properties, etc.

Similarly, data items are usually written to a sequential data file via the Print # statement, which in general terms is written as

Print #*n*, *data items*

where the data items can be constants, variables, expressions, array elements, control properties, etc.

Now consider the arrangement of the data items within the input data file. Within any line, consecutive numeric constants must be separated by commas. Strings are usually (but not always) enclosed in quotation marks. However, if a string includes commas or blank spaces as a part of the string, it *must* be enclosed in quotation marks. Consecutive strings that are enclosed in quotation marks need not be separated by commas.

EXAMPLE 9.2 TEXT FILE FUNDAMENTALS

In this example we present a Visual Basic project that will read data from a sequential file, write the data to a new sequential file, and/or print out the data. In developing this project we will make use of the Open, Save As and Print common dialog boxes discussed in Sec. 9.1.

Let us begin with the preliminary control layout shown in Fig. 9.7. Note that the form includes a menu labeled File, a label, a combo box, and a common dialog control. The individual menu items, Open, SaveAs, Print and Exit, are shown in Fig. 9.8.

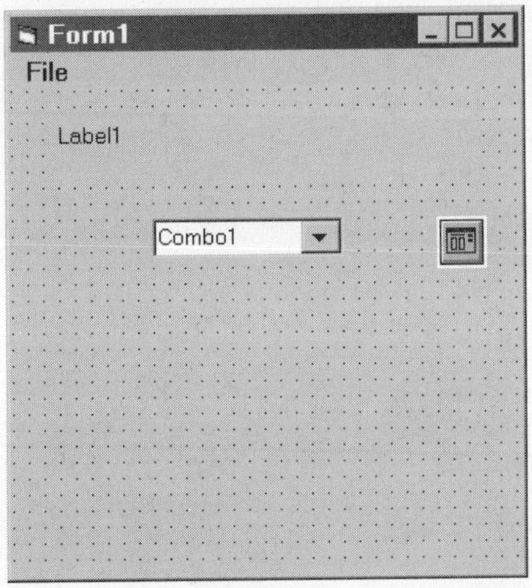

Fig. 9.7

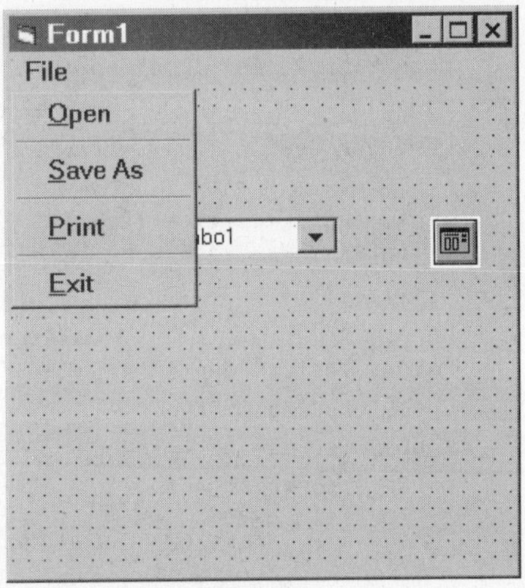

Fig. 9.8

The entries in the menu editor, used to generate the File menu, are shown below (see Chap. 5).

Caption	Name
File	mnuFile
....&Open	mnuOpen
....-	mnuSep1
....&Save As	mnuSaveAs
....-	mnuSep2
....&Print	mnuPrint
....-	mnuSep3
....&Exit	mnuExit

Recall that each menu item is associated with event procedure. Here is the complete list of event procedures.

```
Private Sub Form_Load()
    Form1.Caption = "Text File 1"

    Label1.Caption = "Text File Fundamentals"
    Label1.FontSize = 12
    Label1.Alignment = 2     'Center

    Combo1.Text = ""

    mnuSaveAs.Enabled = False
    mnuPrint.Enabled = False
End Sub


Private Sub mnuOpen_Click()
    Dim OldFile As String, Item As String
    Dim i As Integer

    CommonDialog1.CancelError = True     'activate error detection
    On Error GoTo CancelButton           'error trap for Cancel button
    CommonDialog1.Filter = "Text files (*.txt)|*.txt"
    CommonDialog1.ShowOpen
    OldFile = CommonDialog1.FileName
    Open OldFile For Input As #1
    i = 0
    Do Until EOF(1)
        Input #1, Item
        Combo1.List(i) = Item
        Combo1.Tag = i           'tag the number of file entries
        i = i + 1
    Loop
    Combo1.Text = "Contents"
    Combo1.Locked = True         'prevent user changes to combo box entries
    mnuSaveAs.Enabled = True
    mnuPrint.Enabled = True
    Close #1
CancelButton:
    Exit Sub
End Sub
```

```
Private Sub mnuSaveAs_Click()
    Dim NewFile As String
    Dim i As Integer, n As Integer

    CommonDialog1.CancelError = True      'activate error detection
    On Error GoTo CancelButton            'error trap for Cancel button
    CommonDialog1.Filter = "Text files (*.txt)|*.txt"
    CommonDialog1.ShowSave
    NewFile = CommonDialog1.FileName
    Open NewFile For Output As #2
    n = Val(Combo1.Tag)
    For i = 0 To n
        Print #2, Combo1.List(i)
    Next i
    Close #2
CancelButton:
    Exit Sub
End Sub

Private Sub mnuPrint_Click()
    Dim i As Integer, n As Integer

    CommonDialog1.CancelError = True      'activate error detection
    On Error GoTo CancelButton            'error trap for Cancel button
    CommonDialog1.ShowPrinter
    n = Val(Combo1.Tag)
    For i = 0 To n
        Printer.Print Combo1.List(i)
    Next i
    Printer.EndDoc
CancelButton:
    Exit Sub
End Sub

Private Sub mnuExit_Click()
    End
End Sub
```

The Form_Load procedure is straightforward. Note, however, that we initially generate an empty heading for the combo box (Combo1.Text = ""), and that we initially disable the SaveAs and Print menu items. These menu items will be enabled during program execution, once an input file has been opened.

In contrast, the mnuOpen_Click procedure requires considerable explanation, mostly because of the statements associated with the Open common dialog box. The commands

```
CommonDialog1.CancelError = True
On Error GoTo CancelButton
```

activate error trapping, so that an error trap can be initiated if the user clicks on the Cancel button within the Open dialog box. The actual error trap, shown at the bottom of the procedure, simply causes the program to exit the mnuOpen_Click procedure if the Cancel button is selected.

The next statement,

```
CommonDialog1.Filter = "Text files (*.txt)|*.txt"
```

restricts the list of available files to those with the .txt extension, as in Fig. 9.4. There are many other variations of this statement, including one that causes all available files within the current folder to be displayed; namely,

```
CommonDialog1.Filter = "All files (*.*)|*.*"
```

We then generate the Open dialog box, assign a filename to the variable OldFile, and then open the file as an input text file on channel #1.

We then enter a loop that reads data items from the input file via the Input #*n* statement, until an end-of-file condition has been detected. The EOF library function is used to detect the end-of-file condition.

The statement

```
Combo1.Tag = i
```

causes the current value of the index i to be assigned to the tag property. After the last pass through the loop, Combo1.tag will then represent the number of data items read from the file.

The two disabled menu items, Save As and Print, are enabled near the end of the procedure. This is followed by the Close statement, which closes the open text file.

The mnuSaveAs_Click and mnuPrint_Click procedures are similar. Note, however, that each of these procedures includes a For To-Next loop, in which the number of passes is known in advance. The value of Combo1.tag, assigned in mnuOpen_Click, provides the number of passes through each loop.

When the program is executed, we first see the form shown in Fig. 9.9. We can then select either Open or Exit from the drop-down menu, as shown in Fig. 9.10.

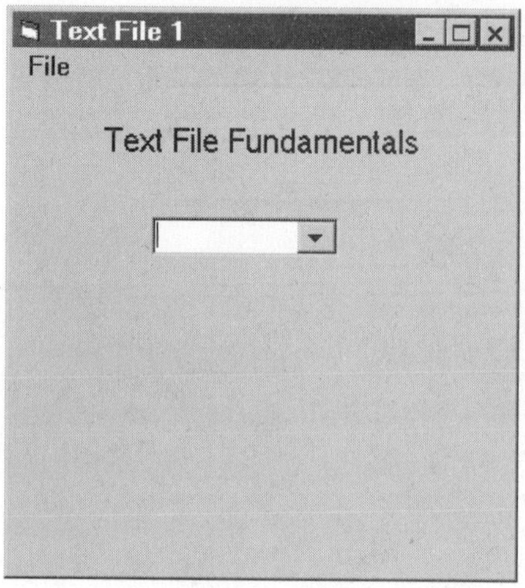

Fig. 9.9 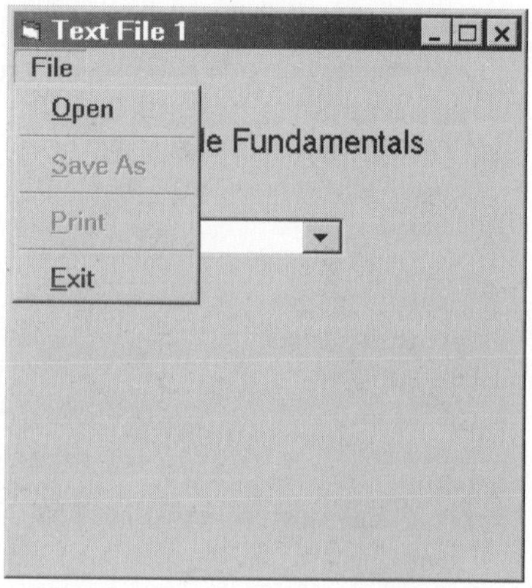   Fig. 9.10

Now suppose we select Open from the drop-down menu, resulting in an Open dialog box similar to that shown in Fig. 9.4. Suppose we then select the data file Sample.txt, containing the following information.

```
red white blue
green yellow black
123 456 789
```

The number of data items read from the file and the content of the data items will depend on the manner in which the data items are written within the text file. If the data items are entered exactly as shown above, then each complete line of information will be entered as a single data item, as shown in Fig. 9.11. The reason for this is the absence of commas separating the individual data items within the text file. Thus, if we alter the data file so that it appears as

```
red, white, blue
green, yellow, black
123, 456, 789
```

then each individual data item within the data file will be read into the computer separately, as shown in Fig. 9.12. This is the result that is most likely to be desired when reading simple data items (i.e., numeric constants and/or strings not containing any commas or blank spaces).

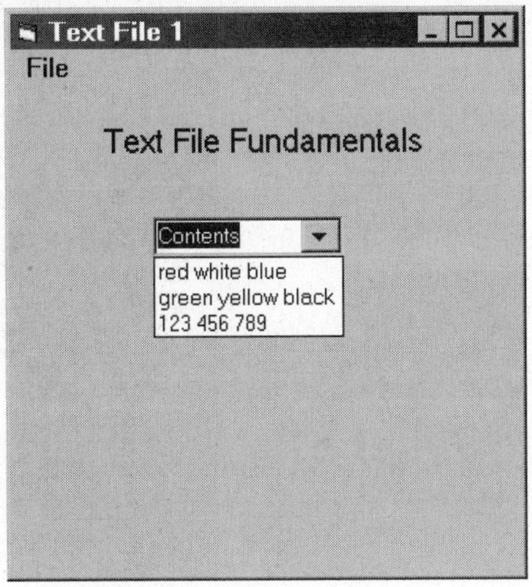

Fig. 9.11 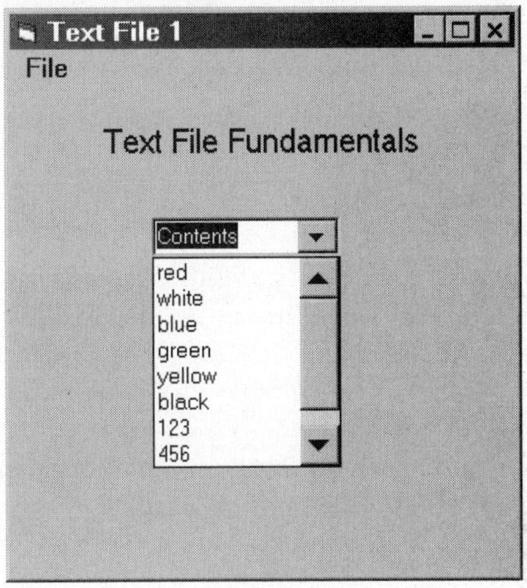   **Fig. 9.12**

Placing quotes around the individual data items, i.e.,

```
"red" "white" "blue"
"green" "yellow" "black"
"123" "456" "789"
```

will produce the same results as those shown in Fig. 9.12, thus replacing the need for commas as separators. Furthermore, commas and quotes may be combined; i.e.,

```
"red", "white", "blue"
"green", "yellow", "black"
"123", "456", "789"
```

though the results will still be the same as those shown in Fig. 9.12.

Until now, we have focused on entering data from a text file via the Input #*n* statement, and writing data to a text file via the Print #*n* statement. However, there are other ways to enter and write data that are convenient in certain situations. For example, the Line Input statement; i.e.

Line Input #*n data item*

enters an entire line of text as a single data item. Any commas or quotation marks that are included as separate data item delimiters are simply entered as a part of the text, along with everything else.

The Input library function is also useful under certain conditions. This function returns a specified number of bytes from a given data channel. The function is written in general terms as

Input(*number of bytes*, #*n*)

When combined with the LOF (length-of-file) library function, the Input function can be used to read an entire text file as a single data item, as shown in the following example.

EXAMPLE 9.3

Suppose we have opened an input text file on data channel #1. Then the following assignment statement will cause the contents of the entire data file to be assigned to the string variable Message.

```
Dim Message As String
. . . . .
Message = Input(LOF(1), #1)
```

When writing data to a text file, we may wish to use the Write #*n* statement rather than the Print #*n* statement. This statement is very useful when generating a text file from information entered from the keyboard.

The Write #*n* statement is written in general terms as

Write #*n*, *data items*

This statement causes the data items to be separated by commas. In addition, each string item will be enclosed in quotation marks. The following example illustrates the use of the Write #*n* statement.

EXAMPLE 9.4 CREATING A SEQUENTIAL DATA FILE: DAILY HIGH TEMPERATURES

We now develop a Visual Basic program that accepts information from the keyboard via a series of input boxes, and writes the information to a sequential text file. We will use the program to enter the following list of daily high temperatures for a typical summer week in Pittsburgh, Pennsylvania.

Day	High Temperature, °F
Sunday	77
Monday	76
Tuesday	81
Wednesday	87
Thursday	84
Friday	79
Saturday	74

We begin with the preliminary control layout shown in Fig. 9.13. The File menu contains the entries New and Exit, as shown in Fig. 9.14.

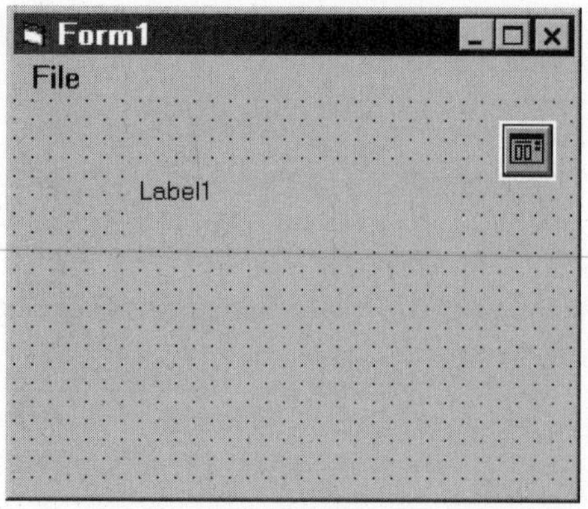

Fig. 9.13 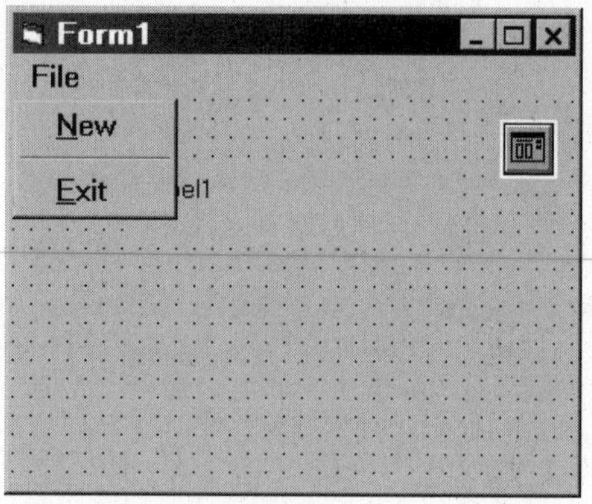   Fig. 9.14

Here are the corresponding menu editor entries.

Caption	Name
File	mnuFile
....&New	mnuNew
....-	mnuSep1
....&Exit	mnuExit

The associated event procedures are shown below.

```
Private Sub Form_Load()
    Form1.Caption = "Creating a Data File"

    Label1.Caption = "Daily Temperatures"
    Label1.FontSize = 12
    Label1.Alignment = 2     'center text

End Sub

Private Sub mnuNew_Click()
    Dim NewFile As String, Day As String
    Dim HiTemp As Single

    CommonDialog1.CancelError = True
    On Error GoTo CancelButton
    CommonDialog1.Filter = "Text file (*.txt) |*.txt"
    CommonDialog1.ShowSave
    NewFile = CommonDialog1.FileName
    Open NewFile For Output As #1
    Day = InputBox("Please enter the day of the week _
                                    (type END when finished):", "Day")
    Do While UCase(Day) <> "END"
       HiTemp = Val(InputBox("Please enter the high temperature:", "High Temp"))
       Write #1, Day, HiTemp
       Day = InputBox("Please enter the day of the week _
                                    (type END when finished):", "Day")

    Loop
    Close #1
CancelButton:
    Exit Sub
End Sub

Private Sub mnuExit_Click()
    End
End Sub
```

Event procedure mnuNew_Click uses the SaveAs dialog box to name the output file. A Do While loop is used to enter the data and save it to the output file. Two input boxes, one for the day of the week and the other for the daily high temperature, are generated for each day. The looping action continues until the user enters the string "End" (in either upper- or lowercase) when prompted for the day. Notice that the first weekday is entered before entering the loop, so that the logical condition within the Do While statement can be evaluated during the first pass through the loop.

Once a string representing the day and a value for the high temperature have been entered, the information is written to the output file via the Write #n statement. Each day's information is written on a separate line in the output file.

When the program is executed, the form shown in Fig. 9.15 first appears. We then select New from the File menu, as shown in Fig. 9.16. This results in the SaveAs dialog box, shown in Fig. 9.17. (Note that the purpose of the SaveAs dialog box in this application is simply to provide a file name.)

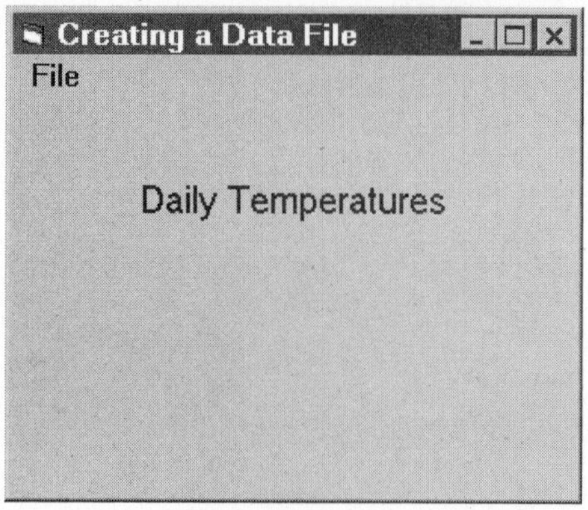

Fig. 9.15

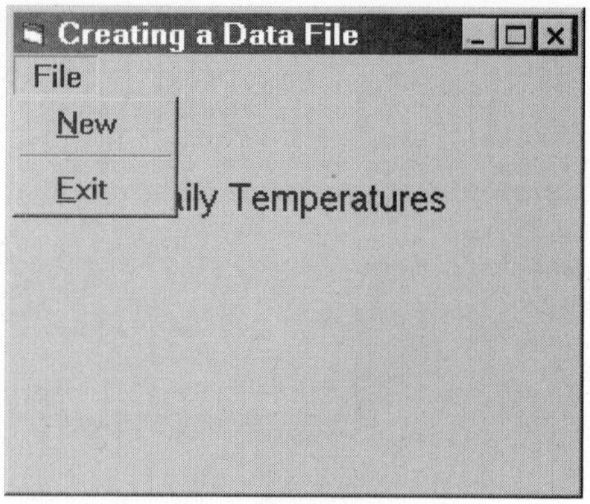

Fig. 9.16

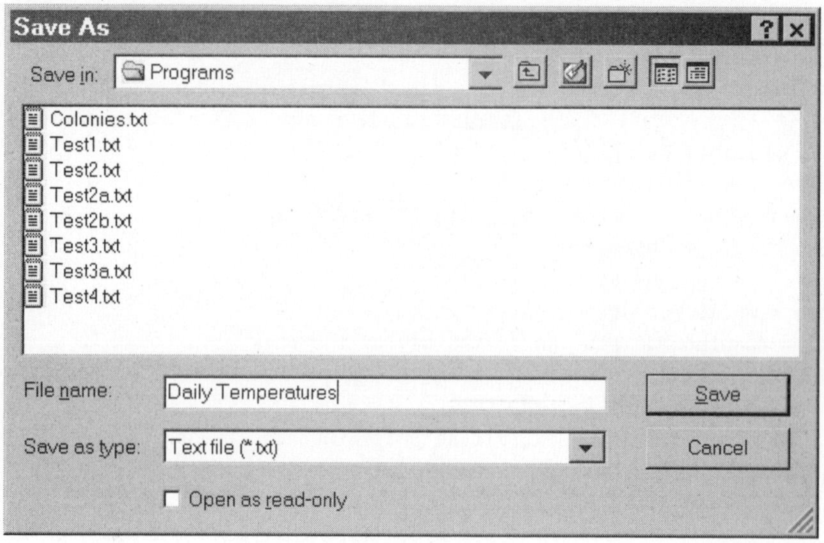

Fig. 9.17

Once a file name has been provided a pair of dialog boxes appears, prompting for the day, as shown in Fig. 9.18, and the corresponding daily high temperature, as shown in Fig. 9.19. This process continues until the user enters "End" as the day of the week, as shown in Fig. 9.20. The program execution is then terminated by selecting Exit from the File menu.

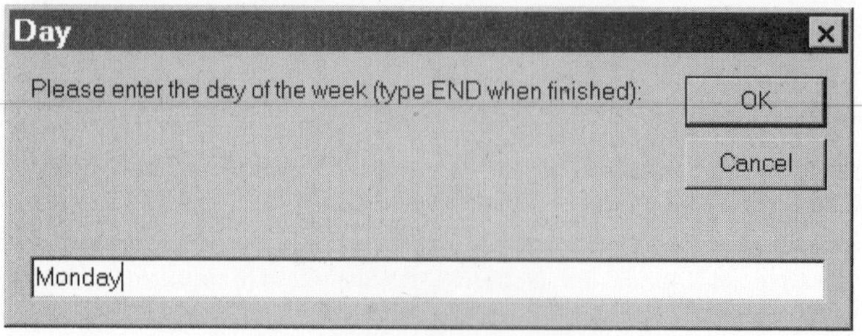

Fig. 9.18

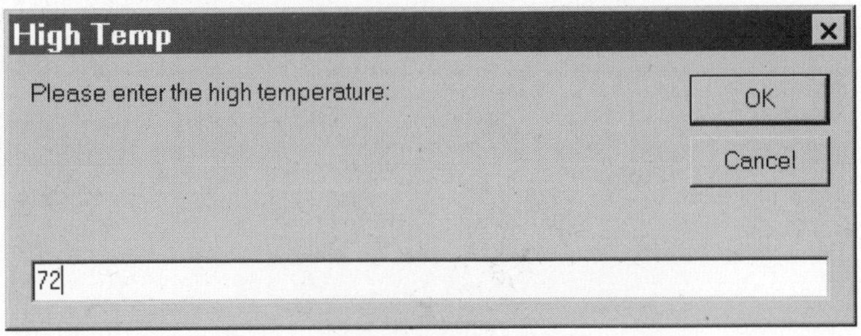

Fig. 9.19

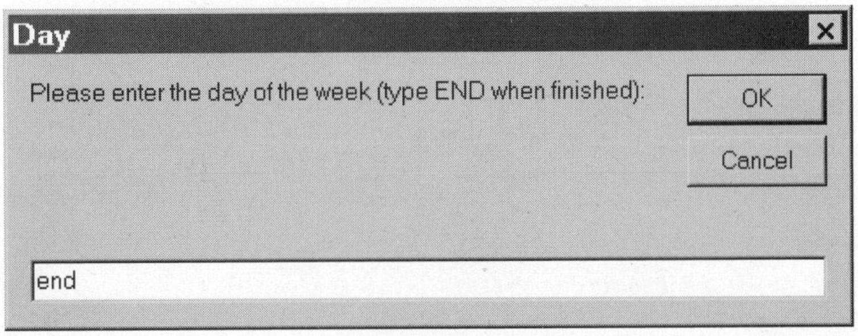

Fig. 9.20

After the program execution has been completed, a sequential text file called Daily Temperatures.txt will have been created. The contents of this text file are shown below. Note that the final string, "End," is not included in the text file.

```
"Sunday",77
"Monday",76
"Tuesday",81
"Wednesday",87
"Thursday",84
"Friday",79
"Saturday",74
```

A program that creates a new text file can easily be altered so that it also appends additional information to an existing text file. To do so, simply open an existing text file as an Append file; then proceed as you would if you were creating a new text file. The following example illustrates the technique.

EXAMPLE 9.5 APPENDING A SEQUENTIAL DATA FILE: MORE DAILY TEMPERATURES

Let us modify the Visual Basic program created in the last example so that it can now append new information to an existing sequential text file as well as create a new text file. Hence, we will add a new menu item, Append, as shown in Fig. 9.21.

The corresponding event procedure, mnuAppend_Click, is shown beneath Fig. 9.21. This event procedure is very similar to mnuNew_Click, presented in the last example. Now, however, we refer to the filename as OldFile rather than NewFile; we use the Open common dialog box to open the existing file, and we open it as an Append file rather than an output file.

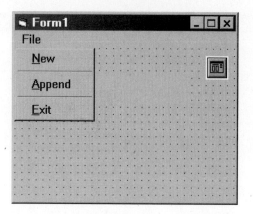

Fig. 9.21

```
Private Sub mnuAppend_Click()
    Dim OldFile As String, Day As String
    Dim HiTemp As Single

    CommonDialog1.CancelError = True
    On Error GoTo CancelButton
    CommonDialog1.Filter = "Text file (*.txt) |*.txt"
    CommonDialog1.ShowOpen
    OldFile = CommonDialog1.FileName
    Open OldFile For Append As #1
    Day = InputBox("Please enter the day of the week _
                                  (type END when finished):", "Day")
    Do While UCase(Day) <> "END"
        HiTemp = Val(InputBox("Please enter the high temperature:", "High Temp"))
        Write #1, Day, HiTemp
        Day = InputBox("Please enter the day of the week _
                                  (type END when finished):", "Day")
    Loop
    Close #1
CancelButton:
    Exit Sub
End Sub
```

Suppose we wish to append the following data to the file `Daily Temperatures.txt`, which was created in the last example.

Day	High Temperature, °F
Sunday	70
Monday	67
Tuesday	74
Wednesday	79
Thursday	83
Friday	86
Saturday	85

If we execute the program and select Append from the File menu (see Fig. 9.22), the Open menu appears. We then specify the filename `Daily Temperatures.txt`, as shown in Fig. 9.23.

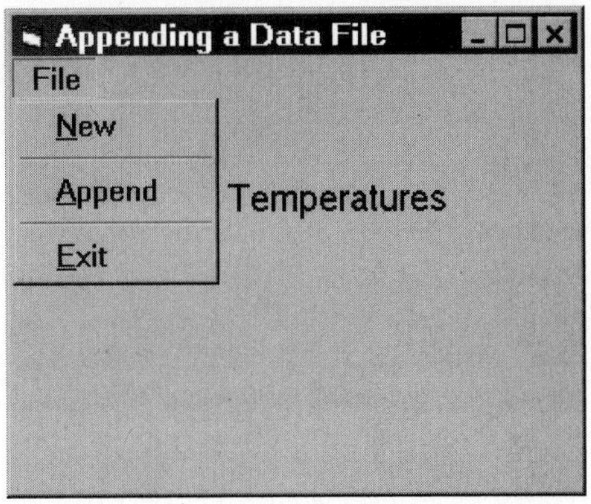

Fig. 9.22

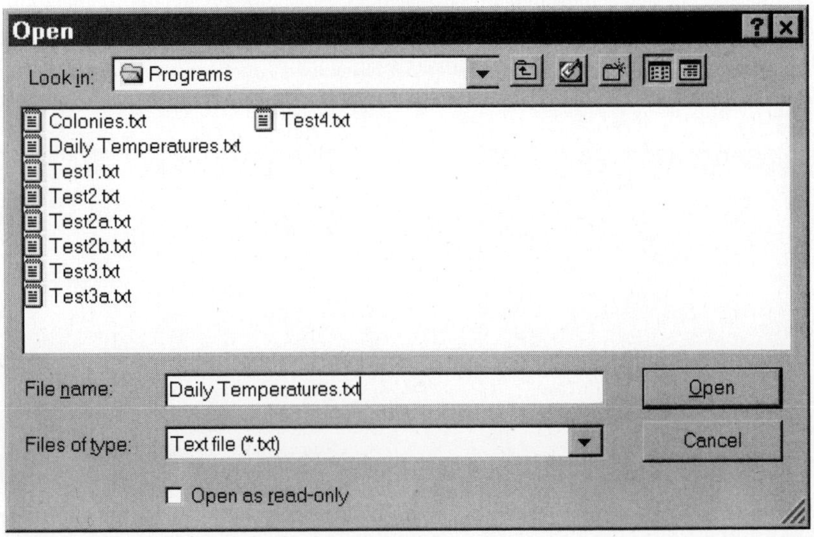

Fig. 9.23

This is followed by a series of input boxes, prompting for the day of the week and the corresponding high temperature, as shown in Example 9.4. At the conclusion of the data entry, the user must type "End" when prompted for the day of the week. Selecting Exit from the File menu then concludes the program execution.

Once the program execution has been completed, the data file will appear as shown below.

```
"Sunday",77
"Monday",76
"Tuesday",81
"Wednesday",87
"Thursday",84
"Friday",79
"Saturday",74
"Sunday",70
"Monday",67
"Tuesday",74
"Wednesday",79
"Thursday",83
"Friday",86
"Saturday",85
```

In many applications, the information stored in a data file will be read and then processed by a Visual Basic program. The data items in a sequential data file must be read in the same order they are stored, starting at the beginning of the file. All of the information within the data file will be preserved in its original form for subsequent use.

EXAMPLE 9.6 PROCESSING A SEQUENTIAL DATA FILE: AVERAGING DAILY TEMPERATURES

In this example we present a Visual Basic program that will read the daily high temperatures from the sequential data file Daily Temperatures.txt and determine an average daily high temperature. We will read from the appended form of the data file, as shown in the preceding example.

We begin with the preliminary control layout shown in Fig. 9.24. This is an extension of the control layout presented in Example 9.5, with the addition of a text box, an additional label, and two command buttons. The text box and its accompanying label (Label2) will display the average temperature. Command button Command1 will be used to read the data file and calculate the average, and command button Command2 will be used to end the computation. (Note that we are introducing some redundancy into the program, since the File menu also includes a menu item that will end the computation. Many commercial applications include such redundancy.)

When the program is executed, the form will take on the appearance shown in Fig. 9.25.

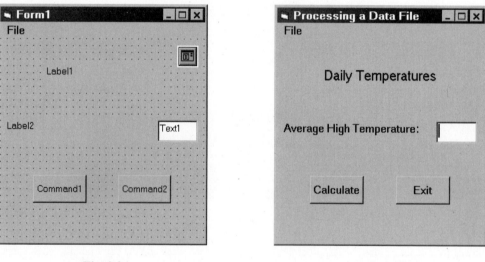

Fig. 9.24   Fig. 9.25

The event procedures included in this program are shown below. Note that event procedures mnuNew_Click, mnuAppend_Click, and mnuExit_Click are identical to those presented in Examples 9.4 and 9.5. However, event procedure Form_Load has been modified from its earlier versions, and event procedures Command1_Click and Command2_Click are new.

```
Private Sub Form_Load()
    Form1.Caption = "Processing a Data File"

    Label1.Caption = "Daily Temperatures"
    Label1.FontSize = 12
    Label1.Alignment = 2     'center text
    Label2.Caption = "Average High Temperature:"
    Label2.FontSize = 10
    Text1.Text = ""
    Text1.FontSize = 10
```
(Continues on next page)

```
        Command1.Caption = "Calculate"
        Command1.FontSize = 10
        Command2.Caption = "Exit"
        Command2.FontSize = 10

End Sub

Private Sub mnuNew_Click()
        Dim NewFile As String, Day As String
        Dim HiTemp As Single

        CommonDialog1.CancelError = True
        On Error GoTo CancelButton
        CommonDialog1.Filter = "Text file (*.txt) |*.txt"
        CommonDialog1.ShowSave
        NewFile = CommonDialog1.FileName
        Open NewFile For Output As #1
        Day = InputBox("Please enter the day of the week _
                                      (type END when finished):", "Day")

        Do While UCase(Day) <> "END"
            HiTemp = Val(InputBox("Please enter the high temperature:", "High Temp"))
            Write #1, Day, HiTemp
            Day = InputBox("Please enter the day of the week _
                                      (type END when finished):", "Day")

        Loop
        Close #1
CancelButton:
        Exit Sub
End Sub

Private Sub mnuAppend_Click()
        Dim OldFile As String, Day As String
        Dim HiTemp As Single

        CommonDialog1.CancelError = True
        On Error GoTo CancelButton
        CommonDialog1.Filter = "Text file (*.txt) |*.txt"
        CommonDialog1.ShowOpen
        OldFile = CommonDialog1.FileName
        Open OldFile For Append As #1
        Day = InputBox("Please enter the day of the week _
                                      (type END when finished):", "Day")

        Do While UCase(Day) <> "END"
            HiTemp = Val(InputBox("Please enter the high temperature:", "High Temp"))
            Write #1, Day, HiTemp
            Day = InputBox("Please enter the day of the week _
                                      (type END when finished):", "Day")

        Loop
        Close #1
CancelButton:
        Exit Sub
End Sub
```

(Continues on next page)

```
    Private Sub mnuExit_Click()
        End
    End Sub


    Private Sub Command1_Click()
        Dim OldFile As String, Day As String
        Dim i As Integer, n As Integer
        Dim HiTemp As Single, Sum As Single, Average As Single

        CommonDialog1.CancelError = True
        On Error GoTo CancelButton
        CommonDialog1.Filter = "Text file (*.txt) |*.txt"
        CommonDialog1.ShowOpen
        OldFile = CommonDialog1.FileName
        Open OldFile For Input As #1
        i = 0               'loop counter
        Sum = 0
        Do Until EOF(1)
            Input #1, Day, HiTemp
            Sum = Sum + HiTemp
            i = i + 1
            n = i          'number of items read from data file
        Loop
        Average = Sum / n
        Text1.Text = Format(Average, "##.#")
        Close #1
    CancelButton:
        Exit Sub
    End Sub


    Private Sub Command2_Click()
        End
    End Sub
```

Event procedure Command1_Click causes the data file to be read and the average to be calculated. The data file is opened as an input file, after its file name has been selected via the Open common dialog box, as illustrated in Fig. 9.26. The Do Until loop then reads information sequentially from each line within the data file. Note that the day of the week and the corresponding high temperature must both be read from each line, though only the temperature is used in the calculations.

As the loop progresses, the integer variable n records the number of daily temperatures that have been read. This variable will represent the total number of data values once the loop has been completed. Note that the final value of n is used at the completion of the loop, in order to calculate the average.

Once the average daily temperature has been calculated, its formatted value (one decimal place) is displayed within the text box, and the data file is closed. Fig. 9.27 shows the final result, based upon the 14 temperatures recorded within the version of the data file Daily Temperatures.txt presented in Example 9.5. We see that the average daily high temperature is 78.7 °F.

Many applications require that the information in a data file be upgraded by modifying the information in the data file or by adding new information. The general procedure for updating a sequential data file is to copy the contents of the old data file to a new data file, incorporating any additions or changes to the data during the copy procedure. After the updating has been completed, the old data file can be deleted and the new (updated) data file renamed as the old data file. The procedure is illustrated below in Example 9.7.

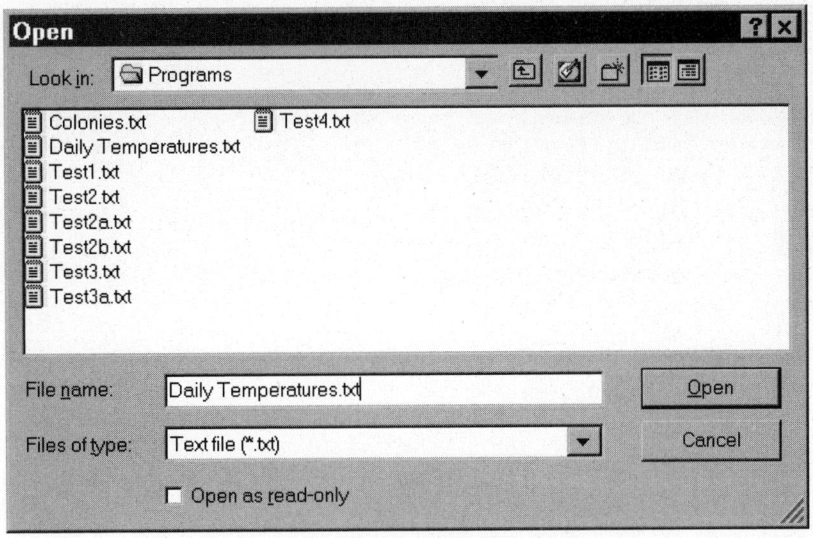

Fig. 9.26

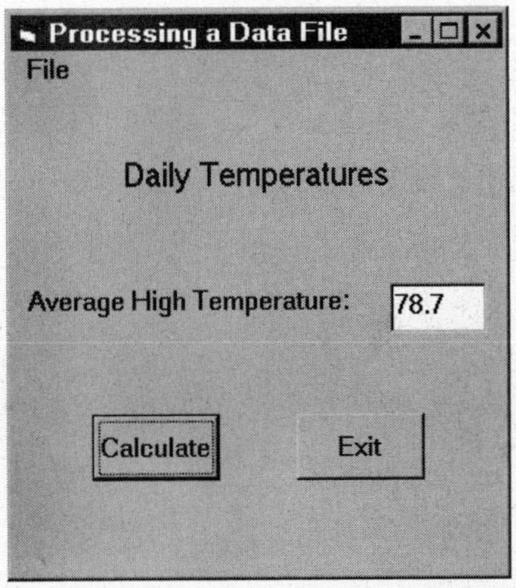

Fig. 9.27

EXAMPLE 9.7 MODIFYING A SEQUENTIAL DATA FILE: RECORDING DAILY HIGH AND LOW TEMPERATURES

Let us now alter the Visual Basic program presented in Example 9.6 so that new information can be added to each line of a sequential data file. To do so, we will read a line of information from an existing data file, enter additional information from the keyboard via an input box, and then write everything out to a new data file. This process will continue on a line-by-line basis, until the entire original data file has been modified. (Note the distinction between adding new information to each line of a data file, and appending information to the end of a data file, as we did in Example 9.5.)

In particular, suppose we want to add a daily low temperature to each of the daily high temperatures in the data file Daily Temperatures.txt shown in Example 9.5. Recall that this file contains only the day of the week and the corresponding high temperatures. Therefore, for each line in Daily Temperatures.txt, we will carry out the following steps.

1. Read the day of the week and the daily high temperature.

2. Enter a corresponding daily low temperature from the keyboard.

3. Write the day of the week, the daily high temperature, and the daily low temperature to a new data file, with the file name New Daily Temperatures.txt.

Here are the low temperatures corresponding to the high temperatures recorded in `New Daily Temperatures.txt`.

Day	Low Temperature, °F
Sunday	61
Monday	63
Tuesday	64
Wednesday	71
Thursday	68
Friday	65
Saturday	62
Sunday	58
Monday	55
Tuesday	61
Wednesday	66
Thursday	70
Friday	72
Saturday	70

We begin with the preliminary control layout shown in Fig. 9.28. Notice that we have added an additional text box and an accompanying label, compared with the layout shown in the previous example. Also, the File menu now contains a new entry, called Modify, as shown in Fig. 9.29. This new menu entry will initiate the desired data file modification.

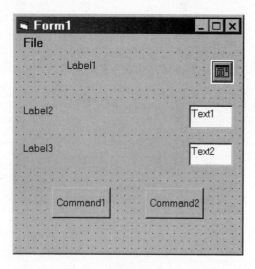

Fig. 9.28   **Fig. 9.29**

Here are the corresponding menu editor entries.

Caption	Name
File	mnuFile
....&New	mnuNew
....-	mnuSep1
....&Append	mnuAppend
-	mnuSep2
&Modify	mnuModify
-	mnuSep3
....&Exit	mnuExit

The corresponding event procedures are shown below.

```
Private Sub Form_Load()
    Form1.Caption = "Modifying a Data File"

    Label1.Caption = "Daily Temperatures"
    Label1.FontSize = 12
    Label1.Alignment = 2     'center text
    Label2.Caption = "Average High Temperature:"
    Label2.FontSize = 10
    Label3.Caption = "Average Low Temperature:"
    Label3.FontSize = 10

    Text1.Text = ""
    Text1.FontSize = 10
    Text2.Text = ""
    Text2.FontSize = 10

    Command1.Caption = "Calculate"
    Command1.FontSize = 10
    Command2.Caption = "Exit"
    Command2.FontSize = 10

End Sub




Private Sub mnuNew_Click()
    Dim NewFile As String, Day As String
    Dim HiTemp As Single

    CommonDialog1.CancelError = True
    On Error GoTo CancelButton
    CommonDialog1.Filter = "Text file (*.txt) |*.txt"
    CommonDialog1.ShowSave
    NewFile = CommonDialog1.FileName
    Open NewFile For Output As #1
    Day = InputBox("Please enter the day of the week _
                            (type END when finished):", "Day")
    Do While UCase(Day) <> "END"
        HiTemp = Val(InputBox("Please enter the high temperature:", "High Temp"))
        Write #1, Day, HiTemp
        Day = InputBox("Please enter the day of the week _
                            (type END when finished):", "Day")
    Loop
    Close #1
CancelButton:
    Exit Sub
End Sub
```

(Continues on next page)

```
Private Sub mnuAppend_Click()
    Dim OldFile As String, Day As String
    Dim HiTemp As Single

    CommonDialog1.CancelError = True
    On Error GoTo CancelButton
    CommonDialog1.Filter = "Text file (*.txt) |*.txt"
    CommonDialog1.ShowOpen
    OldFile = CommonDialog1.FileName
    Open OldFile For Append As #1
    Day = InputBox("Please enter the day of the week _
                            (type END when finished):", "Day")
    Do While UCase(Day) <> "END"
        HiTemp = Val(InputBox("Please enter the high temperature:", "High Temp"))
        Write #1, Day, HiTemp
        Day = InputBox("Please enter the day of the week _
                            (type END when finished):", "Day")
    Loop
    Close #1
CancelButton:
    Exit Sub
End Sub

Private Sub mnuModify_Click()
    Dim OldFile As String, NewFile As String, Day As String
    Dim Message As String
    Dim HiTemp As Single, LoTemp As Single

    CommonDialog1.CancelError = True
    On Error GoTo CancelButton
    CommonDialog1.Filter = "Text file (*.txt) |*.txt"

    CommonDialog1.ShowOpen
    OldFile = CommonDialog1.FileName
    Open OldFile For Input As #1

    CommonDialog1.ShowSave
    NewFile = CommonDialog1.FileName
    Open NewFile For Output As #2

    Do Until EOF(1)
        Input #1, Day, HiTemp
        Message = "Please enter " & Day & "'s low temperature:"
        LoTemp = Val(InputBox(Message, "Low Temp"))
        Write #2, Day, HiTemp, LoTemp
    Loop
    Close #1
    Close #2
CancelButton:
    Exit Sub
End Sub
```

(Continues on next page)

```
Private Sub mnuExit_Click()
    End
End Sub

Private Sub Command1_Click()
    Dim OldFile As String, Day As String
    Dim i As Integer, n As Integer
    Dim HiTemp As Single, LoTemp As Single
    Dim HiSum As Single, LoSum As Single

    CommonDialog1.CancelError = True
    On Error GoTo CancelButton
    CommonDialog1.Filter = "Text file (*.txt) |*.txt"
    CommonDialog1.ShowOpen
    OldFile = CommonDialog1.FileName
    Open OldFile For Input As #1
    i = 0            'loop counter
    HiSum = 0
    LoSum = 0
    Do Until EOF(1)
        Input #1, Day, HiTemp, LoTemp
        HiSum = HiSum + HiTemp
        LoSum = LoSum + LoTemp
        i = i + 1
        n = i      'number of items read from data file
    Loop
    Text1.Text = Format(HiSum / n, "##.#")
    Text2.Text = Format(LoSum / n, "##.#")
    Close #1
CancelButton:
    Exit Sub
End Sub

Private Sub Command2_Click()
    End
End Sub
```

Event procedures `mnuNew_Click`, `mnuAppend_Click`, `mnuExit_Click` and `Command2_Click` are unchanged from the previous examples. Procedure `Form_Load` includes some additional property assignments to accommodate the new controls.

Event procedure `mnuModify_Click` is new. It opens both an existing sequential data file (the input file) and a new sequential data file (the output file). The loop reads information from the old data file, adds new information entered from the input box, and then writes the combined information to the new data file. This process proceeds on a line-by-line basis, until an end-of-file condition is encountered on the old data file.

In addition, event procedure `Command1_Click` has been modified to calculate two averages – one for the daily high temperatures, and the other for the daily low temperatures. This event procedure first opens a designated data file as an input file, and then reads all of the data on a line-by-line basis. A `Do Until` loop is used for this purpose. Once the looping action has been concluded, the averages are computed, formatted, and assigned to the appropriate text boxes.

Note that the Modify feature could have been initiated from a new control button rather than an additional File menu entry. Similarly, the calculation of the averages could have been initiated from a menu entry rather than a control button. The use of both types of controls in this example was intended to illustrate the mechanics of each control type.

Now let us turn our attention to the program execution. Figs. 9.30 and 9.31 show the opening user interface and the entries within the File menu. If we then select Modify from the File menu, we see the Open dialog box shown in Fig. 9.32.

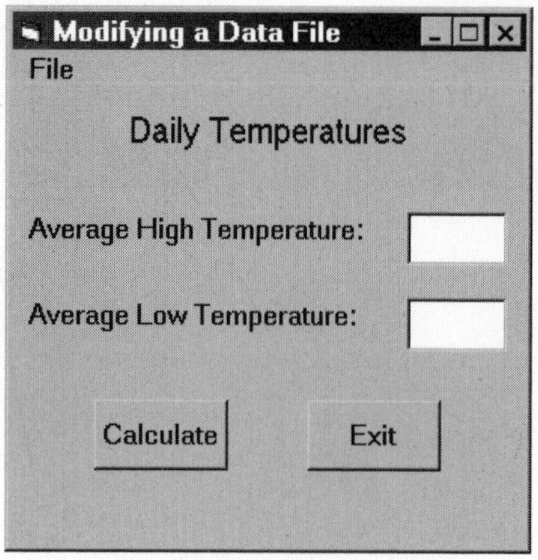

Fig. 9.30

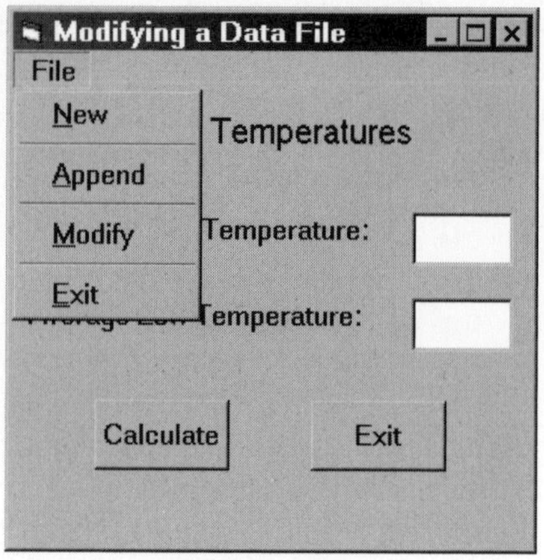

Fig. 9.31

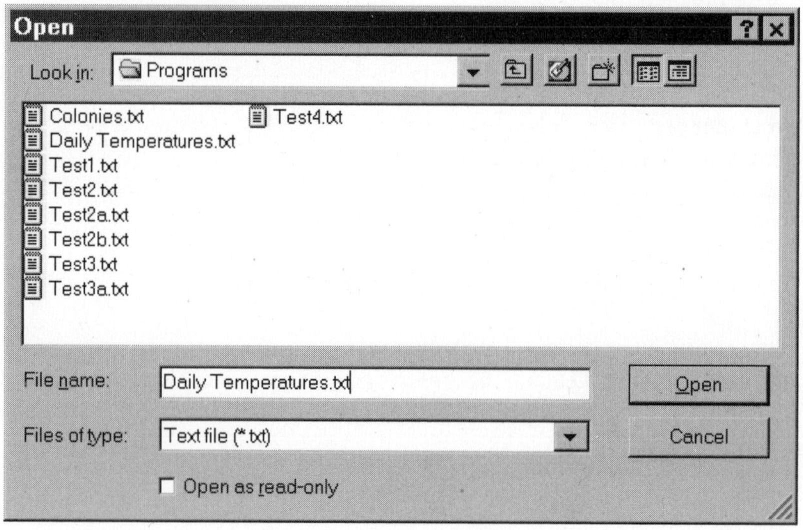

Fig. 9.32

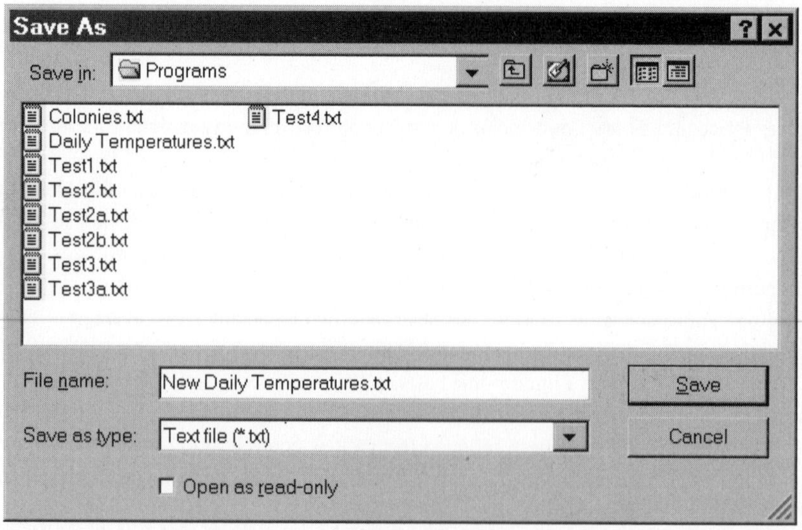

Fig. 9.33

Once an existing text file has been selected within the Open dialog box, the Save As dialog box appears, prompting for the name of the new text file, as shown in Fig. 9.33. Note that we have selected the existing text file Daily Temperatures.txt from the Open dialog box (Fig. 9.32), and the new text file name New Daily Temperatures.txt within the Save As dialog box (Fig. 9.33).

A series of input boxes will then appear, each prompting for a daily low temperature. The first two input boxes are shown in Figs. 9.34(a) and 9.34(b). A total of 14 such input boxes will appear, one for each line of text within data file Daily Temperatures.txt.

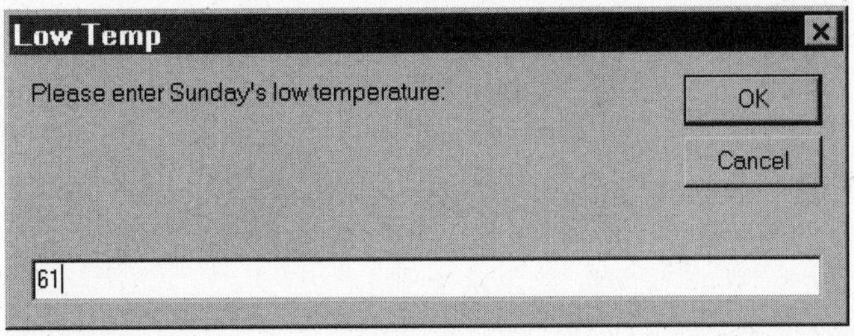

Fig. 9.34(a)

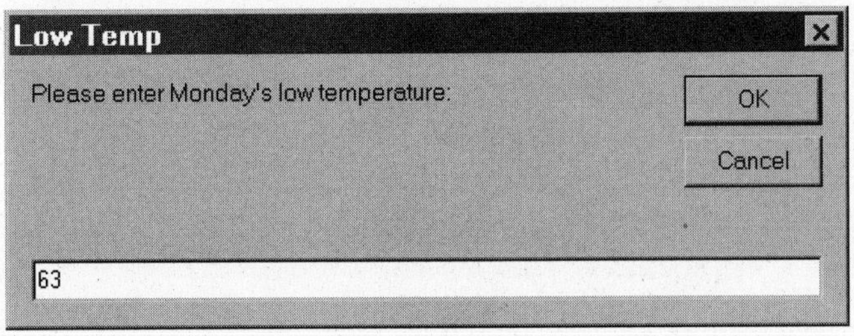

Fig. 9.34(b)

Upon completion of this process, we will have generated the data file New Daily Temperatures.txt, whose contents are shown below.

```
"Sunday",77,61
"Monday",76,63
"Tuesday",81,64
"Wednesday",87,71
"Thursday",84,68
"Friday",79,65
"Saturday",74,62
"Sunday",70,58
"Monday",67,55
"Tuesday",74,61
"Wednesday",79,66
"Thursday",83,70
"Friday",86,72
"Saturday",85,70
```

We now press the Calculate button, which again displays the Open dialog box, as shown in Fig. 9.35. We must then select an existing text file from the Open dialog box. The file selected must be a modified data file, containing both high and low temperatures for each day. Fig. 9.35 shows that we have selected the recently created data file New Daily Temperatures.txt.

Once an appropriate data file has been selected, the averages will be calculated and displayed, as shown in Fig. 9.36. Thus, for the data contained in data file New Daily Temperatures.txt, we see that the average daily high temperature is 78.7 °F, and the average daily low temperature is 64.7 °F.

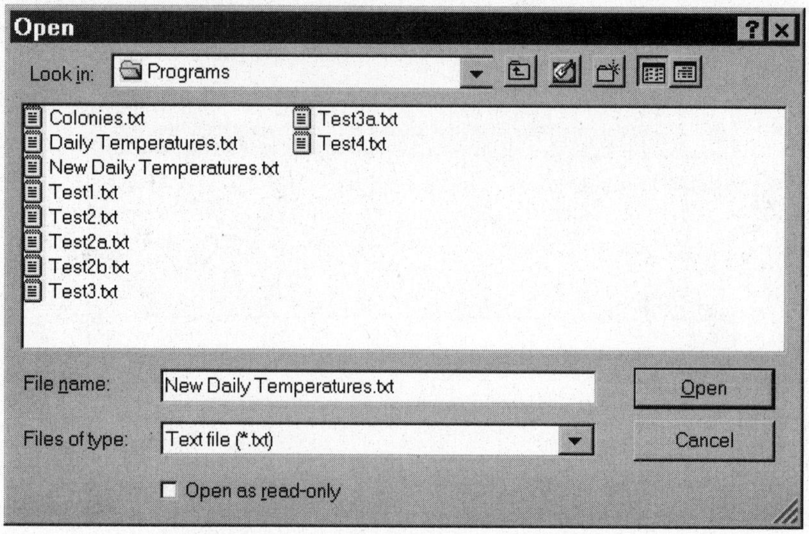

Fig. 9.35

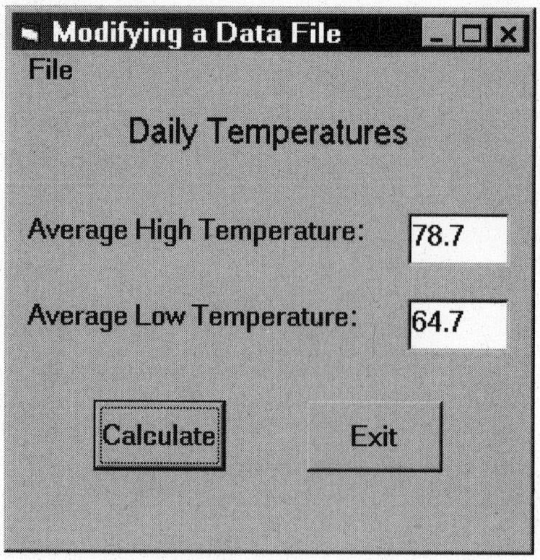

Fig. 9.36

9.5 RANDOM ACCESS (DIRECT) DATA FILES

Random access data files consist of a collection of fixed-length records, each of which is assigned a unique record number. Once a random access file has been opened, an individual record can be accessed by referencing its record number. Information can then be read from the record or written to the record, as required by the individual application.

With random access files, the Open statement takes on the form

> Open *filename* For Random As #*n* Len = *record length*

or simply

> Open *filename* As #*n* Len = *record length*

since Random is the default file type, in the absence of an explicit specification.

The *record length* (expressed in bytes) must be large enough to accommodate each of the fixed-length data items that will be stored within the random access data file. The record length may be written as an integer constant or an expression. It is particularly common to use the library function Len to return the length, in bytes, of a previously defined data item.

Records are usually defined as user-defined data types (see Sec. 2.4). The size of each string member must be included within the data type declaration.

EXAMPLE 9.8

A Visual Basic program that utilizes a random access data file. The program includes the following record declarations.

```
Private Type Customer
    Customername As String * 20
    AcctNo As Integer
    Balance As Single
End Type

Dim OldCustomer As Customer, NewCustomer As Customer
```

Thus, OldCustomer and NewCustomer are user-defined variables that will be used to represent records.

Note that we have specified the maximum length of the string member, since strings do not have a predefined standard size. Thus, each record will consist of 26 bytes (20 bytes for the string member, 2 bytes for the integer member, and 4 bytes for the single-precision member).

Data items are read from a random access data file, one record at a time, via the Get # statement. This statement is written in general terms as

> Get #*n*, *record number, data item*

or simply

> Get #*n*, , *data item*

If the record number is not stated explicitly, it is taken to be that of the record following the last Get # statement or the last Put # statement (see below).

Data items are written to a random access data file, one record at a time, via the Put # statement. Syntactically, this statement resembles the Get # statement. It is written in general terms as

> Put #*n*, *record number, data item*

or simply

> Put #*n*, , *data item*

As with Get #, the record number is taken to be that of the record following the last Get # or Put # statement if it is not shown explicitly.

EXAMPLE 9.9 CREATING A RANDOM-ACCESS DATA FILE: STATES AND THEIR CAPITALS

The following Visual Basic program creates a random access data file containing the names of the 50 states within the USA and their capitals. Each record will consist of the name of one state and the corresponding state capital. The records will be stored alphabetically, in the same order they are created, although the individual records need not be accessed in this order once the file has been created (see Example 9.10).

Fig. 9.37 shows the preliminary control layout. The File menu entries are shown in Fig. 9.38.

Fig. 9.37 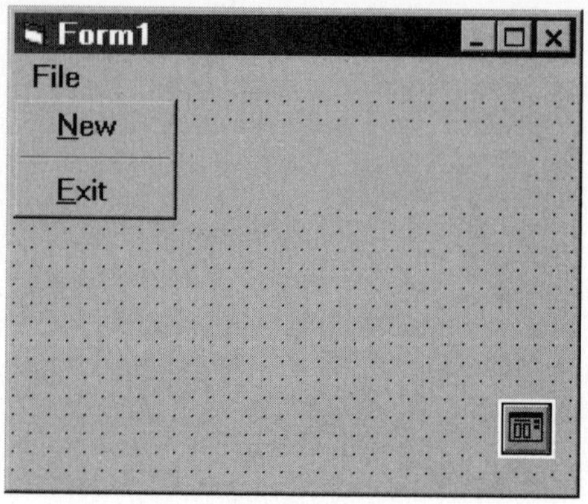   **Fig. 9.38**

Here are the corresponding menu editor entries.

Caption	Name
File	mnuFile
....&New	mnuNew
....-	mnuSep1
....&Exit	mnuExit

The required Visual Basic instructions are shown below. Note that the program defines a 30-byte, user-defined record type called StateRecord, consisting of two 15-byte strings, Name and Capital. Event procedure mnuNew_Click utilizes a variable of this type, called State. Hence, State will consist of two members, called State.Name and State.Capital.

In all other respects the program logic should be straightforward, as it is similar to that utilized in earlier programs. Note, however, the use of the Put # statement, rather than the Input # statement, within event procedure mnuNew_Click.

```
Private Type StateRecord
    Name As String * 15
    Capital As String * 15
End Type

Private Sub Form_Load()
    Form1.Caption = "Creating a Random Access Data File"

    Label1.Caption = "States and their Capitals"
    Label1.FontSize = 12
    Label1.Alignment = 2     'center text

End Sub
```

(Continues on next page)

```
Private Sub mnuNew_Click()
     Dim State As StateRecord, RecordNumber As Integer
     Dim NewFile As String

     CommonDialog1.CancelError = True
     On Error GoTo CancelButton
     CommonDialog1.Filter = "Data file (*.dat) |*.dat"
     CommonDialog1.ShowSave
     NewFile = CommonDialog1.FileName
     Open NewFile For Random As #1 Len = Len(State)

     RecordNumber = 1
     State.Name = InputBox("State (type END when finished):", "State")
     Do While UCase(Mid(State.Name, 1, 3)) <> "END"
          State.Capital = InputBox("Capital:", "Capital")
          Put #1, RecordNumber, State
          RecordNumber = RecordNumber + 1
          State.Name = InputBox("State (type END when finished):", "State")
     Loop
     Close #1
     MsgBox (NewFile & " has been created")
CancelButton:
     Exit Sub
End Sub

Private Sub mnuExit_Click()
     End
End Sub
```

When the program is executed, we first see the form shown in Fig. 9.39. If we then select New from the File menu, the Save As dialog box shown in Fig. 9.40 appears. This dialog box allows us to specify a name for the new file. Note that we are currently selecting the name States.dat.

Fig. 9.39

Once the new file name has been specified, a pair of input boxes is generated, prompting for the name of the state and the state capital, respectively, as shown in Figs. 9.41 and 9.42. This process continues until the user enters the word "End" for the name of the state, as shown in Fig. 9.43. The message box shown in Fig. 9.44 then appears, indicating that the new file has been created.

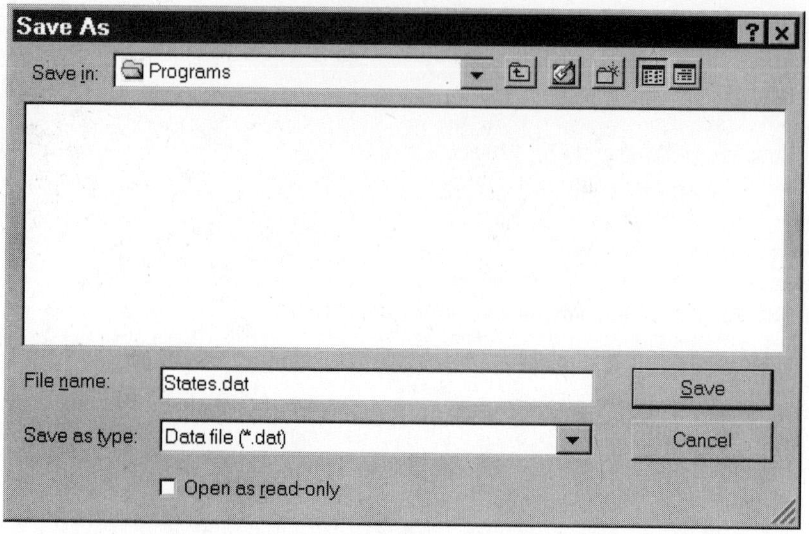

Fig. 9.40

Fig. 9.41

Fig. 9.42

Fig. 9.43

Fig. 9.44

Upon completion of the program execution, the random access data file shown in Fig. 9.45 will have been created. This particular data file consists entirely of strings; hence, it can be viewed within a text editor, as in Fig. 9.45. However, this is not true of all random access files. If some of the data items had been numeric rather than strings, we would not have been able to view the file within the text editor.

States.dat - Notepad					_ □ ×
File Edit Search Help					
Alabama	Montgomery	Alaska	Juneau	Arizona	Phoenix
Arkansas	Little Rock	California	Sacramento	Colorado	Denver
Connecticut	Hartford	Delaware	Dover	Florida	Tallahassee
Georgia	Atlanta	Hawaii	Honolulu	Idaho	Boise
Illinois	Springfield	Indiana	Indianapolis	Iowa	Des Moines
Kansas	Topeka	Kentucky	Frankfort	Louisiana	Baton Rouge
Maine	Augusta	Maryland	Annapolis	Massachusetts	Boston
Michigan	Lansing	Minnesota	St. Paul	Mississippi	Jackson
Missouri	Jefferson City	Montana	Helena	Nebraska	Lincoln
Nevada	Carson City	New Hampshire	Concord	New Jersey	Trenton
New Mexico	Santa Fe	New York	Albany	North Carolina	Raleigh
North Dakota	Bismark	Ohio	Columbus	Oklahoma	Oklahoma City
Oregon	Salem	Pennsylvania	Harrisburg	Rhode Island	Providence
South Carolina	Columbia	South Dakota	Pierre	Tennessee	Nashville
Texas	Austin	Utah	Salt Lake City	Vermont	Montpelier
Virginia	Richmond	Washington	Olympia	West Virginia	Charleston
Wisconsin	Madison	Wyoming	Cheyenne		

Fig. 9.45

Although the records within a random access data file are not arranged in any special order, the *locations* of the records are numbered consecutively from the start of the file, beginning with record number 1 and increasing by one unit for each consecutive data item. A *pointer* is used to to indicate the location of any particular record. The pointer must be positioned properly before a record can be read from or written to a direct data file. We have already encountered some use of pointer control in the previous example, where the pointer location is determined by assigning values to the variable RecordNumber.

Visual Basic uses the LOF function to determine the file size and the Loc function to determine the pointer location. In addition, Visual Basic uses the Seek function to set the pointer for the next file I/O operation.

EXAMPLE 9.10 READING A RANDOM-ACCESS DATA FILE: LOCATING STATE CAPITALS VIA BINARY SEARCH

In this example we present a Visual Basic program that will allow the user to specify the name of a state and have the computer return the name of the state capital. In fact, the user will not have to enter the entire name of the state, but only those first few letters that uniquely identify each state (e.g., Alas for Alaska, Ca for California, Tex for Texas). The search procedure will make use of the random access data file States.dat, created in the last example.

The basic idea will be to search the data file until the record containing the desired state has been found and then display the corresponding state capital. We will make use of an efficient search technique known as *binary search* to locate the desired record as quickly as possible. The method is based upon the assumption that the the records are stored in alphabetical order with respect to the names of the states. Thus, the method is intended for a random access data file in which the records are arranged consecutively with respect to the search parameter.

To see how the binary search technique works, consider a search interval consisting of several consecutive records within the file. Our overall strategy will be to compare the desired state with the state within the middle record. One of three possible conditions will be obtained.

1. The desired record will be the middle record, in which case we display the corresponding state capital and end the search.

2. The desired record will be in the first half of the search interval. Hence we eliminate the second half of the search interval and compare the desired state with the state within the middle record of the remaining subinterval.

3. The desired record will be in the second half of the search interval. In this case we eliminate the first half of the search interval and compare the desired state with the state within the middle record of the remaining subinterval.

This process is repeated until either the desired record has been found or it has been determined that the desired state cannot be found.

The relationship between a given search interval and its two possible subintervals is illustrated in Fig. 9.46.

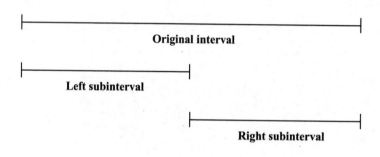

Fig. 9.46

Because the computational strategy is somewhat complicated, we present a detailed program outline. First, however, let us define the following variables.

OldFile = the name of the random access data file (States.dat)

State.Name = the name of the state contained in the record State.

State.Capital = the name of the state capital contained in the record State.

Target = the uppercase equivalent of the desired state (or the first few letters of the state)

Current = the uppercase equivalent of the state in the current record (or the first few letters of the state)

RecordNumber = the current record number

First = pointer to the first record in the current search interval

Last = pointer to the last record in the current search interval

The computation will proceed as follows.

1. Type the name of the desired state into a text box. The uppercase equivalent of the state name will be assigned to Target.

2. Prior to the first search, select and open the random access data file containing the list of state names and state capitals. (This should only be done once.)

3. Assign 1 to `First` and the quantity `LOF(1) / Len(State)` to `Last`. These assignments define the initial search interval. (Note that `LOF(1) / Len(State)` represents the number of the last record.)

4. Carry out the binary search as follows.

   (*a*) Determine the record at the middle of the search interval and assign its record number to `RecordNumber`.

   (*b*) Locate the middle record and read the values of the state name and the state capital. Then assign the uppercase equivalent of the leftmost characters of the state name to `Current`.

   (*c*) If `Current = Target`, the desired state has been located. Hence, display the state capital and end the binary search routine.

   (*d*) If `Current > Target`, the desired state will be located in the *first* half of the search interval. Hence, define a new subinterval by assigning `RecordNumber – 1` to `Last` and repeat this step.

   (*e*) Otherwise (i.e., if `Current > Target`), the desired state will be located in the *last* half of the search interval. Hence, define a new subinterval by assigning `RecordNumber + 1` to `First` and repeat this step.

   (*f*) If the search interval has been narrowed down to one remaining record (`First = Last`), then read the state name and the state capital from this record and assign the uppercase equivalent of the leftmost characters of the state name to `Current`.

   　　(*i*) If `Current = Target`, the desired state has been located. Hence, display the state capital and end the binary search routine.

   　　(*ii*) Otherwise, display an error message indicating that the desired state cannot be found. Then end the binary search routine.

To implement this strategy in Visual Basic, we will utilize two text boxes (one for the name of the state, the other for the capital) and three command buttons (to initiate the search, clear the text boxes, and end the computation). Fig. 9.47 shows the initial control layout. We will assign appropriate properties to the controls so that the form appears as in Fig. 9.48 when the program is executed.

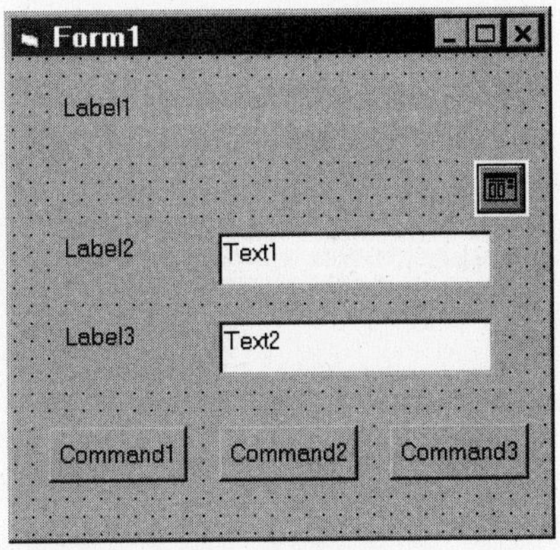

Fig. 9.47

Fig. 9.48

Here is the complete Visual Basic code listing, including the property assignments.

```
Private Type StateRecord
    Name As String * 15
    Capital As String * 15
End Type
```

(*Continues on next page*)

```
Private Sub Form_Load()
    Form1.Caption = "State Capitals"

    Label1.Caption = "Finding a State Capital"
    Label1.FontSize = 12
    Label1.Alignment = 2      'center text
    Label1.Tag = 0            'Set up data file selection
    Label2.Caption = "State:"
    Label2.FontSize = 10
    Label3.Caption = "Capital:"
    Label3.FontSize = 10
    Label3.Enabled = False
    Text1.Text = ""
    Text1.FontSize = 10
    Text2.Text = ""
    Text2.FontSize = 10
    Text2.Enabled = False
    Command1.Caption = "Find"
    Command1.FontSize = 10
    Command2.Caption = "Clear"
    Command2.FontSize = 10
    Command3.Caption = "Quit"
    Command3.FontSize = 10
End Sub


Private Sub Command1_Click()
    Dim State As StateRecord
    Dim OldFile As String, Target As String

    If Label1.Tag = 0 Then
        CommonDialog1.CancelError = True
        On Error GoTo CancelButton
        CommonDialog1.Filter = "Data file (*.dat) |*.dat"
        CommonDialog1.ShowOpen
        OldFile = CommonDialog1.FileName
        Open OldFile For Random As #1 Len = Len(State)
        Label1.Tag = 1     'disable data file selection
    End If
    Target = UCase(Text1.Text)
    Call Search(Target)
CancelButton:
    Exit Sub
End Sub


Private Sub Command2_Click()
    Text1.Text = ""
    Text2.Text = ""
    Text2.Enabled = False
    Label3.Enabled = False
End Sub
```

(*Continues on next page*)

```
        Private Sub Command3_Click()
            Close #1
            End
        End Sub


        Private Sub Search(Target As String)
            Dim State As StateRecord
            Dim RecordNumber As Integer, First As Integer, Last As Integer
            Dim Current As String

            First = 1
            Last = LOF(1) / Len(State)

            Do   'binary search routine
                RecordNumber = Int((First + Last) / 2)
                Get #1, RecordNumber, State
                Current = UCase(Left(State.Name, Len(Target)))
                If (Current = Target) Then        'found the target state
                    Label3.Enabled = True
                    Text2.Enabled = True
                    Text2.Text = State.Capital
                    Exit Do
                ElseIf (Current > Target) Then    'retain first half of search interval
                    Last = RecordNumber - 1
                    If (Last < First) Then Last = First
                Else                              'retain last half of search interval
                    First = RecordNumber + 1
                End If

                If (First = Last) Then            'try the remaining end point
                    RecordNumber = First
                    Get #1, RecordNumber, State
                    Current = UCase(Left(State.Name, Len(Target)))
                    If (Current = Target) Then
                        Label3.Enabled = True
                        Text2.Enabled = True
                        Text2.Text = State.Capital
                    Else
                        MsgBox ("Cannot find this state - please try again")
                    End If
                End If
            Loop Until (First = Last)
        End Sub
```

The event procedures are similar to those presented in earlier examples, and require little additional explanation. Note, however, that within event procedure Command1_Click, the name of the state, originally entered in text box Text1 by the user, is converted to uppercase and then assigned to the string variable Target. Target is then passed to sub procedure Search, where the binary search process outlined earlier is actually carried out.

Also, notice that the access to the Open dialog box is controlled by the value assigned to property Label1.Tag. Initially, Label1.Tag is assigned a value of 0, within event procedure FormLoad. This allows the Open dialog box to be accessed within Command1_Click. Once the Open dialog box is accessed, however, Label1.Tag is reassigned the value 1, thus preventing any further (and unnecessary) reference to the Open dialog box.

When the program is first executed, the user must enter the name of a state, as shown in Fig. 9.49. Clicking on the Find button causes the Open dialog box to appear, as shown in Fig. 9.50. (Note that the data file States.dat is selected in Fig. 9.50.) The Open dialog box appears only at the beginning of the first search. It is not required for subsequent searches, since it is assumed that all subsequent searches will be carried out within the same data file (States.dat).

Fig. 9.49

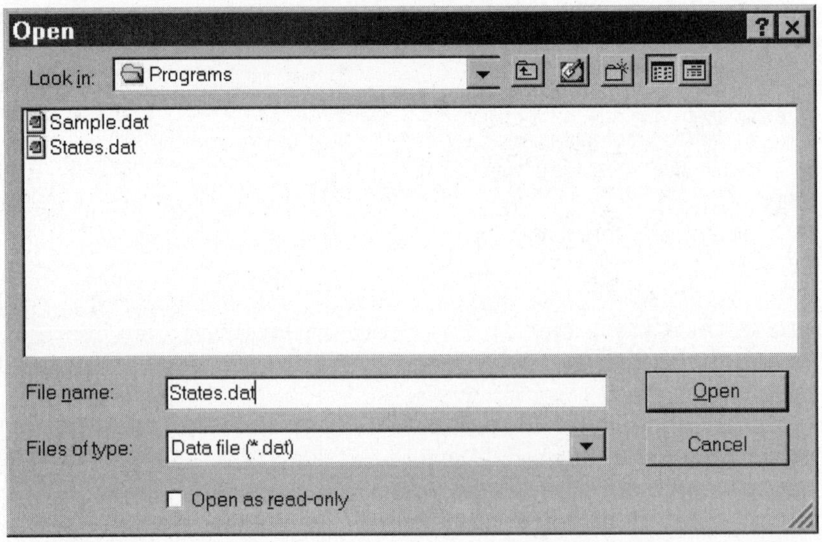

Fig. 9.50

Fig. 9.51    **Fig. 9.52**

Once a state has been specified and a data file has been selected, the corresponding state capital appears in the lower text box, as shown in Fig. 9.51. Thus, we see that the capital of Ohio is Columbus.

The search procedure may be carried out repeatedly by clicking on the Clear button, entering the name of a new state, and again clicking on the Find button. The user need not enter the entire name of the state. Only the first few letters are required – enough to uniquely identify the state. Thus, Fig. 9.52 shows the capital Sacramento in response to the abbreviated name Cal, which uniquely identifies California. (Note that ambiguous abbreviations, such as Ala, Miss, or New, cannot be used.)

Now suppose the user enters a string that cannot be identified as a part of a state name, as shown in Fig. 9.53 (NY is not an acceptable abbreviation for New York). Then the binary search process will be unable to locate a matching record. Hence, an error message will appear within a message box, as shown in Fig. 9.54.

Fig. 9.53

Fig. 9.54

Since this example deals with a relatively small data file, it would have been easier to copy the file contents into arrays and then locate the desired state by scrolling through a list box or a combo box. The corresponding state capital could then easily be located and displayed. This method works well when the resulting arrays do not consume an inordinate amount of memory. If the data file were very large, however (i.e., if it contained thousands of records), the resulting arrays would most likely be too large to store in the computer's memory. In such situations, the use of the binary search procedure is a much better strategy.

Random access data files are well-suited for applications that require periodic record updates, because information can be read from and written to the same data file. (Recall that a *sequential* data file can be opened in an input mode or an output mode, but not both). Thus, for any given record, old information can be read from a random access data file and displayed on the screen. Updated information can then be entered from the keyboard and written to the data file. This procedure can be repeated for all of the records in the file, or for a selective number of records that specifically require updating. The procedure is illustrated in the following example.

EXAMPLE 9.11 UPDATING A RANDOM-ACCESS DATA FILE: BASEBALL TEAM RECORDS

A Little League manager keeps records of all teams within the league on a personal computer. The records are maintained in a random access data file. Each record contains the team name, the number of wins and the number of losses.

After each round of new games, the manager updates the records by reading each record from the data file and adjusting the total number of wins and losses for each team. Each updated record is written to the data file as soon as it is adjusted. To make the adjustments, the current team status (team name, number of wins, number of losses and percentage of games won) will displayed on the screen, within labeled text boxes.

This program is used to update a file called Teams.dat, containing the following information. (Presumably, the file containing this information will have been created with another Visual Basic program.)

Team Name	Wins	Losses
Giants	3	4
Jets	1	6
Nerds	3	4
Rockets	5	2
Sluggers	4	3
Techies	5	2

The preliminary control layout is shown in Fig. 9.55, and the File menu entries are shown in Fig. 9.56.

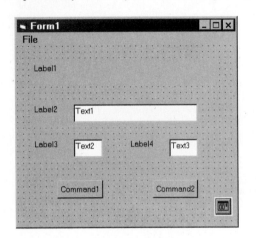

Fig. 9.55   **Fig. 9.56**

The corresponding menu editor entries are shown below.

Caption	Name
File	mnuFile
....&Open	mnuOpen
....-	mnuSep1
....&End	mnuEnd

We will assign values to the control properties during runtime so that the opening form appears as shown below, in Fig. 9.57.

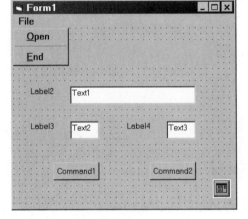

Fig. 9.57

Here is the complete program listing.

```
Private Type RecordType
    Name As String * 8
    Wins As Integer
    Losses As Integer
End Type

Private Team As RecordType
Private Last As Integer, RecNo As Integer

Private Sub Form_Load()
    Form1.Caption = "Record Updates"

    Label1.Caption = "Updating Little League Records"
    Label1.FontSize = 12
    Label1.Alignment = 2      'center text
    Label2.Caption = "Team:"
    Label2.FontSize = 10
    Label2.Enabled = False
    Label3.Caption = "Wins:"
    Label3.FontSize = 10
    Label3.Enabled = False
    Label4.Caption = "Losses:"
    Label4.FontSize = 10
    Label4.Enabled = False

    Text1.Text = ""
    Text1.FontSize = 10
    Text1.Enabled = False
    Text2.Text = ""
    Text2.FontSize = 10
    Text2.Enabled = False
    Text3.Text = ""
    Text3.FontSize = 10
    Text3.Enabled = False

    Command1.Caption = "Update"
    Command1.FontSize = 10
    Command1.Enabled = False
    Command2.Caption = "Next"
    Command2.FontSize = 10
    Command2.Enabled = False
End Sub

Private Sub mnuOpen_Click()
    Dim TeamFile As String

    CommonDialog1.CancelError = True
    On Error GoTo CancelButton
    CommonDialog1.Filter = "Data file (*.dat) |*.dat"
```

(Continues on next page)

```
            CommonDialog1.ShowOpen
            TeamFile = CommonDialog1.FileName
            Open TeamFile For Random As #1 Len = Len(Team)
            Last = LOF(1) / Len(Team)
            RecNo = 1
            Get #1, RecNo, Team
            Text1.Text = Team.Name
            Text2.Text = Str(Team.Wins)
            Text3.Text = Str(Team.Losses)

            Label2.Enabled = True
            Label3.Enabled = True
            Label4.Enabled = True
            Text1.Enabled = True
            Text2.Enabled = True
            Text3.Enabled = True
            Command1.Enabled = True
            Command2.Enabled = True
    CancelButton:
            Exit Sub
    End Sub

    Private Sub mnuEnd_Click()
            Close #1
            End
    End Sub

    Private Sub Command1_Click()

            Team.Name = Text1.Text     'update the current record
            Team.Wins = Val(Text2.Text)
            Team.Losses = Val(Text3.Text)
            Put #1, RecNo, Team

            If RecNo < Last Then       'get the next record
                RecNo = RecNo + 1
                Get #1, RecNo, Team
                Text1.Text = Team.Name
                Text2.Text = Str(Team.Wins)
                Text3.Text = Str(Team.Losses)
            Else
                Label2.Enabled = False
                Label3.Enabled = False
                Label4.Enabled = False
                Text1.Enabled = False
                Text2.Enabled = False
                Text3.Enabled = False
                Command1.Enabled = False
                Command2.Enabled = False
            End If
    End Sub
```

(Continues on next page)

```
      Private Sub Command2_Click()
          If RecNo < Last Then       'get the next record
              RecNo = RecNo + 1
              Get #1, RecNo, Team
              Text1.Text = Team.Name
              Text2.Text = Str(Team.Wins)
              Text3.Text = Str(Team.Losses)
          Else
              Label2.Enabled = False
              Label3.Enabled = False
              Label4.Enabled = False
              Text1.Enabled = False
              Text2.Enabled = False
              Text3.Enabled = False
              Command1.Enabled = False
              Command2.Enabled = False
          End If
      End Sub
```

This program utilizes a record type consisting of the team name, the number of wins, and the number of losses. Note that the record-type variable `Team`, the integer variables `Last` and `RecNo` are defined as global variables so that they can be accessed in multiple event procedures.

Event procedure `Form_Load` assigns values to various control properties and disables most of the controls until a data file has been identified and opened. This occurs in event procedure `mnuOpen_Click`. In addition, the first record is read from the data file and its contents displayed on the screen, and the disabled controls are enabled in `mnuOpen_Click`. The `Get #` statement is used to read from the data file.

Event procedure `Command1_Click` corresponds to the `Update` button. It writes the values displayed on the screen (which are assumed to have been modified) back to the data file. The `Put #` statement is used to write to the data file. If additional records remain in the data file, the next record is then read and displayed on the screen. Otherwise, most of the controls are again disabled. Note that the modified record is written to the same data file from which it was read, on channel 1.

Event procedure `Command2_Click` corresponds to the `Next` button. It is similar to the event procedure called `Command1_Click`, but it does not write the values displayed on the screen to the data file. This event procedure is used when the record currently displayed is to remain unchanged.

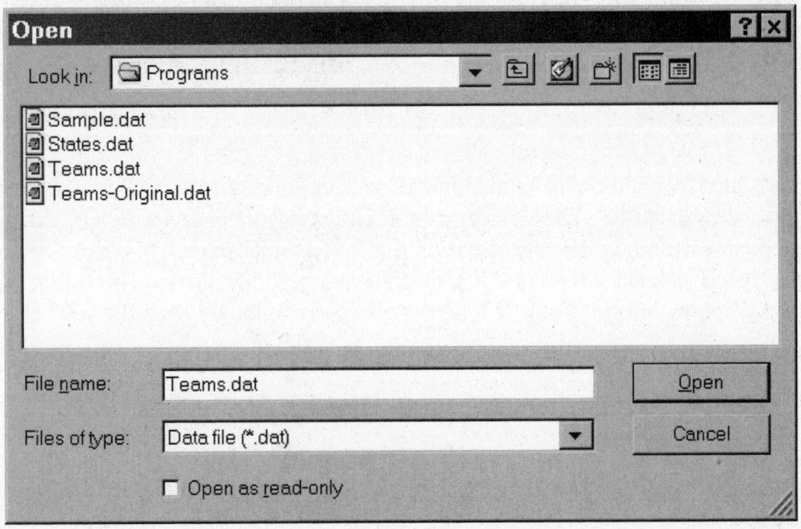

Fig. 9.58

When the program is executed, the Open dialog box appears, as shown in Fig. 9.58. Once data file Teams.dat is selected, the first record is displayed, as shown in Fig. 9.59(a). Any changes to this record can then be entered within the appropriate text box, as shown in Fig. 9.59(b), where the number of losses has been increased from 4 to 5. Clicking on the Update button then causes the new values to be saved to the data file. The next record then appears, as shown in Fig. 9.60. (The user may also click on the Next button, which results in the next record being displayed without saving the values from the previous record.) The process continues until the last record has been processed, resulting in the controls being disabled, as shown in Fig. 9.61.

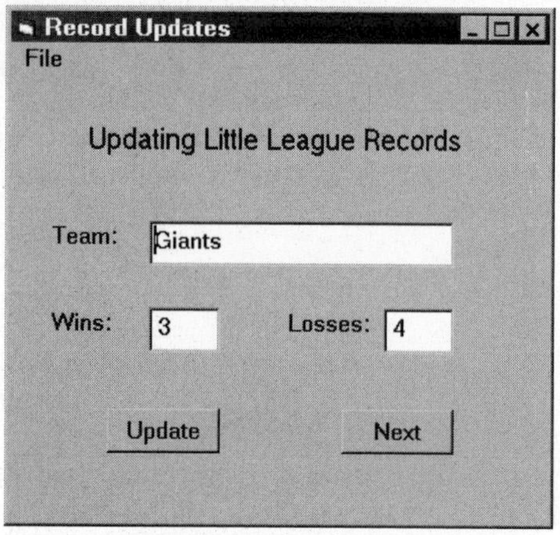

Fig. 9.59(a)

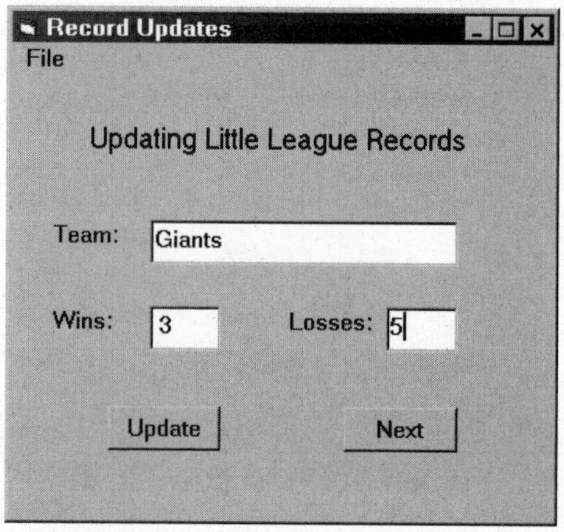

Fig. 9.59(b)

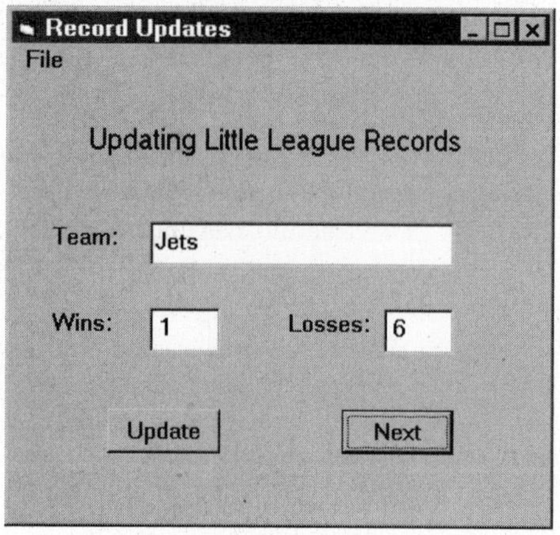

Fig. 9.60

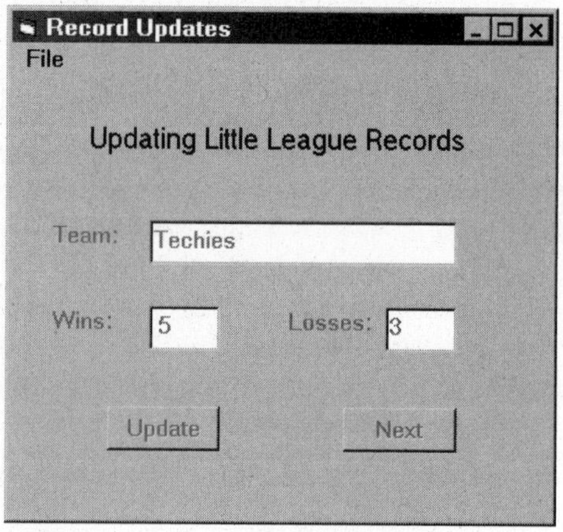

Fig. 9.61

Visual Basic includes two additional library functions, Loc and Seek, which may be useful in programs that process random access data files. The Loc function returns the pointer location (i.e., the record number) of the record last read or last written within the specified file. The pointer location is expressed as a long integer. Similarly, the Seek function returns the current pointer location within the specified file. Again, the pointer location is expressed as a long integer. Table 9.1 summarizes the commonly used file-related functions.

9.6 BINARY FILES

Binary files contain information expressed as a stream of consecutive, unformatted bytes. A binary file may represent a graphic, a sound file, or compiled code (i.e., a set of machine language instructions). Applications that make use of binary files are typically complicated very specialized in nature, and hence beyond the scope of this book.

Table 9.1 File-Related Library Functions

Function	Application	Description

EOF	`Do While Not EOF(1)`
	`· · · · ·`
	`Loop`
		Checks for an end-of-file condition within a specified file. Returns True if an end-of-file has been detected, and False otherwise.

Len	`n = Len(Record)`	Returns the length (in bytes) of the object specified as the argument. Frequently, the argument will represent a record.
Loc	`RecNo = Loc(1)`	Returns the pointer location of the last record read or the last record written (whichever is most recent) within the specified file.
LOF	`n = LOF(1)`	Returns the length (in bytes) of the specified file.
Seek	`RecNo = Seek(1)`	Returns the current pointer location within the specified file.

To open a binary file, we use the Open statement in the following manner.

> Open *filename* For Binary As *#n*

where *filename* represents the file name and *n* represents the data channel number, as before.

Information is read from a binary file as consecutive bytes. To read from a binary file, we again use the Get # statement, though in a slightly different form than that used with random access files. With binary files, the Get # statement is written in general terms as

> Get *#n*, *first byte*, *data item*

where *first byte* is a positive integer that represents the number of the first byte read. If this field is left blank (i.e., if the *first byte* is not shown), the byte following the last Get # or the last Put # is read. The surrounding commas must be present if *first byte* is omitted; i.e.,

> Get *#n*, , *data item*

Information is written to a binary file in the same manner, using the Put # statement. The general form of this statement for a binary file is

> Put *#n*, *first byte*, *data item*

where *first byte* is a positive integer that represents the number of the first byte written. If this field is left blank, the byte following the last Get # or the last Put # is written. The surrounding commas must be present if *first byte* is omitted; i.e.,

> Put *#n*, , *data item*

The Get # and/or Put # statements are usually included within a loop, so that the binary file is read and/or written on a consecutive byte-by-byte basis. The following example illustrates the overall process.

EXAMPLE 9.12 READING FROM AND WRITING TO A BINARY FILE

Here is a skeletal outline of a Visual Basic program that reads data from a binary file and later writes to the same binary file, presumably after performing some modification to the information within the file. Graphics and sound editing programs often make use of this overall read/process/write strategy.

```
Private Sub Command1_Click()
    Dim FileLength As Integer, Count As Integer
    Dim FileName As String
    Dim FileByte() As Byte

    'determine the file name
    FileName = . . . . .

    Open FileName For Binary As #1
    FileLength = LOF(1)
    ReDim FileByte(FileLength)

    'read the file
    For Count = 1 To FileLength
        Get #1, , FileByte(Count)          'note that second field is empty
    Next Count

    'process the file contents

    'write to the file
    For Count = 1 To FileLength
        Put #1, Count, FileByte(Count)     'note that second field is not empty
    Next Count

    Close #1
End Sub
```

Note that the second field of the Get # statement is empty. Hence, the loop containing the Get # statement begins by reading the first byte within the file, and then reads each successive byte during each consecutive pass through the loop. On the other hand, the second field of the Put # statement contains the variable Count. This resets the file pointer so that the file contents are overwritten by the modified bytes. If the second field of the Put # statement had been left empty, the modified bytes would have been written at the *end* of the original file, thus appending rather than overwriting the original file.

Review Questions

9.1   What is a file? What kinds of information can be contained within a file?

9.2   What type of components comprise a sequential (text) file? What are the advantages of a sequential file? What are its disadvantages?

9.3   What is a record? What is a field? What is the relationship between records and fields?

9.4   What type of components comprise a random access file? What are the advantages of a random access file? What are its disadvantages? Compare with the answers to Question 9.2.

9.5   What type of components comprise a binary file? What are the advantages of a binary file? What are its disadvantages? Compare with the answers to Questions 9.2 and 9.4.

9.6   Summarize the method used to add the common dialog control to the toolbar.

9.7　What is the purpose of each of the following common dialog control methods: `Filter`, `ShowOpen`, `ShowSave`, and `ShowPrint`?

9.8　Describe, in general terms, the three principal steps involved in processing the information within a data file.

9.9　What happens when a data file is opened? What happens when it is closed?

9.10　Describe each of the following file-related terms: channel number, mode, access type, restrictions.

9.11　What modes can be selected when opening a sequential data file?

9.12　How are numeric constants stored within a sequential data file?

9.13　How are consecutive numeric constants separated within the same line of a sequential data file?

9.14　Under what conditions must a string be enclosed in quotation marks within a sequential data file?

9.15　Are separators required for consecutive strings within the same line of a sequential data file?

9.16　Within a sequential data file, what is the difference between the `Input #` statement and the `Line Input #` statement? When is each used?

9.17　What is the purpose of the `Input` library function? How does it differ from the `Input #` statement?

9.18　Within a sequential data file, what is the difference between the `Print #` statement and the `Write #` statement? When is each used?

9.19　What is the purpose of the `EOF` function? What does this function return?

9.20　What is the purpose of the `LOF` function? What does this function return?

9.21　How is new information appended to an existing sequential data file?

9.22　Describe a strategy involving two separate data files that is often used when updating the information in a sequential data file.

9.23　How is a particular record in a random access data file identified? How can a particular record be accessed?

9.24　How is the composition of the records within a random access data file defined?

9.25　What is the purpose of the `Len` function? What does this function return?

9.26　How is the `Get #` statement used with a random access data file? How is this statement interpreted if the record number is not explicitly shown?

9.27　How is the `Put #` statement used with a random access data file? How is this statement interpreted if the record number is not explicitly shown?

9.28　What is meant by a pointer? How can the location of a pointer be determined? How can a pointer be repositioned?

9.29　Can the records in a random access dataa file be read sequentially? Can they be written sequentially? Why might one want to do this?

9.30 Can a text editor or word processor be used to edit a random access data file?

9.31 Describe a strategy for updating the information in a random access data file. Compare with the strategy used with a sequential data file (see Question 9.22).

9.32 What is the purpose of the Loc function? What information is returned by this function?

9.33 What is the purpose of the Seek function? What information is returned by this function? How does this function differ from the Loc function?

9.34 How is the information within a binary file organized?

9.35 How is the Get # statement used with a binary file? How is this statement interpreted if the *first byte read* is not explicitly shown? Compare with the answer to Question 9.26.

9.36 How is the Put # statement used with a binary file? How is this statement interpreted if the *first byte written* is not explicitly shown? Compare with the answer to Question 9.27.

Problems

9.37 Describe the data file associated with each of the following statements.

 (*a*) `Open "demo.dat" For Input As #3`

 (*b*) `Open FileName For Output As #5`

 (*c*) `Open DataFile For Random As #2 Len = Len(RecName)`

 (*d*) `Open "customers.dat" For Append As #1`

 (*e*) `Open "c:\myfiles\students.dat" For Binary As #2`

9.38 Write an Open statement for each of the following situations.

 (*a*) Open an existing sequential file called `"students.dat"` as an input file on data channel number 2.

 (*b*) Open a new sequential file called `"grades.dat"` as an output file on data channel number 3.

 (*c*) Open an existing sequential file whose name is given by FileName as an append file on data channel number 4.

 (*d*) Open a random access data file called `"orders.dat"` with a record size of 72 bytes on data channel number 1.

 (*e*) Open a random access data file whose name is given by FileName and whose record size is given by RecSize on data channel number 2.

 (*f*) Open a binary file whose name is given by BinFile on data channel number 1.

9.39 Outline a Visual Basic program that will read the values of the variables Name, Salary, Taxes and NetPay from a record in the sequential (text) file oldrecs.dat; update the values as required; and write them to the sequential file newrecs.dat. Include a loop that causes the process to be repeated for every record in the file. Show the Open and Close statements and the skeletal structure of the loop. Do not show the details of the updates.

9.40 Outline a Visual Basic program that will read the values of the variables Name, Salary, Taxes and NetPay from a record in the random access data file salaries.dat; update the values as required;

and write them back to the data file. Include a loop that causes the process to be repeated for every record in the file. Show the Open and Close statements and the skeletal structure of the loop, including the pointer positioning statements. Do not show the details of the updates. Compare with the outline written for Prob. 9.39.

9.41   Outline a Visual Basic program that will ask the user for a record number (i.e., a pointer value) and locate that record from the random access data file oldrecs.dat. Then read the values of the variables Name, Salary, Taxes and NetPay from the record and display them on the screen. Show the Open and Close statements and the main features, including the statements used to locate the record. Include the required event procedures as a part of your outline.

Programming Problems

9.42   Modify the Visual Basic program shown in Example 9.7 so that it utilizes random access files rather than sequential data files.

9.43   Combine the Visual Basic programs shown in Examples 9.9 and 9.10 into one program that can either create a new random access data file or search an existing data file for the capital corresponding to a given state.

9.44   Modify the Visual Basic program written for Problem 9.43 so that each record includes the name of a state, its population, and its capital. Include the ability to carry out either of the following operations.

   (*a*)   Display both the population and the capital for a given state.

   (*b*)   Display the state name and population for a given state capital. (Note that a binary search cannot be carried out for this option, since the state capitals are not arranged alphabetically.)

9.45   Write a Visual Basic program that will allow the state populations in the data file created for Problem 9.44 to be updated periodically.

9.46   Modify the program written for Problem 9.44 so that it will read the data file and then do either of the following.

   (*a*)   Sort the data file so that the states are listed in the order of decreasing populations (largest to smallest).

   (*b*)   Sort the data file so that the state capitals rather than the state names are arranged alphabetically.

   Use a sort strategy similar to that described in Example 8.10 to carry out the sorts.

9.47   Write a single Visual Basic program that combines all of the features described in Problems 9.44, 9.45 and 9.46.

9.48   Write a program that will read a random access data file containing baseball team records, as described in Example 9.11, and do any one of the following.

   (*a*)   Update the team standings, as described in Example 9.11.

   (*b*)   Sort the teams with respect to the percentage of games won (highest to lowest) and display the sorted list. Include complete information (i.e., name, games won, games lost and percentage of games won) for each team.

   Use a sort strategy similar to that described in Example 8.10.

9.49 Expand the program described in Problem 9.48 so that new records (new baseball teams) can be added, old records can be deleted and existing records can be modified. Be sure to maintain the records in alphabetical order.

9.50 Write a program that will create a sequential data file containing baseball team records. Include the information described in Example 9.11 for each team.

9.51 Write a program that will read the sequential data file containing baseball team records created in Prob. 9.50 and do any one of the following.

  (*a*) Update the team standings, as described in Example 9.11.

  (*b*) Sort the teams with respect to the percentage of games won (highest to lowest) and display the sorted list. Include complete information (i.e., name, games won, games lost and percentage of games won) for each team.

  Use a two-file update procedure, as described in Example 9.7. Also, use a sort strategy similar to that described in Example 8.10. Test the program with the sequential data file created in Problem 9.50.

9.52 Modify the multilingual hello program shown in Example 4.9 so that it utilizes a sequential data file. The program should be able to read the data file and display the appropriate greeting for a selected language, as in the earlier example. (See also Example 8.6.)

  Create the data file with a text editor or a word processor. Place each language and its accompanying greeting on a separate line.

9.53 A group of students earned the following scores for the six examinations taken in a Visual Basic programming course.

Name	*Exam Scores (percent)*					
Adams	45	80	80	95	55	75
Brown	60	50	70	75	55	80
Davis	40	30	10	45	60	55
Fisher	0	5	5	0	10	5
Hamilton	90	85	100	95	90	90
Jones	95	90	80	95	85	80
Ludwig	35	50	55	65	45	70
Osborne	75	60	75	60	70	80
Prince	85	75	60	85	90	100
Richards	50	60	50	35	65	70
Smith	70	60	75	70	55	75
Thomas	10	25	35	20	30	10
Wolfe	25	40	65	75	85	95
Zorba	65	80	70	100	60	95

Write a Visual Basic program that will accept each student's name and exam scores as input and then determine an average score for each student. Place the names and exam scores, including the student average, in an appropriate data file. Use a separate dialog box for entering and displaying information for each student. (See Problem 8.50, which emphasizes the use of arrays rather than data files for this application.)

9.54   Create a Visual Basic program that will read the data file created in Problem 9.53 and calculate an overall class average (i.e., the average of the individual student averages) and the deviation of each student's average about the overall class average. Display the class average, followed by the following information for each student:

Student name.

Individual exam scores.

Student average.

Deviation of the student average about the class average.

9.55   Extend the Visual Basic program written for Problem 9.54 so that the student exam records can be modified after they have been created. Include a provision for each of the following features.

(*a*)   Change an existing exam score.

(*b*)   Add a new exam score.

Write the modified information to a new data file before ending the program execution.

9.56   Modify the craps game simulator given in Example 7.10 so that it simulates a specified number of games and saves the outcome of each game in a data file. At the end of the simulation, read the data file to determine the percentage of wins and losses that the player has experienced.

Test the program by simulating 1000 consecutive games. Based upon these results, estimate the odds of winning when playing craps.

9.57   Extend the Visual Basic program written for Problem 8.39 (reordering a list of numbers four different ways) so that the original set of numbers is written to a random access data file, which is later updated by replacing the original set of numbers with the sorted numbers. Include all of the following features.

(*a*)   Enter a set of numbers from the keyboard and write it out to the data file.

(*b*)   Read the numbers from the data file, sort the numbers in one of the four ways indicated in Problem 8.39 and write the sorted numbers out to the data file.

(*c*)   Read the numbers (either sorted or unsorted) from the data file and display them on the screen.

Test the program using the following values, originally presented in Prob. 8.39.

43	−85	−4	65
−83	10	−71	−59
61	−51	−45	−32
14	49	19	23
−94	−34	−50	86

9.58   Extend the Visual Basic program written for Problem 4.52 (U.S./foreign currency equivalents) so that the list of currency equivalents is stored alphabetically in a random access data file. Place the name of each country and its currency equivalent in a separate record. Include a provision for each of the following features.

(*a*)   Enter the list of countries and currency equivalents from the keyboard, with the countries in alphabetical order. Write each record to the data file as it is entered.

(*b*)   Convert a specified amount of money from one currency to another. Use a binary search routine to locate each record, as required.

(*c*)   Read the entire data file and display its contents on the screen.

For your convenience, the list of U.S./foreign currency equivalents originally presented in Problem 4.52 is presented below.

1 U.S. dollar =	0.6	British pounds
	1.4	Canadian dollars
	2.3	Dutch guilders
	6.8	French francs
	2.0	German marks
	2000	Italian lira
	100	Japanese yen
	9.5	Mexican pesos
	1.6	Swiss francs

9.59 Expand the Visual Basic program written for Problem 9.58 to include the following addition features.

(*a*) Enter a new record (a new country and its currency equivalent).

(*b*) Delete an existing record.

(*c*) Modify the U.S. dollar equivalent for any existing record.

Remember to maintain the records in alphabetical order so that the binary search procedure can be used for the conversions.

9.60 Extend the Visual Basic program written for Problem 6.53(*c*) (areas of triangles, largest inscribed circles and smallest circumscribed circles) so that the sides of each triangle and the corresponding areas are written out to a random access data file. Each record should include a field for the three sides of a triangle and the corresponding three areas. Include the following features in the program.

(*a*) Enter the three sides of each triangle from the keyboard and write them to one record of the data file.

(*b*) Read each record, calculate the corresponding three areas, and write the areas within the record.

(*c*) Display the three sides and the corresponding areas for any specified record number.

Test the program using the following data, originally presented in Prob. 6.53(*c*).

a:	11.88	5.55	10.00	13.75	12.00	20.42	7.17	173.67
b:	8.06	4.54	10.00	9.89	8.00	27.24	2.97	87.38
c:	12.75	7.56	10.00	11.42	12.00	31.59	6.66	139.01

9.61 Write a Visual Basic program that will encode or decode multiple lines of text, using the encoding/decoding procedure described in Problem 8.56. Store the encoded text within a sequential data file, so that it can be retrieved and decoded at any time. Include the following features.

(*a*) Enter text from the keyboard, encode the text and store the encoded text in the data file.

(*b*) Retrieve the encoded text and display it in its encoded form.

(*c*) Retrieve the encoded text, decode it and then display the decoded text.

Test the program using several lines of text of your choice.

9.62 Extend the program described in Problem 9.61 so that multiple keys can be entered, where each successive key is used to encode each consecutive line of text. Thus, the first key will be used to encode the first line of text, the second key will be used to encode the second line of text, and so on. Test the program using several lines of text of your choice.

9.63 Write a Visual Basic program that will create and utilize a sequential data file containing names, addresses and telephone numbers. Include a provision for each of the following features.

(a)   Add a new record (i.e., a new name, address and telephone number) to the file.

(b)   Delete an existing record.

(c)   Find and display the contents of a record corresponding to a particular name.

(d)   Modify the contents of an existing record.

(e)   Display a complete list of all names, addresses and telephone numbers.

Be sure to rearrange the records whenever a new record is added or an existing record is deleted, so that the records are always maintained in alphabetical order.

9.64 Repeat Problem 9.63 utilizing a random access data file. Compare with the sequential data file version from a standpoint of programming ease and execution speed.

9.65 Extend the BINGO program written for Problem 8.60 so that each letter-number combination is stored in a data file as it is drawn, in addition to displaying the letter-number combination. Include the following features.

(a)   Display each letter-number combination as it is drawn.

(b)   Display the entire game history (i.e., display the contents of the data file).

Remember to initialize (erase) the data file at the beginning of each new game.

Appendix A

The ASCII Character Set

The first 128 characters are the most commonly used. They are tabulated below.

ASCII Value	Character	ASCII Value	Character	ASCII Value	Character	ASCII Value	Character
0	NUL	32	(space)	64	@	96	`
1	SOH	33	!	65	A	97	a
2	STX	34	"	66	B	98	b
3	ETX	35	#	67	C	99	c
4	EOT	36	$	68	D	100	d
5	ENQ	37	%	69	E	101	e
6	ACK	38	&	70	F	102	f
7	BEL	39	'	71	G	103	g
8	BS	40	(	72	H	104	h
9	HT	41	)	73	I	105	i
10	LF	42	*	74	J	106	j
11	VT	43	+	75	K	107	k
12	FF	44	,	76	L	108	l
13	CR	45	−	77	M	109	m
14	SO	46	.	78	N	110	n
15	SI	47	/	79	O	111	o
16	DLE	48	0	80	P	112	p
17	DC1	49	1	81	Q	113	q
18	DC2	50	2	82	R	114	r
19	DC3	51	3	83	S	115	s
20	DC4	52	4	84	T	116	t
21	NAK	53	5	85	U	117	u
22	SYN	54	6	86	V	118	v
23	ETB	55	7	87	W	119	w
24	CAN	56	8	88	X	120	x
25	EM	57	9	89	Y	121	y
26	SUB	58	:	90	Z	122	z
27	ESC	59	;	91	[	123	{
28	FS	60	<	92	\	124		
29	GS	61	=	93	]	125	}
30	RS	62	>	94	^	126	~
31	US	63	?	95	_	127	DEL

Note: The first 32 characters and the last character are control characters. Usually, they are not printed.

Appendix B

Incompatibilities with Visual Basic.NET

Like all commercial software products, Visual Basic is revised periodically to include new features, and occasionally to modify existing features that users have found problematic. Normally, these revisions have minimal effect on the underlying fundamentals of the language. Hence, introductory textbooks describing Visual Basic fundamentals usually remain valid over several years, spanning multiple revisions with minimal disruption.

As this book is about to go to press, however, Microsoft has published a preliminary set of specifications describing its next release of Visual Basic, which will be know as *Visual Basic.NET*. Microsoft intends to introduce significant changes in this forthcoming release, in order to provide greater compatibility between Visual Basic and other programming languages in Microsoft's Visual Studio suite. Many of these changes involve advanced features within Visual Basic and will therefore have little or no impact on the material discussed in this book. However, certain of the proposed new features are incompatible with the long-standing Visual Basic fundamentals presented in this book. The more significant incompatibilities, based upon Microsoft's preliminary specifications, are briefly summarized below.

1. The Visual Basic environment has a different appearance in Visual Basic.NET.

2. Some control properties are changed and some new properties added in Visual Basic.NET.

3. The location and appearance of the menu editor is changed in Visual Basic.NET.

4. The Variant data type is replaced by the *Object* data type in Visual Basic.NET.

5. Integer constants are redefined as follows.

   (*a*) Ordinary integer constants (two bytes) are referred to as *short integers* in Visual Basic.NET.

   (*b*) Long integer constants (four bytes) are referred to simply as *integers* in Visual Basic.NET.

   (*c*) Visual Basic.NET also supports eight-byte integers, referred to as *long integers*.

6. Visual Basic.NET strongly encourages the use of named constants rather than numerical values or variables with assigned values.

7. Arrays must be defined differently in Visual Basic.NET, as indicated below.

   (*a*) All arrays must have a lower bound of zero. Thus, the `Dim` statement

   ```
   Dim x(10) As Integer
   ```

   defines a 10-element integer array whose subscript values run from 0 to 9.

   (*b*) The `ReDim` statement can be used only with variables that are explicitly declared as arrays. The array declaration must precede the `ReDim` statement.

   (*c*) `Option Base 1` is not supported in Visual Basic.NET. Moreover, the use of `Option Base 0` is unnecessary and is strongly discouraged.

8. User-defined data types cannot include fixed-length arrays or fixed-size strings in Visual Basic.NET. However, workarounds are available. Thus, the code segment

```
Type Customer
    CustomerName As String * 20
    Items(10) As Integer
End Type

Dim OldCustomer As Customer
```

can be replaced by

```
Type Customer
    CustomerName As String
    Items() As Integer
End Type

Dim OldCustomer As Customer

ReDim OldCustomer.Items(10) As Integer
OldCustomer.CustomerName = String(20, " ")
```

(*Note*: String is a library function that returns a repeated string of the specified character. In this particular example, String returns a string consisting of 20 blank spaces.)

For more extensive and detailed information, consult appropriate Visual Basic.NET reference material when it becomes available.

Answers to Selected Problems

Chapter 1

1.19 Modify the program in the following ways.

    (*a*)   Change Form1.Caption to "Area and Circumference of a Circle"

    (*b*)   Add an additional label (Label3) and an additional text box (Text3). Resize and position these new objects accordingly within the form.

    (*c*)   Assign the caption "Circumference:" to Label3.Caption. Assign appropriate values to Label3.Font and Text3.Font.

    (*d*)   Change event procedure Command1_Click to the following:

```
Private Sub Command1_Click()
    Dim Pi, R, A, C As Single

    Pi = 3.141593
    R = Val(Text1.Text)
    A = Pi * R ^ 2
    C = 2 * Pi * R
    Text2.Text = Str(A)
    Text3.Text = Str(C)
End Sub
```

Chapter 2

2.43   (*a*)   7350, 7.35E3, etc.

    (*b*)   −12

    (*c*)   1000000, 1E6, etc.

    (*d*)   −2053180, −2.05318E6, etc.

    (*e*)   0.00008291, 8.291E−5, etc.

    (*f*)   9.563E12

    (*g*)   0.1666667

2.44   (*a*)   Comma not allowed.

    (*b*)   Double sign not allowed.

    (*c*)   Exponent too large.

    (*d*)   Too many significant figures (excess digits will be ignored).

    (*e*)   Exponent cannot include a decimal point.

2.45   (*a*)   Correct.

    (*b*)   Correct.

    (*c*)   The string is not enclosed in quotation marks.

    (d)   Correct.

    (e)   Quotation marks are not allowed within a string constant.

    (f)   Correct.

    (g)   Trailing quotation mark is missing.

2.46 *(a)*   Correct.

    (b)   Correct.

    (c)   Blank spaces are not allowed.

    (d)   Correct.

    (e)   First character must be a letter.

    (f)   Period is not allowed.

    (g)   Question mark is not allowed.

    (h)   Correct.

    (i)   Correct.

    (j)   Correct.

2.47 *(a)*   `Dim x1 As Single, x2 As Single`

    (b)   `Dim CustomerName As String, Address As String`

    (c)   `Dim Counter As Integer, Sum As Double, Variance As Double`

    (d)   `Const Factor As Single = 0.80`

    (e)   `Const City As String = "New York"`

2.48 *(a)*   Simply refer to `x1` and `x2` as `x1!` and `x2!`.

    (b)   Refer to `CustomerName` and `Address` as `CustomerName$` and `Address$`.

    (c)   Refer to the variables as `Counter%`, `Sum#` and `Variance#`.

    (d)   `Factor! = 0.80`

    (e)   `City$ = "New York"`

2.49
```
Type MachinePart
     Color As String
     PartNo As Long
     Length As Single
     Cost As Single
End Type
```

2.50 *(a)*   `3 * x + 5`   *(e)*   `(u + v) ^ (k - 1)`

    (b)   `i + j - 2`   *(f)*   `(4 * t) ^ (1 / 6)` or `(4 * t) ^ 0.1666667`

    (c)   `x ^ 2 + y ^ 2`   *(g)*   `t ^ (n + 1)`

    (d)   `(x + y) ^ 2`   *(h)*   `(x + 3) ^ (1 / k)`

2.51 (*a*) 5.666667   (*e*) 4   (*i*) 0

(*b*) 5   (*f*) 0   (*j*) 3.944444

(*c*) 2   (*g*) 5.461538   (*k*) 3

(*d*) 4.333333   (*h*) 7   (*l*) 1

2.52 (*a*) StrA & StrB & StrC   or   StrA + StrB + StrC

(*b*) Client & " " & Street & " " & City   or

Client + " " + Street + " " + City

(*c*) "Hello, " & StudentName

2.53 (*a*) C = 2.54

(*b*) xmin = 12

(*c*) Nstar = N

(*d*) Date = "January 31"

(*e*) Tag = Str1

(*f*) squares = A ^ 2 + B ^ 2 + C ^ 2

(*g*) count = count + 0.01

(*h*) I = I + J

(*i*) City = "PITTSBURGH, PA."

(*j*) Ratio = X / (A + B − C)

(*k*) K = K − 2

(*l*) Prize = 2 * Prize

2.54 (*a*) z = x / y + 3

(*b*) z = x / (y + 3)

(*c*) w = (u + v) / (s + t)

(*d*) f1 = 2 * a * b / (c + 1)
f2 = t / (3 * (p + q))
f = (f1 − f2) ^ 0.3333333

(*e*) y1 = a1 − a2 * x + a3 * x ^ 2 − a4 * x ^ 3 + a5 * x ^ 4
y2 = c1 − c2 * x + c3 * x ^ 2 − c4 * x ^ 3
y = y1 / y2

(*f*) P = A * i * (1 + i) ^ n / ((1 + i) ^ n − 1)

2.55 If the value of y is less than the value of z, there will be a problem because a negative number cannot be raised to a fractional power.

2.56 −16

2.57 16

2.58 (a) PRINT C1, C2, C3, C4, C5

(b) PRINT A, B, C
     PRINT
     PRINT X, Y, Z

(c) PRINT A; B; C; X; Y; Z

(d) PRINT "X ="; X, "Y ="; Y, "Z ="; Z   or
     PRINT "X ="; X; "Y ="; Y; "Z ="; Z

(e) PRINT N$; N; A ^ 2 + B ^ 2 or PRINT N$; N, A ^ 2 + B ^ 2

2.59 (a) Name: George Smith 7000   1500   5500

(b) Name: George Smith 7000 1500 5500

(c) 3   6   9   12
     5   10   15   20

(d) 3 6 9 12 5 10 15 20

(e) 9 1.333333 .1666667

2.60 (a) w = Log(v)

(b) p = q * Exp(–q * t) or p = q / Exp(q * t)

(c) w = Abs(Abs(u – v) – Abs(u + v))

(d) r = (p + q) ^ 0.5 or r = Sqr(p + q)

(e) y = a * Exp(b * x) * Sin(c * x)

(f) y = Sqr(Abs(Sin(x) – Cos(x)))

2.61 (a) y = Sgn((a * b – c * d) / (f + g))

(b) m = n / 2 – Int(n / 2)   (If the value of m is zero, n is even; otherwise, n is odd.)

(c) The method still works properly.

(d) IZ = Int(X ^ 2 – Y ^ 2)

(e) –34

2.62 (a) 24

(b) 1600 PENNSYLVANIA AVENUE

(c) venue

(d) Pennsyl   (Note the blank space preceding the first letter P)

(e) 0.2

(f) 1.25

2.63 (a) 'Area and Circumference of a Circle

(b) 'Averaging of Air Pollution Data

(c) Area = Pi * Radius ^ 2   'Area
     Circumference = 2 * Pi * Radius   'Circumference

(d) 'Loop to Calculate Cumulative Sum

(e) Avg = Sum / n   'Calculate an Average Value

Chapter 3

3.33 (*a*) `If sum > 100 Then sum = 100`

(*b*)
```
If sum > 100 Then
    Print sum
    sum = 100
    Flag = "Maximum Amount Exceeded"
End If
```

(*c*)
```
If sum <= 100 Then
    sum = sum + v
Else
    sum = 100
    v = 0
End If
```

3.34 (*a*) `If hours > 40 Then pay = 9.50`

(*b*)
```
IF hours <= 40 Then
    pay = 6.00
    Status = "Regular"
Else
    pay = 9.50
    Status = "Overtime"
End If
```

3.35
```
If Flag = "True" Then
    count = 0
    Msg1 = "Resetting the Counter"

    If Z > Zmax Then
        Msg2 = "Maximum Value Exceeded"
        Z = Zmin
    Else
        Z = Z + W
    End If

Else    'Flag <> "True"
    count = count + 1

    If Type = "A" Then
        Z = Z + U
    ElseIf Type = "B" Then
        Z = Z + V
    Else
        Z = Z + W
    End If

    Flag = "True"
End If
```

3.36
```
Select Case Flag
    Case 1
        Message = "Hot"
    Case 2
        Message = "Luke Warm"
    Case 3
        Message = "Cold"
    Case Else
        Message = "Out of Range"
End Select
```

3.37
```
Select Case Color
    Case "r", "R"
        Message = "Red"
    Case "g", "G"
        Message = "Green"
    Case "b", "B"
        Message = "Blue"
    Case Else
        Message = "Black"
End Select
```

3.38   Yes, Select Case can be used.

```
Select Case Temperature
Case Is < 0
    Print "Ice"
Case 0 To 100
    Print "Water"
Case Is > 100
    Print "Steam"
End Select
```

3.39   (*a*)
```
sum = 0
For i = 2 To 99 Step 3
    sum = sum + i
Next i
```

(*b*)
```
sum = 0
i = 2
Do While (i < 100)
    sum = sum + i
    i = i + 3
Loop
```

(*c*)
```
sum = 0
i = 2
Do Until (i >= 100)
    sum = sum + i
    i = i + 3
Loop
```

(d) ```
     sum = 0
     i = 2
     Do
         sum = sum + i
         i = i + 3
     Loop While (i < 100)
     ```

(e)  ```
     sum = 0
     i = 2
     Do
         sum = sum + i
         i = i + 3
     Loop Until (i >= 100)
     ```

3.40 (a) ```
          sum = 0
          For i = nstart To nstop Step n
              sum = sum + i
          Next i
          ```

(b)  ```
     sum = 0
     i = nstart
     Do While (i <= nstop)
         sum = sum + i
         i = i + n
     Loop
     ```

(c) ```
     sum = 0
     i = nstart
     Do Until (i >= nstop + 1)
         sum = sum + i
         i = i + n
     Loop
     ```

(d)  ```
     sum = 0
     i = 2
     Do
         sum = sum + i
         i = i + n
     Loop While (i <= nstop)
     ```

(e) ```
     sum = 0
     i = nstart
     Do
         sum = sum + i
         i = i + n
     Loop Until (i >= nstop + 1)
     ```

**3.41**  (a)  ```
          sum = 0
          For i = nstart To nstop Step n
              sum = sum + i
              If sum > maxsum Then Exit For
          Next i
          ```

   (b)
```
sum = 0
i = nstart
Do While (i <= nstop)
    sum = sum + i
    If sum > maxsum Then Exit Do
    i = i + n
Loop
```

   (c)
```
sum = 0
i = nstart
Do Until (i >= nstop + 1)
    sum = sum + I
    If sum > maxsum Then Exit Do
    i = i + n
Loop
```

   (d)
```
sum = 0
i = 2
Do
    sum = sum + i
    If sum > maxsum Then Exit Do
    i = i + n
Loop While (i <= nstop)
```

   (e)
```
sum = 0
i = nstart
Do
    sum = sum + i
    If sum > maxsum Then Exit Do
    i = i + n
Loop Until (i >= nstop + 1)
```

3.42   *(a)*
```
For j = 2 To 13
    sum = 0
    For i = 2 To 99 Step j
        sum = sum + i
    Next i
Next j
```

   (b)
```
For j = 2 To 13
    sum = 0
    i = 2
    Do While (i < 100)
        sum = sum + i
        i = i + j
    Loop
Next j
```

   (c)
```
For j = 2 To 13
    sum = 0
    i = 2
```

(Continues on next page)

```
            Do Until (i >= 100)
                sum = sum + i
                i = i + j
            Loop
        Next j
```

```
(d)  For j = 2 To 13
         sum = 0
         i = 2
         Do
             sum = sum + i
             i = i + j
         Loop While (i < 100)
     Next j
```

```
(e)  For j = 2 To 13
         sum = 0
         i = 2
         Do
             sum = sum + i
             i = i + j
         Loop Until (i >= 100)
     Next j
```

3.43
```
sum = 0
i = 2
Do While (i < 100)
   If (i Mod 5 = 0) Then sum = sum + i
   i = i + 3
Loop
```

3.44
```
n = . . . . .
k = . . . . .
sum = 0
i = nstart
Do While (i <= nstop)
   If (i Mod k = 0) Then sum = sum + i
   i = i + n
Loop
```

3.45
```
letters = 0
digits = 0
blanks = 0
others = 0
For i = 1 To Len(Text)
   c = Mid(Text, i, 1)
   If (Ucase(c) >= "A" And Ucase(c) <= "Z") Then
      letters = letters + 1
   ElseIf (c >= "0" And c <= "9") Then
      digits = digits + 1
   ElseIf (c = " ") Then
      blanks = blanks + 1
```

(*Continues on next page*)

```
        Else
            others = others + 1
        End If
    Next i
```

3.46
```
    vowels = 0
    consonants = 0
    For i = 1 To Len(Text)
        c = Ucase(Mid(Text, i, 1))
        If (c >= "A" And c <= "Z") Then        'character is a letter
            If (c = "A" Or c = "E" Or c = "I" Or c = "O" Or c = "U") Then
                vowels = vowels + 1
            Else
                consonants = consonants + 1
            End If
        End If
    Next i
```

3.47
```
    For i = Len(Text) To 1 Step -1
        Print Mid(Text, i, 1);
    Next i
```

3.48

(a)	30	(d)	25	(g)	30	(j)	20
(b)	4	(e)	20	(h)	6	(k)	23
(c)	5	(f)	1	(i)	0		

Chapter 7

7.32 (a)
```
    Function Fnp(t As Single, a As Single) As Single
        If (t ^ 2 > a) Then
            Fnp = Log(t ^ 2 - a)
        Else
            Fnp = Log(t ^ 2)
        End If
    End Function
```

(b)
```
    Function TwoLetters(L1 As String, L2 As String) As String
        If (L1 <= L2) Then
            TwoLetters = L1 & L2
        Else
            TwoLetters = L2 & L1
        End If
    End Function
```

(c)
```
    Function Average(a As Single, b As Single) As Single
        Dim r1 As Single, r2 As Single

        r1 = a + (b - a) * Rnd
        r2 = a + (b - a) * Rnd
        Average = (r1 + r2) / 2
    End Function
```

(*d*)
```
Function SignIs(X As Double) As String
    If (X < 0) Then
        SignIs = "Negative"
    ElseIf (X > 0) Then
        SignIs = "Positive"
    Else
        SignIs = "Zero"
    End If
End Function
```

(*e*)
```
Function First(Word As String) As String
    Dim c As String, i As Integer

    First = "z"
    For i = 1 To Len(Word)
        c = Lcase(Mid(Word, i, 1))
        If (c < First) Then First = c
    Next i
End Function
```

7.33 (*a*) `q = Fnp((a + b), c)`

(*b*) `NewString = Ucase(TwoLetters(LC1, LC2))`

(*c*)
```
V1 = Average(1, 10)
V2 = Average(1, 10)
V = (V1 + V2) / 2
```

(*d*) `V = (Average(1, 10) + Average(1, 10)) / 2`

(*e*)
```
V = Average(-1, 1)
MsgBox(SignIs(V))       or, combining statements,       MsgBox(SignIs(Average(-1, 1)))
```

7.34 (*a*)
```
Sub SignIs(X As Single, Message As String)
    If (X < 0) Then
        Message = "Negative"
    ElseIf (X > 0) Then
        Message = "Positive"
    Else
        Message = "Zero"
    End If
End Sub
```

(*b*)
```
Sub Reorder(a As Integer, b As Integer, c As Integer, d As Integer)
    Dim min As Integer, mid As Integer, max As Integer

    min = a
    If (b < min) Then min = b
    If (c < min) Then min = c
    max = c
    If (a > max) Then max = a
    If (b > max) Then max = b
    mid = (a + b + c) - (min + max)
```

```
            If (d = 1) Then            'arrange smallest to largest
                a = min
                b = mid
                c = max
            ElseIf (d = 2) Then        'arrange largest to smallest
                a = max
                b = mid
                c = min
            Else                       'assign zeros
                a = 0
                b = 0
                c = 0
            End If
        End Sub
```

Note: This problem can be solved more efficiently using arrays.

(*c*)
```
        Sub Averages(a As Single, b As Single, c As Single, d As Single)
            c = Sqr(a ^ 2 + b ^ 2)
            d = Sqr(a * b)
        End Sub
```

7.35 (*a*)
```
        Dim X As Single, Message As String

        Randomize
        X = -1 + 2 * Rnd
        Call SignIs(X, Message)
        MsgBox(Message)
```

(*b*)
```
        Dim i1 As Integer, i2 As Integer, i3 As Integer, i4 As Integer

        i1 = . . . . .
        i2 = . . . . .
        i3 = . . . . .
        i4 = . . . . .
        . . . . .
        Call Reorder(i1, i2, i3, i4)
```

or

```
        Reorder i1, i2, i3, i4
```

(*c*)
```
        Dim a As Single, b As Single, c As Single, d As Single

        Call Averages(a, b, c, d)
        a = c
        b = d
        Call Averages(a, b, c, d)
```

7.36 (*a*) Text = "'Hello, There!'"

(*b*) z = 11

(*c*) z = 146

(d)   z = 25

(e)   Message = "Ifmmp-!Uifsf""   (the repeated double quote at the end is correct)

(f)   Str2 = "1600 pENNSYLVANIA aVENUE nw, wASHINGTON, dc 20500"
      Str3 = "1600 Pennsylvania Avenue NW, Washington, DC 20500"

(g)   First = 21
      Second = 18

Chapter 8

8.34   (a)   cost is a 100-element, one-dimensional single-precision array; items is a 100 x 3, two-dimensional string array.

(b)   P is a one-dimensional numeric array; Q is a two-dimensional numeric array.

(c)   Message is a one-dimensional string array.

(d)   Z is a two-dimensional numeric array.

(e)   A is a one-dimensional string array.

8.35   (a)   One element of the one-dimensional, single-precision array Values is passed to subroutine Sub1.

(b)   The entire one-dimensional, single-precision array Values is passed to subroutine Sub1.

(c)   The entire one-dimensional, single-precision array Values is passed to subroutine Sub1. The array is later dynamically resized, and the newly dimensioned array is again passed to Sub1.

(d)   The entire one-dimensional, single-precision array Values is passed to subroutine Sub1. The array is later dynamically resized, preserving the values originally assigned to the remaining array elements. The newly dimensioned array is then passed to Sub1.

(e)   All of the elements of the one-dimensional, single-precision array Values are assigned values within a loop. (The actual values assigned to the array elements are not shown explicitly.)

(f)   A value is assigned to the Font property of each element within the control array Button.

8.36   (a)
```
sum = 0
For i = 1 To n
    sum = sum + Costs(i)
Next i
```

(b)
```
sum = 0
For i = 1 To 60
    sum = sum + Values(i, 3)
Next i
```

(c)
```
sum = 0
For j = 1 To 20
    sum = sum + Values(5, j)
Next j
```

```
(d)   sum = 0
      For i = 1 To m
         For j = 1 To n
            sum = sum + Values(i, j)
         Next j
      Next i

(e)   For i = 2 To 60 Step 2
         Print Names(i)
      Next i

(f)   sum = 0
      For i = 1 To 199 Step 2
         sum = sum + X(i) ^ 2
      Next i
      root = sqr(sum)

(g)   Dim H(8, 12)
      . . . . .
      For i = 1 To 8
         For j = 1 To 12
            H(i, j) = 1 / (i + j - 1)
         Next j
      Next i

(h)   Call Search(H())
      . . . . .
      Sub Search(H() As Single)

(i)   Print "i", "K(i)"      'Column headings
      For i = 1 To n
         If K(i) <= Kmax Then Print i, K(i)
      Next i

(j)   Prod = 1
      For i = 1 To k
         Prod = Prod * W(i, i)
      Next i

(k)   Dim Colors(32) As String
      . . . . .
      ReDim Preserve Colors(20)

(l)   Dim min As Integer, tag As Integer, i As Integer, Colors(32) As String
      . . . . .
      ReDim Preserve Colors(20)
      min = Len(Colors(1))
      For i = 2 To 20
         If Len(Colors(i)) < min Then
            min = Len(Colors(i))
            tag = i
         End If
      Next I
      MsgBox("Element " & Str(tag) & " contains the shortest string")
```

```
(m)   Dim Count As Integer, Index As Integer
      Count = 0
      For Each Index In Labels
         If Label(Index).FontSize = 10 Then
            Count = Count + 1
         End If
      Next Index
```

Chapter 9

9.37 (a) A sequential data file called demo.dat is opened as an input file on data channel 3.

(b) A sequential data file whose name is represented by the string variable FileName is opened as an output file on data channel 5.

(c) A random access data file whose name is represented by the string variable DataFile is opened on data channel 2. The record size is determined by the variable RecName.

(d) A sequential data file called customers.dat is opened as an append file (i.e., an output file set for writing new data at the end of the file) on data channel 1.

(e) A binary file whose name and path are c:\myfiles\students.dat is opened on data channel 2.

9.38 (a) `Open "students.dat" For Input As #2`

(b) `Open "grades.dat" For Output As #3`

(c) `Open FileName For Append As #4`

(d) `Open "orders.dat" For Random As #1 Len = 72`

(e) `Open FileName For Random As #2 Len = Len(RecSize)`

(f) `Open BinFile For Binary As #1`

9.39
```
Dim Name As String, Salary As Single, Taxes As Single, NetPay As Single

Open "oldrecs.dat" For Input As #1
Open "newrecs.dat" For Output As #2

Do Until EOF(1)
   Input #1, Name, Salary, Taxes, NetPay

   . . . . .              'update the data

   Print #2, Name, Salary, Taxes, NetPay
Loop

Close #1
Close #2
```

9.40
```
Private Type RecordType
     Name    As String * 20
     Salary As Single
     Taxes  As Single
     NetPay As Single
End Type

Private Sub Command1_Click()
   Dim Employee As RecordType, RecNo As Integer, Last As Integer

   Open "salaries.dat" For Random As #1 Len = Len(Employee)

   Last = LOF(1) / Len(Employee)    'Last record number
   RecNo = 1
   Do
      Get #1, RecNo, Employee

      . . . . .         'update the data

      Put #1, RecNo, Employee
      RecNo = RecNo + 1
   Loop Until RecNo > Last

   Close #1
End Sub
```

9.41
```
Private Type RecordType
     Name    As String * 20
     Salary As Single
     Taxes  As Single
     NetPay As Single
End Type

Private Sub Command1_Click()
   Dim Employee AS RecordType, RecNo As Integer

   Open "oldrecs.dat" For Random As #1 Len = Len(Employee)

   RecNo = Val(InputBox("Record Number:"))
   Get #1, RecNo, Employee
   Print Employee.Name, Employee.Salary, Employee.Taxes, Employee.NetPay
End Sub

Private Sub Command2_Click()
   Close #1
   End
End Sub
```

Index

Programming examples are indicated in italics.